MODERN GREATS

TIMEFORM

First Published in 2013
by Timeform Limited
Halifax West Yorkshire HX1 1XF
Tel: 01422 330330 Fax: 01422 398017
Email: timeform@timeform.com
www.timeform.com

© Timeform Limited

ISBN 1 901570 92 2

Printed and bound by
Charlesworth Press
Wakefield West Yorkshire WF2 9LP

*Nearly all of the photographs used in Modern Greats originally appeared in Racehorses or
Chasers & Hurdlers, where acknowledgement is given. We are particularly grateful to those
photographers who have made such a contribution to the Timeform Annuals down the years,
including Ed Byrne, John Crofts, Alec Russell, George Selwyn and Bill Selwyn. The essay extracts
are reprinted in their original form, with a few minor amendments, mostly to avoid repetitions.*

Contents

INTRODUCTION

A Timeform Publication

Introduction

The absolute racehorse would have to possess a combination of the salient qualities of such as Abernant, Frankel, Brigadier Gerard, Sea-Bird and Alycidon. There is no such animal, there are simply racehorses with different capabilities and racing characteristics, and with different requirements. By the standards of their day—in the years just after World War II—Abernant and Alycidon undoubtedly proved themselves great racehorses, but they were as different as chalk and cheese. Abernant was the fastest horse in training and a champion at two, three and four, and Alycidon became the outstanding horse over extreme distances, assisted by pacemakers to ensure his races were run at a cracking gallop. Abernant and Alycidon were virtually unbeatable in their specialist spheres, Abernant beaten only once (trying to concede 23 lb to Tangle) when reverting to sprinting after just failing to last out the mile in the Two Thousand Guineas, and Alycidon remaining undefeated at three and four after not even being trained for the Derby and being beaten for speed in the St Leger (he galloped his St Leger conqueror Black Tarquin into the ground in the following year's Gold Cup in which he had two pacemakers).

Comparisons between champions of the same era are difficult enough to make and those between champions of different eras are even more so. Claims can never be substantiated to everyone's satisfaction, but comparisons are bound to be made, and they are essential in reaching a serious estimate of a horse's true merit. Horseracing is fortunate in having access to a wealth of historical information about the performances of the top horses. The first *Racehorses* annual covered the 1947 Flat season and became the forerunner of a series that is acknowledged around the world as the sport's most authoritative source of reference on the achievements of all Britain's thoroughbreds (National Hunt fans had to wait a further twenty-eight years for the appearance of the first *Chasers & Hurdlers* annual which has gone on to become equally renowned).

Fifty editions of *Racehorses* and twenty-two of *Chasers & Hurdlers* had appeared when Timeform brought out a glossy, landscape-format anthology in 1997 under the title *Favourite Racehorses*. Most of the top horses of the previous half century were celebrated using the 'favourite' extracts from the Timeform Annuals reprinted in their original form, linked by passages expanding the contemporary accounts with sequels where relevant. *Favourite Racehorses* was awarded the ultimate accolade in a *Racing Post* countdown, in September 2005, of the best racing books ever written. Racing annuals were ineligible for the list, but *Favourite Racehorses* was lauded as 'a fascinating, erudite and entertaining record of half a century of racing' and 'a magnificent substitute for the series of books that represent the pinnacle of turf literature.'

When *Favourite Racehorses* was published, few would have been found to dispute Sea-Bird's position as number one among the horses seen in Europe in the extensive era since World War II. The classic crop in 1965 was one of superlative merit and Sea-Bird won the Derby without coming off the bit. He then spreadeagled his field in the Prix de l'Arc de Triomphe by an official six lengths and five lengths, with three-year-olds filling the first three places. Sea-Bird was one of five current Derby winners in an Arc field that was arguably the strongest ever assembled for a race in Europe, either before or since. Sea-Bird's performance in the Arc was widely regarded as being at the limit of what the thoroughbred can achieve, his Timeform rating of 145 putting him 1 lb ahead of the next-highest-rated champions of the *Racehorses* era up to that time, the runaway 1947 Two Thousand Guineas winner Tudor Minstrel and that paragon of the early-'seventies Brigadier Gerard who won seventeen of his eighteen races and put up top-class performances at a mile, a mile and a quarter and a mile and a half.

Sea-Bird, Tudor Minstrel and Brigadier Gerard were supplanted at the top of the Timeform Flat ratings in 2012 by the phenomenal Frankel; the first horse since Abernant to be champion in each of the three seasons that he raced. Frankel's career is the starting point for *Modern Greats* which reviews the achievements of the best thoroughbreds of the past fifteen years or so—the period since *Favourite Racehorses*. Although there are subtle differences in the presentation and content of *Modern Greats* and that of *Favourite Racehorses*—the last-named was primarily a selection of the *best reading* (not necessarily the *best horses*) from the Timeform annuals—the contemporary accounts of Frankel and other top horses have been selected to entertain and inform in equal measure. Dubai Millennium, Sea The Stars and Harbinger are others whose careers are dealt with in detail, while *Modern Greats* also covers the successors to Golden Miller, Arkle and Desert Orchid. Heading that roll-call of jumping big names are Sprinter Sacre—who like Frankel has a chapter to himself—and Kauto Star.

The horses mentioned are among the small number that have earned the accolade 'great' over the years in *Racehorses* or *Chasers & Hurdlers*, but what exactly is the definition of a great horse? There is no completely objective test of greatness in the racehorse—a multitude of factors have to be taken into account—but it might help if the customary narrow definition used in *Racehorses* and *Chasers & Hurdlers* is reproduced here. Quality of performance has always been the thing that has mattered most and the definition of a great horse used in the Timeform Annuals has been 'one of such superlative merit as to make him, or her, far superior to the general run of classic winners [substitute "winners of top championship races" for "classic winners" as the rule of thumb for National Hunt performers].' Even that definition is not all-encompassing, and therefore not wholly satisfactory, since it would be perverse to deny greatness to the unique Red Rum, for example, whose three victories and two seconds in the Grand National, a degree of domination unmatched by any horse in the history of that great race, transformed the perception of the sport among the wider public. The adjective 'great' is so overused nowadays that it has virtually lost its original meaning but, if nothing else, the restrictive definition applied in the Timeform Annuals has resulted in 'great' never being used thoughtlessly in those pages.

Horseracing has become even more international in the twenty-first century, and there is a special chapter devoted to 'the globetrotters', including British horses which have achieved notable success elsewhere in the world, as well as foreign horses which have made a name for themselves far beyond their own countries. As well as covering horses which have set themselves apart from the rest by their sheer ability—as defined by Timeform's handicappers and writers—*Modern Greats* also gives space to others. Readers and racing correspondents also offer a personal view on horses which, in their opinion, have made a special contribution to racing in the modern era.

The Timeform essays themselves have stood the test of time and the cornucopia of extracts from *Racehorses* and *Chasers & Hurdlers* sets the major achievements of Timeform's highest-rated horses of the twenty-first century into historical perspective. When the esteemed *Racing Post* historian John Randall named *Favourite Racehorses* as the number-one racing book of all time, he wrote: 'On *Desert Island Discs*, any discerning racing person would choose a set of Timeform annuals to accompany them on their tropical retreat.' *Modern Greats* is a splendid substitute for the thirty editions that have appeared since those words were written.

November 2013

*The Timeform Jury Stakes
(John of Gaunt) - Haydock, 2011*

FRANKEL

A Timeform Publication

Frankel

'Plainly has a lot going for him and will surely be competing in some of the Group races he's entered in by the end of the season, creating a very good impression starting out and with the prospect of a whole lot more to come, travelling comfortably off the pace and making easy headway to join the runner-up, his rider not needing to go for his whip to get the better of that one as they pulled clear; an excellent prospect, he'll peak over middle distances next year.'

So read Timeform's report on Frankel's debut in a Newmarket maiden in August 2010. Positive as it was, in truth, the same write-up could apply just as easily to a number of well-bred two-year-olds from top stables that have made winning debuts over the years. What nobody could have foreseen on that rather wet Friday evening was that this half-length victory (from Nathaniel, who himself proved a high-class colt) was the beginning of a career that would see Frankel become the highest-rated—the greatest— among the many thousands of racehorses Timeform has assessed in more than sixty years of assigning ratings to their performances. Tom Queally's whip was rarely required in the remainder of Frankel's races either as he went unbeaten through his remaining thirteen starts after that Newmarket debut, the only occasion, incidentally, that he started at odds against. Wide-margin wins in a minor event at Doncaster and the Royal Lodge Stakes at Ascot soon followed before Frankel ended his two-year-old season with victory in a much-anticipated Dewhurst Stakes at Newmarket.

Frankel's trainer Henry Cecil (to be knighted the following year), who from his wealth of experience in handling classic prospects, knew better than most that a degree of caution was required, even with a colt as exciting as Frankel. 'I'm not going to do the usual thing and say he's the best I've ever trained—that's alright before they go to stud but there is a long way to go.' Keeping a lid on expectations was understandable on the part of his connections, though a rating of 133p as a two-year-old, implied, as *Racehorses of 2010* made clear, that 'Frankel has the potential to develop into one of the greats of the sport.'

But one of the greats at what distance? His breeding might have suggested middle distances, but Frankel's style of racing as a young horse lent itself more to tests of speed than stamina, and his three-year-old campaign was that of a miler. In fully living up to all that early promise, by the end of his three-year-old season Henry Cecil was prepared to acclaim Frankel as not just the best he had ever trained himself, but the 'best I have seen in my lifetime.' Now rated 143, Frankel's rating had only ever been bettered by three horses. Next best behind Sea-Bird on Timeform's list of greats were Brigadier Gerard and Tudor Minstrel, both rated 144 and each of them winners of the Two Thousand Guineas. Brigadier Gerard (rated 141 as a three-year-old before proving better still at four) beat another high on the list, Mill Reef (rated 141), for his Guineas win in 1971, but it was the manner of Tudor Minstrel's eight-length win at Newmarket in the spring of 1947 that was recalled when Frankel spread-eagled his field in similar fashion in the same race sixty-four years later. The Timeform annuals and ratings were still in the process of taking their current form in Tudor Minstrel's day, as some of the opening paragraphs in Frankel's 2011 essay explained:

> . . . Tudor Minstrel was a flamboyant performer who captured the imagination, his destruction of the field in the 1947 Two Thousand Guineas a scarcely credible performance in a classic. Tudor Minstrel only came to be allotted a Timeform rating because Timeform's founder Phil Bull, who gave up teaching and began racing on the courses in earnest in the 'thirties, encountered problems producing his *Best Horses of 1947* on time.

> Bull started the *Best Horses* series in 1942, providing a review of the Flat-racing year which examined the performances of the best two hundred and fifty horses individually in essay form. The 'vigour and clarity' of *Best Horses*, in the words of the *Daily Telegraph*'s reviewer, 'adds a new dimension to racing writing in this country.' *Best Horses* grew in size as the years passed—covering four hundred and fifty horses in 1943, five hundred and fifty in 1945 and so on. The principal measure of the merit of the horses in that period were their racefigures—timefigures as they came to be known—calculated from times taken for individual races and adjusted mathematically for each horse to take into account factors such as how far the horse had won or been beaten by, what weight it had carried and the prevailing conditions on the day, such as the going and wind speed and direction. The racefigures were expressed in seconds and hundredths of seconds (per five furlongs) faster or slower than a defined standard. Tudor Minstrel's 1.74 fast in the Two Thousand Guineas was the best recorded up to that time, and it has been surpassed only once, when Troy recorded 1.79 fast in the 1979 Derby.

> The production problems associated with the burgeoning *Best Horses* became acute when racing started to return to normal after wartime restrictions (*Best Horses of 1946*, written by Bull single-handedly, didn't appear until November 1947). Outside help was called in for the writing of *Best Horses of 1947*, contributors including Quintin Gilbey of the Sporting Chronicle who was commissioned to write the essay on Tudor Minstrel, among others—though nothing could prevent Bull from having his own say in *Best Horses of 1947*, sometimes at greater length than the contributor's own essay, when he felt the need to express it. *Best Horses of 1947* was still late but Bull and his righthand man Dick Whitford, who assisted with the last three editions of *Best Horses*, came up with a temporary answer. The *Best Horses of 1947 Timeform Supplement* appeared in

April 1948 and featured thumbnail commentaries on 3,800 horses and the first Timeform ratings (including Tudor Minstrel's 144).

Whitford served in the navy during the war and had whiled away the long months of 'mind-blowing' naval patrol by conducting research on horseracing, examining the results of races and producing evidence that 'racehorses were figurable, not approximately or roughly, but almost exactly.' Whitford compiled a row of 'ratings' in a series of ledgers, showing how each horse had run on consecutive outings, and he later devised a scale to measure the differences between horses of different merit, producing a 'universal handicap'—based on each horse's best runs—of the horses in training during 1941, connecting stayers with sprinters, two-year-olds with three-year-olds, and so on. Whitford submitted his research to Bull in 1943 and correspondence continued between them until Whitford was demobbed in 1945 and joined Bull.

While writing brief comments on all the horses that ran in 1947—as part of the preparation for *Best Horses of 1947*—Whitford pencilled in, for his own guidance, alongside Bull's time-based racefigures, the form ratings he had compiled. The ratings were expressed in pounds, specifically the number of pounds that a horse would be entitled to receive in an average Free Handicap (a horse worth 9-7—the maximum weight in an average Free Handicap in those days— received a rating of 133; Tudor Minstrel's rating meant he was regarded as 11 lb superior to the top horse in an average year). Time and form came together for the first time when the two figures both eventually appeared—along with a table of equivalents—in the *Timeform Supplement* published to recompense subscribers for the lateness of *Best Horses of 1947.* Timeform was born and *Best Horses* and the *Supplement* gradually evolved into *Racehorses* . . .

Tudor Minstrel had just a few lines devoted to him in the *Best Horses of 1947 Timeform Supplement* but *Best Horses* included a ten-page, fully illustrated appreciation, written in the first-person-singular as was the style in all the *Best Horses* editions. Quintin Gilbey's essay began: 'However good one's memory may be, a number of races, even important ones, become erased from the mind with the passing of time. On the other hand, there are races which are quite unforgettable, and such a one was the Two Thousand Guineas of 1947. Never have I seen a Guineas which can bear comparison with it, and I never expect to do so again. We have all seen races which were a foregone conclusion some way from home, but it was inconceivable that the Two Thousand Guineas should have been over and done with before the horses had travelled half a mile' . . . Phil Bull advised readers not to underestimate Tudor Minstrel's merit 'nor be misled by the fact that his failures in the Derby and the Eclipse Stakes robbed him of much of his "glamour" . . . So far as I know I have never yet described any horse as a world-beater, but, with the reservation about distance [Tudor Minstrel remained unbeaten at up to a mile], I think I am prepared so to describe Tudor Minstrel . . . The memory of Tudor Minstrel's strolling home the length of a street in front of everything else will remain with me for the rest of my life. Like Quintin Gilbey, I don't expect to see such a thing in a classic race again.'

Bull and Gilbey would have been centenarians had they lived to see Frankel scatter his opponents in the latest Two Thousand Guineas in a style strikingly reminiscent of Tudor Minstrel's. Like Tudor Minstrel, Frankel was an exceptional two-year-old who looked very much like becoming just as outstanding a champion at three. He won his four starts by an aggregate margin of over twenty-five lengths, which included romping home by ten in the Royal Lodge Stakes at Ascot (one of the best performances by a juvenile in recent years) before beating the subsequent Criterium International winner Roderic O'Connor by two and a quarter in a much-hyped Dewhurst in which Frankel's main opponent, the wide-margin Middle Park winner Dream Ahead, failed to give anything like his true running. Dream Ahead was a very good two-year-old, rated as highly in *Racehorses* as any juvenile since Xaar in 1997, but the World Thoroughbred Rankings still did Frankel a disservice by making the pair joint champion two-year-old. *Racehorses* had 5 lb between them.

Odds on over the winter for the Two Thousand Guineas (and a warm favourite—with a run—for the Derby), Frankel reappeared in the totesport.com Greenham Stakes at Newbury in April with the full range of superlatives already heaped on him by the Newmarket gallops watchers in the spring, including one bizarre-sounding claim that he had outpaced the Cambridge to Newmarket train during one of his workouts! Frankel landed odds of 4/1-on with the minimum of fuss in the Greenham, his intended pacemaker Picture Editor not really fulfilling his role and the exuberant Frankel being committed for home over two furlongs out after the early part of the race had been steadily run. Frankel looked at full stretch for a moment or two in the penultimate furlong, his rider administering a couple of sharp cracks of the whip as the 25/1-shot Excelebration stuck with him before Frankel forged ahead to win smoothly in the end by four lengths (Excelebration pulled six clear of the third to record a performance that was itself on a par with the normal standard for the winner of the race).

The list of beaten Two Thousand Guineas favourites in modern times is as long as your arm. In the previous twenty years, Zafonic and George Washington had been the only successful favourites in the race, with odds-on shots Celtic Swing and Xaar among those beaten, along with other hotpots such as Machiavellian, Marju, Hawk Wing, One Cool Cat, Dubawi, New Approach and St Nicholas Abbey, all of whom started at shorter than 2/1. Frankel was sent off at 2/1-on in the thirteen-runner field, the shortest-priced favourite for the Two Thousand Guineas for thirty-seven years (Apalachee finished third in 1974 at 9/4-on when he himself started the shortest-priced Guineas favourite since Colombo, who had landed odds of 7/2-on forty years before that). Qipco took over sponsorship of the Two Thousand Guineas and One

Thousand Guineas but prize money for both was down on the year before, the first prize for the Two Thousand Guineas £198,695, compared to £227,080 the previous year. With Dream Ahead's preparation held up by the dry spring at Newmarket, the main opposition to Frankel, who looked immaculate in the paddock, seemed likely to come from the two Irish-trained challengers, Roderic O'Connor and another Group 1-winning two-year-old Pathfork, who had won Ireland's premier juvenile event the National Stakes at the Curragh. They were joint second favourites at 8/1, with the Racing Post Trophy winner Casamento (transferred to Godolphin after winning that race) next at 11/1. Godolphin's challenge also included the Champagne Stakes winner Saamidd, who had run disappointingly behind Frankel in the Dewhurst and was sent off at 22/1 on Guineas day, one of only four others in the line-up who started at shorter than 66/1, the remaining trio being the Tattersalls Millions winner Fury (12/1), the clear-cut Craven Stakes winner Native Khan (16/1) and the dual listed winner on the all-weather Dubawi Gold (33/1).

Frankel's trainer said before the Two Thousand Guineas that he wanted the race to be run at a 'decent, sensible pace' and that Frankel 'could make the running if he has to,' although the Free Handicap runner-up Rerouted, in the same ownership but a different stable, was in the Guineas field and presumed to be there in a pacemaking role. In the event, Rerouted would have had to have been champion sprinter material to have performed the job. Frankel has a ground-devouring stride when allowed to use himself and his jockey Tom Queally quickly signalled his intention not to mess about, letting Frankel bowl along from the start. Frankel's tendency to fight his rider had been a feature of his two-year-old races and, when let loose in the Guineas, he really took the bit between his teeth and seemed at first to be running away. He was quickly out clear, burning up the Rowley Mile at a gallop that, while seemingly comfortable for him once Queally got him to settle, was too strong for his

*A never to be forgotten performance from Frankel
in the Two Thousand Guineas*

rivals to cope with. Frankel took about forty-seven and a half seconds to reach halfway, setting the sort of pace more likely to be seen in a top sprint than in a championship race over a mile (although not on the same part of the course, he actually covered the first five furlongs in a time over a second inside the winner's time in the Palace House Stakes thirty-five minutes later). Provision had been made in the original Two Thousand Guineas conditions for the runners to carry speed sensing equipment, but plans to reintroduce sectional timing for the races in the new British Champions' Series, which got under way with the Two Thousand Guineas, did not come to fruition until British Champions' Day itself at Ascot in October, the climax to the series. The Two Thousand Guineas has had sectional timing before, however, and Frankel's time to halfway was significantly faster than in earlier editions for which electronic sectionals were recorded, including some run under conditions that were more favourable for fast times (the latest Guineas was run into a stiff headwind).

Frankel was at least ten lengths clear at halfway and almost everything else in the field was under pressure, the other Group 1 winners Roderic O'Connor, Pathfork and Casamento among those trying in earnest to give chase (all three eventually paid the price and finished out on their feet down the field). Understandably, considering the prevailing headwind and the fact that he had nothing to race with, Frankel could not keep up the same pace all the way and the hand-timed sectionals for his last three furlongs were his slowest of the race, apart from the opening furlong from a standing start. Queally glanced back between his legs three furlongs out but, if he was having thoughts that Frankel might have gone off too fast, he would have been reassured to see how far in front he was. The Two Thousand Guineas had been turned into a procession and there wasn't the slightest threat to him. Applause began in the stands as Frankel reached the Bushes, just over two furlongs from home, and he came home unchallenged, though Queally had to get to work on him in the final furlong. It was only late in the race, though, that the placed horses began to make inroads into Frankel's substantial lead. After looking for so long as if he would win by a record margin, he eventually won by six lengths—the second longest official margin of victory in the history of the race (behind Tudor Minstrel's eight)—chased home by Dubawi Gold who had been dropped out last and finally made his move as most of the others had run their race; Native Khan was only half a length behind Dubawi Gold in third, doing easily the best of those who raced close up in the main body of the field. There was an astonishing eleven lengths further back to the fourth, rank outsider Slim Shadey who was never in the hunt, with fifth-placed Fury the only other to finish within twenty lengths of Frankel. Pathfork was twenty-six lengths behind Frankel in seventh, with Casamento and Roderic O'Connor beaten over thirty-five lengths into tenth and eleventh. There was nearly a furlong between Frankel and the last horse, the strung-out field having more in common with the finish of a top steeplechase than a top Flat race, especially one over a mile on good to firm going.

Frankel's performance was simply stunning and there is not the slightest doubt that he was even better than the bare form on the day. Taking into account all the circumstances, not least how much energy Frankel must have used up in the first half of the race, the Two Thousand Guineas put Frankel on the threshold of being one of the very best Flat racehorses in Timeform's long experience, already almost up there with Tudor Minstrel and Brigadier Gerard, Two Thousand Guineas winners themselves who stand at the top of the list of great milers. The form assessment of Frankel's Guineas was backed up by an outstanding final time which, even on the bare result, produced the fastest timefigure of the twenty-first century so far, over any distance, 1.43 fast (equivalent to a timerating of 136). Frankel's timefigure was the best recorded in the Two Thousand Guineas itself since El Gran Senor's 1.54 fast (139) in 1984. The 2011 Two Thousand Guineas was, in so many ways, an epochal event in the history of Flat-racing in Britain and a race that will be talked about for years.

After creating such a deep impression at Newmarket, it was perhaps ironic that Frankel's next outing, in the St James's Palace Stakes at Royal Ascot, was the closest he would come to defeat other than on his debut, run to three quarters of a length by Zoffany after being sent for home too soon by Tom Queally, who later claimed that the colt had idled in front. A close shave, and one that gave encouragement to prospective opponents, among them top older miler Canford Cliffs, whose defeat of star mare Goldikova in the Queen Anne seventy-five minutes earlier had heightened expectation of a meeting

between the two to such an extent that the bookmakers couldn't agree on a favourite in the early betting. The Sussex Stakes at Goodwood six weeks later soon put to bed any doubts as to where the balance of power lay, however:

> . . . The eagerly-anticipated 'Duel on the Downs' pitched the dominant three-year-old miler against the dominant older miler in a head-to-head to decide 'the title'. The clash was promoted to the wider public in a comparable way to similar contests in more popular sports. Unfortunately, only a minority of head-to-heads between sporting heavyweights live up to the seemingly general expectation of a closely-fought battle and a tight finish. Frankel v Canford Cliffs—the pair 13/8-on and 7/4 respectively on the day—was emphatically one of those that failed to follow the script. It wasn't even close.

> Only four lined up for the Sussex at Goodwood and Frankel was forced into making his own running. After a little hesitation among the jockeys in the very early stages, Frankel went on and, with Queally judging the pace perfectly and gradually stepping up the gallop, Canford Cliffs—who had won five Group 1s in a row—looked in trouble even before Frankel produced an instant and most decisive turn of foot when given the office inside the two-furlong marker. Feeling the whip only once, Frankel streaked clear to win by five lengths, a winning margin equalled in the race in the last forty years only by Brigadier Gerard and Kris. Canford Cliffs hung left, markedly so, under strong pressure but there was still a further two and a half lengths back to third-placed Rio de La Plata, with the smart French-trained challenger Rajsaman the same distance away. Canford Cliffs was far from discredited on form but he certainly did not run to his absolute peak and a scan a week later revealed a shadow on the joint running into his near-fore pastern, an injury put forward to explain why he hung so badly at Goodwood (although he had done so before, in the Greenham as a three-year-old). The exemplary Frankel gave his trainer a record sixth Sussex

Frankel impressively accounts for Canford Cliffs (right) in the
'Duel on the Downs'

Stakes winner, following Bolkonski, Wollow, Kris, Distant View and Ali-Royal, all except the last-named successful in the race as three-year-olds.

After Goodwood there was again talk of Frankel going up in trip (a Derby bid had been debated in the media after Newmarket), but a run in the Juddmonte International was ruled out and Frankel didn't reappear until mid-October, when kept to a mile for the Queen Elizabeth II Stakes on the newly-instituted British Champions' Day, a new climax to the season brought about by the controversial rearrangement of four weeks of racing in the autumn:

Frankel was the centre of attention on Champions' Day for the second year running, having stolen the limelight twelve months earlier from the older horses when winning the Dewhurst—a race transferred in the latest season to a new Future Champions' Day card at Newmarket which was staged the previous weekend. Frankel had seven opponents in the Queen Elizabeth II Stakes Sponsored By Qipco. Three-year-olds have almost as impressive a record in the Queen Elizabeth II—twenty-five winners in the previous forty years—as they have in the Sussex and, with no Canford Cliffs or Goldikova to oppose them, the classic generation dominated the betting on the latest running. Frankel started at 11/4-on with Excelebration, who had won the Moulin, at 6/1 and the Coronation Stakes winner Immortal Verse, who had won the Jacques le Marois from Goldikova, at 7/1. The Hannon-trained pair, four-year-old Dick Turpin and Dubawi Gold, came next, ahead of Poet's Voice and Side Glance, with Frankel's half-brother and pacemaker Bullet Train the rank outsider. The four three-year-olds filled the first four places, Frankel producing another 140-plus performance to win by four lengths from Excelebration. Excelebration is a top-class miler whose only defeats during the season came in races won by Frankel and he had Immortal Verse a further three and a half lengths away in third, just ahead of fourth-placed Dubawi Gold. Frankel never looked in any trouble, settling well and quickening to take over from Bullet Train two furlongs out before drawing away, still keeping on strongly pushed out almost to the line.

The principals in the Queen Elizabeth II did not start to race in earnest until around halfway and the overall time was nothing out of the ordinary. Frankel's winning margin wasn't a record either—Brigadier Gerard (in his second appearance in the race), Bahri (under an inspired ride on a track that had been unevenly watered) and Dubai Millennium all won the Queen Elizabeth II Stakes by six lengths, with Warning a five-length winner, in the forty years since Brigadier Gerard won it as a three-year-old by eight lengths (from that year's Jacques le Marois winner). Reform won by ten lengths four years before that. The origins of the Queen Elizabeth II Stakes, which was first run in 1955, are to be found back in Tudor Minstrel's day, in the Knight's Royal Stakes over the Ascot mile. That race was the last of Tudor Minstrel's career and it was framed with the specific object of settling the much discussed question of the day about which was the better horse, Tudor Minstrel or the four-year-old The Bug who had proved himself one of the fastest sprinters for years (The Bug, looking for his eleventh successive victory, ran unaccountably badly in the Knight's Royal, also his last race). Frankel's performance in the Queen Elizabeth II Stakes—Europe's richest mile race (£567,100 to the winner)—needed no embellishment. 'We were not trying to catch pigeons,' his trainer said afterwards, 'we were just trying to win the race nicely.' A victory by four lengths and three and a half from two very good Group 1-winning milers was more than enough to consolidate Frankel's reputation as a phenomenon.

Thoroughbreds on the Flat are not reckoned to have reached full maturity until their four-year-old season, hence the weight-for-age scale which dictated, for example, that when Frankel won the Queen Elizabeth II Stakes on his final start as a three-year-old, he was entitled to carry 3 lb less than his older male rivals in the line-up. Already with an imposing physique at two, Frankel matured into a strong, well-made colt, but it was arguably his increased maturity in the mental, rather than physical, sense that played the greater part in his duly becoming 'the best there has ever been' in Timeform's experience.

Rated 147 as a four-year-old, a much more tractable Frankel was given the opportunity to prove himself beyond a mile for the first time in his final season. But Frankel's unbeaten status, whilst confirming his standing as the perfect racehorse for some, left others wondering what more he might have achieved had he been set still more demanding goals—at a mile and a half, for example, or overseas. The other significant development during Frankel's final season was that his profile became such that he achieved the rare feat for a racehorse, and a Flat performer at that, of becoming front-page news at a time when, in some quarters, racing is struggling just to maintain its traditional presence in the back pages of the newspapers. Frankel's essay in *Racehorses of 2012*, most of which is reprinted here, examines those points, as well as drawing comparisons with greats of the past whom he supplanted at the top of Timeform's all-time rankings:

> According to legend, when Alexander the Great saw the breadth of his domain he wept because there were no more worlds to conquer. By the time of Alexander's death at the age of thirty-two, his empire stretched from Greece, through what is now Turkey, into the Middle East and south to Egypt, and further east through Persia to the borders of India. Alexander's armies did not suffer a single defeat and his empire was the biggest ever known up to that time, though, as those who came after him discovered, there were indeed more worlds to conquer. Horizons are limited only by men's imagination and, as the annals of sport show, for example, there are no fixed boundaries to human achievement. Ever—the biggest ever, the best ever—is not really a word to use in a world in which records and milestones come along all the time. But for Frankel, the best racehorse of his generation in each of the three seasons that he raced (the first in Britain since the sprinter Abernant to be a champion at two, three and four), the description 'best ever' may well turn out

to be justified. Many of the current generation of British racegoers will be lucky to see another as good.

Frankel was invincible, unbeaten in fourteen races before most of which the speculation was not about whether he was going to win, but by how far, and how impressively he was going to do so. The answer was usually: by a comfortable margin, like a chainsaw going through balsa wood. In the latest season, he earned the highest rating ever awarded to a horse in *Racehorses*, supplanting the 145 achieved by the majestic 1965 Derby and Prix de l'Arc de Triomphe winner Sea-Bird, who recorded two of the most stunning performances in racing history in those races, his victory in the Arc a phenomenal one which became widely regarded as being at the limit of what the thoroughbred can achieve. In the end, Frankel was not given so expansive an examination as a four-year-old as the great Brigadier Gerard, another of the highest-rated champions of the *Racehorses* era. But the quality of Frankel's best performances, in Timeform's view at least, had the edge on the pick of Brigadier Gerard's and also surpassed the best form shown by Tudor Minstrel.

Frankel's performances justified all the superlatives used about them but, in line with Thomas Fuller's famous observation 'there is no banquet but some dislike something in it,' some felt that Frankel was not given a full opportunity to be tested to the limit of his potential. The Greek philosopher Diogenes, the inventor of cynicism, dared to mock Alexander the Great who looked down on him when he was relaxing in his barrel and said 'Ask me for anything you want.' Alexander received the reply 'Stop blocking my sunlight.' If there were modern cynics who did not stand quite so much in awe of Frankel's achievements as they were expected to, it was perhaps because the racing world is a more exciting place than it was in Sea-Bird's and Brigadier Gerard's day and today's champions have more chances to prove themselves on the global stage. Frankel's horizons did not stretch much beyond his own doorstep, the 170-mile journey from Newmarket to York being the longest he undertook.

In the world of modern communications—Facebook is said to be approaching a billion active users—Frankel's connections could have been forgiven for thinking that his achievements were being more widely appreciated. However, events always feel bigger when they take place on your own shores. Black Caviar's connections saw her worldwide popularity soar as a result of her 10,500-mile journey from Australia to take on the best of Britain's sprinters at Royal Ascot, while the Japanese triple crown winner Orfevre was a challenger for the Prix de l'Arc de Triomphe, the richest race in Europe, in a quest for international prestige. Neither the Arc nor the Breeders' Cup, the two most prestigious occasions in the world's autumn programme, was on the agenda for Frankel. Frankel's trainer Sir Henry Cecil and his horses tend not to venture abroad very often. The Arc is a race Cecil has never won (Ardross was narrowly beaten) while his profile in North America was memorably illustrated on a rare

Breeders' Cup visit in the 'nineties when an American TV journalist began an interview with the ten-times champion by asking him how he spelt his name, followed by 'Have you been training long?'

Cecil's masterly handling of Frankel deserves nothing but praise, especially in the second half of the latest season when he was fighting the all-too-evidently debilitating effects of the treatment for the stomach cancer he has had for the last six years. Watching him at York and Ascot it was clear that making the journey to Longchamp, let alone Santa Anita, might well have been a strain, something which would have made it extremely difficult for connections to change their long-term plans for a purely domestic campaign for Frankel, even if they had wanted to. Their decision, though, meant that the old showbusiness saying 'always leave them wanting more' certainly applied to Frankel at the time of his retirement, though some of his supporters might claim that asking for more from Frankel—who had already recorded the year's five best individual performances—would have been asking the near-impossible.

Frankel reappeared at Newbury in May for the JLT Lockinge Stakes after suffering an injury scare when he struck into himself on the gallops a month before the race (BBC TV jumped the gun and announced his retirement during its Grand National coverage). A scan revealed, however, that Frankel had not damaged the tendon in his off-fore and, when he returned to training after ten days, his connections were always optimistic that he would be ready in time. After putting Frankel through a workout before racing on Two Thousand Guineas day, his trainer announced that 'he seems fine now.' Frankel, who looked to have grown stronger over the winter, had beaten his two main Lockinge rivals before, both of them three times. Those rivals Excelebration and Dubawi Gold had actually met each other four times as three-year-olds, Excelebration coming out on top each time, including when winning the Hungerford Stakes (by six lengths) and the Prix du Moulin. Excelebration had changed stables over the winter and had won his warm-up race for Aidan O'Brien. He started at 100/30, the shortest odds in any of the five races in which he met Frankel during his career, but Frankel was still a 7/2-on shot to retain his unbeaten record. Frankel produced top form after seven months off the course and won by five lengths and four from Excelebration and Dubawi Gold after tracking his pacemaker and close relation Bullet Train until taking over two furlongs out. Both second and third were patiently ridden and might have finished a little nearer if they had started their challenges from a closer position, though Frankel's outstanding timefigure was itself testament to the fact that the Lockinge was a true test in which neither Excelebration nor Dubawi Gold would have had the slightest chance with Frankel, however they had been ridden.

The plans announced for Frankel involved a move from a mile up to a mile and a quarter, though that was not envisaged until much later in the season, possibly not until the Juddmonte International—a race sponsored by his owner—at York in August. There were some who became impatient, though, especially after the announcement that Frankel's next race would be at a mile in the Queen Anne Stakes at Royal Ascot, where he met some familiar rivals and was sent off at 10/1-on against ten opponents, only two of whom had also been successful in Group 1 company, Excelebration and the Caulfield Guineas winner Helmet who was having his first start in Britain since being imported from Australia. Frankel delivered the perfect answer to those clamouring for something new. Instead of beating Excelebration by four and five lengths, he beat him by eleven!

The Queen Anne, which opened the meeting, was only ever going to be about Frankel who, without feeling the full force of the whip, produced a breathtaking performance that stretched his dominance as far as it was manifested in any of his fourteen races. The rout arguably settled the question about whether he really was the best there has ever been. Always travelling strongly, Frankel went past Bullet Train with less than three furlongs to go, Excelebration staying in touch with him at first before Tom Queally unleashed Frankel, who burst clear from the two-furlong pole and galloped on remorselessly. Excelebration was four or five lengths in front of the rest until he faltered inside the final furlong, almost certainly paying the penalty for trying to keep up with Frankel and eventually holding on for second by just a neck from Side Glance, with the German-trained challenger Indomito a further length back in fourth, followed by Windsor Palace, Bullet Train, Helmet, Premio Loco, Red Jazz, a well below form Strong Suit and Worthadd. Excelebration, incidentally, beat Side Glance and Indomito by wide margins when they met again later in the season in Group 1 races that Excelebration won. Frankel's trainer was the centre of

A truly breathtaking performance as Frankel routs his rivals in the Queen Anne Stakes at the Royal meeting

attention after the Queen Anne. 'I wanted Tom to produce him between the two-and-a-half marker and the two-furlong pole, because he's got a good stride on him and takes some catching, keeping going when other horses don't ... he's a great horse, he's exceptional but I don't like comparing them. I don't see how people can judge horses from different generations, in different countries and over different distances, and put them a pound ahead of each other, I think it's all double dutch.'

Cecil was partly alluding to the comparisons being made between Frankel and Black Caviar. 'They are both champions in their own right, one a sprinter, the other a miler/middle-distance horse, you can't compare them, why can't we just appreciate what we've got?' Comparisons between past and present champions are usually even more contentious than comparisons between contemporary champions, and they can be particularly unfair when the horses concerned have raced decades apart. Times change, with improvements in nutrition and training techniques, and in the general level of competition, and claims about the respective merits of exceptional champions forty or fifty years apart can never be substantiated to everyone's satisfaction. The population of three-year-olds and upwards dealt with in the *Racehorses* annual has roughly doubled since the days of Sea-Bird and Brigadier Gerard and, statistically, it might be reasonable to expect the number of highly-rated horses in that category to have increased as the population has increased. Would it not be equally reasonable to expect the rating of the highest-rated horse to have gone up too? If so, it is testament to the immense ability of Brigadier Gerard, and of Sea-Bird just before him, that it has taken so long for their feats to be surpassed. They were far superior to the norm in their eras, as can be illustrated by a brief summary of selected performances which represent their best.

Take Sea-Bird's performance in the 1965 Prix de l'Arc de Triomphe. The classic crop that year was one of superlative merit and the first three in the Arc were all three-year-olds. Sea-Bird was the only horse to beat the Arc runner-up Reliance

(unbeaten up to the Arc), and only Sea-Bird and Reliance beat the Arc third Diatome that season. The twenty-strong field had tremendous strength in depth, containing the best middle-distance performers of the year (including five current Derby winners) from France, Britain, Ireland, Italy, the United States and Russia, and was arguably the strongest ever assembled for a race in Europe, either before or since. Sea-Bird was officially credited with winning the Arc by six lengths, with Reliance finishing five lengths ahead of Diatome, though photographic evidence subsequently suggested that the official distances were exaggerated (the Timeform ratings accorded to Sea-Bird, Reliance [137] and Diatome [130] are more in line with distances of four and a half lengths and four). The form is nonetheless cast iron and was franked afterwards when Diatome and Arc eighth Carvin went on to fill the first two places in the Washington International (the summit of European ambition in North America in the era before the Breeders' Cup). The Arc fifth Anilin (beaten nearly twelve lengths at Longchamp) won the Preis von Europa next time by four lengths and the Arc seventh Demi Deuil (beaten over twenty at Longchamp) went on to win the Premio Roma by seven. Carvin, beaten nearly twenty-five lengths in Sea-Bird's Arc, came sixth the following year, four and a half lengths behind the winner; second place went to Sigebert who couldn't make the first ten in Sea-Bird's Arc.

Brigadier Gerard's career had a surfeit of tip-top performances but his second victory in the Queen Elizabeth II Stakes was one of his very best. The Queen Elizabeth II Stakes was a Group 2 in those days (thirteen of the races won by Brigadier Gerard are now designated as Group 1s) and Brigadier Gerard had to concede 7 lb to that year's Queen Anne Stakes winner Sparkler (who had run Brigadier Gerard to a head on atrocious ground in the St James's Palace Stakes the previous season). There was only one other serious contender, the 120-rated three-year-old Redundant, a notably genuine miler who had proved himself a very smart horse in handicaps. Brigadier Gerard was pushed right out to win in tremendous style by six lengths and five lengths from Sparkler and Redundant, the winning time a full second inside the track record. On the bare result, using the scale then applied by Timeform's handicappers, Brigadier Gerard gave Sparkler (rated 129 in that year's *Racehorses*) a 19-lb beating and Redundant a 30-lb beating. The margins that separate the finest competitors of any generation in top-class sport are usually small but the selected performances of Sea-Bird and Brigadier Gerard provide an accurate reflection of the gulf between them and most of their contemporaries, which is the only worthwhile way of comparing the great performers of different eras, given the various changes in circumstances that take place from one generation to the next.

. . . Frankel's tearaway style had been a feature of some of his races as a three-year-old—he was at least ten lengths clear at halfway in the Two Thousand Guineas with almost everything else off the bridle. However, he became more tractable as a four-year-old, in the words of his trainer 'learning that it had to be the rider who said "go", not him.' Frankel's jockey in all his races was Tom Queally, who always maintained that he 'didn't want to play the film star' and sometimes seemed a little wary of interviews, though, in the saddle, he came out of his partnership with Frankel with enormous credit.

… A crowd of 21,363 turned up at Goodwood to see Frankel win the four-runner Sussex Stakes, an attendance that compared with 16,748 in 2010, and 19,674 when Frankel beat Canford Cliffs in the 'Duel on the Downs' in 2011. Racegoers witnessed another one-horse race as Frankel turned the Group 1, which had £300,000 added prize money, into a procession. He strolled home by six lengths from his only worthy opponent Farhh to become the first dual winner of the Sussex Stakes since it was opened to four-year-olds in the 'sixties, in the process also equalling Rock of Gibraltar's seven Group 1 wins in succession. There was only three weeks to the International, for which the Sussex, one of the most prestigious races of the season, had seemingly served as little more than a stepping stone ('It felt like a piece of work, a nice prep for his next race,' Queally said afterwards).

The headline 'Frankel set for International stardom' did indeed signal that Frankel was travelling to tackle a fresh challenge—but only as far as York. The fresh challenge was to win at his first attempt beyond a mile, in a race in which Brigadier Gerard suffered his only defeat, at the hands of the Derby winner Roberto when the race was run as the Benson and Hedges Gold Cup. There was no Derby winner in the latest edition, in fact there wasn't a single representative of the classic generation. Frankel started at 10/1-on, his most dangerous opponent looking to be the Breeders' Cup Turf and dual Coronation Cup winner St Nicholas Abbey, one of three Ballydoyle runners, who was sent off second favourite at 5/1, with Farhh and Frankel's stablemate Twice Over (winner of the race the previous year) the only others at shorter than 20/1.

The marketing build-up—featuring adverts on Yorkshire Television 'Come and see Frankel, the greatest horse in the world'—contributed to a clamour for tickets for what York's chief executive William Derby described afterwards as 'the most memorable day we have ever had here.' There had, he said, never been so many cars parked on the Knavesmire—the approach roads were jammed before racing—and the crowd of 30,163 was fifty per cent up on the same day the previous year (19,457 in 2011). As racegoers packed in around the paddock to get a sight of Frankel, the emotionally-charged atmosphere was heightened by the sight of his trainer looking gaunt and walking with the aid of a stick, appearing on a racecourse again after missing the Sussex. Frankel's owner Khalid Abdulla was at York too, after missing Frankel's appearances at Royal Ascot and Goodwood. Entering the paddock with a police escort, Frankel looked well muscled up and very fit. He never turned a hair, either in the paddock preliminaries (though he was sweating between his back legs as so often) or going to post. A fluent mover, as was his sire, Frankel floated over the ground on the way to the start. He proved a class apart from his rivals in the race itself, recording one of his finest victories, one that will have left an indelible mark on the memory of those who witnessed it (the number of Channel 4 TV viewers and the audience share were both up by over forty per cent, the 845,000 who were watching equivalent to a twelve per cent share of the terrestrial TV audience at the time).

Ridden as patiently in the International as in any race since his two-year-old days, Frankel slipped through quickly from the rear soon after the runners had turned into the home straight, steered towards the stand rail by a motionless Queally. He took up the running on the bridle around two furlongs out, after cruising up alongside St Nicholas Abbey, who had also been waited with and had himself yet to be asked a serious question after moving very smoothly into contention. Farhh had also travelled well from the start in a truly-run race (the pace set by the Ballydoyle pacemakers), but neither he nor St Nicholas Abbey was able to go with Frankel once he produced his now-customary burst, after one tap with the whip, to go clear with over a furlong to go. Ridden out only with hands and heels, Frankel was value for more than the seven lengths by which he beat very close finishers Farhh and St Nicholas Abbey, with Twice Over coming six lengths further back in fourth. The reception Frankel received from the Yorkshire crowd was rapturous as his jockey trotted him down in front of the stands before returning to the unsaddling enclosure. As well as recording another performance that merited a Timeform rating of over 140, Frankel also put up the best time performance of the year, his 1.45 fast (equivalent to a timerating of 136) displacing his 1.43 fast in the Two Thousand Guineas as the fastest timefigure of the twenty-first century. Frankel's performances on the clock were as impressive as his form ratings and he was responsible for the three highest timefigures recorded by any horse over any distance in the latest season, returning 1.36 fast in the Champion Stakes on his final appearance, following his 1.34 fast in the Lockinge. Frankel was his trainer's fourth winner of the International and in a post-race interview—his cancer treatment having left his voice faint—he said 'That was great, wasn't it? It's fantastic. It's great for Yorkshire. They are very supportive of racing and they deserve to see him.'

There was some discussion in the media straight after York about the possibility of Frankel stepping up to a mile and a half for the Prix de l'Arc de Triomphe (for which he would have had to be supplemented). Both his owner and trainer had seemed reluctant, however, in the immediate aftermath of the International and it always seemed likely that Frankel would have his final outing before retirement in the Champion Stakes on British Champions' Day at Ascot thirteen days after the Arc. Frankel was quoted at 4/1-on with a run for the Arc, though conditions on the day were very soft, placing the emphasis firmly on stamina, and he might well have been pulled out anyway even if connections had decided to target Longchamp. Finishing his career in the Breeders' Cup Classic at Santa Anita against North America's top dirt performers would have been

Champion Stakes—Frankel is made to work a bit harder than usual but still bows out unbeaten

fitting, given that he takes his name from the legendary American trainer who enjoyed so many fine victories at the course, but Cecil ('Do I really want to run him on dirt?') was not in favour and, with only a fortnight between British Champions' Day and the main day of the Breeders' Cup, it was unlikely that Frankel would be asked to take in both. All of Frankel's races at four were part of the fledgling British Champions' Series—'We need to support it,' said Cecil—and, although he was certainly missed from Europe's Breeders' Cup challenge, his presence at Ascot resulted in a sell-out crowd of 32,348 (it wasn't financially viable for Ascot to increase the capacity for a single day by erecting temporary facilities, as for the five days of Royal Ascot, all of which had significantly bigger crowds than Champions' Day).

The Qipco Champion Stakes originally looked as if it might prove something of a lap of honour, but it turned out to be anything but. Frankel's appearance, on a day when the curtain came down on BBC TV's long-standing Flat racing coverage, hung in the balance at one time as heavy rain hit Ascot and turned the going testing. Some of Frankel's connections walked the track on the morning of the race before finally giving the thumbs up. Frankel looked tremendous, probably in the best shape we had ever seen him (he didn't get warm between his back legs until leaving the paddock), and he started at 11/2-on despite the concerns over ground conditions and the fact that he was up against two of the best middle-distance horses around. They were the previous year's winner Cirrus des Aigles, the best horse in France who was barred from the Arc because he is a gelding, and the Eclipse Stakes winner Nathaniel, who had been an intended runner in the Arc until being ruled out by a temperature. The other overseas challenger in the six-strong line-up was the Deutsches Derby winner Pastorius, having his first race outside Germany.

Unlike some of Frankel's previous races, in which most of the pleasure had been derived from witnessing a sublime demonstration of his superiority, the Champion Stakes turned into more of a competition than a demonstration. Frankel missed the break and his pacemaker Bullet Train was quickly restrained, resulting in a steady early pace with Cirrus des Aigles left in front until Frankel recovered the two or three lengths he had lost. Bullet Train pressed on again after three furlongs or so, with Frankel poised in mid-field until making up ground in the straight. He drew almost alongside the leaders Cirrus des Aigles and Nathaniel with two furlongs to run, looking as if he could take it up when his jockey wanted. After edging ahead of Cirrus des Aigles, however, Frankel had to be ridden at the furlong pole to assert himself—a very rare sight for him—and was then pushed along to win, with a little in hand, by a length and three quarters. It was the smallest margin of victory in any of his races since the St James's Palace Stakes. Nathaniel, a fully established Group 1 performer who also had a King George VI and Queen Elizabeth Stakes victory on his record, ran right up to his best to finish third in the Champion, a further two and a half lengths behind Cirrus des Aigles and three and a half ahead of fourth-placed Pastorius. The remarkable scenes that followed Frankel's tenth Group 1 win, and ninth in succession, provided a fitting farewell for a horse described afterwards by his worryingly frail trainer, barely able to raise his voice above a whisper, as 'the best I've ever had, the best I've ever seen, I can't believe that in the history of racing there has ever been better.'

Frankel takes up stallion duties at Banstead Manor Stud, Newmarket, in 2013, valued at more than £100m and set to command a fee of £125,000, just over half as much again as the fee set in 2013 for the stud's current stallion stars Dansili and Oasis Dream. Although he will be provided with plenty of the best mares, there is no guarantee that Frankel will shine at stud, where he will have to start building his reputation all over again, with all eyes on his first two-year-olds when they reach the racecourse in 2016. Frankel certainly has plenty in his favour, being by the extremely well-bred Galileo, currently the world's number-one sire whose fee is 'private' (when it was last advertised, in 2007, it was €150,000, but has now probably doubled). Galileo sired twenty-two individual European pattern winners in the latest season and was champion sire in the *Racing Post* combined table for Britain and Ireland for the fourth time in five years, his prize money earnings of £5,774,558 beating his own record. Frankel's grandsire and his great grandsire both achieved legendary status at stud. His grandsire Sadler's Wells was combined British and Irish champion fourteen times, and his great grandsire Northern Dancer, who was active before the days of three-figure books and never had a crop larger than thirty-six, commanded a stud fee of 500,000 dollars in the mid-'eighties. Northern Dancer, Sadler's Wells and Galileo are among only eight stallions who have sired the winners of a hundred or more European pattern races since the official pattern was introduced in 1971. Galileo (137) already ranks third in that list behind Sadler's Wells (327) and Danehill (198), having overtaken Nureyev (121)

. . . It would have provided added fascination if Frankel, who acted on soft and good to firm going, had been given the chance to prove that he stayed a mile and a half, the classic European distance over which many of his greatest predecessors cemented their reputations in races that are now fixed in the national consciousness, races such as the Derby, the King George and the Arc. Frankel was too keen and pulled too hard as a three-year-old to have stayed the trip in the Derby, but the more settled and tractable Frankel on show in the latest season would surely have got the extra distance. His dominant display in the International, after which he took some pulling up, showed that he was equally as devastating at ten and a half furlongs as at a mile. But, in the end, did it really matter that Frankel never ran at a mile and a half, or that he never raced abroad, or on any surface other than turf? It is necessary to go back to the nineteenth century, when Ormonde won sixteen out of sixteen, to find an undefeated champion on the Flat in Britain who retired with such an extraordinary record. In terms purely of the quality of his performances, the measure used by this Annual to compare horses, Frankel had nothing left to prove. He was a phenomenon for the racing world to wonder at and his legend is powerful enough to endure, and even to blossom, with the passing years.

Frankel's setting of a new standard of excellence was something for most to marvel at. But for others, that presented its own problems and caused a rethink in terms of how past champions had been assessed. The 'official' handicappers responsible for the World Thoroughbred Rankings (formerly the International Classifications, first published in 1977) were forced to 'recalibrate' the assessments of some of the champions of years past to ensure that the rating accorded to Frankel tallied with their assessment of him as the best horse in their experience (the ratings had been allowed to slip over time, with the aim of the 'recalibration' being to 'level the playing field for comparisons to be made'). Left as they were, the WTR assessment would have put Frankel only joint-second on their all-time list behind Dancing Brave and level with Alleged and Shergar. 'Let's trust', concluded the postscript to Frankel's final essay, 'that, having 'recalibrated' some of its historical form assessments, the World Rankings Supervisory Committee isn't tempted to move on to some of the race results themselves, perhaps by producing an amended list of Derby winners containing El Gran Senor and Dancing Brave!'

By all accounts, Frankel has made an excellent start in his new career, covering 133 mares in all in the first half of 2013, as well as a limited book of mares to southern hemisphere time later in the year. Meanwhile, a full brother to Frankel was foaled in February 2013, while his younger siblings Morpheus and Joyeuse are winners themselves and useful ones at that. Joyeuse's winning debut at the end of May came just days after Frankel's full brother Noble Mission landed a listed race at Goodwood. They proved to be a couple of the very last winners trained by Sir Henry Cecil who lost his lengthy battle with his illness in June 2013, in the week before Royal Ascot. Frankel's wins at successive Royal meetings in the St James's Palace Stakes and Queen Anne Stakes were just two of a record 75 winners the trainer sent out at the meeting during his career. The Queen's Vase, one of the Royal Ascot races in which Sir Henry Cecil had the most success, was run in his memory. The trophy for the Queen's Vase was presented by Sir Henry's widow Lady Cecil, who took over the licence at Warren Place, and saddled two winners of her own at Royal Ascot. One of them, the Ribblesdale Stakes winner Riposte, was another related to Frankel, being a close relative of his dam Kind.

Sea The Stars

THE OTHER GREATS

The Other Greats

Highest Annual Timeform Ratings (Flat)

147 **Frankel**

145 **Sea-Bird**

144 **Brigadier Gerard, Tudor Minstrel**

142 **Abernant, Ribot, Windy City**

141 **Mill Reef**

140 **Dancing Brave, Dubai Millennium, Harbinger, Sea The Stars, Shergar, Vaguely Noble**

Since Timeform started publishing ratings in 1948, only fourteen horses have achieved a Timeform rating of 140 or higher on the Flat, defining them as outstanding performers. As outlined in the previous pages, Frankel now leads the way on the 'all-time' Timeform list, though three others this century have also surpassed the 140 mark, namely Dubai Millennium, Sea The Stars and Harbinger. The following recalls their achievements, reproducing large parts of their essays in *Racehorses* from their defining season:

Sea-Bird spread-eagles his field in the 1965 Prix de l'Arc de Triomphe

*A stunning performance from Dubai Millennium
in the Dubai World Cup*

Dubai Millennium

It all began at Brighton for Sheikh Mohammed. His colours were carried to victory for the first time when his two-year-old filly Hatta won the Bevendean Maiden Stakes there in June 1977. The John Dunlop-trained Hatta, who won the Molecomb Stakes at Goodwood later that summer, had cost just 6,200 guineas as a yearling and the Brighton race was worth £968.60. Those are trifling sums compared with the investment in bloodstock and the prizes won by Sheikh Mohammed in the thirty-five years or so since then as the owner's ambitions have taken on global proportions. According to its website, Sheikh Mohammed's Godolphin operation, represented by 348 horses, won 214 races worldwide in 2012, earning nearly $26m in prize money. From experimental beginnings in the mid 'nineties involving the wintering of a select number of Maktoum family-owned horses in Dubai before bringing them back for European campaigns,

Godolphin has grown out of all recognition. The same could be said of Dubai itself as a racing nation in the same period, due largely to Sheikh Mohammed's creation of the Dubai World Cup in 1996 as the world's richest race. Sheikh Mohammed had seen his own colours carried to success in the second running of that race by Singspiel, while the 2000 renewal of that contest became the long-term aim for another of his home-bred colts, a grandson of the outstanding broodmare Fall Aspen, originally named Yaazer. But it was as Dubai Millennium that the same colt had made an impressive winning debut as a two-year-old (in 1998) in a back-end maiden at Yarmouth for trainer David Loder in Sheikh Mohammed's colours.

Rated 132 and by then in the care of Godolphin's trainer Saeed bin Suroor, Dubai Millennium became the best horse over a mile of any age in Europe in 1999, though a couple of his fellow three-year-olds had better form at different distances. Stravinsky proved a top-class sprinter, but the outstanding three-year-old that season, over middle distances, was Montjeu. The prospect of Dubai Millennium crossing swords at some point with the French colt, who was also being kept in training at four, was something to relish, but a more pressing engagement was the race that had prompted his change of name and one that would prove, one way or the other, if Sheikh Mohammed's exalted view of him, that he was the best horse to have carried the Godolphin colours, was justified.

'Set your sights further than your feet can take you.' So wrote Sheikh Mohammed in his May message for the opulent and instructive Godolphin 2000 desk diary. 'No barrier can withstand strength of purpose' he revealed in June. At the start of each month the calendar has a section for annotation marked 'Goals', 'Actions' and 'Dates of Achievements'. In the latest season the Sheikh's goals for one horse exceeded those held for any other among the thousands he has been associated with, and his ambition once again operated well beyond the sport's traditional parameters. Even as the outstanding Daylami had completed his victory in the inaugural Emirates World Series Racing Championship in 1999, Sheikh Mohammed was telling the world that he had something better.

Having Dubai Millennium in your team was an excellent spur to positive thinking. By the start of the latest season, he had victories in a maiden, a minor event, the Predominate Stakes, the Prix Eugene Adam, the Prix Jacques le Marois (at two and a half lengths his smallest winning margin) and the Queen Elizabeth II Stakes on his record, the only blemish being his ninth place in the Derby. All of those wins were gained with ease and, in our book, he was clearly the season's top miler, and behind only Montjeu and Stravinsky among three-year-olds over any distance. As had been well publicised, though, this colt's career target was the 2000 Emirates Dubai World Cup on dirt. Top-notch American dirt performers Cigar and Silver Charm had won the race in 1996 and 1998, while Singspiel and Almutawakel had shown that it could be won by a horse making its first public appearance on the surface. Dubai Millennium was not asked to emulate the latter feat, instead being given a warm-up over the Dubai World Cup course and distance in a listed event at the start of March. In a six-runner race, he had the field well strung out at the finish, and with good reason, as he too showed high-class form at the first time of asking on dirt, registering a new track record in the process as he went on to beat Lear Spear by four and a half lengths, leading on the bridle two furlongs out and eased close home.

There were twelve rivals for Dubai Millennium in the world's most valuable race (worth £2,286,427 to the winner) just over three weeks later, the most dangerous of which appeared to be the US-trained six-year-old Behrens. Although he had disappointed in the previous November's Breeders' Cup Classic, Behrens was good enough to have started favourite that day and had been back to his best when registering an easy five-length win, conceding weight all round, in the Grade 1 Gulfstream Park Handicap at the end of February. He was a better horse now than when a well-beaten fifth to Silver Charm in the Dubai World Cup in 1998. Four other US-trained challengers for the latest running were Grade 1 winners Ecton Park and Puerto Madero, Grade 2 winner Saint's Honor and the former Andre Fabre-trained Public Purse, who had just won a Grade 2. Worldly Manner and Gracioso carried the Godolphin second and third colours, while 1999 Japan Cup runner-up Indigenous had come from Hong Kong and eight-time winner World Cleek from Japan; furthering the truly international aspect to this line-up, Strudel Fitz had won a Grade 1 on dirt in Argentina the previous summer and was now trained in Saudi Arabia. From Britain, Lear Spear and globetrotting Running Stag did not represent the cream of European talent, but if this failed to excite much interest for the racing public in Britain, the race itself, once under way, proved eye-catching in the extreme.

'Stride on, and the world will make way for you'—it looked as though Frankie Dettori had already read Sheikh Mohammed's missive for the month of April as Dubai Millennium went to the front inside the first furlong, eased across to the rail from his outside draw, and was thereafter in a class of his own. It was a rout, and the ease with which Dubai Millennium administered it was a cause for disbelief. Racing apparently well within himself until the straight, he had the rest struggling to keep up well before that point and then sprinted away once in line for home. Behrens, Running Stag and Saint's Honor had been within two lengths of him off the final turn, three furlongs out, but Dubai Millennium was well clear over the last furlong and a half, and what was supposed to be a race had turned into a ceremony of acclamation. He had already gone clear before Dettori started pushing on him about two furlongs out, and felt three slaps with the whip over the next furlong before the jockey looked round and, as he put it, nearly broke his neck. At the post, in the midst of Dettori's energetic celebrations, Dubai Millennium held an official winning margin of six lengths over Behrens, who had himself drawn five and a half clear of Public Purse and Puerto Madero. In our estimation, these distances were more like seven lengths and six and a half. Either way, and why mince words, the winner had put on a display of sheer brilliance.

The Other Greats

Standing back from the astounding visual impression left by this performance, an analysis of the form produces a conclusion to match. Even if one accepts that virtually all bar the first four performed well below the best form they had shown during the previous twelve months, and that the second, third and fourth did little better than they had on other occasions, this has to be form of the highest order. In relation to each other, Behrens, Public Purse and Puerto Madero finished very much where their previous form entitled them to, so, to conclude, unless one believes that not one horse behind him ran to its form, Dubai Millennium performed to a level which is seen with extreme rarity. Dubai Millennium had, by the way, set another course record for the mile and a quarter dirt track at Nad Al Sheba with his time of 1m 59.5sec. If the television advertisements are to be believed this is also the time it takes to pour a perfect pint of Guinness. One might say that with this performance, Dubai Millennium came as close to perfection as any horse that Timeform has rated in more than a quarter of a century.

Dubai Millennium's winning margin in the Dubai World Cup might have been bettered subsequently, but no horse has rivalled his performance—which was worth a Timeform rating of 140—in form terms, with Curlin's 134 in 2008 the highest winning rating recorded in the race since. Dubai Millennium was the second of six Dubai World Cup winners so far for Godolphin (the first of its winners Almutawakel carried the colours of Hamdan Al Maktoum). Five of those came with Dubai Millennium's handler Saeed bin Suroor, Godolphin's main trainer for much of the time since its inception in 1992, though the latest, Monterosso in 2012, was under the care of Mahmood Al Zarooni, who was appointed as Godolphin's second trainer in Britain in 2010 but was banned from racing in April 2013 after eleven horses in his yard tested positive for anabolic steroids.

Of the plan for Dubai Millennium after the Dubai World Cup, Godolphin racing manager Simon Crisford stated: 'He's equally good on turf as on dirt, and Sheikh Mohammed is very keen to parade him as the first champion on both surfaces. We tried it with Swain and nearly made it, but this horse has the potential to do it—he's top of the range on turf in Europe and he was ruthless and relentless here.' The Breeders' Cup Classic, in which dual King George winner Swain had controversially been beaten a length in 1998, was now 'the ultimate goal', Crisford reported, 'and we will work back from that.' Dubai Millennium would have two or three more races on turf in Europe. For some, he still had something to prove. As mentioned earlier, Dubai Millennium had done enough to persuade Timeform of his status as champion miler in 1999, but he was a diplomatic joint top-rated with French champion Sendawar in the International Classifications, on 127, and then of course, over middle distances, there was the peerless Montjeu. The form of Montjeu's victory in the Arc de Triomphe stood well above that shown by any other three-year-old in 1999. In 2000, while Dubai Millennium was rested after the Dubai World Cup, Montjeu reverted to a mile and a quarter with a virtuoso success in the

Tattersalls Gold Cup and Sendawar reappeared with an impressive triumph in the Prix d'Ispahan over an extended nine furlongs.

Sendawar had been pencilled in for a clash with Dubai Millennium twice as a three-year-old but failed to meet either engagement, withdrawn at a late stage when the ground turned soft for both the Prix Jacques le Marois and the Queen Elizabeth II Stakes. At Royal Ascot 2000, the upgrading of the Prince of Wales's Stakes to Group 1 status was rewarded spectacularly when both Dubai Millennium and Sendawar were declared as runners. Rain on the Tuesday morning resulted in good ground and, with no further significant rainfall, Sendawar took his chance. In hindsight, the betting for this race will cause some frenzied scratching of heads: Dubai Millennium opened at evens and was sent off at 5/4, with Sendawar the solid 6/5 favourite. The rest of the field was made up of smart colt King Adam (9/1), a winner eleven days earlier; the 1999 Derby third Beat All (backed to 14/1 from 20/1); a second Godolphin runner in Rhythm Band (50/1); and German four-year-old Sumitas (66/1), who had been a standing dish in pattern races in his own country the previous season. Most unusually, the form of Dubai Millennium's stable did not at the time inspire any confidence. Since May 27th, when Bachir won the Irish Guineas, Saeed bin Suroor had had thirty-three runners worldwide before the Prince of Wales's Stakes and only one winner, Slickly at Longchamp on June 15th. Additionally, with Frankie Dettori unable to take the mount following his plane crash earlier in the month, Dubai Millennium was ridden by leading US jockey Jerry Bailey, which might also have prompted some reticence in British punters, particularly following the reaction to Best of The Bests' performance in the Derby under another American, Chris McCarron, and Godolphin's and Bailey's strictly limited impact earlier at the Royal meeting.

After the Prince of Wales's Stakes, Bailey explained: 'Frankie and Sheikh Mohammed talked to me and said the best thing was not to get in his mouth, let him have his head—he will relax better that way.' The result was another spectacular display of front-running. After something of a phoney war through the first furlong, Dubai Millennium was warmed up and Bailey let him loose. Cracking on at a furious pace, they rapidly had the field well strung out with Gerald Mosse on Sendawar the only jockey who attempted to stay in close touch at this stage. Coming out of Swinley Bottom, six and a half furlongs from home, Sendawar was two and a half lengths behind the leader but he never got any closer; the other chasers were a further six lengths off the pace, and they did not get any closer to the winner either. While Bailey sat still and pointed Dubai Millennium in the right direction, Sendawar was clearly straining to keep up, and fighting a losing battle, from a long way out. The margins entering the straight were Dubai Millennium ahead of Sendawar by four lengths and Sendawar ahead of the rest by five. Bailey first gathered up the reins and began pushing just inside the two-furlong marker, at which point Sendawar was backpedalling and Dubai Millennium was left to complete

Another exhilarating display of front running from Dubai Millennium in the Prince of Wales's Stakes

on his own. Astonishment at the sight was not diminished by the earlier, very similar denouement to the Dubai World Cup. Dubai Millennium now had an exceptional performance on turf to go with the one he had produced on dirt.

The finishing order among the also rans in the Prince of Wales's Stakes was Sumitas from Beat All, Sendawar, King Adam and Rhythm Band. Sumitas was beaten eight lengths, with another half length back to Beat All. With the exception of Sendawar, who finished two and a half lengths behind Beat All, the result fits in with that of other races. The timefigure for Dubai Millennium, equivalent to a rating of 113, is unexceptional, and that can be put down to the punishing pace that followed that steady first furlong. The winner was tired in the final furlong and gave one flash of his tail, but Sumitas, whose jockey had tried to save something for the finish, and Beat All, who had been outpaced in the early stages, were unable to make significant inroads into his advantage. Various excuses were made for Sendawar. One week after the race, it was reported that there was nothing abnormal with the horse but that he had been 'rather playful in the paddock and became a little hot . . . he was not very concentrated on the task ahead and was possibly troubled by the condition of certain members of the opposite sex.' Even for Royal Ascot, it sounds like clutching at straws. Others suggested that Sendawar did not stay, and it is entirely possible to agree with that suggestion without taking anything away from the performance of Dubai Millennium. Sendawar's performance in the Prince of Wales's Stakes should be recalled as that of a top-class miler who tried to keep tabs on an even better horse, could not do so from a point well before stamina became a factor, and then paid the price for trying.

Sendawar was again below par on his only subsequent start, when runner-up (at odds on) back over a mile in the Prix Jacques le Marois, and he was retired the following

month after rain-softened ground ruled him out of the Prix du Moulin. With Sendawar vanquished, thoughts now turned to a possible clash with Montjeu:

As a rival to Dubai Millennium then, Sendawar had been dispensed with. But Montjeu carried all before him. For his second and third starts of the season, Montjeu hacked up in the Grand Prix de Saint-Cloud and did the same against much stronger opposition, including Beat All, in the King George VI and Queen Elizabeth Stakes. These two races at Ascot, one won by Dubai Millennium, the other by Montjeu, generated a burgeoning hope and anticipation for a third race, one in which the two champions would meet. Even as Montjeu was in the Ascot winner's enclosure, however, with plans for the Irish Champion Stakes and Arc de Triomphe next, Sheikh Mohammed stated that Dubai Millennium was being targeted at the Prix Jacques le Marois, Queen Elizabeth II Stakes and Breeders' Cup Classic. The plan was to give Dubai Millennium five weeks between races and, as Simon Crisford reiterated, 'the aim is to produce the horse at his very best on Breeders' Cup day . . . It's not lost on us that the public wants to see a match with Montjeu but the programme that suits us is dropping back to a mile.' The following day, Montjeu's owner, Michael Tabor, said: 'I wish there was some carrot that could be dangled to make Sheikh Mohammed change his mind—I'm open to suggestions and maybe someone will think of something.'

Five days later, someone did. Referring perhaps to his dispatch for the month of February—'At the root of all creation is imagination; Because before you achieve, you must first conceive'—Sheikh Mohammed now proposed a race which would break some more of the conventions of modern racing; Dubai Millennium and Montjeu would meet in a match over a mile and a quarter under Jockey Club rules at either York on August 24th, Newmarket on August 26th or Ascot on September 23rd. The prize would be $6m from loser to winner, with perhaps half of it going to charity. 'We've thought long and hard,' said Sheikh Mohammed, 'and I would like it to be a match, horse against horse, one champion against another . . . Horses like Dubai Millennium and Montjeu come along only every twenty years or so—perhaps once in a lifetime. Everyone wants to see them race against each other and that includes me. I want to bring this race to the nation and the racing world.' Two rich men each wagering that his horse was better than the other—the concept of the match—provided the sport with its foundations. They were commonplace in the early days of racing. Hambletonian beating Diamond narrowly for 3,000 guineas at Newmarket in 1799 and The Flying Dutchman beating Voltigeur by a length for £1,000 at York in 1851, both in front of crowds which those racecourses could nowadays only dream of—these were races which have entered the sport's folklore. Derby winner Papyrus meeting Kentucky Derby winner Zev at Belmont Park in 1923, and going down by five lengths, was the putative start of competition between racehorses which spanned the continents. The most famous match in the States in the last thirty years was the tragic Ruffian versus Foolish Pleasure in 1975, when the undefeated filly Ruffian broke down after three and a half furlongs whilst leading against the Kentucky Derby winner. Cheltenham Gold Cup winner Dawn Run beat the Queen Mother Champion Chase winner Buck House in a specially arranged match at Punchestown in 1986, but, in recent decades, European Flat racing has relegated the match to novelty status. Willie Shoemaker making all on Princes Gate against Lester Piggott on Spanish Pool at Ascot in 1982 was an entertaining clash, rather more so than those in 1988 and 1990 between supposed speed record-holder Klute, the non-thoroughbred stallion, and two of Jack Berry's sprint handicappers who thoroughly outclassed him. A charity match between Tony McCoy and Frankie Dettori at Sandown in April, 1999 was a light-hearted affair won by the National Hunt champion. These recent matches do not provide fair comparisons, of course. By any standards, Dubai Millennium against Montjeu would have been a sensation. But it did not happen. One day after Sheikh Mohammed made his proposal, and even as the public were reading about it for the first time over their breakfasts, Dubai Millennium fractured a leg on the gallops. He underwent a five and a half hour operation on a complicated 'lateral condylar fracture' of the off-hind, which required the insertion of three screws. Sheikh Mohammed was reportedly present throughout the operation and also present until the horse got to his feet after emerging from the anaesthetic. Dubai Millennium's racing career was over.

One hundred broodmares, including the dams of Lammtarra, Agnes World and Stravinsky, as well as Group 1 winners Embassy and Cherokee Rose, are lined up for a visit to Dubai Millennium at Dalham Hall in 2001. His fee is in the £100,000 to £120,000 range, with thirty-five mares chosen from Europe, thirty-five from the United States and thirty from those owned by the Maktoums. 'No person or organisation can achieve outstanding results without organised and efficient planning'. Those were Sheikh Mohammed's tidings for November, and the previous month it was reported in *The Observer* that free travel was being offered for any mare visiting Dubai Millennium and that a Boeing 747 had been purchased for the job and was in Frankfurt being painted in the Godolphin colours. If looks, pedigree and performance, as well as planning, are anything to go by, Dubai Millennium will be a major success as a stallion. He is a tall, good-looking colt, with a short unimpressive action, and he constantly took the eye in physique and condition, although there were a few occasions (notably on Derby Day) when he got rather excitable in the preliminaries. Hardly any offspring of Seeking The Gold stay a mile and a half and Dubai Millennium was not one of them. He would have been at least as good at a mile as a mile and a quarter in the latest season had he been given the chance. Indeed connections repeatedly stated that a mile was his best trip. He acted on any turf going and on dirt, in all probability being equally good on either surface. There is absolutely no cause to doubt his resolution, though it is questionable whether one can label any horse game and genuine when he has never been involved in a close finish!

In sheer ability, as already stated, Dubai Millennium was one of the very best racehorses in our experience. Lack of opposition in his turf races and the injury as a four-year-old meant that he could not build as extensive a record in the highest class as several of his peers in the last fifty years, but we have no doubt that he realised Sheikh Mohammed's ambition for him in being a champion on both turf and dirt. Fusaichi Pegasus came and went, and there were some other high-class performers in the United States, but they achieved nothing on dirt to match Dubai Millennium's success in the Dubai World Cup. Neither did anything else in the world, and Tiznow, who recorded Timeform's second highest dirt rating for the season, is rated fully 7 lb his inferior. Strictly on form, Dubai Millennium also recorded the best turf performance of the year, but we cannot be sure that Montjeu would not have at least matched it had he been ridden out when enjoying his afternoon stroll in the King George. That the match between Dubai Millennium and Montjeu—with Dubai Millennium, of course, able to dictate the pace—did not take place was a massive disappointment. The interest it would have generated is hard to exaggerate. Montjeu, however, had a minor set-back in the summer and would probably not have been fit for the clash either. Dubai Millennium's far more serious injury will have been a huge blow to Sheikh Mohammed, but, as his December message in the Godolphin desk diary would have reminded him, 'You don't fail when you fall. You fail when you refuse to get up.' It is likely to be a long time before Sheikh Mohammed owns a horse so good as Dubai Millennium, if indeed he ever does, but it will probably not be for want of trying.

Dubai Millennium was Sheikh Mohammed's favourite horse, as well as his best one, with a rating of 140. If the injury that curtailed Dubai Millennium's racing career was a huge blow to his owner, then even worse followed when his stud career was soon cut short too. That first book of mares yielded what proved to be Dubai Millennium's only crop of foals (numbering 54) as he fell victim to grass sickness in the spring of 2001 before the end of the covering season. 'He was a very special horse, the best I have ever owned, the best I have ever seen' said Sheikh Mohammed. 'If you could ever describe a horse as a friend or a counsellor, that was him.' But one member of that reduced crop did at least turn out to be a high-class colt. Dubawi was unbeaten at two and then emulated his sire by winning the Prix Jacques le Marois at three, along with the Irish Two Thousand Guineas, all in the Godolphin colours. Like Dubai Millennium, Dubawi failed to stay in the Derby but finished third at Epsom nonetheless. Dubawi is also enjoying the highly successful stud career that was largely denied his sire, his progeny including the aforementioned 2012 Dubai World Cup winner Monterosso.

Sea The Stars

It was only two years before Frankel's three-year-old season that another colt's outstanding campaign prompted debate about his own place among the all-time greats. Two years is the blink of an eye in historical terms, and, in hindsight, Frankel's emergence soon afterwards quickly rendered academic some of the judgements made, at the time, about Sea The Stars' place in racing history. But as far as the wider racing public was concerned, Sea The Stars had the sort of three-year-old campaign fully befitting a 'great' horse, in the mould of a Mill Reef or Dancing Brave. In Europe at least, a mile and a half remains the 'classic' test, the distance of races that traditionally carry the most prestige. Dubai Millennium tried and failed at a mile and a half, while Frankel was never even tested at the trip, whereas Sea The Stars won both the Derby, Britain's richest race, and the Prix de l'Arc de Triomphe, one of the world's most valuable races on turf. Those victories certainly added weight to his claims to greatness, but purely in terms of form, it was in his races over a mile and a quarter that Sea The Stars put up his very best performances in Timeform's view. As a Two Thousand Guineas winner as well, Sea The Stars showed more versatility too, than the other modern greats, though the fact that he was not asked to demonstrate that quality still further by contesting the St Leger, in pursuit of the triple crown, showed that the classics are no longer necessarily the be-all and end-all of a top colt's three-year-old campaign.

'I was always reading about racing and great horses of the past. So when you grow up with the history of racing and the history of breeding, the landmark horses that came along over a century—to train one that's in that league gives you the greatest satisfaction.' John Oxx was careful not to get too closely involved in the academic debate about the place of his 'landmark horse' Sea The Stars in the pantheon of the Flat-racing greats, but he showed a keen appreciation of racing history. 'Sea-Bird was the flashiest Arc winner in my time. Mill Reef was such a generous sort, he could stretch clear and win by wide margins. Brigadier Gerard ran a lot of races over a variety of distances and was outstanding. Nijinsky was a triple crown winner. They are the ones . . . it's marvellous just that Sea The Stars is up there with them.' . . .

Comparisons between past and present champions are always difficult to make but, when an exceptional horse like Sea The Stars comes along, the desire to make them becomes well-nigh irresistible. Absolute comparisons between top horses of different generations are notoriously unfair, more so when the horses are separated by decades. The present learns from the past and no sport stands still, each succeeding generation of performers shaped by an ever-changing environment with, for example, advances made in nutrition and training methods. The story in most sports is of modern-day, professional competitors generally bettering the achievements and skills of their predecessors, sometimes with the help of technological advances in equipment and kit (and, it has to be said, sometimes with the help of performance-enhancing drugs). It should almost go without saying that the average thoroughbred racehorse is superior to its ancestors from half a century ago. But by how much? How can any intrinsic improvement—if there has been any—be quantified accurately, given the unevenness of the landscape of the sport over the years? A general improvement in the racing surfaces, and the use of artificial watering, is a stumbling block to using the stop-watch to measure improvement. Worthwhile comparisons can be made only by accurate assessment of what the sport's great horses achieve against their own generations and by putting them in historical context. To this end, the level of the ratings in the Timeform Annuals has been carefully monitored, and maintained or amended as required, to allow valid comparisons to be made between crops.

… Sea The Stars had shown progressive form in three races as a juvenile, winning the Beresford Stakes at the Curragh on the last of them and being promoted towards the head of the ante-post Derby lists. His stable's main hope for the Two Thousand Guineas seemed to be another choicely-bred prospect the Futurity Stakes winner Arazan, who had taken the place of Sea The Stars in the National Stakes and started odds on, finishing third to Mastercraftsman. Sea The Stars began fast work in March but he missed a fortnight after running a high temperature in the middle of that month and his participation in the Two Thousand Guineas was still in the balance two weeks before Newmarket when he worked upsides with Arazan—who was as short as 10/1 for the Guineas at the time—in a gallop at Leopardstown. With Newmarket having to water, Arazan's connections eventually decided the going would be too firm (he missed the whole season), while the trainer reported at the start of Guineas week that Sea The Stars had 'failed to sparkle' in a gallop at home. 'It's very soft and he hasn't worked as well as he has been working on good ground, or as well as he worked at Leopardstown eight days ago.' Oxx spoke more encouragingly, however, as the race approached and Sea The Stars was sent off at 8/1, half the odds he had been after his gallop with Arazan at Leopardstown (25/1 had been generally available at the start of April). Sea The Stars was still only sixth choice in the betting on the day, behind the impressive Craven Stakes winner Delegator (a stablemate of the previous year's top two-year-old Crowded House, who was headed for the Derby via the Dante Stakes at York). Rip Van Winkle, Evasive, Mastercraftsman and Gan Amhras also started at shorter odds than Sea The Stars. The race was truly run, the field keeping together up the centre of the course after the stalls were positioned in the middle. Sea The Stars took a while to settle but produced a strong run on the stand-side flank coming out of the Dip and won, without his rider having to go for everything, by a length and a half and three quarters of a length from Delegator and Gan Amhras. Rip Van

Sea The Stars comes home ahead of four Ballydoyle challengers in the Derby

Winkle, Mastercraftsman and Evasive came next in an above-average Guineas. Sea The Stars really took the eye beforehand, towering over most of his rivals in the paddock, and he was made Derby favourite immediately after the Guineas.

'The Derby is the Derby' was John Oxx's reply when asked at the end of the season to nominate his personal highlight of the magnificent campaign enjoyed by Sea The Stars. The Derby has the most distinguished roll of honour of any event in the sport and is still the biggest draw in Britain's Flat calendar (watched on the BBC by 2.8m in the latest season). However, until the banking group Investec stepped in to sign a five-year deal in early-May, Jockey Club Racecourses seemed resigned to the latest Derby being run without a sponsor, just as a major grandstand redevelopment costing £38m was being completed at Epsom. The Derby is still the richest prize in British racing—Sea The Stars earned £709,625 for winning the latest edition—but the weakness of the pound saw the race fall from thirteenth to forty-second in the list of the world's most valuable races compiled by the International Racing Bureau. The Tokyo Yushun (Japanese Derby), the Kentucky Derby, the Prix du Jockey Club, the Irish Derby, the Hong Kong Derby and the UAE Derby were all worth more than the Derby at Epsom. Crowded House's Derby aspirations took a knock when he ran disappointingly in the Dante and the market was monopolised by Irish-trained runners, with Fame And Glory, one of six representing Ballydoyle, advancing his claims with an impressive win in the Derrinstown Stud Derby Trial at Leopardstown and supplanting Sea The Stars as Derby favourite. Ballydoyle's number-one Johnny Murtagh stuck with Rip Van Winkle at Epsom and he started third favourite, ahead of the Dante winner Black Bear Island (another representing Ballydoyle) and the Two Thousand Guineas third Gan Amhras, half of the field of twelve—only four of whom were trained in Britain—starting at odds ranging from 20/1 to 40/1. It was a smaller field than usual, no Derby having had fewer runners since Nijinsky's race in 1970, when there were eleven, the race having had twelve runners in 1989 (Nashwan), 2001 (Galileo) and 2002 (High Chaparral) in the period since.

Sea The Stars became the first since Nashwan, and only the second since Nijinsky, to win both the Two Thousand Guineas and the Derby. His trainer's stated misgivings about whether Sea The Stars would stay a strongly-run mile and a half must have been relieved somewhat by the steady pace over the first three furlongs, though the strong-travelling Sea The Stars did himself no favours by pulling his way to the front of the main pack as two of the Ballydoyle contingent, Golden Sword and Age of Aquarius, eventually quickened and opened up a clear lead. The result was never in much doubt after Sea The Stars responded really well when ridden halfway up the straight, catching and overtaking the leaders approaching the final furlong. Nothing ever looked like coming from behind, Fame And Glory (after tracking Sea The Stars throughout) outpaced in the penultimate furlong when Sea The Stars began to quicken, but still emerging best of the Ballydoyle challengers. Sea The Stars won with something in hand by a length and three quarters from Fame And Glory who was all out to hold on to second by a neck in a very close finish with three of his stablemates, Masterofthehorse, Rip Van Winkle and Golden Sword, the last-named collared by his compatriots only in the dying strides. The first British-trained finisher was Crowded House, six lengths behind Golden Sword in sixth; Black Bear Island and Gan Amhras came tenth and eleventh, neither making any impression, the latter's performance blamed by his jockey on his inability to handle Epsom's gradients.

Sea The Stars was a second Derby winner for his trainer, following Sinndar, and a third for Mick Kinane, his forty-nine-year-old rider (the oldest winning jockey since Willie Carson, successful at fifty-one on Nashwan). Kinane also won the Derby on Commander In Chief and on Galileo, a half-brother to Sea The Stars. Galileo's win came during Kinane's five years as number one at Ballydoyle when he also rode High Chaparral in most of his races, though he partnered runner-up Hawk Wing instead at Epsom, and when he also rode French-trained Montjeu, another of the stars associated with the Coolmore partners at that time. Kinane, who retired at the end of the latest season, won the Irish jockeys' title thirteen times and he was very much a jockey for the big occasion, as his outstanding record in the major races showed. The performance of Sea The Stars at Epsom, judged strictly on the form-book, didn't match those of Galileo and High Chaparral and was also not up with the Derby-winning efforts of Motivator, Authorized or the previous year's winner New Approach. Kinane, though, privately already had no doubts that Sea The Stars was the best he had ever ridden; John Oxx revealed later in the year that Kinane whispered to him, as he dismounted at Epsom, 'This is one of the greats.'

. . . Connections of Sea The Stars were quick to pour cold water on the idea that he might be aimed at the triple crown. The passing in Derby week of Nijinsky's trainer Vincent O'Brien, one of the legends of the turf, was another poignant reminder of an era when the Derby was still almost universally regarded as the greatest race in the world (O'Brien saddled the winner six times between 1962 and 1982) and when the highest status attainable by a thoroughbred on the British turf was that of triple crown winner. Since Nijinsky, the filly Oh So Sharp is the only horse to win three English classics (One Thousand Guineas, Oaks and St Leger). The decision four years after Oh So Sharp's achievement of Nashwan's owner to bypass the St Leger in favour of an Arc preparatory race in France caused a stir among traditionalists, whose criticism—some of it vitriolic— ranged from 'unadventurous' to 'defying any sporting explanation'. But there was no wholesale criticism of the connections of Sea The Stars. The St Leger, the oldest classic, faces much stiffer competition on the international stage nowadays for the best of the classic horses than it did, for example, in Nijinsky's day. It is fair to question whether Nijinsky himself would have contested the St Leger had the richly-endowed Irish Champion Stakes been in existence in 1970. John Oxx is among those who think the triple crown will be won again. He points to the make-up of Coolmore's current stallion band, which includes the influential Sadler's Wells stallions Montjeu, Galileo and High Chaparral, and is resulting in more staying-breds coming through to Ballydoyle. Sea The Stars would have been a red-hot favourite had he turned up at Doncaster but, in the opinion of his trainer, he was not another genuine all-rounder like Nijinsky. 'I am a believer in the triple crown, it's a nice dream, but it might be a bridge too far for this fellow,' he said straight after the Derby. The position became even clearer when Oxx gave a further interview shortly after Sea The Stars returned home from Epsom. 'The St Leger is a great race, but it's a gruelling race and a big test of stamina, and I don't think this is the horse to do it,' he said. 'Cape Cross [sire of Sea The Stars] is Cape Cross and our fellow is just not bred for the St Leger—you can't ignore it. In any case, we want Sea The Stars to run in the Irish Champion Stakes [a week before the St Leger], ground permitting . . . if he doesn't run there he could run in the Arc if the ground is suitable.'

John Oxx's views on the future of the triple crown were made to look somewhat prophetic when Ballydoyle's Camelot, by Montjeu, attempted the feat just three years later, though it remains to be seen what effect that colt's failure at Doncaster has for the future of the concept.

. . . Sea The Stars was pulled out of the Irish Derby following heavy rain in the lead up to the race, and instead took the path taken by Nashwan after his Two Thousand Guineas and Derby successes, dropping back to a mile and a quarter after Epsom. Conditions at Sandown for the Coral-Eclipse, a week after the Curragh, were on the firm side and odds-on Sea The Stars, again looking in excellent shape beforehand, faced nine opponents, headed by the previous year's St Leger and Breeders' Cup Turf winner Conduit and by Rip Van Winkle, whom he was meeting for the third time in three outings as a three-year-old. No Derby winner had been successful in the Eclipse since Nashwan—Reference Point, Erhaab, Benny The Dip, Motivator and Authorized those beaten in the interim—but Sea The Stars put up a top-class performance, his effort, on form, better than those in winning the Two Thousand Guineas and the Derby and matched by his timefigure of 1.28 fast (equivalent to a timerating of 132) which was the fastest recorded by any horse over any distance in Britain in the latest season. With pacemakers for Rip Van Winkle and Conduit ensuring an unrelenting gallop, Kinane again had Sea The Stars at the head of the main pack and the response in the home straight was as impressive as it had been at Epsom. Sea The Stars quickened really well and was two lengths clear entering the penultimate furlong before idling a little in front and briefly allowing Rip Van Winkle almost alongside, before reasserting himself to win by a length, the shortest distance between the pair in their three meetings. Sea The Stars and Rip Van Winkle pulled clear of the rest, Conduit finishing four and a half lengths away in third after challenging briefly in the home straight, with the rest stretched right out (the only other runners to start at odds shorter than 50/1, Cima de Triomphe and Twice Over, were well beaten in fourth and seventh respectively).

In a further indication of the changed fashions in racing, the King George VI and Queen Elizabeth Stakes wasn't mentioned as a target for Sea The Stars after the Derby, though John Oxx did say that the colt would have been aimed at the Ascot race had he been able to run in the Irish Derby, and he next appeared at York in the Juddmonte International:

By the time Sea The Stars lined up against Mastercraftsman and two Ballydoyle pacemakers in a rather disappointing four-runner, all Irish line-up at York, his Timeform rating had gone up a further 3 lb to 136p after Rip Van Winkle and Conduit went on to boost the Eclipse form with winning performances in the Sussex Stakes (the best in the race for thirty years) and the King George VI and Queen Elizabeth Stakes respectively. Mastercraftsman had won the Irish Two Thousand Guineas and the St James's Palace Stakes since finishing fifth to Sea The Stars at Newmarket. Sea The Stars landed odds of 4/1-on at York but not before his supporters had endured an anxious moment when he briefly looked short of room while following Mastercraftsman through a gap between the two pacemakers early in the straight. Steadied again once through the gap, before Kinane asked him for his final effort, Sea The Stars took a while to hit top gear but swept through in the closing stages to beat Mastercraftsman (the pair a distance clear) with something in hand by a length, first and second both inside the previous time record for the course and distance (the time value of the performance was excellent, only a fraction behind the effort of Sea The Stars in the Eclipse).

'I'll see you at Leopardstown' was Johnny Murtagh's parting shot as Sea The Stars and Mastercraftsman were being pulled up at York. The Tattersalls Millions Irish Champion Stakes, with a first prize of £518,646 (over £200,000 more than the St Leger), certainly lived up to its billing, with Ballydoyle launching its biggest challenge yet to Sea The Stars. The management and staff at Leopardstown produced the track in very good shape, taking the precaution of preparing an inner and an outer course (the less-used latter circuit kept for the two Group 1s). Fortunately, the racecourse missed much of the heavy rain that led to several meetings elsewhere in Ireland being lost to the weather during the week, though the appearance of Sea The Stars wasn't finally confirmed until two hours before the race, which may have contributed to the fact that just 9,000 Irish racegoers took their only chance to get a view of Sea The Stars in the flesh as a three-year-old. The race provided a fascinating prospect, with Ballydoyle saddling both Mastercraftsman (pulled out of the Prix du Moulin to take part) and Fame And Glory (ridden by Murtagh), in addition to three others. Sea The Stars started at 6/4-on, Fame And Glory at 9/4 and Mastercraftsman at 6/1, with the Tattersalls Gold Cup winner Casual Conquest at 16/1 the only other runner in the nine-strong line-up at shorter than 100/1.

One of the best performances in Europe in recent times - Sea The Stars beating Fame And Glory in the Irish Champion Stakes

What established Sea The Stars as a great horse was not just the fact of his winning six Group 1 races in a row, but rather his performances in some of those races. His Eclipse performance was that of a true champion, but his performance at Leopardstown was even better, arguably the best on turf in Europe since Dancing Brave in the 1986 Prix de l'Arc de Triomphe. Any fears that Sea The Stars might be inconvenienced by the prevailing good to soft ground proved absolutely ill-founded. He completed his Group 1 five-timer in spectacular fashion, settled in mid-field and not beginning his unanswerable finishing run until after Fame And Glory had been sent clear early in the straight. Sea The Stars forged ahead over a furlong out and won by two and a half lengths, merely kept up to his work after taking the lead, drifting slightly left but giving the distinct impression he could have found more if needed. Mastercraftsman finished third, a further two and a half lengths behind Fame And Glory, with another nine back to Ballydoyle's third string Grand Ducal in fourth, Casual Conquest managing only seventh. Sea The Stars returned to the type of reception usually reserved for an Irish-trained winner of one of the championship events at Cheltenham's National Hunt Festival. It was thoroughly deserved—seeing that he had just proved himself the best Flat horse trained in Ireland in the now-extensive period since the Second World War, surpassing Nijinsky and dual Arc winner Alleged, the last-named also trained by Vincent O'Brien. John Oxx and his team at Currabeg deserved great credit for their handling of Sea The Stars, who was turned out once again in the pink of condition, while the unflappable Mick Kinane kept his nerve admirably when Fame And Glory suddenly surged past Sea The Stars early in the home straight. 'I wasn't worried. I was happy to let Fame And Glory go past me because my fellow was still running away. This is a hell of a racehorse,' he said afterwards.

Next step was the Qatar Prix de l'Arc de Triomphe, the world's richest race on turf (£2,096,881 to the winner). The race was, at one time, said to be an unlikely port of call but, with the Irish Champion showing that softish ground did not inconvenience Sea The Stars (he had won on soft at two), and the horse himself still thriving, he was sent to Longchamp with an outstanding chance…Dancing Brave was the outstanding example between Mill Reef (who won the Derby, Eclipse, King George and Arc as a three-year-old) and Sea The Stars of a top three-year-old winning the Arc after following a full programme of top races beforehand. Dancing Brave suffered an unlucky defeat in the Derby, eating up the ground to finish second, after winning the Two Thousand Guineas (before which he was warmed up in the Craven) but he swept the board otherwise until managing only fourth in the Breeders' Cup Turf on his eighth outing as a three-year-old. Dancing Brave had a similar record to Sea The Stars, winning the Eclipse (the first Derby winner to run in it since Mill Reef), turning the tables decisively on Derby winner Shahrastani in the King George and, after a warm-up in the Select Stakes at Goodwood, taking the Arc in breathtaking fashion from one of the best fields ever assembled for the race. The comparisons with Mill

Reef and Dancing Brave became irresistible after Sea The Stars duly extended his one-a-month sequence of Group 1 victories to six.

The prestige of the Arc and the attention focussed on Sea The Stars—who was cheered when he came into the paddock—led to the victory being lauded as the finest of his career though, judged solely on the quality of performance, it wasn't on a par with his Eclipse and Irish Champion efforts. The going at Longchamp was good, if anything on the firm side, and with his main rival on form Fame And Glory proving difficult to settle and then never really threatening, Sea The Stars effectively had 10 lb in hand of the rest of the Arc field. Although there was an anxious moment when Sea The Stars looked like being crowded on the inside in the home straight, the incident was never going to cost him the race. Kinane had eventually anchored the hard-pulling Sea The Stars about halfway down the main field, the two Ballydoyle pacemakers essentially ignored as they raced a long way clear, and, once extricated in the straight, Sea The Stars quickened between the leaders Stacelita and Dar Re Mi to take command a furlong out. He was well on top at the finish, winning by two lengths from the running-on Youmzain in second. The impression that Sea The Stars had plenty left was confirmed when Sea The Stars took off again as Stacelita came alongside after the leaders had crossed the line; it took Kinane some time to pull him up. The Grand Prix de Paris winner Cavalryman was the

Sea The Stars and Mick Kinane round off a superb campaign in the Prix de l'Arc de Triomphe at Longchamp

first home-trained runner to finish, a head behind Youmzain and the same in front of Conduit, with Dar Re Mi (whose dam Darara finished sixth in Dancing Brave's Arc) a further length away in fifth. Fame And Glory came sixth and Stacelita dead-heated for seventh. Sea The Stars, who received the expected rousing reception, was the first Derby winner to go on to success in the Arc since Sinndar in 2000; he was the third Arc winner ridden by Mick Kinane ('I was never worried, when I got the gap the race was over, I was on the fastest horse in the race'), following Carroll House and Montjeu. Sea The Stars carried very similar colours to those worn by his dam Urban Sea when she won the race for the Hong Kong-based Tsui (pronounced Choy) family in 1993 (Christopher Tsui, registered owner of Sea The Stars, was in the Longchamp winner's circle as an eight-year-old to greet Urban Sea with his father David). Urban Sea is the second Arc winner in the post-war era to produce a winner of the race, following Detroit who became the dam of 1994 winner Carnegie.

. . . The achievements of Raven's Pass, Henrythenavigator and New Approach in 2008 provided a timely reminder that top three-year-olds can have a full campaign and still be at their best for autumn's big championship races. Raven's Pass and Henrythenavigator finished first and second in the Breeders' Cup Classic, North America's richest race, and, with that race being staged on Santa Anita's synthetic surface for the second year running, the connections of Sea The Stars faced an awkward decision about whether or not to take up the challenge. Victory for Sea The Stars would have been a real feather in his cap, adding further to his reputation by succeeding where Dancing Brave had failed and, in the process, successfully completing just about the toughest programme that could be set for a European classic three-year-old. Sea The Stars's Arc performance clearly indicated that he was still in peak form. Kinane reported that the horse had been 'scintillating' in his homework leading up to the race, though the fact that he was starting to go in his coat at Longchamp and sweated up at the start seemed to put his rider off the idea of going on to the Breeders' Cup. 'Does he need to achieve anything more? It's questionable,' said Kinane . . . The announcement that Sea The Stars was being retired came nine days after the Arc, his trainer saying that the horse had come out of the race 'in his usual good form' but connections felt it was 'unfair to keep him going any further given his unprecedented record of achievement in the last six months.' Although some writers sought to set Sea The Stars apart as the only winner of the Two Thousand Guineas, Derby and Arc, which they dubbed 'the modern triple crown', it was Sea The Stars's unparalleled, sustained excellence, in remaining unbeaten in six genuine championship events as a three-year-old, that underpinned his claims to greatness.

Hardly any regrets were expressed in the mainstream media that Sea The Stars would not be in training at four. He was very mature physically as a three-year-old and it is unlikely he would have made more than the regulation progress from three to four and, in any event, what could he have achieved at four that would have added significantly to his record as a racehorse—or to his value? Sea-Bird, Tudor Minstrel, Nijinsky, Vaguely Noble, Sir Ivor, Shergar and Dancing Brave are among those who laid claims to immortality without running beyond the age of three. One last hurrah in the Breeders' Cup Classic—and a clash with the unbeaten American mare Zenyatta—would have brought Sea The Stars to an even wider audience, as well as giving him a chance to conquer North America, in addition to Britain, Ireland and France (not to mention one last opportunity to show whether he might indeed have proved capable of an even higher Timeform rating than the one he has been given). As it was, Sea The Stars left the stage just as the general public was getting an inkling of his greatness.

Some of those thwarted by Sea The Stars at three benefitted from the colt's retirement; Rip Van Winkle came back and landed the Juddmonte International in 2010, whilst stablemate Fame And Glory landed two Group 1s as a four-year-old, including the Coronation Cup, before later tackling staying trips, winning the Ascot Gold Cup the following season.

Sea The Stars is a big, lengthy, good sort who developed into a real power-house through his three-year-old season, very much taking the eye with his appearance and displaying a most relaxed disposition in the preliminaries. He has the pedigree to go with his good looks, being by the high-class miler Cape Cross, who stands under the Darley banner at Kildangan Stud in County Kildare, out of Urban Sea, who won the Arc at 37/1 as a four-year-old. Urban Sea ran for an unfashionable stable and her four-year-old campaign was unorthodox. She won the Prix Exbury at Saint-Cloud in March in preparation for a tilt at the Hong Kong International Cup (in which she came sixth) at Sha Tin four weeks later, running again at Saint-Cloud before looking a shade unlucky when beaten in the Prince of Wales's Stakes at Royal Ascot and then kept busy in the summer, winning at Le Lion d'Angers in the Provinces in July and in the Prix Gontaut-Biron at Deauville in August, before lining up for the Arc against fifteen Group 1 winners (she herself had never won a Group 1).

. . . Galileo has followed his own sire Sadler's Wells in becoming a star of the Coolmore stallion band, but his half-brother Sea The Stars won't be standing under the Coolmore banner, or that of its great rival Darley. He will stand at the Aga Khan's 'neutral' Gilltown Stud in Ireland where he is expected to cover between one hundred and twenty and one hundred and thirty mares at a fee of €85,000. Among the first mares to visit him will be the Aga Khan's 2008 Arc winner Zarkava. The outstanding Sea The Stars was effective at a mile to a mile and a half and he showed tip-top form on going ranging from good to firm to good to soft (also won on soft). Patiently ridden to make the most effective use of his fine turn of foot, Sea The Stars is the embodiment of that hardy Timeform epithet, tough, genuine and consistent, and he thoroughly deserves his place among the select group of horses who have fulfilled the time-honoured

Timeform definition of greatness, being 'a horse of such superlative merit as to make him, or her, far superior to the general run of classic winners.'

With his first set of two-year-olds making the track in 2013, it's too early of course to assess what impact Sea The Stars will have as a stallion, though unsurprisingly his progeny proved very popular at the sales in 2012, with his thirty-four yearlings that went through the ring selling for an average of nearly €320,000. At the time of writing Sea The Stars has already sired a pattern winner in the shape of juvenile filly My Titania, who fittingly races for the same connections of John Oxx and owner Christoper Tsui. Sea The Star's dam, the outstanding broodmare Urban Sea, died early in 2009 following complications after foaling a colt by Invincible Spirit. Born To Sea, as the colt became known, went into training with Oxx and Tsui but failed to match the achievements of some of his illustrious siblings, running his best race when runner-up to Camelot in the Irish Derby.

Harbinger

Harbinger—'one that indicates or foreshadows what is to come.' The horse of that name actually gave little prior notice that he had in him a performance that would elevate him to a place alongside some of the best horses in Timeform's experience. Harbinger belonged to the same crop as Sea The Stars, but the notion at the end of their three-year-old seasons in 2009 that Harbinger would go on to equal his great contemporary's rating as a four-year-old would have taken some believing. The pair could conceivably have met in the Derby, though Harbinger was only a twice-raced maiden winner at the time, while later in the season Harbinger was briefly ante-post favourite for the St Leger, another engagement which he didn't take up. Harbinger was rated 118 at three, when around fifty other horses of the same age earned a higher rating in *Racehorses* that year. But while Sea The Stars had no more left to prove after the end of his three-year-old season and was already at stud, the later-maturing Harbinger enjoyed an unbeaten campaign of his own as a four-year-old, albeit one ended abruptly by injury which left his claims to greatness resting on one performance. Further evidence of Harbinger's brilliance would have been welcome, if only to make those claims less open to dispute, but at the same time, in the absence of anything else to go on, the subsequent performances of those he beat in the King George VI and Queen Elizabeth Stakes did nothing to make his Ascot win look any less remarkable.

'The King is dead. Long live the King.' With champion racehorses, as with monarchs, the throne is never empty. Harbinger's reign as 'the world's best racehorse' lasted a mere sixteen days. He became the world's top-rated horse overnight with a record-breaking eleven-length victory in the King George VI and Queen Elizabeth Stakes, having gone into that race not even acknowledged as the best horse in his own stable. The transformation at Ascot sent Harbinger's reputation sky-high, the status of the King George combined with the quality of his performance on the day virtually proving Harbinger a great champion in a single performance. But sixteen days afterwards his racing career was over, the owners confirming Harbinger's retirement two days after he sustained a condylar fracture of his near-fore cannon bone in a routine piece of work on the Newmarket gallops. The King George was Harbinger's fourth straight victory in a season which had seen his performances becoming more impressive with each race.

Wide-margin victories in a top race are always hard to follow and Harbinger would have done very well to have bettered his performance on King George day, though, at the time, there seemed every possibility that Ascot would still be the precursor of other outstanding performances from a racehorse who seemed to be only just reaching the height of his powers at the age of four. That Harbinger didn't get the opportunity to prove himself further in the top open-aged championships—he was set to run in the International at York next and was a very short-priced favourite for the Arc—may well lead to his King George performance being gradually devalued as it is judged by posterity. The previous year's outstanding champion Sea The Stars proved himself time and time again, tested against the best six times during a memorable campaign— at a mile, a mile and a quarter and a mile and a half—and passing every test with flying colours. By contrast, Harbinger contested only one Group 1 race in his life but, on any rational reading of the form-book, there is very little reason to doubt that the performance he gave was one of the greatest in Timeform's very long experience. Harbinger's career may eventually stand as testament to the fleeting nature of fame but his one-off performance in the King George is worthy of being rated at least the equal of the pick of the individual performances recorded by Sea The Stars. One of the others among a select band rated at 140 or higher in the *Racehorses* series is Shergar, with whom Harbinger now shares the distinction of being the best horse trained by ten-times champion Sir Michael Stoute. Shergar's official margin of victory in the Derby, which he won by ten lengths in 1981, is also a record for that race, his performance at Epsom the pinnacle of his career, though he went on to cement his reputation by following up in the Irish Derby and the King George, both of which he won by four lengths, before an unexpected defeat in the St Leger, after which he was retired.

Sir Michael Stoute is a particularly fine trainer of late-developing older horses but Harbinger's successful four-year-old season did not owe so much to the renowned patient approach which has produced so many other big winners for the stable down the years. 'He was quite well developed as a young horse, we had him ready to run in the September of his two-year-old season but he got shin-sore,' said Stoute of Harbinger, adding that the stable had been 'very optimistic' about him before he finished last when a short-priced favourite in the Great Voltigeur as a three-year-old. Harbinger progressed well at three after finishing second on his debut in the Wood Ditton at Newmarket, one of the most historic maiden races in the Calendar. He won a maiden at Chester on his second start, after which he was as low as 16/1 for the Derby, but returned from Chester with a pulled muscle in his quarters. After being given time, he eventually reappeared in the Gordon Stakes at Goodwood in July, beating his field with something to spare and going to the head of the St Leger betting until his poor run in the Voltigeur. Harbinger had his tongue tied on his only subsequent outing at three, coming a creditable third on heavy going in the St Simon Stakes at Newbury without showing any obvious sign of what was to come at four.

Harbinger began his unbeaten run in the new season in the Group 3 Dubai Duty Free Finest Surprise Stakes, better known as the John Porter, at Newbury in April. Starting third favourite in a fifteen-strong line-up, Harbinger was always going smoothly and quickened well to win by three lengths from Manifest, whose season was being mapped out around the major staying events. It was on to Chester for Harbinger and the Boodles Diamond Ormonde Stakes over an extended mile and five furlongs, in which he started odds on and again travelled well throughout before winning in eye-catching style by a length and a half from another Gold Cup-bound stayer, Age of Aquarius, the pair clear. Harbinger was making up for lost time and rattled up his third win of the season in the Hardwicke Stakes at Royal Ascot (two days after Age of Aquarius went down by a neck in the Gold Cup). Royal Ascot was a good meeting for punters generally—thirteen winning favourites and only six of the thirty winners returned at double-figure odds—but the estimate of industry-wide losses of £50m circulated by the bookmakers needed taking with the proverbial pinch of salt. Harbinger started the shortest-priced favourite of the week—11/8-on—and ran out one of the easiest winners. The field for the Hardwicke was above average and Harbinger showed he was well and truly ready to take on the very best, cruising smoothly into contention before the straight and again producing a fine turn of foot to hit the front two furlongs out. He beat Duncan with the minimum of fuss by three and a half lengths, with front-running Barshiba six lengths further back in third, Sans Frontieres fourth and Redwood fifth. Harbinger's win crowned a fine week for the various syndicate members of Highclere Thoroughbred Racing, the two-year-olds Memory and Approve also carrying the colours to success, with Theology nearly making it four winners when just touched off in the Queen's Vase.

The King George VI and Queen Elizabeth Stakes, in its second year sponsored by Betfair, had already been announced as the next race for Harbinger's stablemate, the very impressive Derby winner Workforce, but their trainer kept his cards close to his chest when asked after the Hardwicke whether Harbinger would be taking on Workforce, who had won at Epsom in record time. It wasn't too long, though, before confirmation was forthcoming that both Workforce and Harbinger would be running at Ascot. Ryan Moore had partnered Harbinger in all eight of his races but his decision to ride Workforce in the King George, after the pair had twice worked together in early-July, led to Olivier Peslier taking over (he had ridden the 2008 runner-up Papal Bull for the stable when Moore rode Ask). With Cape Blanco, the only horse to have beaten Workforce, also earmarked for the King George after winning the Irish Derby, the classic generation had two strong representatives in a race that had not been won by a three-year-old since Alamshar in 2003, the last time the winners of the Derby at Epsom and the Curragh had clashed in Britain's most important open-aged middle-distance race (Kris Kin, the Derby winner, came third). The latest edition of the King George was the sixtieth and, after Harbinger's victory, the older horses, as a group, now lead the three-year-olds by thirty-three victories to twenty-seven, the roll of honour extended by seven successive four-year-old winners since Alamshar's year. The King George was inaugurated—strategically placed at the end of July—with the purpose of providing an opportunity for the leading classic middle-distance horses to meet, on weight-for-age terms, the best of their older counterparts that had remained in training. The return of the Derby winners restored the latest edition to a much more genuine clash of the generations than most of its recent predecessors, though there were only six runners (one of them a pacemaker for the Stoute stable). Harbinger's form in the Hardwicke was virtually good enough to have won any of the most recent King Georges, while the two other representatives of the older generation were both Group 1 winners, namely Youmzain and the French-trained Hong Kong Vase winner Daryakana, that pair having finished a close second and third respectively in the Grand Prix de Saint-Cloud on their latest outing. The five-year-old mare Dar Re Mi, winner of the Dubai Sheema Classic, was a late absentee because of a foot abscess.

Workforce's presence at Ascot as a Derby winner proved to be little more than a blip in the long-term trend, however, with the three Epsom winners since (all owned by Coolmore) notable by their absence at Ascot, and he remains the only Derby winner since Kris Kin (2003) to tackle the King George. Galileo in 2001 was the last to complete the double, though Alamshar was third at Epsom prior to his win in 2003.

With Workforce at 11/8-on and Harbinger second favourite at 4/1 (Cape Blanco started 9/2), a record-equalling fifth King George winner for the Stoute stable seemed very much on the cards, to add to Shergar, Opera House, Golan and Conduit. The prevailing popular view that Workforce would reinvigorate the profile of the race by romping to victory proved very wide of the mark. His

An outstanding performance - Harbinger crushes his rivals, headed by Irish Derby winner Cape Blanco, in the King George VI And Queen Elizabeth Stakes

performance, managing only fifth of six, was as big a letdown as Harbinger's exhilarating victory was a revelation. The look on Sir Michael Stoute's face after the King George said it all! Harbinger didn't just win, he annihilated the opposition. He could be named the winner turning for home and the sublime manner in which he cruised up to Cape Blanco and Workforce early in the straight and strode right away, with Peslier barely having to move a muscle, took the breath away. His margin of victory over Cape Blanco eclipsed the seven lengths by which Generous won in 1991 (Mill Reef, Dahlia and St Jovite were six-length winners, Ribot and Daylami won by five, and Ragusa, Shergar and Dylan Thomas by four). Harbinger's winning time was a record since the revamped Ascot track reopened in 2006, though record times in themselves are not particularly significant, often just an indication that the prevailing conditions were favourable for the setting of time records. The time value of Harbinger's performance indicated, however, that he had put up an exceptional display, his computer timefigure of 1.38 fast the best recorded in a British middle-distance race since Generous clocked 1.41 fast in the same race. In terms of form, Harbinger's performance earned him a higher annual rating than all the winners of the King George except Ribot, Mill Reef, Brigadier Gerard, Shergar and Dancing Brave. In other words, purely in terms of racing merit, Harbinger joined the list of post-war racing greats.

'One performance proves nothing' is sometimes the reaction to a wide-margin winner of a major race but Harbinger's untimely injury meant that, effectively, he does have to be judged on one race. The job of handicapping—and allocating largely academic ratings for top horses who have finished their careers—involves a degree of subjective judgement, more so in some cases than others. In day-to-day handicapping, no-one would dream of ignoring the performance of a wide-margin winner and allowing him an unpenalised chance to repeat the form. Likewise, Harbinger's King George performance cannot simply be dismissed as being too good to be true, or as being inexplicable. Had Workforce won in similar manner, following on from his stunning Derby win, there is not the slightest doubt that the eulogies would have been fulsome. It would certainly have been better to have had a bigger field, especially as two of the six runners were Workforce, clearly not the horse he had been on Derby Day, and Confront, who was used as a pacemaker. However, this wasn't a victory for which too much credit could be placed on the frailties of the winner's opponents. Harbinger's eleven-length margin of victory over Cape Blanco (rated 125 after the Irish Derby) translated to a 20-lb beating, while Timeform's historical race standards, applied to the result, indicated that it would be unusual for the rating of Harbinger to fall outside the range of 135 to 140—admittedly giving some scope for 'subjective judgement'. Analysis of the overall time of the race, as already mentioned, revealed a time performance right out of the top drawer which provided further valuable independent evidence (the wind was light on the day and the going over the three-day meeting uniform, which reduced the complications involved in arriving at a reliable timefigure). Sectional timing analysis is also used by Timeform's handicappers, and their hand-held times—sadly the raw data is not available on a plate—for the individual horses in the King George revealed that those behind Harbinger were fading relatively quickly in the closing stages. This almost certainly exaggerated the winning distance, and, in arriving at Harbinger's final rating, the three horses in the frame behind him— Cape Blanco, Youmzain (who finished a further three and a quarter lengths back in third, placed in the race for a third time) and Daryakana (another neck behind in fourth)—were all taken as running several pounds below their very best in the King George.

Timeform ratings are always subject to review in the light of subsequent performances but any idea that Harbinger might turn out to be too high at 140—the rating published for him after the King George—was not too long in being dispelled. Cape Blanco franked the form by winning the Irish Champion Stakes at Leopardstown by five and a half lengths from the two principals in the International at York, Rip Van Winkle and Twice Over (who had won the Eclipse and went on to win the Champion Stakes at Newmarket for a second time). Cape Blanco's victory may have been as much of a surprise to his stable (stablemate Rip Van Winkle started odds on) as Harbinger's had been to his in the King George, but both performances are there in the form-book. The form of another of the races won by Harbinger, the Hardwicke Stakes, also received a further boost when runner-up Duncan won the Prix Foy on Longchamp's 'day of trials', the day after the Hardwicke fourth Sans Frontieres stretched his winning run since Royal Ascot to three by taking the Irish St Leger. Harbinger would have had to be supplemented at a cost of £50,000 to contest the International (in which he was to have been reunited with Ryan Moore), but, by the time that race was being run, negotiations were well under way for Harbinger's sale as a stallion. Harbinger came through surgery—involving the insertion of a plate to repair the hairline fracture—without complications and in early-September it was announced that he had been sold to Japan, following in the footsteps of two other Stoute-trained King George winners, Opera House and Conduit. The twelve shareholders in the Admiral Rous Highclere syndicate were entitled to receive the proceeds of the sale, as Highclere Thoroughbred Racing operates ownership groups, not a club. Highclere Thoroughbreds does not retain horses for breeding and two of its earlier Group 1-winning colts, the sprinters Lake Coniston and Tamarisk, were sold to Coolmore. Harbinger will start his stud career at Shadai Farm where the roster of around two dozen stallions includes a number of sons of Kentucky Derby winner Sunday Silence, whose purchase by the founder of Shadai Farm, the late Zenya Yoshida, changed the face of Japanese breeding and made Shadai one of the world's most successful studs.

Harbinger's record-breaking King George win

BLACK CAVIAR

A Timeform Publication

Black Caviar

Still a relative unknown beyond her own shores, Black Caviar was a late addition to the main A to Z section of *Racehorses of 2010*, though a rating of 128 (the equal of the best sprinter in Europe that year, Starspangledbanner, himself an import from Down Under) and a record of eight wins from as many starts were good arguments for her inclusion as one of the more interesting overseas performers. She was summed up, like the vast majority of horses in the annual, in note form, but a year later she demanded more in-depth attention. Black Caviar's career had still to take her beyond Australia, but by the time more than 85,000 turned up at Flemington to see her final appearance of 2011, it was clear she was on the way to becoming more than just an Australian phenomenon— and, all being well, she was on the way to Royal Ascot as well. A poll conducted just beforehand showed that seventy-eight per cent of Australians had read, seen or heard of Black Caviar, but her fame was spreading further:

Despite never having set foot outside Australia, Black Caviar has already made a name for herself more widely, among racing fans at least. The fact that she is racing in the era of the internet—she has her own web site and all her big wins can be watched on-line—has undoubtedly helped to spread Black Caviar's name around the world much more readily than those of Australia's greatest horses of the past; the likes of Tulloch, Kingston Town and Manikato were all top-notchers as well, but their names are unlikely to have anything like the same resonance outside Australia. Black Caviar is also performing at a time when racing links between Australia and Europe have never been closer. The make-up of the field for the latest Melbourne Cup is one indication of that. Another is the great success of Australian sprinters in Britain in recent years, and Black Caviar's overwhelming superiority over the sprinters in her own country has resulted in her progress being followed all the more keenly from Britain in anticipation of her one day following in the footsteps of Choisir, Takeover Target, Miss Andretti and Scenic Blast. Royal Ascot is said to figure very much in the plans for Black Caviar in 2012. Another reason for the attention being paid to Black Caviar beyond her own shores is her unbeaten record, which she had extended to sixteen by the end of 2011. Unbeaten records attract media interest and capture the imagination, and Black Caviar's unblemished record has played its part in making her famous, in the same way as it has in recent years with Silent Witness, Overdose and Zenyatta—and will almost certainly do with Frankel in 2012.

Frankel v Black Caviar or Frankel x Black Caviar? Speculation that the unbeaten champions might meet on the track, or failing that, at a later date in the breeding shed, was simply that, and a distraction from the main focus of Black Caviar's 2012 campaign:

Royal Ascot. Another demonstration of her superiority, but to a new set of rivals, was widely anticipated, though as it turned out, Black Caviar's win in the Diamond Jubilee Stakes was the one occasion when the dwindling supply of superlatives did not need to be called upon:

'She looks at the 30,000-strong crowd and she says "Jeez I'm good, no I'm not good, I'm the best you've ever seen in the world" . . . she's twenty out of twenty . . . Black Caviar by four lengths.' The racing year was packed with so many monumental achievements that even experienced pundits expressed concerns that they might 'run out of superlatives'. No danger though of the climactic race commentator at Morphettville in Adelaide failing to reflect the excitement when Black Caviar produced the first of the year's 'were you watching?' moments. It came at the end of April (on her fourth start of the calendar year) when she broke the Australasian metropolitan record for the number of successive wins with a comfortable four-and-a-half-length victory in the Sportingbet Classic (registered as the Robert Sangster Stakes) for fillies and mares. Black Caviar was 20/1-on for an event claimed beforehand by the same commentator to be 'the most anticipated race of the century', a description that might have been better left to garnish her appearance two races later in the Diamond Jubilee Stakes at Royal Ascot. Morphettville was packed to the rafters again when Black Caviar made it twenty-one in a row in the Distinctive Homes Goodwood Stakes—again landing odds of 20/1-on—before being flown halfway round the world to seal her place in racing history in front of a sell-out 77,863 at the Royal meeting. The crowd featured something of an invasion of Aussie racegoers numbering between 3,500 and 5,000—many with flags in Black Caviar's colours of salmon with black spots—in the largest influx of visitors from outside Europe for a major raceday since Deep Impact's Japanese fans took Longchamp by storm on Arc day in 2006.

Black Caviar's 10,500-mile journey (which took thirty hours) is regularly undertaken nowadays with Australia's top sprinters, who have built up an impressive Royal Ascot record since Choisir became the first Australian-trained horse to win in Britain when taking the King's Stand Stakes in 2003, when he went on to complete an historic Royal Ascot double in the Golden Jubilee Stakes (renamed Diamond Jubilee in 2012 to mark the sixtieth year of the Queen's reign). The Group 1 Golden Jubilee was in its second year when Choisir won it, the race having been introduced when Royal Ascot was extended to a fifth day to commemorate the fiftieth anniversary of the Queen's accession. It replaced the Cork And Orrery Stakes and was run on the Saturday to ensure there was at least one Group 1 event on each of the five days. The Golden Jubilee has been a great success—Saturday attracts the biggest crowd of the week—and the first prize of £283,550 under its new name again made it the joint most valuable race at the meeting, with the Prince of Wales's Stakes. Black Caviar had won bigger prizes at home—in top weight-for-age sprints like the Coolmore Lightning Stakes and the Patinack Farm Classic, both of which she

*Diamond Jubilee Stakes, Royal Ascot - it all looks plain sailing
on Black Caviar's British debut….*

had won twice—and her trainer Peter Moody was keen to emphasise the point. 'It's a massive risk for the mare's owners to bring her over here—really for very little gain. It doesn't add up that we have to travel across the world to stamp her greatness by racing inferior opposition and for inferior prize money,' he said.

Black Caviar arrived at Royal Ascot generally acknowledged as the second best horse in the world, behind Frankel, whom Moody pointed out had 'done what he has done only on his own patch and is never going to leave the UK.' Frankel and Black Caviar, both virtually unbackable, were the star attractions at Royal Ascot, though attempts to divert attention to a possible meeting between them in the Sussex Stakes at Goodwood got in the way during the build-up. Qipco, sponsors of the Sussex, offered to raise the prize money to £1m if both Frankel and Black Caviar contested their race, though the prospect was never realistic, if for no other reason than, as Moody said, 'We could find sponsors in Australia to put up £10m if they bring Frankel down to run over seven furlongs at Flemington or Caulfield. How about it? Winner takes all.' For some reason, Black Caviar's connections were accused in some quarters of 'sidestepping' or 'ducking' a meeting with Frankel in the Sussex, though any such meeting would have been on terms that very much favoured Frankel (Frankel's connections didn't come under fire for 'swerving' a meeting with Black Caviar in the Diamond Jubilee, or for going for the less valuable Queen Anne Stakes).

Modern Greats

Black Caviar's reputation as a wonder mare—'The Wonder From Down Under'—meant that she was feted like a pop star on her stay in Britain, with daily bulletins from her temporary quarters at Abington Place stables in Newmarket. With Black Caviar reported as being 'as bright as a button' in the days after her arrival, the trainer's racing manager supplied the big media presence with enough stories to keep Black Caviar's name in the headlines ('Her track work is like nothing you've ever seen . . . she runs times that have you scratching your head, once or twice in the early days we thought our watches were playing up'). The anticipation of Black Caviar's appearance in the paddock before the Diamond Jubilee was palpable, though, having come from an Aussie winter, her coat didn't quite have the shine of her rivals and she was sweating. There was an enthusiastic reception as she was led in from the pre-parade ring, and loud applause as she made her way out on to the track. Down Under, where Black Caviar is a household name and regularly appears on the general news pages, there was enormous interest in her challenge. The Diamond Jubilee was shown live on TV across Australia and on a giant screen in Melbourne's Federation Square, even though the race took place well after midnight, local time. Australian sprinters Takeover Target, Miss Andretti and Scenic Blast had all followed in the footsteps of Choisir by winning at Royal Ascot, but Black Caviar was by far the best to have made the journey and stood out a mile on form in the Diamond Jubilee, sent off at 6/1-on against thirteen rivals headed

. . . but, after prematurely stopping riding, jockey Luke Nolen has to shake her up to hold off the challengers

Black Caviar

by the high-class French-trained filly Moonlight Cloud and the previous year's winner Society Rock, that pair and the Bahrain-trained Golden Shaheen winner Krypton Factor (making up a quartet of overseas challengers) the only ones to start at shorter than 20/1. Royal Ascot's top sprints both form part of the Global Sprint Challenge and it was unusual that none of the runners from the King's Stand Stakes on the opening day doubled up in the Diamond Jubilee— Australian-trained Star Witness had been placed in both the previous year.

If Frankel's astounding eleven-length victory in the Queen Anne provided Royal Ascot with its most brilliant moment, then Black Caviar certainly provided the meeting with its most dramatic one. On her first start outside Australia, she was nowhere near her best and, in the end, had to pull out all the stops to survive a near-calamitous error by her regular jockey Luke Nolen, who stopped riding with around fifty yards to go after pushing Black Caviar into the lead over a furlong out. Black Caviar was over a length in front at one stage but her jockey elected to let Black Caviar coast in, seeming to underestimate the stiffness of the uphill finish, until realising in the nick of time that Moonlight Cloud and 40/1-shot Restiadargent were finishing strongly. Shaken up again in the last few strides, Black Caviar scraped home by a head and a neck, though there was an anxious wait for the result of the photo finish. The ex-Australian-trained Soul, who was up there all the way, finished fourth, only a further three quarters of a length behind, just in front of Society Rock, who would have gone very close but for missing the break, and Krypton Factor. It wasn't the performance everyone had come to see and, even if she had been ridden right out, Black Caviar would probably not have won by much further than half a length. It transpired the next morning that she was 'quite sore behind' and was found to have suffered damage to a suspensory ligament and torn some muscles in her back, connections at first hinting that she might be headed for retirement. 'I had concerns half a mile out because she wasn't travelling with the zip she shows at home, and only her grit got her home,' said her trainer afterwards. 'Fortunately she was able to get the job done and, if she is retired, she has ended on a high.' (Peter Moody revealed some time afterwards that he 'knew on the morning of the race that she wasn't right but I didn't want to be making excuses before the race was even run so I kept my feelings to myself, and didn't even let on to the owners'). Black Caviar's jockey had his explanation 'noted' at a subsequent stewards' inquiry and his attention drawn to the rules governing negligence by a rider. Nolen faced a possible 42-day suspension if Black Caviar had been beaten and he admitted to the media that he had made 'an error that every apprentice is taught to avoid', saying that he had been trying to 'look after' his mount who 'stopped and came back underneath me.'

Black Caviar was seen on a racecourse again, but not in 2012. Her first race back in Australia in 2013 came just before _Racehorses of 2012_ went to press and was covered in this postscript to her essay:

'And the legend lives on . . . ' to quote the course commentator when Black Caviar made it twenty-three wins from twenty-three starts in the Black Caviar Lightning Stakes in February 2013, winning the race for the third time and breaking the track record in the process when returning 55.43sec for Flemington's straight five furlongs. Asked about the possibility of Black Caviar returning to Royal Ascot in 2013, trainer Peter Moody said 'It's a case of never say never, if the owners were mad keen and maybe it tied in with a mating with, say, Frankel, then who knows?' He also revealed that, in the albeit seemingly unlikely event of a second Royal Ascot appearance, Black Caviar would appear in the King's Stand Stakes, rather than the Diamond Jubilee. 'We ran her in the wrong race in 2012,' he said.

The legend lived on for another two races before time was called on Black Caviar's racing career but there was to be no return trip to Royal Ascot. After winning the William Reid Stakes at Moonee Valley for the second time, Black Caviar bowed out with win number twenty-five in the T J Smith Stakes at Randwick in April 2013, in the process setting a new Australian record of fifteen for the most number of Group 1 victories. She begins her broodmare career with a visit to leading shuttle stallion Exceed And Excel. Like Black Caviar, Exceed And Excel features on the Newmarket Handicap's roll of honour in Australia, and he too made one appearance in Britain, though he beat only one home in the 2004 July Cup after making much of the running.

So where does Black Caviar, on a rating of 136, fit in the wider scheme of things among the best fillies and mares of the Timeform era?

Black Caviar has been the best filly or mare in the world over the last two years (in each of which she has been Australia's Racehorse of the Year) and she is the joint-highest-rated filly or mare aged three or above in the history of the *Racehorses* series, equal with the great French-trained middle-distance performer Allez France and the tip-top British sprinter Habibti. Next in the list come Allez France's contemporary Dahlia, the 1949 Prix de l'Arc winner Coronation V ('won in brilliant style by four lengths from a very strong field, leaving them all standing with a great final run') and the very fine British middle-distance filly Pebbles, all rated 135, just ahead of Petite Etoile and All Along on 134. The long list of illustrious mares and fillies rated 133 is: Dunfermline, Goldikova, Hula Dancer, Indian Skimmer, Lianga, Marwell, Miesque, Noblesse, Pistol Packer, Rose Bowl, San San, Three Troikas, Triptych and Zarkava.

Favourite Racehorses called Habibti, Timeform's Horse of The Year in 1983 and winner of that season's July Cup, Nunthorpe, Sprint Cup and Prix de l'Abbaye, 'the best female sprinter of the last fifty years'. With the exception of the colt Dayjur in 1990, there has not been a better sprinter of either sex to race in Europe since Habibti, whose rating Black Caviar equalled.

Oasis Dream

SPRINTERS

Modern Greats

A Timeform Publication

Sprinters

Speed might be the most obvious quality a racehorse should possess, and as two-year-olds, it is, by and large, the quality that they are most often asked to demonstrate. But for good three-year-olds, the racing programme offers little opportunity, at least in the early part of the season, for the out-and-out sprinter. For that reason—and there are commercial pressures too with stud careers in mind—a number of leading sprinters have been campaigned first as Guineas horses before ultimately proving best when brought back to shorter distances. The alternative means taking on seasoned older horses in the big sprints. There have even been some good sprinting two-year-old colts in recent seasons—Dark Angel in 2007, Zebedee in 2010—which have been retired to stud at the end of their juvenile careers, not due to injury, but simply because they had little prospect of proving anything other than sprinters at three. Perhaps it is not surprising, therefore, that a number of sprinters who have gone on to success at Group 1 level have graduated from the handicapping ranks, instead of pattern company, as younger horses.

Stravinsky (rated 133) was not originally considered a sprinter by his trainer Aidan O'Brien and was campaigned accordingly, racing exclusively over seven furlongs on his next four starts after making a winning debut as a two-year-old in 1998, including finishing third in the Dewhurst Stakes on his final start at two. Stravinsky's two outings as a three-year-old prior to the July Cup had seen him finish a neck second in a minor event at the Curragh, after which he lost his position as favourite for the Two Thousand Guineas, and fourth in the Jersey Stakes, where he didn't convince with his finishing effort and was again well below his two-year-old form—'I was asking him to do something he just wasn't able to do' his trainer later conceded, referring to the colt's inability to produce his best over a trip further than six furlongs.

In what was a vintage year for racing in Britain and Ireland—there were unforgettable performances over longer distances from the likes of Montjeu, Daylami, Royal Anthem and Dubai Millennium which are covered elsewhere in these pages—Stravinsky produced one of his own by not just beating his rivals in the July Cup but destroying them, as detailed in *Racehorses of 1999*:

> So, Stravinsky arrived at Newmarket for the July Cup with the record of one win from five starts, in the Convivial Maiden at York the previous August, and the suspicion that he would never take high rank. His star was not so low, however, as

to make him an outsider in a most open July Cup, for which he started 8/1 third favourite. The sixteen other runners included thirteen pattern winners, among them proven speed merchants Bold Edge, successful in the Cork And Orrery Stakes and second favourite at 7/1, King's Stand Stakes winner Mitcham, Duke of York Stakes winner Sampower Star and 1998 Nunthorpe winner Lochangel. There were also several other three-year-olds coming back in distance, headed by the 11/2 favourite Wannabe Grand, placed in the One Thousand Guineas and Coronation Stakes, and 9/1-shot Bertolini, who had finished one place ahead of Stravinsky at Royal Ascot. The best sprinter of 1979, Thatching, had been trained at Ballydoyle (by Vincent O'Brien) and had improved dramatically when tried in blinkers, storming home in the Cork And Orrery Stakes and the July Cup, which he won by five lengths. Another Ballydoyle inmate, Marinsky, had been blinkered (and muzzled) when winning the 1977 July Cup, only to be disqualified. Stravinsky was fitted with a visor for the first time—he wore this headgear in his remaining starts as well—and, combined with the shorter trip, the result was devastating. Cool as a cucumber in the preliminaries, Stravinsky was held up, travelling smoothly, as Bold Edge and Bertolini set a good pace. Cruising through on the bridle from halfway, he unleashed a spectacular turn of foot to lead inside the final furlong and strode away to score by four lengths. The time was a track record (if not an outstanding time performance), beating that set by Elnadim the year before, and the winning margin equalled Lake Coniston's in 1995, with only Thatching having scored by further in recent times. For the record, Bold Edge was second and Bertolini third, a neck away, but nothing really mattered besides the winner, who was in a class of his own and clearly very much at home on firm going.

'The composer was different but the outcome was the same' noted *Racehorses of 2001* in reference to the fact that just two years after Stravinsky had been brought back in distance to develop into one of the best sprinters of the modern era, the same connections' **Mozart** (rated 131) followed suit. Mozart had actually succeeded where Stravinsky had failed in winning the Jersey Stakes, and he matched Stravinsky's feat of winning Europe's two most strongly-contested races for sprinters, the July Cup and Nunthorpe Stakes, on successive starts. Mozart's essay endeavoured to answer the question of what makes a sprinter:

> Stamina in the thoroughbred is dependent on various factors, including heredity, temperament and conformation, but usually the most important element is how the horse's muscles are arranged. There is a mix between 'fast-twitch' and 'slow-twitch' muscles in all thoroughbreds and the division crucially affects the greatest distance over which a runner is effective. Fast-twitch muscles, which use glycogen, not oxygen, are able to expand and contract quickly, providing rapid movement for short periods of time. If dominant, they make for a sprinter. A preponderance of slow-twitch muscles, which use oxygen for power and have a slower expansion and contraction time, enables a horse to receive energy at a steadier pace and to stay further. Unfortunately, even allowing for

differences in appearance or temperament, there is no easy way for a trainer to ascertain precisely how the muscles of any of his horses are arranged. Once the racecourse has given a clear indication, though, skilful training can change the balance and enhance one type of muscle at the expense of the other. In other words, a sprinter doesn't have to be born, he can be made, providing the ability (and sufficient fast-twitch muscles) are there in the first place.

Unlike Stravinsky, Mozart appeared to have prospects of staying further on breeding, the Dewhurst fourth being talked of as a possible Kentucky Derby contender (his dam's half-brother Sea Hero had won the race) by Aidan O'Brien even after his three-year-old season had begun, and he actually produced a very smart—if ultimately non-staying—performance when second to stablemate Black Minnaloushe in the Irish Two Thousand Guineas. But his natural calling was clearly sprinting, and Mozart's essay emphasised just how dominant he was over a good batch of sprinters:

The form of the Jersey Stakes was not so good as that of the Irish Guineas, but, given O'Brien's expertise, the signs were there that by the time of the colt's next intended start, the July Cup, he would be even sharper and faster—O'Brien said at Ascot: 'I've never seen a horse with his pace. Speed is his thing.' So it proved, and in astonishing fashion, at Newmarket, where eighteen runners faced the starter. Besides Mozart they included horses who had won two Group 2 races (Cassandra Go, Harmonic Way), three Group 3 races (Gorse, Shibboleth, Volata) and two listed events (Mount Abu, Misraah) on their last start, so there was no shortage of in-form contenders. Mozart, who very nearly got away from his rider on the way to post, proved ideally drawn on the stand side—the low-drawn runners who raced towards the far side were seriously disadvantaged—and, away like lightning, he soon left the others trailing when asked to quicken approaching the two-furlong pole, storming clear to defeat Cassandra Go by three and a half lengths with Misraah third. A breathtaking display, comfortably the best by a sprinter all year, and in the second-fastest time in the race's history. After this it looked as though only ill-luck could prevent Mozart's adding the five-furlong Victor Chandler Nunthorpe Stakes to his tally at York the following month. His nine opponents, six of whom started at 20/1 or longer, were not so good a bunch as at Newmarket—the second favourite, Nuclear Debate, seemed to be struggling to recapture the form which had won him the race the previous year. After just missing the break, Mozart was niggled along to find his stride, improved to lead two furlongs out and responded well when given a couple of reminders in the final furlong to run out a comfortable two-length winner from Nuclear Debate. Mick Kinane finished the race with his saddle having slipped a long way back after Mozart left the stalls awkwardly, which cannot have helped the colt's cause and paid tribute to the jockey's balance—this only four years after Kevin Darley's heroics riding without reins on Coastal Bluff in the same race. With the saddle in the right place Mozart would surely have won more cosily, but to claim, as his owner did, that the margin might have been ten lengths is fanciful in the extreme.

Oasis Dream (rated 129) was another colt for whom Guineas ambitions were seemingly held at the beginning of his three-year-old season. However, speed had been the dominant characteristic in his juvenile campaign, highlighted by his win in the Middle Park Stakes, and he became the third horse in five years to land the July Cup-Nunthorpe double, a feat that hasn't been repeated since.

Oasis Dream failed to come to himself in time for the classics, and was undone by a combination of needing the run and trying five furlongs for the first time when returning in the King's Stand Stakes, for which he was sent off favourite despite carrying a penalty, and finished third. Oasis Dream, one of nine Juddmonte-bred horses to win Group 1 or Grade 1 races in 2003, won a strong July Cup on his next start, with his beaten rivals including the first two from the King's Stand, Choisir and Acclamation, and Airwave, who had finished fourth to Choisir in the Golden Jubilee Stakes. Oasis Dream's July Cup victory was the first in a Group 1 sprint by a champion two-year-old since the pattern system was introduced in 1971. His win in the Nunthorpe Stakes was arguably more impressive, though, as explained in *Racehorses of 2003*:

> The form of the July Cup was not far behind that shown by the two best recent winners of the race, Stravinsky and Mozart. Unfortunately, by the time of the Nunthorpe Stakes at York six weeks later, Choisir had been retired to stud and Airwave was under the weather, leaving Oasis Dream with an apparently straightforward task. He had the beating of four of his seven rivals—Acclamation, Bahamian Pirate, Continent and Orientor—on Newmarket form and of Dominica and The Trader on King's Stand form, while King George Stakes victor The Tatling had to improve considerably to pose a threat. Oasis Dream put on a performance that was a shade reminiscent of Dayjur's in the Nunthorpe thirteen years earlier. Again looking at the peak of condition and on very good terms with himself, Oasis Dream left the stalls like lightning, clearly had the legs of the others after only two furlongs and surged clear when shaken up over a furlong out to beat The Tatling by two and a half lengths. Although not driven out fully, Oasis Dream put up a timefigure equivalent to a rating of 133, better than any sprinter had managed for over a decade, and his time of 56.20sec came within four hundredths of a second of Dayjur's course record. In fact, Oasis Dream would have broken the record but for a course alteration in the meantime which added three yards to the distance, so it was surprising that certain journalists took this particular opportunity to pooh-pooh Oasis Dream's claims to being 'the fastest horse in the world'. Comparisons with Dayjur were inevitable but, good as Oasis Dream's victory was, Dayjur's was better; he recorded a timefigure equivalent to a rating of 142, beating the very smart Statoblest by four lengths. Dayjur covered himself in glory in his remaining starts, the Haydock Sprint Cup and the Prix de l'Abbaye de Longchamp, both of which he won, and the Breeders' Cup Sprint, which he unluckily lost. The same cannot be said of Oasis Dream, but the fact that he tasted defeat in both his remaining races did little to diminish his standing.

July Cup - Oasis Dream reverses King's Stand form with Choisir (rail)

For the record, Oasis Dream was undone by softish ground when runner-up to Somnus in the Sprint Cup at Haydock, and then failed to stay in the Breeders' Cup Mile.

Another high-class sprinting three-year-old who was tried over further than sprint trips was Dream Ahead, who quickly put a poor return in the St James's Palace Stakes behind him when winning both the July Cup and Sprint Cup. Dream Ahead's best performance—the one that gave him a rating of 133—was achieved when beating Goldikova in the Prix de la Foret back over seven furlongs, and therefore the best performance in a sprint in 2011 according to *Racehorses* came from **Deacon Blues** (rated 130) who progressed from a win in the Wokingham Handicap to four victories from as many starts at Group level.

> The Wokingham was the last handicap that Deacon Blues contested. He was 11 lb off top weight on the day and feasibly might have gone on to contest the Stewards' Cup (the Wokingham seventh Hoof It produced an outstanding handicap performance to land that race by two and a half lengths off a BHA mark of 111). However, connections decided to step him straight up to pattern company and the move paid dividends straight away. A month after Ascot, Deacon Blue won the Hackwood Stakes, run under the title of the Shadwell Stakes, at Newbury, easily beating a field of smart sprinters—Markab was second, beaten two and three quarter lengths—and producing form a stone in advance of that he had shown to win the Wokingham. Deacon Blues could still have gone for the Stewards' Cup, looking well in under top weight even with a penalty. However, connections were by now aiming at the Sprint Cup at Haydock in early-September, so, instead of Goodwood, Deacon Blues was sent to Ireland for the Patrick P. O'Leary Memorial Phoenix Sprint at the Curragh. The field wasn't so strong as that for the Hackwood but Deacon Blues, starting at 11/4-on, was still most impressive, winning by seven lengths from the second

favourite Empowering, the performance by Deacon Blues good enough to have won just about any Group 1 sprint run in 2011. Deacon Blues travelled strongly under a patient ride before drawing clear as soon as he was asked to do so. With Society Rock a good second in the Prix Maurice de Gheest at Deauville on the same afternoon, the Fanshawe stable looked to have two strong contenders for the Sprint Cup at Haydock. However, Deacon Blues was forced to miss the race after an unsatisfactory scope, though it proved no more than a temporary setback. Two weeks after the Sprint Cup (in which the July Cup winner Dream Ahead edged out Bated Breath and Hoof It in a very tight finish), Deacon Blues completed a Group 3 hat-trick in the Dubai International World Trophy at Newbury. It was his first run at a bare five furlongs—he had come third in the Portland Handicap over slightly further at three—and he won every bit as convincingly as he had in the Hackwood and the Phoenix Sprint, ridden for a turn of foot and quickening ahead under no more than hands and heels to win by a length from Masamah.

While Deacon Blues, who rounded off his 2011 campaign with a success in the British Champions Sprint Stakes at Ascot, was prevented from showing what he could do in Group 1 company—he missed the following season due to a tendon injury, and his retirement was announced in June 2013 after a recurrence when being prepared for a possible return in the Diamond Jubilee Stakes—fellow geldings Marchand d'Or (rated 127) and Borderlescott (125) both enjoyed long and fruitful careers. French-trained Marchand d'Or won three consecutive renewals of Deauville's Prix Maurice de Gheest, the last of those (in 2008) coming in a season in which he also won the July Cup and Prix de l'Abbaye. That same year, Borderlescott matched the form of his excellent third under a big weight in the Stewards' Cup (he had won the Goodwood handicap in 2006 and was runner-up in 2007) when taking the Nunthorpe Stakes—run that year at Newmarket after York's Ebor meeting was abandoned because of a waterlogged track—and he landed the race again the following year.

Borderlescott was aged seven when winning his second Nunthorpe, making him one of the oldest recent winners, but another noteworthy Nunthorpe winner was the two-year-old Kingsgate Native, who in 2007 took advantage of the generous weight allowance to become the first of that age to be successful since Lyric Fantasy in 1992, losing his maiden tag in the process. Runner-up against older horses again later in the year in the Prix de l'Abbaye, Kingsgate Native (rated 124 at his best) defied odds of 33/1 in the following season's Golden Jubilee Stakes. Both Borderlescott and Kingsgate Native, incidentally, were still racing in 2013 aged eleven and eight respectively despite both having been 'retired' at one time, Kingsgate Native having failed at stud.

Rock of Gibraltar

MILERS

Milers

Even after the various alterations to the Flat racing calendar in recent years, the Two Thousand Guineas has retained its position as the season's first big race, usually providing the first platform for a potentially top miler to display his full talent. Frankel's stunning success in the 2011 renewal has become the new benchmark, but of course there have been plenty of other notable winners and performances in the modern era. Frankel went on to record a series of superlative efforts, but for others success at Newmarket ends up being their career pinnacle, and that description certainly applies to another well-above-average Guineas winner, **King's Best** (rated 132), as explained in *Racehorses of 2000*:

> There was a lot of the flawed genius about King's Best, the extent of his strengths and failings both far exceeding general expectations. Compare and contrast him with Sinndar, the season's top three-year-old: Sinndar was something of a paragon, a relatively uncomplicated racehorse, but there was nothing uncomplicated about King's Best. He might just have been as good as Sinndar, but, whereas the Derby winner was still going strongly at Longchamp in October, King's Best had long gone, leaving only the one race on which to judge the true extent of his ability. The Sagitta Two Thousand Guineas was the first of Britain's Group 1 races. In the normal course of a season, there is a danger that the merits of the Guineas winner might be subsumed in the course of subsequent events, events more fresh in the memory, but anyone who saw the latest Guineas is unlikely to be forgetting the performance of King's Best in a hurry . . .
>
> Twenty-seven lined up on the Rowley Mile, a near-record field (twenty-eight had taken part in 1930), and it seemed as if King's Best had to weave his way through the lot of them. With Primo Valentino setting a strong pace, Kieren Fallon had King's Best anchored at the back of the field and that is more or less where he remained until the three-furlong marker, with only a few stragglers now behind him. While Zoning and Giant's Causeway were being galvanised to throw down their challenges up front, with Cape Town, Umistim and Summoner trying to join the firing line as well, King's Best still had most of the field ahead of him two furlongs out, fighting for his head under heavy restraint as he threatened to run into the rear of struggling rivals. Trying to manoeuvre a way through, Fallon found that some breaches in the wall

appeared but, a furlong and a half out, King's Best was only thirteenth with still six or seven lengths to make up on Giant's Causeway who was about to take over in the lead. Barathea Guest was also making headway but King's Best, showing a remarkable turn of foot, went past him after seeing clear daylight for the first time just before the furlong marker, made up the three-length leeway on Giant's Causeway in another hundred yards and was three and a half lengths clear at the line. There was another length and a half back to third-placed Barathea Guest, with Zoning two lengths behind him and just in front of Compton Bolter, Umistim, Primo Valentino and Distant Music. 'I was planning his next race at the Bushes because I thought today was over,' observed trainer Sir Michael Stoute afterwards. Of King's Best's scintillating finishing run, jockey Kieren Fallon reported 'I've never felt acceleration like that before on any horse I've ridden' . . .

In a bizarre postscript to his Newmarket win, King's Best became known as Kings Best for a short spell due to a saga about the apostrophe which, apparently, had been added by Weatherbys to make it grammatically correct when the horse was first named. After some further deliberation, the name was changed back, avoiding a second classic winner having his name changed within twelve months; the previous year, following his success in the Irish Two Thousand Guineas, Saffron Waldon became Saffron Walden in order to match the correct spelling of the Essex town.

Unfortunately, King's Best never got the chance to confirm the striking impression made in the Guineas. He missed the Derby (had been favourite) after a recurrence of a slight muscle problem, and worse was to follow in the Irish Derby when the colt was pulled up and dismounted with a career-ending fracture of the off-fore cannon bone. Possible lack of stamina might well have done for him in either of those two races—it was Timeform's calculated guess that King's Best wouldn't have stayed a mile and a half—but temperament was also an issue. Though clearly a top-class miler, vastly superior to his contemporaries at the time of the Guineas, King's Best had contrived to lose his two starts prior to Newmarket, racing so freely in a slowly-run Dewhurst that he was later described as a 'head-case' by his owner's racing manager, and looking the best horse for much of the race in the Craven Stakes only to hang left into the whip when it mattered.

In contrast, the horse that King's Best beat into second on Guineas day, **Giant's Causeway** (also rated 132), went on to win five Group 1 races on the bounce in the summer, spanning the St James's Palace Stakes through to the Irish Champion Stakes, and inspired the admiration of the racing public like few horses in recent times, primarily due to his toughness and consistency—he even attracted a couple of hundred spectators to watch him gallop on a non-racing day at Southwell in preparation for the Breeders' Cup!

> Racing has unique qualities, yet in common with all spectator sports it benefits from star performers capable not only of catching and keeping the hearts and minds of existing fans but of adding to the stock. Occasionally horses who are not champions can achieve the desired effect—a case in point is Provideo,

rated 112 in Racehorses of 1984 when Horse of the Year after breaking the twentieth-century record for races won by a two-year-old. The reason for this is simple, since, much as in political elections, equine popularity is proof of majority opinion, not necessarily of exceptional merit. There's no doubt that Giant's Causeway was one of the most popular and most talked-about horses in Europe within recent memory. He put more into the latest season than any of the top horses in terms of effort and this, together with his admirable record of five Group 1 victories and four places from nine starts in such company, means it matters not one iota that he fell a touch short of being the best of his generation. Being a touch short of Sinndar, and the same as King's Best, is a credit, not a debit, and neither of those colts, nor the pick of the older horses, Dubai Millennium, Montjeu and Kalanisi, could outscore him in toughness, determination and the ability to maintain form at the topmost level for the best part of seven months without a break and without a single easy race. That, and the number of nail-biting finishes in which he was involved, is what set Giant's Causeway apart from his peers, that is what entitles him to unstinting praise, and that is what led to his being voted Horse of the Year in a poll carried out by the Racehorse Owners Association.

In a series of close finishes—the biggest winning margin in his five wins was three quarters of a length—the Eclipse at Sandown was perhaps the most memorable:

. . . The Eclipse provided a magnificent finish between colts from different generations as Giant's Causeway just got the better of Kalanisi. Close up from the start, Giant's Causeway led two furlongs out only to wander a bit and start idling. When Kalanisi caught him inside the final furlong that would have been it for most horses, but not for Giant's Causeway who, in what was on the way to becoming customary fashion, responded tenaciously to strong handling by George Duffield, deputising for the injured Mick Kinane, to rally and get up again for a head victory. The form was first-class—Shiva was two and a half lengths away third, with Sakhee, who had been left behind in the straight, fourth—and this was by some way the best run of Giant's Causeway's career to that point.

Whilst unstinting in its praise of the colt's constitution, *Racehorses of 2000* still took issue with the widespread use of the moniker attached to Giant's Causeway, 'The Iron Horse':

The unquestioning way in which the media collectively referred to 'The Iron Horse' whenever Giant's Causeway was mentioned became tiresome. What precisely does the term mean? Used about a thoroughbred, rather than a railway engine, it has to be taken as implying superior constitution and toughness in a top performer—plenty of lesser lights run a lot more often than Giant's Causeway in a season (Nineacres' thirty-five runs in the latest season, or Noukari's thirty-eight in the previous year, for example)—but to be valid the application needs to be universal, not just applicable to the present. By the end of his campaign Giant's Causeway had certainly been given more opportunities to show his mettle than classic colts normally receive in an era when specialisation, infirmity or an over-cautious approach by connections based on a fear of defeat for commercial reasons can all play a part in keeping the best runners off the track. All praise to his owners and trainer for that. But even if this makes the colt an iron horse relatively, it doesn't give him universal claims. He answered some tough questions, but not of the type posed to some top horses in earlier periods. For instance, he did not have to travel all over Europe by train, as Kincsem did in winning all her fifty-four starts in the 1850s, including seventeen at three and fifteen at four, carrying up to twelve stone. He did not have to do as Sceptre did in 1902, when the filly contested the Derby, Oaks, Grand Prix de Paris, Coronation Stakes and St James's Palace Stakes in just over a fortnight, winning two of them. He did not have to do as Tristan did as a four-year-old in 1882, when winning three events at Royal Ascot, including the Gold Vase, before landing the July Cup. Abroad, Phar Lap won fourteen races in a row in 1930/31, headed by the Melbourne Cup under 9-12, Donau won fifteen of forty-one outings at two in 1909 before succeeding in the Kentucky Derby, 1966 American Horse of the Year Buckpasser won thirteen in a row that season, and the redoubtable five-year-old New Zealand mare Sunline has a record of twenty-three wins from thirty-one starts including eight Group 1s and eight Group 2s. We defer to no-one in our admiration of Giant's Causeway's achievements, but the description 'The Iron Horse' should have been consigned to the scrapheap as soon as it appeared. He needed no nickname; his proper name was quite sufficient to send a frisson up the racing public's spine . . .

Giant's Causeway's career ended with a memorable, if agonising defeat by Tiznow in the Breeders' Cup Classic, beaten a neck after Mick Kinane lost the reins twice in the final one hundred yards, though his quest to become the first since Mill Reef to land six consecutive Group 1s had come to an end on his previous start, when going down to 14/1-shot **Observatory** (rated 131) in the Queen Elizabeth II Stakes at Ascot:

Observatory received nothing like the credit he deserved for winning the Queen Elizabeth II Stakes at Ascot in September, principally because it was widely seen less as a race which he won than as one which Giant's Causeway, going for his sixth straight Group 1 victory, lost. Such an interpretation, along with the puzzling idea that his defeat of the very popular runner-up was something akin to an act of betrayal perpetrated by a spoilsport, owed everything to emotion and nothing to logic. In the wake of the race, excuses for Giant's Causeway were wheeled out and grudging praise was awarded to Observatory's connections for what were widely seen as sound tactics, but few people seemed ready to acknowledge that this was a first-rate display by the winner, one that put him— judged on form—close to the season's best miler King's Best . . .

Encouraging as his progress had been, most observers felt Observatory was up against it in the Queen Elizabeth II Stakes, in which his eleven rivals included

Giant's Causeway with two pacemakers, Medicean, in-form Indian Lodge, Crimplene and the Godolphin pair, Best of The Bests and Diktat. Observatory started at 14/1—Giant's Causeway was 11/10 favourite—and after being held up in fifth most of the way while the pacemaker Lermontov took them along at a good gallop, he was asked to make ground early in the straight. By this time Giant's Causeway had hit the front and was making the best of his way home, but Observatory produced a relentless run up the middle of the course to collar the leader in the final fifty yards and beat him by half a length. Best of The Bests finished three and a half lengths away third, with Medicean fourth. A cracking finish and a worthy winner, despite all the silly remarks in the media afterwards. Observatory undoubtedly benefited from the way the race was run and was given an intelligent ride by Kevin Darley to capitalise on this, since lying off the strong pace gave him the opportunity to attack Giant's Causeway when the latter probably was nearing the end of his tether after being prominent from the start. But there could be no doubt that Giant's Causeway ran somewhere close to his best and the other runners were soundly held, so anyone casting doubt on the quality of the winner or the value of the form was wide of the mark.

Observatory didn't get much of an opportunity to confirm the form in the following season, the colt's racing career ended after he was found to have suffered a hairline fracture of the pelvis after returning from his second outing of the year at Royal Ascot.

Mill Reef's record of six consecutive Group 1 wins wasn't to last much longer. In the 2002 season Ballydoyle unearthed another colt who attracted something of a cult following, **Rock of Gibraltar** (rated 133). He put together a then record-breaking series of seven consecutive Group 1 victories over two seasons, starting with the Grand Criterium and Dewhurst at two years, and followed by the Two Thousand Guineas, Irish Two Thousand Guineas, St James's Palace Stakes, Sussex Stakes and Prix du Moulin at three. Arguably his most striking performance came in the Sussex, though in form terms Royal Ascot was his best effort, as *Racehorses of 2002* outlined:

> Rock of Gibraltar faced anything but a straightforward task on form, though he started at 5/4-on. He was up against his very smart stablemate Landseer and the Andre Fabre-trained Bowman, a fast finishing third to Landseer in the Poule d'Essai des Poulains. Bowman was sent off second favourite at 4/1 in a field of nine for the St James's Palace which also included Dupont, who had landed the Guineas double in Italy and Germany, and three who had finished behind Rock of Gibraltar at Newmarket, sixth-placed Aramram, ninth-placed King of Happiness and eleventh-placed Where Or When. Rock of Gibraltar and Landseer provided another first and second in a Group 1 for Ballydoyle, whose classic colts were carrying all before them (High Chaparral and Hawk Wing had filled the first two places in the Derby). The patiently-ridden Rock of Gibraltar gave arguably his best performance, producing an excellent turn of foot to sweep aside Landseer entering the final furlong, winning largely

under hands and heels by a length and three quarters, the first two pulling clear. Aramram came third, four lengths behind Landseer, with Dupont a neck away fourth, just ahead of Where Or When and Bowman. The early stages of the St James's Palace were not run at a breakneck gallop by any means, making Rock of Gibraltar's effort in cutting down the leaders in such striking style even more praiseworthy. Handicappers who rigidly adhere to the result, accepting the relationship between the horses as they cross the line are accepting self-imposed limitations. To say Rock of Gibraltar was 'probably better than anyone was able to rate him', as one leading handicapper did, is an abdication of responsibility. Rock of Gibraltar was a better horse than was simply reflected by the results of most of his races. Using tools such as time analysis to support observation and traditional handicapping methods, it is possible to quantify with a fair degree of accuracy how much better a horse like Rock of Gibraltar is than the bare result. We rated Rock of Gibraltar as a four-length winner of the St James's Palace . . .

Having showered the stock superlatives on Rock of Gibraltar at Royal Ascot, the reviewers might well have had to reach for a thesaurus after his next race, but for the fact that Mick Kinane virtually did their job for them. Rock of Gibraltar continued his triumphal progress with another splendid performance in the Sussex Stakes at Goodwood, his first encounter with some of the leading older milers, headed by Noverre and No Excuse Needed who had filled the first two places in the race as three-year-olds the previous year. The field of five included a pacemaker for odds-on Rock of Gibraltar, who would have faced a sterner test had the French-trained four-year-old Keltos, impressive conqueror of Noverre in the Lockinge, taken up his Sussex entry. Rock of Gibraltar could, however, do no more than win with ease against the best of those that took him on—and win with ease he did, closing effortlessly on the bridle after being waited with and cruising past Noverre inside the final furlong. Rock of Gibraltar treated the opposition like handicappers, winning without turning a hair by two lengths from Noverre, though the fact that the subsequent Hungerford winner Reel Buddy was only another two lengths behind in third limited the view that could be taken of the bare form. Kinane's post-race comment that Rock of Gibraltar had put up a 'great performance' and proved himself 'the ultimate racehorse' was widely reported . . .

As an aside, Reel Buddy returned to win the Sussex the following year, a penultimate Group 1 success for Pat Eddery, who retired at the end of the season. In a further parallel with Giant's Causeway, Rock of Gibraltar's career also ended with a defeat at the Breeders' Cup, and a controversial one at that, going down by a length to the French-trained Domedriver after being left with a lot to do by regular jockey Mick Kinane, who again came in for criticism in some quarters, especially from the American pundits—leading critic Andrew Beyer was particularly scathing: 'Ever since International racing began we've been seeing your European pinheads lose races like this . . . any reasonably competent American jockey would have won easily.' *Racehorses* took a more balanced view:

> ... the critics rounded on Kinane at Arlington, particularly the American experts who were vitriolic. Another way of looking at Kinane's handling of his mount, however, is that he employed more or less the same tactics that had proved successful in most of Rock of Gibraltar's earlier races and was simply unlucky the way the race went. Even after the steadier than usual early pace, Rock of Gibraltar might still have won—though only narrowly—had the momentum of his finishing run not been affected by the sudden manoeuvre to avoid Landseer (his stablemate who suffered a fatal injury entering the straight). Punters were left to lick their wounds but Rock of Gibraltar's failure to extend his run of consecutive Group 1s scarcely harmed his reputation or his stud value. Rock of Gibraltar was widely hailed as the moral victor of the Breeders' Cup Mile, though it seemed incongruous that defeat in a race he was expected to win should be hailed in some quarters as his finest moment, one newspaper going so far as to ask whether any race had ever witnessed such equine heroics!

Few would have predicted such a record-breaking campaign back in the spring after Rock of Gibraltar's Two Thousand Guineas win, as much of the kudos post-Newmarket had gone to his stable-companion, the well-touted **Hawk Wing**, who had been sent off 6/4 favourite in a field of twenty-two and looked most unlucky in what was a somewhat unsatisfactory renewal:

> Hawk Wing's spectacular late surge just failed to win him the Guineas, but his reputation blossomed in defeat more than any horse beaten in a classic since Dancing Brave in the Derby in 1986. For most at Newmarket, or among those watching on television either at home or in betting shops, the issue probably wasn't whether or not Hawk Wing should have won the Guineas, but by how far. So, what went wrong? ... For some, the explanation for Hawk Wing's defeat at Newmarket lay in the state of the going. The suggestion wasn't that Hawk Wing had failed to cope with the ground, officially good to firm, but that the ground had been firmer on the far side of the course than it had been where Hawk Wing raced in the centre. Newmarket opened a fresh strip of ground on the stand side on Guineas day, but all the riders shunned it in the big race, some doing so in favour of the more 'down-trodden' ground on the far side, where four of the first five raced from the start.

> 'Ground bias' is a fashionable theory, but, at many meetings throughout a season, trying to establish an advantage for one part of the track over another frequently proves to be like chasing rainbows. The impression that one side of a track is favoured often has another plausible explanation—in the subtle differences to a result that can be accounted for by pace and tactics, the run of the race. Races take different shapes, and the shape of a race early on often gives a strong clue as to how the race might unfold. Racegoers and TV viewers alike have become accustomed to the varieties of fields that head towards

A much discussed finish to the Two Thousand Guineas - stablemates Rock of Gibraltar (nearest camera) and Hawk Wing are separated by half the width of the track

them in a race: on straight courses, for example, all the horses cramming to one rail; the field splitting into two groups, one on each rail; or 'rogue' horses racing in isolation from the rest. To give another example: in races in which the field forms an arrowhead up the centre, those on the wings usually prove at a disadvantage. The tip of the arrowhead becomes the 'focal point' of the race, and a disadvantage lies in being the most detached from the focal point once the race begins in earnest, particularly if it is run at something less than a true gallop.

The field soon split into three groups in the Two Thousand Guineas. The early pace wasn't strong, but it was set by Redback in a small, far-side group. Belief in a 'ground bias' can be a powerful incentive for some jockeys to ride more enterprisingly than usual early on so as to secure a position on the part of track considered favoured. This was undoubtedly behind Darryll Holland quickly having Redback across to the far rail from stall sixteen in the Guineas. Other riders were less premeditated, restraining their mounts more than usual early on, while assessing how the race might be shaping up. Such diverse approaches can quickly lead to significant disparities between the pace and momentum of individual groups in the early stages of a race. Not far into the Guineas, it was clear that the larger group up the centre, which included Hawk Wing, was trailing those racing on the far side, where the other two groups had eventually merged. This spelt danger for the favourite. As the race unfolded, Redback was kicked for home over two furlongs out against the rail, where

Rock of Gibraltar, drawn highest in stall twenty-two, began his move in the same group. Soon after, Jamie Spencer (deputising for suspended stable jockey Mick Kinane), who had dropped Hawk Wing out from stall ten, still seemed under the impression that he had only those in his group to worry about, sitting confidently as Hawk Wing moved easily under him approaching the Dip. Once finally unleashed Hawk Wing responded magnificently, storming clear of his group and producing a turn of foot rarely seen in a classic. The line came too soon. Hawk Wing was still a neck down on his stable-companion Rock of Gibraltar, the two still racing half the width of the track apart.

Despite capturing the public's imagination in the spring, Hawk Wing was in need of rescuing from his detractors by the end of the campaign despite a record that included a win in the Eclipse and seconds in the Derby, Irish Champion Stakes and Queen Elizabeth II Stakes, when sent off favourite each time. By way of an explanation, *Racehorses of 2002* noted that:

Public perception can be hard on sporting figures who fail to deliver all they might have promised, whose achievements in the end don't quite match their perceived talents. And, those whose reputations soar highest to begin with can suffer the biggest backlash.

Hawk Wing returned as a four-year-old with a spectacular eleven-length success in the Lockinge at Newbury, a performance which may not have satisfied all his critics but was, by any measure, top class, earning the colt a Timeform rating of 136, the best recorded over a mile since Mark of Esteem's success in the Queen Elizabeth II Stakes in 1996, and seemed finally to vindicate Aidan O'Brien's faith in the colt:

O'Brien, it seemed, was resolved to let Hawk Wing's performances as a four-year-old largely speak for themselves, though privately he forecast that 'two televisions will be needed to watch the Lockinge'—one to follow Hawk Wing and the other to pick out the opposition. The prophecy wasn't far out. When the normally trail-blazing Desert Deer was withdrawn after refusing to go into his stall, Mick Kinane decided on a change in his normal riding tactics on Hawk Wing, allowing him to stride along in front from the start and gradually stepping up the tempo. None of his five rivals was ever in the race with him or ever even looked like getting into the race from halfway, all of them toiling in Hawk Wing's wake from fully three furlongs out. Stretching further and further clear through the last furlong, edging right late on, Hawk Wing recorded a majestic victory, which, albeit belatedly, lived up to his home reputation. It was an extraordinary performance, Hawk Wing's Queen Elizabeth II Stakes conqueror Where Or When finishing eight lengths clear of third-placed Olden Times, who had shown himself every bit as good as ever when returning from nearly twelve months on the sidelines to win an up-to-scratch renewal of the Earl of Sefton Stakes at Newmarket on his reappearance. French-trained Domedriver, who had ended Rock of Gibraltar's seven-race sequence of Group 1 victories in the Breeders' Cup Mile, finished a length behind Olden Times in fourth, with

Reel Buddy fifth, after racing alone on the stand rail, and Tillerman bringing up the rear.

Hawk Wing's four-year-old campaign, and career, ended in humiliating fashion, however, trailing home in the Queen Anne Stakes at Royal Ascot (later found to have suffered a near-fore knee ligament strain), and although the highest-rated horse in 2003 based on his Newbury performance, the accolade of Horse of the Year in *Racehorses* went to Falbrav, reflecting that rival's greater number of top-class-performances through the year.

Another Ballydoyle-trained miler who proved something of an enigma was **George Washington** (rated 133). Superior to run-of-the-mill classic winners, and champion miler in 2006, George Washington also had his share of temperament to go with his undoubted talent:

> To his credit, George Washington twice lit up the season with his performances, but in terms of his racing character the bottom line was this: he could be reluctant at the stalls, he could be slowly away, he could pull hard and he could hang both ways and carry his head awkwardly under pressure . . .

> George Washington made his first public appearance as a three-year-old in a racecourse gallop at the Curragh in early-April, a traditional starting point for Ballydoyle classic candidates in the spring. He again made headlines with his antics, jinking left and out through a gap in the running rail on his way to the six-furlong start before cantering with a stable-companion. His behaviour,

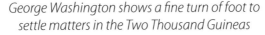

George Washington shows a fine turn of foot to
settle matters in the Two Thousand Guineas

combined with a paucity of winners for Ballydoyle, saw George Washington drift briefly from his winter odds of around 2/1 for Newmarket, though there was no lack of market confidence in him for the Stan James Two Thousand Guineas on the day. In a representative field of fourteen, George Washington was backed down to 6/4. There were eight pattern-race winners in opposition, but only the Dewhurst first and second, the unbeaten Sir Percy, a 4/1-shot, and 6/1-chance Horatio Nelson, a stable-companion of the favourite and winner of the Prix Jean-Luc Lagardere at two, were seriously backed against him. Despite the concerns surrounding the form of the stable, George Washington looked in fine shape at Newmarket. He was attended by a posse of handlers in the paddock, but took most of the preliminaries in his stride, though joined at the start by his trainer and needing to be manhandled into the stalls. In the race, he outclassed the opposition from start to finish. Soon travelling supremely well under Kieren Fallon in a race run at only a fair pace, George Washington cruised through from towards the rear before the Dip as the field began to fan to the far rail and, ridden along, quickly settled matters, showing a fine turn of foot to go clear, despite drifting sharply right with the race won. He scored by two and a half lengths from Sir Percy, who rallied once passed, with the front-running Olympian Odyssey, a 33/1-shot, a length and a half further away in third and another outsider Araafa fourth at 66/1, three quarters of a length further back. Since Zafonic, the last successful favourite, scored by three and a half lengths in 1993, George Washington's winning margin has been bettered only by King's Best, also a three-and-a-half-length winner in 2000.

If George Washington had taken the preliminaries at Newmarket in his stride for the most part, he was in no mood to co-operate on his return to the winner's enclosure, turning in an almost unique display of temperament for a classic winner, rooting himself to the spot on the walkway to the paddock, refusing to be led forward even when his trainer took the reins, eventually being taken via the pre-paddock but still failing to appear in the designated area, delaying his rider weighing in.

Defeats at odds on in his two starts after Newmarket, in the Irish Two Thousand Guineas and the Celebration Mile, damaged George Washington's reputation, with the latter even bringing him close to receiving a Timeform "squiggle" (§) to indicate his unreliability from a betting point of view. Success later in the Queen Elizabeth II Stakes at Ascot put to bed any doubts over his merit, though the race wasn't without controversy:

George Washington came close to being given a squiggle by Timeform after Goodwood. At the time, taken together, his two most recent performances certainly raised doubts about his trustworthiness. In the end, he escaped the ignominy. As a matter of interest, in the last ten years, only a handful of three-year-olds rated in Timeform's top hundred at the end of the season have received a squiggle, most of them after showing a marked reluctance to race or, as with O'Brien's Antonius Pius, a marked reluctance to go through with their finishing effort. Far more squiggles have been awarded to those lower down the performance scale, but, in general, it seems the upper echelons of the horse population have proved a genuine bunch as three-year-olds, or have been given the benefit of the doubt while their racing character was still being fully established.

With the Goodwood run behind him, it seemed reasonable to expect George Washington to be harder to beat in the Queen Elizabeth II Stakes at Ascot, provided he put his best foot forward, but the question of his temperament dominated the build up to the race. BBC television, which covered the meeting, hired Kelly Marks, a 'horse psychologist', to comment on the horse's antics during the season and on the day. 'Aidan O'Brien has done a wonderful job with George Washington, but he's spinning when he says the horse is arrogant,' she said beforehand, adding: 'Arrogance is purely a human trait. An arrogant horse in the wild would get eaten. To me, George Washington looks insecure and immature. He puts his head in the air, which is what a frightened horse does. He runs like a horse lacking confidence, and when he gets hit he doesn't run on, he runs sideways.' Without an outrider this time, though accompanied by another horse in the saddling area, George Washington was on his best behaviour beforehand and produced another top-class performance. On ground softened by the previous day's rain, he was backed down to 13/8 favourite in a field of eight. Godolphin's Librettist, the first horse since 1997 to complete the Marois/Moulin double, was next best at 3/1 followed by his stable-companion, the joint-champion miler of 2005 Proclamation, a 5/1 chance. Breaking more quickly than at Goodwood, George Washington tracked Araafa through effortlessly in the straight. Once shaken up, he was soon in control, albeit carrying his head high and edging left as he got on top, hardly touched with the whip. In this third meeting between the pair, George Washington won by a length and a quarter (it looked further) from Araafa, a high-class miler in his own right, with the Sussex Stakes winner Court Masterpiece two lengths further away. It is debatable whether George Washington would have found much more had Kinane put him under the strongest pressure. On average, the Queen Elizabeth II Stakes has been Europe's top event over a mile for some time, and the roll of honour reads like a who's who of European miling, including, since 1990, those other top-class performers Markofdistinction, Mark of Esteem, Desert Prince, Dubai Millennium, Observatory and Falbrav. George Washington's performance was at least as good as any in the race in that time except for Mark of Esteem's outstanding victory over Bosra Sham in 1996, and it was the best seen on a European racecourse in 2006.

Mark of Esteem's jockey Frankie Dettori, who rode all seven winners on the card in 1996, was at the centre of a storm over the running of George Washington's stablemate Ivan Denisovich in the Queen Elizabeth II Stakes. Ivan Denisovich's jockey Seamus Heffernan was banned for fourteen days under the rule governing 'team tactics' after being found guilty of interfering with

Dettori's mount Librettist. Ballydoyle ran three horses in the race, including the pacemaker, River Tiber, but claimed that Ivan Denisovich, a 28/1-chance wearing a visor for the first time and a smart horse in his own right, was running on his merits. On appeal, the case against Heffernan under Instruction H1 Pacemakers (Team Tactics), introduced in response to an incident at the Shergar Cup meeting in 2003, was thrown out, the appeal panel concluding that he had not acted as a spoiler, though stopping short of completely exonerating the rider. The panel also found that Heffernan, who raced to the fore on Ivan Denisovich with River Tiber, flanked by Librettist on his outside, did deliberately take a line which had the effect of interfering with Librettist. The panel instead imposed a six-day ban on Heffernan for careless riding. The turnaround, which came against a background of stinging criticism of Dettori's character from O'Brien after Dettori offered the opinion on Caradak at Goodwood that Ballydoyle's pacemaker had gone too fast, came after the production of new evidence from Heffernan's solicitor, including evidence that Ivan Denisovich had been bumped by Araafa in the back straight, causing him to lose his action, and a submission that Heffernan had been looking for better ground. Interestingly, had the original offence been committed in France and the decision upheld, the stewards would have been within their rights to disqualify or demote all the horses in the same, shared ownership as Ivan Denisovich.

George Washington was initially retired following a sixth in the Breeders' Cup Classic on his next outing but his racing career was dramatically resumed after fertility problems cut short his spell at stud. Sadly, George Washington failed to scale the same heights as a four-year-old, winless through four starts, and he had to be put down after breaking down in his second attempt at the Breeders' Cup Classic. The only foal George Washington left behind, to be named Date With Destiny, was sold for 320,000 guineas as a yearling and went into training with Richard Hannon, winning a maiden at Newbury on her debut at two and finishing third in the Oaks Trial at Lingfield at three.

Before we move away from the Two Thousand Guineas, it's worth recounting the background tale to 2010 winner **Makfi**, who ended the year rated 130 following a further Group 1 success in France and proved something of a bargain purchase:

If the stanjames.com Two Thousand Guineas—the last under the bookmakers' sponsorship—was a big disappointment for the team at Ballydoyle (who saddled beaten favourite St Nicholas Abbey), it was nearly as chastening an experience for their great rivals the Maktoums whose three runners all ran well below form. While the inquests in the Ballydoyle and Maktoum camps were getting under way, a representative of Sheikh Hamdan's Shadwell Stud sheepishly collected the breeder's prize of £7,500 for the French-trained 33/1 winner Makfi, who had slipped through the net as part of an annual cull the previous autumn, weeded out of Marcus Tregoning's stable still unraced and sent to the Newmarket Autumn Sales where he fetched 26,000 guineas, his price testament to the fact that the big owner-breeders don't make a habit of discarding future stars. The first four in the latest Two Thousand Guineas all went through the sale-ring relatively cheaply, around £110,000 the combined cost of the quartet as yearlings or two-year-olds, and Makfi's owners enjoyed a huge windfall when he was sold as a stallion at the end of the latest season to Qatar's Sheikh Fahad Al Thani, reportedly for £12m. One of Makfi's owners Mathieu Offenstadt explained that he and his partners had only seen a photo of Makfi before they purchased him—'We felt he had a very expressive head'—and he had been bought 'just to have some fun . . . we never expected we'd end up with a classic winner.'

One of the changes to the programme of races for top milers in the domestic calendar was the upgrading of the Queen Anne Stakes at Royal Ascot to Group 1 status in 2003. Prior to Frankel's 147 in 2012, however, the best performance in the race in recent times judged purely on ratings actually came when it was still a Group 2 back in 1998, the year **Intikhab** ran to a figure of 135 in spread-eagling his rivals by upwards of eight lengths:

Genuine excitement on the track often comes with a close finish, as happened in the Prince of Wales's Stakes, the race immediately after the Queen Anne. But it also comes when one horse imposes itself on a field with massive authority. Only someone with all the feeling of a lump of granite could have failed to find Intikhab's performance thrilling. Favourite again, and preferred by Frankie Dettori to Godolphin's other runner, the narrow Lockinge Stakes winner Cape Cross, he made hacks of his eight rivals, who were a very smart collection. Cape Cross was penalised, as were Almushtarak and Among Men, only sixth in the Lockinge but successful in the Celebration Mile in 1997. Poteen and Centre Stalls, respectively second and third in the Lockinge, also lined up, as did outsiders Muchea and Reunion, plus the improving three-year-old Great Dane, having his first outing in pattern company. After Cape Cross and Great Dane had done the donkey work for six furlongs, Among Men took over, but it was only on sufferance as Intikhab, who had tracked the leaders from the outset, moved smoothly through to challenge at the distance and showed exceptional acceleration to storm clear and win by eight lengths. Poteen stayed on to be one and a quarter lengths away in third, followed by Almushtarak and Cape Cross. Any horse who puts eight lengths between himself and his opponents in the space of a furlong or so deserves close attention whatever the type of race. One who takes eight lengths out of proven pattern performers, none of whom had excuses, deserves all the accolades going. Intikhab's display was, quite simply, flawless, and was supported by the season's best timefigure, 1.38 fast, equivalent to a timerating of 135. We regard him as the best older miler since Northjet in 1981.

Injury kept Intikhab off the track for the rest of that year, and he was retired after fracturing his pelvis on his return the following season, when fourth in the Lockinge at Newbury.

The Queen Anne again became the first race of Royal Ascot in 2008, and in 2011 a vintage renewal certainly got the fixture off to a cracking start with a head-to-head between the two top milers from the previous year, Goldikova and **Canford Cliffs** (both rated 133):

> Their Royal Ascot clash in the Queen Anne Stakes provided a fitting opening to a stunning first-day programme as Ascot celebrated its tercentenary—the race commemorates the monarch who established racing at the course. Goldikova and Canford Cliffs were meeting for the first time, Goldikova having won the Queen Anne the previous year from another top miler trained by Hannon, Paco Boy, who ran against Goldikova five times during his career and failed to finish in front of her. Canford Cliffs had followed in Paco Boy's footsteps when winning the JLT Lockinge Stakes at Newbury, the first Group 1 of the year for older milers, landing the odds after a ten-month absence with a fair bit in hand over the smart Italian challenger Worthadd.
>
> Canford Cliffs' victory was gained in typical style, patiently ridden before producing a late turn of foot, and his eye-catching performance—two weeks after Frankel's destruction of his field in the Two Thousand Guineas—laid the foundations for their much-hyped head-to-head. Both Frankel and Canford Cliffs appeared in different races on Royal Ascot's first day, Frankel running nowhere near his Newmarket form when a fairly narrow winner of the St James's Palace Stakes and sharing the next day's headlines with Canford Cliffs and Goldikova, whose encounter lived right up to its billing. Both were ridden in their usual style, Goldikova always in touch and taking over from front-running Cape Blanco on the bit approaching two furlongs out before Canford Cliffs, who settled well in the rear, cruised up to her a furlong later. Canford Cliffs had to battle after taking the lead but he gamely held off the rallying Goldikova by a length in a grandstand finish. It was a career-best performance by Canford Cliffs, though Goldikova's jockey returned to scale 2 lb overweight (having weighed out 1 lb over) which almost certainly made a difference to the winning margin, though there was a further length and three quarters back to third-placed Cityscape and then another two and a quarter to the fourth Rio de La Plata, their performances testament to the fact that Goldikova ran to her best on the day and was simply not quite a match for Canford Cliffs. It was a third successive triumph at the Royal meeting for Canford Cliffs, whose six-length victory in the Coventry Stakes prompted Richard Hughes even at that stage to call him 'by far' the best horse he had ridden.

Canford Cliffs might have been no match for Frankel in the much-hyped 'Duel on the Downs', which turned out to be his final start after he was later found to have injured a near-fore pastern (veterinary opinion was that Canford Cliffs might sustain a fracture if he kept on racing), the second season running his campaign had been ended prematurely, but there's little doubt he was a top-class miler in his own right, as he showed at Ascot and when landing the Sussex Stakes as a three-year-old the previous season. The Sussex Stakes remains an important race in establishing the season's top

Sussex Stakes—the passing of the baton in the miling division as Canford Cliffs (number 7) beats the previous year's winner Rip Van Winkle

miler, the first opportunity for the better three-year-olds to take on their elders in top company, and Canford Cliffs had firmly established his credentials following wins in the Irish Guineas and St James's Palace Stakes when beating the previous season's winner Rip Van Winkle at Goodwood.

Much as Canford Cliffs ended up in Frankel's shadow as a four-year-old, **Rip Van Winkle**'s achievements at three were also overshadowed to a large extent by the exploits of Sea The Stars, who beat him into fourth in both the Two Thousand Guineas and Derby and got the better of him by a length in the Eclipse. Rip Van Winkle, who was reported by his trainer to have been beset by hoof problems throughout his three-year-old campaign, finally lived up to the expectations held for him when winning the Sussex Stakes on his fourth outing:

> Rip Van Winkle started hot favourite for a vintage Sussex and beat the Queen Anne winner Paco Boy by two and a half lengths, the pair clear of the One Thousand Guineas winner Ghanaati in third in a race that further endorsed the quality of the season's leading three-year-olds in Europe. Rip Van Winkle couldn't have been more impressive or more convincing, sent for home in earnest soon after halfway and galloping on really well to record the best performance in the Sussex for thirty years, since Kris won a memorable renewal by five lengths in a season when he dominated racing at around a mile in a way that no other horse had done since Brigadier Gerard.

Success in the Queen Elizabeth II Stakes on his next outing confirmed Rip Van Winkle's position as 2009's leading miler, and although not quite the same force as a four-year-old, he still won the Juddmonte International at York. A peak rating of 134 puts Rip Van Winkle on a par with his sire Galileo and behind only Hawk Wing on Timeform ratings among the best horses trained by Aidan O'Brien.

In terms of being put in the shade by a top-drawer rival, spare a thought for **Excelebration**, (rated 133) a top-class miler in his own right but one who had the misfortune of being around at the same time as the outstanding Frankel, as the opening paragraph in his essay in *Racehorses of 2012* explained:

> The Newmarket trainer Jane Chapple-Hyam counts the ten-length defeat of her Horris Hill winner Klammer by Frankel in the 2010 Royal Lodge among the highlights of her career. 'At least I can always say one of mine finished second to Frankel,' she quipped. Whether she would have felt so enthusiastic about coming second to the phenomenal Frankel if she had had charge of Excelebration is another matter. Excelebration has been a top-class miler whose victories have included the German Two Thousand Guineas (by seven lengths), the Hungerford Stakes (by six) and the Prix du Moulin, all when trained by Marco Botti as a three-year-old. After being switched to Aidan O'Brien for his four-year-old season, there were two more Group 1s to add to the Moulin in the shape of the Prix Jacques le Marois and the Queen Elizabeth II Stakes. If Frankel hadn't been among his contemporaries, Excelebration would also have won the Greenham and the Queen Elizabeth II Stakes for Botti, and the Lockinge Stakes and the Queen Anne for O'Brien. Victories in the three last-named would have doubled Excelebration's number of Group 1 wins to six. In fact, until running below his best at Santa Anita behind another miler dubbed a 'horse of a lifetime', the tip-top American gelding Wise Dan, Excelebration had been beaten over the past two seasons only in races contested by Frankel (in addition to being runner-up to Frankel four times, Excelebration was also third behind him in the St James's Palace Stakes). Along with Canford Cliffs, whom he has now joined on the stallion roster at Coolmore, Excelebration was close to being the best miler seen in Europe in recent years, with the obvious exception of Frankel.

As detailed in the entry on George Washington, the Queen Elizabeth II Stakes, which now sits later in the calendar after the controversial changes made to the end-of-season programme in 2011, has long held claims to being considered the top event over a mile in Europe, and an average Timeform rating of 129 for the winner of the race since the turn of the century backs that up. Most of the best winners in recent times have already been mentioned, with the notable exception of the 2008 winner **Raven's Pass** (rated 133). His success in the Breeders' Cup Classic the following month might have been a still greater feat, but judged purely on form his Ascot win was a career-best, and in a taste of what was to come in America, it was also the first time he managed to get the better of Henrythenavigator (rated 131) in their season-long rivalry which was summarised in the essay on Raven's Pass in *Racehorses of 2008*:

> The meeting between Raven's Pass and Henrythenavigator in the Breeders' Cup Classic was the fifth of the season between the pair, the first of them in the Two Thousand Guineas at Newmarket, before which Raven's Pass had a preparatory race ('because he was too full of himself') when beaten a short

head by Twice Over in the Craven Stakes over the course and distance a little over a fortnight earlier. That narrow defeat didn't diminish the Guineas chance of Raven's Pass, who had been a very smart two-year-old, third in the Dewhurst on his final start after looking the most likely winner for a long way. Raven's Pass managed only fourth to Henrythenavigator in the Two Thousand Guineas after being switched across the course from a high draw and finding himself having to come from last once the field settled down. There was talk of dropping Raven's Pass back to seven furlongs—the Jersey Stakes was mentioned as his Royal Ascot target, to be followed by a further drop in trip in the July Cup—but he took on Henrythenavigator again in the St James's Palace Stakes at the Royal meeting. Henrythenavigator was odds-on after completing the Anglo-Irish Two Thousand Guineas double and he beat Raven's Pass for the second time, though Raven's Pass was closing on him, after being waited with, and went down only by three quarters of a length. Henrythenavigator made it three out of three against Raven's Pass in the Sussex Stakes at Goodwood but this time the margin of victory was down to a head. Raven's Pass had been beaten by Tamayuz after being dropped out and finishing very well (he would have needed a 'jet engine', according to his trainer) in the Prix Jean Prat at Chantilly in the interim. Connections evidently planned to change riding tactics and have Raven's Pass ridden more prominently in the Sussex. However, the gallop was little more than steady and Henrythenavigator was the better placed, closer to the pace, when the race began in earnest. Raven's Pass again finished strongly but couldn't peg back his rival.

With his persistence rewarded by a first victory of the season in the totesport. com Celebration Mile at Goodwood at the end of August, when he beat Bankable by a length, Raven's Pass met Henrythenavigator for the fourth time in the Queen Elizabeth II Stakes (sponsored by Sony) at Ascot at the end of September. Tamayuz was also in the line-up, having added the Prix Jacques le Marois since beating Raven's Pass in the Jean Prat, and the three three-year olds dominated the betting. Henrythenavigator was 11/8 favourite, Tamayuz 9/4 and Raven's Pass 3/1, with 14/1 Sabana Perdida, winner of the Windsor Forest Stakes at Royal Ascot, and 20/1 and upwards the others in a field of seven. Both Henrythenavigator and Tamayuz were provided with pacemakers who ensured a true gallop, with Raven's Pass, who had dictated in the Celebration Mile, racing in front of Henrythenavigator this time. Raven's Pass came out on top against Henrythenavigator for the first time, taking over about two furlongs out, after travelling strongly from the start, and beating Henrythenavigator, who got in only a brief challenge at the furlong pole, by a length. Sabana Perdida came third, four and a half lengths further back, with Tamayuz, who might have been expected to do better, a further three lengths behind in fourth. The form shown by Raven's Pass in the Queen Elizabeth II Stakes was the best in any race over any distance in Britain all year and settled the title of champion miler of Europe.

Authorized and Frankie Dettori

MIDDLE-DISTANCE PERFORMERS

A Timeform Publication

Middle-Distance Performers

The Derby remains the one race in the Flat calendar which reaches beyond the usual confines of racing as a minority sport to reach a wider public consciousness. But that rarely, if ever, means that the name of even the most recent Derby winner is remembered for very long outside racing's normal boundaries. Derby-winning jockeys are apt to suffer the same fate, though, like the Derby itself, the name of Frankie Dettori is one that carries some resonance with the wider public. After years of trying, Dettori was finally successful in the big race in 2007 on **Authorized**—'not since Gordon Richards ended his so-called Derby "hoodoo" [at the twenty-eighth attempt] on Pinza back in 1953 had there been a Derby which, in the public mind, was so much about the winning jockey' concluded *Racehorses* of that year:

> The Derby may not be so significant as it once was, given racing's broader global horizons, but it continues to provide publicity for British racing on a scale unsurpassed by the coverage for any other race apart from the Grand National. Like the National, the Derby comes in for criticism in some quarters from time to time, but the fact that it provides entertainment on a scale approached by no other event on the Flat far outweighs any other considerations. The latest Derby provided racing with the right type of headlines, a welcome antidote to the clouds of suspicion hanging over the sport because of a series of betting and so-called race-fixing scandals which received wide coverage. The victory of the charismatic Frankie Dettori on the short-priced favourite Authorized showed racing in a good light on the front pages and at the top of the television news bulletins.

Modern Greats

Dettori has transcended his sport in a way few other jockeys have ever managed and Authorized provided him with his first win in the Derby after fourteen losing rides in the race, a saga that was becoming part of the annual Derby ritual. Dettori's historic seven wins on the Queen Elizabeth II Stakes card at Ascot in September 1996 was a once-in-a-lifetime occurrence and made headlines around the world, ensuring that the Dettori name would enter racing folklore. Frequent TV appearances over the years have also helped Dettori to become instantly recognisable to a much wider audience. So much so, that straight after his Derby win, his odds for the BBC Sports Personality of the Year award were cut to 5/1. Dettori finished third in the year of his 'Magnificent Seven', a notable achievement for a racing personality. Lester Piggott, whose long and distinguished career included a record nine Derby victories, never managed higher than fourth, though he was given a special trophy by the programme in 1995. The peerless Tony McCoy's achievements over jumps—which include surpassing Flat champion Sir Gordon Richards' enduring British record of 269 winners in a season (McCoy set the new mark of 289 in 2001/2)—earned him third in 2003, and Bob Champion and Aldaniti received the team award after their 1981 Grand National victory.

Winning the Grand National in 2010 earned McCoy the BBC award later that year, as outlined in the chapter on the Aintree race, but Dettori never even made the shortlist of ten in his Derby-winning year, so it was just as well he made the most of the post-race celebrations.

'All eyes afterwards were on the ecstatic Dettori, who broke with tradition and took Authorized past the photographers for a victory parade in front of the stands, turning back only after going halfway to the furlong marker. The trademark flying dismount was executed in the winner's circle as Authorized and Dettori received a tumultuous reception.'

On balance, Dettori's celebrity status has been to racing's benefit, though it was very much 'the wrong type of headlines' that accompanied his six-month ban incurred after failing a drugs test in France in September 2012, not long before Dettori's split with Godolphin.

As for Authorized himself, he put up one of the best recent Derby-winning performances:

As part of the celebrations for its sixtieth year, Timeform published the ratings recorded in the Derby by all the winners since 1947. The best Derby-winning performances (different from the highest Annual ratings) were recorded by Shergar (140), Pinza, Grundy and Troy (all 137). Authorized ran to a rating of 132 in the Derby which put him joint-fifteenth on the extensive list, alongside the 2001 winner Galileo, among others. Authorized's timefigure in the Derby was 1.24 fast, equivalent to a timerating of 131, the fastest recorded in any race in Britain in 2007. It provided confirmation of the merit of his performance on Derby day, which, along with that of Galileo, was the finest seen in the race since Generous in 1991. The Derby form was upheld by results at Royal Ascot where fourth-placed Lucarno and eighth-placed Yellowstone were placed in the King Edward VII Stakes, seventh-placed Kid Mambo finished a close fourth in the Hampton Court Stakes and the Derby eleventh Mahler won the Queen's Vase. The 2005 Derby winner Motivator had been rated 134 for a time after the Derby but his Epsom form didn't look so good by the end of the season, by which time Motivator's rating had fallen to 131. Authorized emulated Motivator when winning the Derby by five lengths—only Shergar (ten lengths), Troy, Slip Anchor (both seven) and Arctic Prince and Relko (both six) won the race by further in the first sixty years of Timeform—but Authorized's followers must have been hoping that the parallels with Motivator's career would end with Epsom. Motivator had looked set for a fine summer after turning the Derby into a one-horse race, but he failed to win again, beaten in the Eclipse, the Irish Champion and the Arc, the best of him, in hindsight, seen on Derby Day.

Authorized was also beaten in the Eclipse and the Arc, but in between he put up another top-class effort to win the Juddmonte International at York, when beating Dylan Thomas a length, becoming the first Derby victor for five years to win again after Epsom.

Another of the best recent Derby winners, **Galileo** enhanced his reputation still further after victory at Epsom in 2001, earning an annual rating of 134 following further successes over a mile and a half in the Irish Derby and the King George VI and Queen Elizabeth Stakes. Galileo became the seventh horse to complete this particular hat-trick, but none has done so since; the only Derby or Irish Derby winner since Galileo to land the King George was the Curragh winner Alamshar in 2003, while Galileo's son Nathaniel in 2011 is the only other three-year-old to have beaten his elders in the King George this century. Excelling at a mile and a half was all well and good, but by the beginning of the twenty-first century, the top-class performer at the traditional 'classic' distance was in danger of becoming a victim of changing fashions in the bloodstock industry. For the Coolmore-owned Galileo, with his future stud career to consider, this was a particularly pertinent issue:

The traditional European notion of the ideal racehorse is slowly but surely being eroded. For most of the second half of the twentieth century, the popular idea of the consummate thoroughbred was the Derby winner, or the winner of the King George VI and Queen Elizabeth Stakes or the Prix de l'Arc de Triomphe—the top-class mile-and-a-half horse with speed. In the strictest sense, of course, there is no such animal as the ideal racehorse: there are simply horses, horses with different racing characters and different requirements. That's one of the reasons why the long-standing bias in the European racing programme towards middle-distance performers has often come in for criticism in these pages down the years. Middle-distance specialists in general still earn too great a share of racing's prestige and prize money, though the sprinters, milers and even the stayers—in Britain at least—thankfully get a fairer crack of the whip than they used to. Far and away the biggest influence, however, in the steadily

*Irish Derby - another striking performance as Galileo provides
jockey Mick Kinane with his first win in the race from eighteen attempts*

dwindling kudos attached to being a middle-distance champion has been the globalisation of the thoroughbred breeding business. North American racing has been contracted around a seven-furlong to a mile-and-a-quarter centre and potential stallions who make their name as racehorses exclusively or mostly at a mile and a half or further are nowhere near so attractive to American breeders as those who shine over shorter distances . . .

Against this background, the latest season produced the extraordinary story of a top-class dual Derby and King George winner whose connections, judged by some public pronouncements, seemed somewhat constrained by the colt's proven ability at a mile and a half and sought to create the impression that the horse ultimately would prove even better at shorter distances. Was this a calculated way of trying to boost potential stallion value, as some cynically whispered, or purely and simply an honest appraisal of the horse's racing character? It is a sign of the times that such a question has to be put. Galileo's strikingly impressive victory at Epsom over the Two Thousand Guineas winner Golan and the rest of a representative field drew a string of superlatives, under examples of the headline-writers' art such as 'Galileo in orbit', 'Galileo powers to celestial status', 'Galileo the star turn'. The front-page headline in the Racing Post was the single word 'PERFECTION'. For trainer Aidan O'Brien, however, Galileo's Derby victory did not represent the pinnacle of achievement, or anything like it. 'This is a serious horse who is capable of producing the unbelievable; he has the speed of a sprinter and the strength of a miler, and this is something I have never seen before in a horse capable of winning a classic over a mile and a half', said O'Brien. 'He is very explosive and very special.'

Consequently, Galileo was dropped back to a mile and a quarter on his last two starts but met with defeat in both the Irish Champion Stakes and the Breeders' Cup Classic on dirt. Ironically, Galileo's phenomenally successful stud career, in which he has taken over the mantle of his own sire Sadler's Wells as the most sought-after stallion in Europe, has soon rendered academic any debate about whether or not a mile and a half was his best trip. As well as Frankel and Nathaniel, Galileo's numerous Group 1 winners include the 2013 Derby winner Ruler of The World, five years after New Approach became his first Epsom winner, while Soldier of Fortune, Cape Blanco and Treasure Beach have given him a trio of Irish Derby wins—the 2013 winner of the latter race is also a direct descendant of Galileo, Trading Leather sired by Galileo's son Teofilo.

If the mile-and-a-half performer had looked an endangered species at the start of the twenty-first century, then the triple crown horse was looking positively extinct. That was until **Camelot** (rated 128) emerged in 2012, following up a win in the Two Thousand Guineas by matching Authorized's winning margin of five lengths in the Derby, and then starting at 5/2-on for the final leg of the triple crown, the St Leger. As Coolmore boss John Magnier implied, the chance to make history outweighed any commercial considerations on this occasion. 'If you had asked me thirty years ago, I would have looked the other way, but these things mean more as you get older.'

> Before the latest season, no Derby winner since Reference Point in 1987 had even run in the St Leger, a race that has fallen right out of fashion with commercial breeders. The fact that the Coolmore partners, whose commercial priorities are understandable given their enormous outlay, took up the dormant challenge, after Camelot won the Two Thousand Guineas and the Derby, reflected great credit on them for producing a gripping story for racing. Their bold, sporting decision breathed new life into one of racing's great traditional challenges but it did not meet with the success that ideally it deserved. Camelot did win three classics, landing the odds in the Irish Derby between Epsom and Doncaster, but, after starting the shortest-priced St Leger favourite since Reference Point, he was beaten at Doncaster by Encke, a defeat that also denied his trainer Aidan O'Brien the unique feat of saddling all five winners of the British classics in a single season (he won all five Irish classics in 2008). Camelot's defeat emphasised that no St Leger is ever cut and dried, and the result was widely regarded as a fatal blow to the revival of the triple crown in Britain, and another nail in the coffin of the St Leger itself. However, the make-up of Coolmore's current stallion band, which has included a number of influential Sadler's Wells stallions in recent years, such as Galileo, Camelot's sire Montjeu (now sadly deceased) and High Chaparral, is resulting in more staying-breds coming through to Ballydoyle. It requires an exceptional horse to win the triple crown but it may not be too fanciful to speculate that the Coolmore partners could find themselves another

colt in the next few years with the qualities needed. If they do, let's hope their spirit of adventure has not been dampened by their experience with Camelot.

Nijinsky in 1970 had been the last colt to win the three classics open to him and Oh So Sharp in 1985 the last filly to win the One Thousand Guineas, Oaks and St Leger. Nashwan, in 1989, and Sea The Stars twenty years later, had been the only other colts between Nijinsky and Camelot to win the first two legs of the triple crown but neither contested the St Leger. These days, it is the Prix de l'Arc de Triomphe, rather than the St Leger, that has become the focus of attention for Derby winners in the autumn. Camelot took in both races, but his three-year-old season ended in defeat at Longchamp, as it had done for both Authorized and Motivator. High Chaparral, who completed the Derby/Irish Derby double for Aidan O'Brien the year after Galileo, was a good third in the Arc before dead-heating in the Breeders' Cup Turf. But three Derby winners in the twenty-first century have gone on to win the Prix de l'Arc de Triomphe. Sea The Stars did so for John Oxx in 2008, emulating the same stable's **Sinndar** (rated 134) in the millennium season:

> The Arc confirmed Sinndar's position as the season's top three-year-old, ahead of the spectacular Two Thousand Guineas winner King's Best and the prodigious Giant's Causeway, but he beat a far from vintage field at Longchamp—take Montjeu out and Sinndar would have been long odds on—and cannot be rated an outstanding winner of the race. In winning the Arc, however, Sinndar achieved something that only three Epsom Derby winners, Sea-Bird, Mill Reef and Lammtarra, had managed in the modern era from a significant number to try, among them two of the Aga Khan's, Shahrastani (fourth in the 1986 Arc) and Kahyasi (sixth in 1988). Most Derby winners are remembered simply for winning the Derby and the fact that Sinndar, a strong, lengthy colt who did well physically through the year, enhanced his reputation after Epsom sets him apart from the generality. He was an admirably game and genuine racehorse, with a temperament to match, who continued to improve after Epsom and left the impression that he probably had more to give. Murtagh summed him up as a horse 'who fights all the way to the line . . . there is no bottom to him.' Oxx described Sinndar, who wore a tongue tie in his races, as 'a pleasure to train, he almost trained himself . . . an incredible horse, very sound and clean-winded with a terrific constitution . . . he has never missed a beat all year, never been off colour, never been lame.' Oxx's eulogy included the comment that Sinndar would 'make a great four-year-old too', but, consistent with his other Derby winners—and those owned by his grandfather—the Aga Khan announced shortly after the Arc that Sinndar was to be retired.

The Derby was worth more than the Prix de l'Arc de Triomphe when Sinndar won the two races in 2000; he picked up £609,000 at Epsom and £552,995 at the prevailing exchange rate at Longchamp. But the balance had shifted markedly in the French race's favour by the time **Workforce** (rated 133) became the most recent Derby winner to triumph in the Arc ten years later. The Derby was now worth £771,504 (twenty-third on the list of the world's richest races compiled by the International Racing Bureau) compared with the Arc's first prize of £1,953,504. Workforce had just a head to spare when beating the Japanese horse Nakayama Festa in the Arc, but his Derby win had come in clear-cut— and record-breaking—fashion:

> Galileo and Authorized (both 132) put up the best performances in the Derby in the first decade of the new millennium but Workforce got the second decade off to a flying start with an even better one, achieving the highest Timeform rating *in the race* since the 1991 winner Generous (135), and before that the 1985 winner Slip Anchor (136), those two the most highly rated performances in the race since Shergar's. Workforce put up an outstanding performance to win by seven lengths, eclipsing the five-length winning margins of Motivator and Authorized among recent winners, and equalling the margin of victory recorded by Troy and Slip Anchor. Only Shergar, who won by ten lengths in 1981, and the last of Steve Donoghue's six Derby winners Manna, who won by eight in 1925, have won the Derby by further than Workforce, who also set a new time-record for the race, 2m 31.33sec (0.98sec inside the previous mark set by Lammtarra). Immediately after the Derby, it seemed that Workforce would do very well to equal or better his superb performance at Epsom. That looked even less likely when he managed only fifth of six behind his older stablemate Harbinger when odds-on for the King George and Queen Elizabeth Stakes at Ascot in July. However, in what was probably the training performance of the year, Sir Michael Stoute, who had had three previous Derby winners beaten in the Arc, produced a rejuvenated Workforce at Longchamp in October.

Workforce has the Derby all sewn up with half a furlong still to go

Workforce's victory—his long-serving trainer's first in the Arc—set him further apart from the generality of Derby winners, most of whom are remembered purely and simply for winning at Epsom.

Three-year-olds have a very good record in the Arc—only four renewals since 1993 have gone to older horses—and a couple of outstanding French colts, both rated 137, put up a couple of the best Arc-winning performances of recent decades at the very end of the twentieth century. **Peintre Celebre**, already winner of the Prix du Jockey Club and Grand Prix de Paris, drew comparisons with Sea-Bird with his magnificent five-length victory in 1997. A cracking gallop on firm ground resulted in Peintre Celebre smashing the course record (over a second and a half inside the previous best time for the race) from a field that included some top-class older rivals. Runner-up was Pilsudski who went on to win the Champion Stakes and Japan Cup later that autumn, sixth was Helissio, himself an impressive five-length winner of the Arc as a three-year-old the previous year, and seventh was Swain, who had beaten Pilsudski, Helissio and another top-class older horse, Singspiel, in that summer's King George at Ascot.

The Arc turned out to be Peintre Celebre's final race, but there wasn't long to wait before the John Hammond-trained **Montjeu** proved his equal as an outstanding Arc winner. Imperious wins in both the Prix du Jockey Club and Irish Derby in 1999, by four lengths and five respectively, had already established Montjeu as much the best three-year-old over middle distances before his first encounter with older horses in the Arc:

> Over a mile and a half in 1999, a top-form Montjeu was a staggering seven lengths in front of any other three-year-old in Europe. He is the sort of competitor who could give his rivals a healthy start and still beat them, and in this case that claim would be more than mere rhetoric because that is what he usually did. The rest were a lightweight bunch, it's true, but Montjeu was good enough to have dominated in most other seasons as well. For three-year-olds over any distance in the 'nineties, he was almost unsurpassed: Generous had the edge over him but Montjeu is right up there with Dayjur, Mark of Esteem and Peintre Celebre. None of those other paragons saw a racecourse at four, Peintre Celebre being prevented from doing so by injury. Thankfully, Montjeu is due to buck the trend.

> John Hammond reckoned that El Condor Pasa posed the greatest threat in the Arc and was thoroughly vindicated. While Montjeu was ridden further up the field than normal, on the rail in seventh, the Japanese challenger made the running and did so at a strong pace. That, it transpired, was a considerable surprise to his trainer and owner. If they believed afterwards that things could have gone better in different circumstances, perhaps they would have swopped positions with Montjeu who was four lengths off the pace and boxed in as the field entered the straight. Extricated from that pocket, Montjeu set off in pursuit and the race came down to a decision between him and El Condor Pasa; Croco Rouge had also been travelling well as the field turned in but was rapidly competing only for third. El Condor Pasa was not stopping,

but with a furlong to go it became clear that Montjeu was going to reel him in, the inevitable happening with about a hundred yards of the race remaining, Montjeu pushed out to hold on by half a length; there were six lengths back to Croco Rouge and another five to Leggera in fourth. Plenty of Arc de Triomphes end with most of the runners in a bunch. This was not one of them.

Montjeu did buck that trend and proved just as good at four as he was at three. His bid to become the first dual winner of the Arc since Alleged in 1977/78 proved unsuccessful when he finished only fourth behind Sinndar, before further defeats in the Champion Stakes and Breeders' Cup Turf, but he began the 2000 season with three further Group 1 wins in the Tattersalls Gold Cup at the Curragh, the Grand Prix de Saint-Cloud and the King George VI and Queen Elizabeth Stakes. He was impressive in Ireland and France as well, but it was the ease of his Ascot win that left the most lasting impression:

How clear are the public's recollections, many years on, of some of racing's greatest moments? Take that 'race of the century', the famous clash between Grundy and Bustino in the King George VI and Queen Elizabeth Stakes. It is twenty-five years since the pair battled it out, neck and neck, in a titanic duel up the Ascot straight. The image of an outstandingly memorable finish remains vivid, reinforced by occasional replays on television, but only aficionados will recall much else about the race. The latest season saw another King George anniversary, that of the effortless victory thirty years earlier of Nijinsky. According to *Racehorses of 1970* the only three-year-old in the field 'treated his elders like so many selling platers.' Ridden in inimitable fashion by Lester Piggott, Nijinsky had the race won in a few strides about a furlong from home and took the lead travelling strongly on the bridle, Piggott having time for a good look round before easing him in the closing stages. As with Grundy and Bustino, we doubt whether anyone with a sense of racing history who was there believed they were present on 'just another day'. But Nijinsky now has a serious rival for the title of 'easiest' or 'most impressive' winner of the King George VI and Queen Elizabeth Stakes. Montjeu's imperious performance looks equally certain to stand the test of time and become a 'were you watching?' moment in racing history.

Look at a replay of the fiftieth running of the King George VI and Queen Elizabeth as often as you like and you won't find a moment when Montjeu looked in the slightest trouble or his supremely confident rider Mick Kinane showed the faintest signs of anxiety. In front of a record Diamond day crowd of 36,604, nearly ten per cent up on the previous year, Montjeu beat his rivals with contemptuous ease, 'only at three parts pace' in the words of his jockey. Held up in the rear in the first part of a truly-run race—some even thought Kinane was lying out of his ground—Montjeu cruised up on the bit on the outside in the home straight, was eased into the lead just inside the two-furlong marker and drew clear without being asked any sort of question. Montjeu coasted home, barely off the bridle at any stage and eased near the finish after opening up a three-length lead, the greatest strain on his jockey's well-publicised bad back probably coming from trying to pull him up! The margin of Montjeu's victory over Fantastic Light, attempting to give Saeed bin Suroor his fifth success in six years in the race, was a length and three quarters but could have been much more (we rated him accordingly). It took the discerning eye to detect just a hint, as Montjeu drifted right after hitting the front, that Kinane's tender handling might have reflected some concern that the horse was feeling the prevailing good to firm going (there had been some speculation in the week leading up to the race that he might not run). But let's not pick nits. Montjeu's display was a defining moment—perhaps the defining moment—in a highly memorable racing year in Europe, one which produced four or five outstanding candidates for the title of horse of the year.

Montjeu was not Timeform's Horse of The Year in 2000, the accolade given to his great contemporary Dubai Millennium instead, and nor had he been in 1999 when the title had gone to an outstanding older horse in Daylami. But, as Montjeu's essay concluded, 'middle-distance horses of his quality don't come along very often; he is only the sixth to win the King George and the Arc, the two races widely accepted as the principal tests of Europe's middle-distance horses.' Like another son of Sadler's Wells, Galileo, Montjeu produced a regular supply of top performers at stud. Camelot was his fourth Derby winner (just months after Montjeu's death in the spring of 2012) in eight years, following Authorized, Motivator and Pour Moi, while 2009 Derby runner-up Fame And Glory, whose subsequent wins included the Irish Derby and Gold Cup at Royal Ascot, is another of his top-class performers. Montjeu's highest-rated offspring, however, came from his very first crop. **Hurricane Run** (rated 134) not only emulated his sire by winning both the Irish Derby and Prix de l'Arc de Triomphe at three, but followed in his footsteps at four by winning the King George as well. Hurricane Run would almost certainly have won the Prix du Jockey Club too, like Montjeu, had it not been for the controversial reduction in distance of 'the French Derby' from its traditional mile and a half to an extended ten furlongs. Ridden by Kieren Fallon, even the manner of Hurricane Run's Arc win was reminiscent of his sire six years earlier:

> Hurricane Run stamped himself the best middle-distance colt in Europe with a two-length win, but the manner of his victory was eventful. Hurricane Run tended to run in snatches in the first part of the race and turned for home still among the backmarkers, being niggled along by Fallon. Having made a wide run in the Irish Derby, Fallon stuck to the inside in the Arc. Hurricane Run enjoyed a relatively clear passage—squeezing his way through on the home turn—and quickened impressively once fully opened out. Switched inside Motivator, who had led halfway up the straight, as that horse came off the rail over a furlong out, Hurricane Run cut down the always prominent Westerner under pressure and won going away, showing no sign of straying off a true line this time. Bago and Shirocco, both slightly disadvantaged by being brought to challenge wide, finished third and fourth, beaten a further length and a half

and three quarters of a length respectively, with Motivator a short head away fifth and Shawanda, afterwards found to be lame, sixth.

Fallon explained after the Arc that, because the pace was strong, he had not been worried during the race—he was over ten lengths off the leaders at one stage. 'When they go a good pace, it usually opens up in the straight,' he said. 'This is the only way to ride tracks like Longchamp where, on the outside, you lose too much ground because of the sweeping turns. You take risks on the inside—I was really lucky to have a horse to get me out of trouble—but eight times out of ten, it comes off.' As he intimated, Fallon rode his luck in the Arc and it paid off. Hurricane Run responded like a champion, producing one the most striking finishes seen from an Arc winner since Dancing Brave's electrifying burst took him past a particularly strong and representative field in 1986 on the wide outside. Among the others in the interim who have swamped the opposition for speed after being behind in an Arc are the 1987 and 1988 winners Trempolino and Tony Bin, the 1991 winner Suave Dancer and the 1997 winner Peintre Celebre. Montjeu had a similar run to Hurricane Run in his Arc, taken round the inside, being boxed in entering the straight and then quickening.

Hurricane Run's four-year-old season also bore similarities to Montjeu's in that his form tailed off later in the year. But Hurricane Run didn't show quite the same form at four (rated 130) as he had at three, and his Ascot win, by just half a length from Electrocutionist, whilst putting him alongside some of the all-time greats as winners of both the Arc and the King George, was gained with nothing like the same ease as his sire's victory:

Hurricane Run's victory at Ascot put him in illustrious company. He was only the seventh horse to win both the Arc de Triomphe and the King George. Ribot, who won the Arc twice, Ballymoss, Mill Reef, Dancing Brave and Lammtarra completed the double in the same season, while, like his son, Hurricane Run's sire Montjeu won the King George the season after he had won the Arc. Following Montjeu in 2000, Hurricane Run was only the second French-trained winner of the King George since Pawneese in 1976. He was a first success in the race for his trainer Andre Fabre, who expressed concerns over running one of his horses in mid-summer, traditionally used as a break for top middle-distance horses trained in France. Hurricane Run was a first major win in Britain for Belgian-born stable-jockey Christophe Soumillon. Hurricane Run's rider received a six-day ban for excessive use of the whip at Ascot, having hit his mount around twenty times in the straight, including down the shoulder. Soumillon also raised a few eyebrows with his victory celebration shortly after the winning post in which he gestured to his posterior before sticking his tongue out at the stands, presumably in response to those in the media who had questioned his tactical awareness on British tracks beforehand (including earlier in the month on Ouija Board in the Eclipse).

Christophe Soumillon was already a winner of the Prix de l'Arc de Triomphe by this time, having partnered the Alain de Royer Dupre-trained Dalakhani (rated 133) to victory in 2003, giving his owner, the Aga Khan, earlier successful with Sinndar, his second win in the race in four years. Like Sinndar, Dalakhani was beaten only once in his career (he too was retired at three), going down narrowly to the same owner's Alamshar, who went on to win the King George, in the Irish Derby. Dalakhani's other wins included a most impressive success in the Prix du Jockey Club, but the field he beat in the Arc wasn't a vintage one, even if it did contain two Derby winners in High Chaparral and Kris Kin.

Five years later, the same set of connections were successful again in the Arc with another three-year-old rated 133, though, exceptionally this time, the recipient was a filly, **Zarkava**, a direct descendant of the Aga Khan's outstanding racemare of the late 'fifties/early 'sixties Petite Etoile. By the time she lined up for the Arc, Zarkava had won all six of her races against her own sex, including the Prix Marcel Boussac at two, both French fillies' classics in the spring, and the Prix Vermeille three weeks before the Arc. She completely missed the break in the Vermeille and trailed the field for a long way before unleashing a tremendous turn of foot in the straight to win a shade comfortably in the end; there were to be similar elements to her Arc victory too. Incidentally, this was a vintage crop of French fillies given that it also included Goldikova who only emerged as a top-class performer in her own right later on after finishing second to Zarkava in the Poule d'Essai des Pouliches and third in the Prix de Diane.

With her effectiveness at a mile and a half now proven and her spectacular victory confirming her, by some way, the best three-year-old filly in Europe, Zarkava started at evens three weeks later to end the long losing run of three-year-old fillies in the Arc. The four-year-old fillies All Along (1983) and Urban Sea (1993) had been the last to triumph but no filly from the classic generation had won the race since 1982 when victory went to Akiyda, a product of the Aga Khan's purchase of the Boussac bloodstock interests. Zarkava was the first filly since Allez France to win the Poule d'Essai des Pouliches, the Prix de Diane and the Prix Vermeille. Allez France went on to finish a clear second in Rheingold's Arc (before winning the race the following year), but Zarkava went one better, proving herself a filly of the highest class when very confidently ridden to cut down the leaders in eye-catching style, without coming under the whip and despite ducking right immediately after leaving the stalls and making a hesitant start. Zarkava's antics contributed to her having plenty to do, but she moved closer to the middle of the sixteen-runner field as the pace was stepped up after halfway (the runners having ignored Ballydoyle's pacemaker Red Rock Canyon). Taking the gaps as they appeared in the home straight, and twice narrowly avoiding interference, Zarkava swept past the leaders near the finish to win going away by two lengths and half a length from the previous year's runner-up Youmzain and dead-heaters Soldier of Fortune (fifth the year before) and the German-trained outsider It's Gino. Vision d'Etat was the first three-year-old colt to finish, back in fifth, while the King George winner Duke of Marmalade plugged on for seventh.

Christophe Soumillon starts his celebrations as Zarkava passes the post in the Prix de l'Arc de Triomphe; race regular Youmzain finishes second

The field for the latest Arc, sponsored by Qatar, wasn't the strongest that could have been assembled, with Derby winner New Approach and Zarkava's sidelined stable-companion the Grand Prix de Paris winner Montmartre probably the most notable absentees on the day. Zarkava was left as the only filly in the line-up when Oaks winner Look Here, whom it had been announced would be supplemented, was ruled out after an unsatisfactory scope. Nonetheless, the manner of Zarkava's success—the twelfth in the Arc for her sex in sixty years— left no doubt that she was fully deserving of a place among the best of her sex in Timeform's experience. Soumillon's victory celebrations this time included hurling his riding helmet and whip into the crowd and launching himself into a flying dismount in the winner's circle! 'Coming into the straight she was going so easily, she's a real jewel and we are unlikely to see the same quality again for twenty-five or thirty years,' Soumillon said afterwards.

Zarkava, retired to stud as the first unbeaten Arc winner since Lammtarra in 1995, ended a long losing run for three-year-old fillies in the Arc. It was only another three years before the next one, however, though there were other reasons, besides her gender, that made German-trained **Danedream** (rated 132), sent off at 27/1, a noteworthy Arc winner:

> Danedream's five-length victory matched the official margins of Helissio's win in 1996 and Peintre Celebre's a year later, though Peintre Celebre and Danedream's actual margins looked a shade less (four and a half lengths in Danedream's case), whereas Helissio's looked nearer six. No matter, the only other Arc winners who had won by a wider margin officially than Danedream were Ribot in 1956, Sea-Bird in 1965 and Sakhee in 2001, all of them successful by six lengths, which puts Danedream in exalted company. Peintre Celebre smashed the race record in his year on very firm ground and Danedream shaved eleven hundredths of a second off Peintre Celebre's time to stop the clock in 2m 24.49sec . . .

> As shocks go, Danedream's win was not in the same league as Germany's only previous Arc winner, Star Appeal, who started at 119/1 in 1975 and became the longest-priced winner in the history of the race. Ridden to a three-length victory in a rough race by Greville Starkey (coincidentally a near namesake of Danedream's jockey Andrasch Starke), Star Appeal was no stranger to big-race success, having won the Gran Premio di Milano and the Eclipse Stakes earlier that season. But more recent defeats in big races accounted for him being virtually ignored on the pari-mutuel. After finishing down the field in the epic King George fought out by Grundy and Bustino, Star Appeal had finished third to Dahlia in the Benson & Hedges Gold Cup at York and then only fourth in heavy ground in the Grosser Preis von Baden. Before Danedream, third was the closest any German horse had come to winning an Arc since Star Appeal. A year after Borgia in 1997, the Peter Schiergen-trained Tiger Hill emulated her (in the trainer's first year with a licence), and It's Gino dead-heated for that position in controversial circumstances (connections claimed he had finished third outright) behind Zarkava in 2008.

The form of Danedream's Arc win stood up well later that autumn, with So You Think and Snow Fairy, who made the frame at Longchamp, filling the places in the Champion Stakes next time and fifth-placed St Nicholas Abbey going on to win the Breeders' Cup Turf. But Danedream clearly still had her doubters when bidding to become just the sixth filly or mare, and the first horse trained in Germany, to win the King George VI and Queen Elizabeth Stakes at Ascot the following summer:

> None of the runners in the latest King George VI and Queen Elizabeth Stakes had form comparable to Danedream's and yet she started at 9/1, only fifth in the betting behind Sea Moon (2/1), Nathaniel (5/2), St Nicholas Abbey (5/1) and Dunaden (8/1). Only a handful of fillies had won the King George, and perhaps that fact, coupled with Danedream being trained in Germany and having bargain-basement origins (she cost €9,000 as a two-year-old), convinced the British betting public that the Arc win had been something of a 'flash in the

pan'. The Arc, though, had been Danedream's third wide-margin Group 1 win in a row following a five-length victory in the Grosser Preis von Berlin and a six-length romp in Germany's top race, the Grosser Preis von Baden. She had managed only sixth in the Japan Cup on her only outing after the Arc as a three-year-old and, after landing the odds on her reappearance in a Group 2 at Baden-Baden in May, was surprisingly beaten in a four-runner renewal of the Grand Prix de Saint-Cloud, on her last outing before the King George, by Meandre, Shareta and Galikova, all of whom she had beaten comprehensively in the Arc. Connections were quoted before the King George as saying that Danedream was back in top form and so it proved.

The bare form of Danedream's King George victory didn't quite match her Arc performance but she did well to get up to head Nathaniel in the last stride after her jockey was forced to switch wide, conceding first run, when a gap between Nathaniel and 20/1-shot Brown Panther, who was in the lead, closed two furlongs out. Danedream responded really well as Nathaniel also found more after taking the lead over a furlong out and the pair had a memorable set-to, separated at the line by the smallest possible margin, a nose, in the closest finish in the history of the race.

Danedream won a second Grosser Preis von Baden later that summer but she was denied an attempt to win the Arc again in unusual circumstances when an outbreak of equine infectious anaemia, or 'swamp fever', at Cologne racecourse where Danedream was trained, resulted in a ban on the movement of racehorses stabled there and thus prevented Danedream from travelling to Paris. But Germany won a second consecutive King George when Novellist was successful at Ascot in 2013.

Christophe Soumillon probably wasn't alone in believing it would be many years before another filly would come along to rival, let alone surpass, Zarkava. But in 2013, as this book was being put together, Soumillon himself finished second in the Arc on Orfevre behind another three-year-old filly who earned a place among the best of her sex in Timeform's experience. Treve became the next Arc winner to maintain an unbeaten record, she too successful in the Prix de Diane and Prix Vermeille beforehand, while her stunning five-length victory matched Danedream's winning margin.

This chapter has so far concentrated on horses who made a name for themselves as three-year-olds, though unless injury intervened or a stud career beckoned, as we've seen, plenty of them went on to enhance their reputations as older horses. There was a time when top three-year-old colts and fillies were packed off to stud all too soon in their careers, but with the proliferation of valuable prizes worldwide for older horses, the incentives for keeping top middle-distance performers in training that much longer are all the greater. For a long while, at least in Europe, there was little to detain good fillies on the racecourse beyond the age of three, though since 2004 a significantly upgraded programme of races for older fillies and mares has opened up plenty more opportunities for them. All of which is good for competitive racing, and for fans of the sport.

Sheikh Mohammed's Godolphin operation was founded largely on older middle-distance performers, and a number of their international successes are dealt with in the chapter on the 'Globetrotters'. One top-class Godolphin horse who amply rewarded the decision to keep him in training, until the age of six, was **Swain** (rated 134 as a five-year-old). He's already been mentioned as one of Peintre Celebre's victims in the 1997 Arc, a race in which he made the frame in two previous attempts, but some of his biggest successes were domestic ones, notably the King George:

> Those who have campaigned for more good older horses to be kept in training in Europe must have felt they were banging their heads against a brick wall at times. The flow of top performers to stud before they've reached full maturity has continued largely unabated in recent years. However, what might have seemed a rather futile crusade at times received a considerable boost in 1997. What kind of a year would it have been without Pilsudski, Singspiel, Helissio, Bosra Sham, Spinning World and Swain, to mention but a few? Perhaps as much to the point, those horses not only provided a lot of enjoyment while winning a great deal of prize money, but they also, with the possible exception of Helissio, enhanced their reputations and in turn their value for stud. Maybe things are changing for the better, as indicated by the fact that Swain, with little left to prove, is due to race on as a six-year-old in 1998.
>
> Swain has a terrific record overall, having finished out of the frame only once in sixteen races. As a three-year-old, in his first season, he won his first five races, notably the Grand Prix de Deauville, and finished under three lengths third to Lammtarra in the Prix de l'Arc de Triomphe. At four, he won the Coronation Cup and the Prix Foy, as well as finishing second in the Grand Prix de Saint-Cloud, third in the Breeders' Cup Turf and the Prix Ganay and fourth, beaten about six lengths by Helissio, in the Arc. The impression, however, was that Swain wasn't quite out of the top drawer. Although accounting for Pentire and Singspiel for his four-year-old wins, that pair seemed better than Swain overall, as did Pilsudski (the winner of the Breeders' Cup Turf, with Singspiel second) and of course Helissio, who had taken his measure at Saint-Cloud also. At the end of that year Swain was wintered in Dubai and transferred from Andre Fabre to Saeed bin Suroor.
>
> Swain, Pilsudski, Helissio and Singspiel all turned up in 1997 at Ascot in July for the King George VI And Queen Elizabeth Diamond Stakes. The 'race of the year' seems to come round every week nowadays, but this, apparently, was not even the 'race of the decade', nor even of 'the century'. No this was (possibly) 'the greatest horserace ever', according to one headline. Well, probably not, and that's not just with the benefit of hindsight. Racing enthusiasts with longer memories may well champion the likes of Sea-Bird's and Dancing Brave's Arcs and Brigadier Gerard's and El Gran Senor's Guineas, to mention just those in Europe that seemed of even more consequence beforehand and actually lived

up to their promise. All the same, the 1997 King George could boast a most impressive roll call . . .

Swain's three chief rivals had all added further Group 1 races to their tallies in 1997 prior to Ascot whereas Swain himself had been beaten by another member of the King George field, St Leger winner Shantou, in the Princess of Wales's Stakes on his belated return earlier in July. However, with torrential rain turning the ground to soft from good to firm overnight, Swain defied odds of 16/1 to account for Pilsudski by a length. Twelve months later, Swain won the King George again, by a length from that year's Derby winner High-Rise, and followed up with another fine performance to win the Irish Champion Stakes. Aged six in 1998, Swain remains the oldest horse to win the King George and only the second to win it twice, after the French filly Dahlia in 1973/74. Swain's admirable career ended on a controversial note after his participation in (another!) 'race of the decade' at that year's Breeders' Cup, though for all the hubbub over the part played by Frankie Dettori in what happened at Churchill Downs, it's as well to remember the merit of Swain's performance—'a rattling good one in all the circumstances.'

One of Kipling's stipulations for maturing into manhood was the ability to 'meet with Triumph and Disaster and treat those two imposters just the same.' Frankie Dettori has enjoyed a celebrated career and earned such a remarkable place in the affections of the racing public that he can, perhaps, be forgiven for not being able to take the stinging criticism that followed his riding of Swain in the Breeders' Cup Classic. Swain's running and the performance of Dettori dominated the post-race headlines. Swain veered off a true line in the closing stages under a very strong ride from Dettori, ending up on the wide outside, beaten three quarters of a length and a neck by the American four-year-olds Awesome Again and Silver Charm in what had been billed by some in America as 'the race of the decade.' Swain's place in the line-up, after firmly establishing himself as the best middle-distance horse in Europe with a second successive victory in the King George at Ascot in July, was a major boost for the organisers of the Breeders' Cup programme.

The Breeders' Cup Classic, the world's richest race in 1998, also attracted four of America's top five older horses (Skip Away and Gentlemen joined Awesome Again and Silver Charm) and three of their top four three-year-olds (Coronado's Quest, Victory Gallop and Arch). Swain was on the heels of the leaders turning for home, moving as well as anything ('I was quite sure we were going to win at this stage,' Dettori has said since), but as he and the doughty Silver Charm challenged long-time leader Coronado's Quest it was soon apparent that Swain had a real fight on his hands with Silver Charm. Dettori picked up his stick and administered, in rapid succession, a number of severe, left-handed blows to Swain's quarters, some of them out of rhythm with the horse's stride; Swain almost immediately began to wander off a true line, edging to his right at first before veering more sharply away towards the stand rail. The damage had been done and, though Swain ran on again once straightened, any chance of winning had gone. Dettori's initial explanation that 'Swain saw something, probably the bank of television arc lights, which made him run away' was far from convincing, especially as Swain ran *towards* the lights, not away from them. The most likely object for Swain to be 'running away' from was Dettori's whip—or, more specifically, the thrashing which was the cumulative result of his rider's over-eagerness. 'All the people know Frankie made a mistake,' acknowledged Swain's trainer Saeed bin Suroor. 'Frankie is our jockey, we love him: I understand he can't do everything right all the time but, at the same time, I would like to see him ride better than this.' Dettori, himself, had difficulty seeing it from that perspective at first. The normally chirpy Italian took the first plane home and spoke to virtually no-one as an unrelenting attack on him continued for the best part of a week in the Press in Britain (the American media had been scathing the day after the race). 'Come on Frankie, "it's good to talk"' was one headline tried in an attempt to goad him into breaking his silence. Questions at a reception for the video *Frankie Dettori, Horsing Around* brought a curt 'I have no comment to make about Saturday, I'm here to launch this video.' Dettori's stance showed his sensitivity over the issue but his characteristic good humour was never far below the surface. He accepted a Cartier Award for Swain with the line 'I almost wrecked his career, now I'm receiving this prize!' and he was also the subject of *This Is Your Life* while the controversy was still raging ('I was afraid that the doors would open and in would walk Swain!' he said afterwards).

Saeed bin Suroor and Frankie Dettori had won the Arc with the three-year-old Lammtarra in 1995, but it was a pair of older horses who carried the Godolphin colours to victory in the same race in successive years after the millennium. Five-year-old Marienbard won a substandard renewal in 2002, but twelve months earlier four-year-old **Sakhee** (rated 136) was an Arc winner out of the top drawer. Clear of the rest when runner-up in Sinndar's Derby, Sakhee managed only one more run (in the Eclipse) at three—when trained by John Dunlop—before a serious knee injury came to light, but a stunning seven-length win in the Juddmonte International at York on his second start back at four made him the one to beat at Longchamp:

> . . . in testing conditions Sakhee started favourite to beat a field of sixteen. As well as Galileo, there was no Fantastic Light, Nayef nor Morshdi, who was injured, but the runners included the two best mile-and-a-half fillies in France, Aquarelliste and Diamilina; the runner-up from 2000, Egyptband; Two Thousand Guineas winner Golan; St Leger winner Milan; the last two winners of the Prix du Jockey Club, Holding Court and Anabaa Blue; and one of the best older horses in France, Hightori. Not a vintage Arc perhaps, but the paying public (the announcement of a record crowd came as a surprise to many regulars) were treated to a vintage performance in a race in which there were few hard-luck stories and no convincing ones. Sakhee had no difficulty travelling strongly, close to the pace, and he moved through readily to lead soon after entering the straight and proceeded to leave the others for dead, passing the post, pushed out, six lengths clear of Aquarelliste, who hadn't enjoyed an entirely

smooth passage but still got clear in time to catch Sakhee if good enough. Three-year-old Sagacity, putting up his best performance, was a further length back in third, followed by Golan and Milan. It was the first time in eight years the race had not been won by a three-year-old colt. Few championship races, let alone the Arc, are as good as over so far out or are won by as much as six lengths. Sakhee's margin matched the official ones for Ribot in 1956 and Sea Bird II in 1965, while Helissio's official five in 1996 was actually six, but, whichever way one looks at it, this was a magnificent display by a well-above-average Arc winner.

Sakhee and Dettori went agonisingly close to avenging Swain's defeat in the Breeders' Cup Classic when touched off by a nose by Tiznow at Belmont Park but he wasn't done with yet:

> Sakhee might well have been packed off to stud by some owners after the Eclipse, given the level of his form and his injury. Precious few would have decided to keep him in training at five with an Arc under his belt, but Godolphin has a different agenda from most other leading owners, which is why the stable continues landing so many Group 1 races.

Unfortunately, Sakhee's knee problems flared up again and his only win at five came in a warm-up race for the Dubai World Cup in which he finished a below-form third.

Keeping older horses in training was not a policy so widely adopted by Godolphin's chief rivals Coolmore, but things have changed over the years, and the likes of Yeats, winner of four Gold Cups, and St Nicholas Abbey, winner of three Coronation Cups, have gone on to enjoy extended careers, in both cases after their classic seasons were cut short by injury. Stable-companion **Dylan Thomas**, on the other hand, won the Irish Derby and the Irish Champion Stakes at three, but the decision to keep him in training at four (when he was rated 132) was rewarded with a tremendous season which brought him the rare double of the King George and Arc in the same year, along with the Prix Ganay and a second Irish Champion Stakes. His Arc victory came on his eighth start in a ten-race campaign which saw him race in Ireland, France, Britain, the USA and Hong Kong:

> Dylan Thomas set the seal on a magnificent year, for himself and for his stable, when becoming his trainer's first winner of Europe's richest race, the Prix de l'Arc de Triomphe. The victory put him in illustrious company—he is only the sixth horse to win both the King George and the Arc in the same season—and provided a timely reminder that a top horse can have a full campaign and still be at their best for Longchamp in October. Ascot's showpiece, the King George VI and Queen Elizabeth Stakes, has long been the midsummer championship of Europe for the middle-distance performers but the myth has grown up that a mid-season break, involving bypassing the King George, is a pre-requisite for any horse whose principal aim is the Arc. The Arc has understandably always been the main focus for the top French middle-distance horses—with the classic three-year-olds traditionally given a summer break—and its ever-rising status as the more important of the two principal tests of Europe's top middle-

distance horses will be emphasised in 2008 when a new sponsorship deal with the Qatar Racing and Equestrian Club will make the Arc the most valuable global event on turf and the second richest race in the world, behind only the Dubai World Cup.

Before leaving the Arc, a word or two on the horse who finished runner-up to Dylan Thomas at both Ascot and Longchamp. **Youmzain** (rated 131 aged five) won the Great Voltigeur at York and a Group 1 in Germany as a three-year-old and the Grand Prix de Saint-Cloud at five, but it's more likely he'll be remembered for the races he didn't win. Youmzain was runner-up in two Coronation Cups, third in another couple of editions of the King George besides finishing second to Dylan Thomas, and was placed twice more in the Grand Prix de Saint-Cloud, including when beaten just a nose. But it was his record of finishing second in three consecutive runnings of the Arc which earns Youmzain a deserved footnote, if not a chapter, in the race's history, as recounted in *Racehorses of 2009*:

> Who says you get nothing for finishing second? Youmzain has earned a total of £1,884,333 (at prevailing exchange rates) for his three splendid second places in the Prix de l'Arc de Triomphe. The last two editions, sponsored by Qatar, have seen the Arc assume the mantle of the richest race in the world on turf. Youmzain earned £838,899 in the latest Arc, £129,274 more than Arc winner Sea The Stars earned for *winning* Britain's most valuable race the Derby and £271,199 more than the *first* prize won by Arc fourth Conduit in 'Britain's Arc' the King George VI and Queen Elizabeth Stakes. It is said that nobody ever remembers who finishes second, but at least Youmzain's connections should be able to draw comfort from the entries made on their bank balances as a result of the horse's efforts on his three visits to Longchamp. Deep down, though, their feelings were probably similar to those of top American golfer Tom Weiskopf, who was runner-up in four editions of the US Masters between 1969 and 1975, twice to Jack Nicklaus. 'I'm absolutely delighted to have come second,' he said. 'Who cares about winning when you can be second? Oh yeah, how I love being runner-up to Jack Nicklaus.'

For the record, Youmzain was beaten a head by Dylan Thomas in 2007, two lengths by Zarkava in 2008 and two lengths again by Sea The Stars in 2009; his fourth attempt to emulate his sire Sinndar saw him finish down the field as a seven-year-old on his final outing.

The absence of an Arc, King George, or Derby win on a horse's CV does not necessarily preclude him or her from being a top-notch middle-distance performer, of course, and this chapter ends with three prime examples, all of them rated 135. Firstly, **Royal Anthem**, who, until Frankel came along more than a decade later, was the best horse trained by Sir Henry Cecil in the period since *Favourite Racehorses*. Unraced at two, Royal Anthem quickly made into a high-class three-year-old, finishing third in the second of Swain's King Georges and winning the Canadian International impressively. Better still was expected of Royal Anthem at four, and while on balance his 1999 campaign might have been considered disappointing, there was one performance which stood out:

> Stravinsky in the July Cup and Daylami in the King George both put up the best performances seen in their respective divisions in Britain for many a year. This was a remarkable season, however, and after the Juddmonte International at York there were strong grounds for thinking that Daylami's Ascot showing had merely become the best performance in his division for a few weeks. Royal Anthem's International win was another exhibition which took the breath away.

> They went a strong pace at York. Frankie Dettori said later that they had gone too fast, but if that had been the case Royal Anthem would have been inconvenienced a good deal more than most; racing on the outside, he was scarcely any more than two lengths behind the leader from the off and was disputing the lead himself fully five furlongs out. The truth is that from that point onwards Royal Anthem just went too fast for everything else. Greek Dance was the only other runner still on the bridle approaching the three-furlong marker and, when Gary Stevens asked Royal Anthem to show what he could really do soon afterwards, Greek Dance was transformed into an also-ran as well. Royal Anthem was eight lengths clear at the line, if anything still drawing further clear, Greek Dance holding off Chester House for second. It was not a vintage field but, behind the second and third, Royal Anthem had also shown a clean pair of heels to Group 1 winners Almutawakel, Central Park, Compton Admiral (fifth), Golden Snake and Saffron Walden, and to Group 2 winners Almushtarak (fourth), Kissogram and Salford Express. Whatever the accomplishments of those behind him, Royal Anthem had won in such a manner that no-one needed telling this was an outstanding performance. That impression was fully confirmed by a timefigure of 1.53 fast (equivalent to a timerating of 138), which was bettered only once in any race in Britain during the nineties, by Dayjur (1.69 fast) in the 1990 Nunthorpe. Royal Anthem's was the widest winning distance in the International, eclipsing Assert's six lengths in 1982, and also the best form shown in the race's twenty-eight-year history.

By the end of the year, Royal Anthem had joined Bill Mott in the States where he finished second to Daylami in the Breeders' Cup Turf before winning a Grade 1 on his only subsequent start aged five. Royal Anthem might have been on a one-way ticket across the Atlantic, but it was not the last that was seen in Europe of his rider at York, Gary Stevens, even if that initially looked to be the case:

> The International Stakes also represented the highlight of a colourful sojourn in Britain for the champion US jockey Gary Stevens, whose career in 1999 took an even greater number of about-turns than that of Royal Anthem. Arriving to take the job of stable jockey to Sir Michael Stoute, Stevens made his first British ride of 1999 a winning one, just four days before partnering Beat All into third place in the Derby. The respect and enthusiasm he expressed for British racing immediately on his arrival, stating that he hoped to see out the remainder of

his career here, helped to endear Stevens to the racing public before he did so in more tangible fashion by registering a total of forty-five winners from two hundred and ten rides. Ready to admit some of the inevitable teething difficulties, Stevens went on to impress particularly with the knack of putting his mount in front in unflappable fashion where it mattered, something exhibited most clearly when winning the William Hill Mile at Goodwood by a neck on Lonesome Dude. One day earlier he had dictated the pace to win another major prize at the track on Mary Stuart, whilst Zahrat Dubai (Nassau Stakes), Cape Cross (Queen Anne Stakes), Greek Dance (Rose of Lancaster Stakes) and Torgau (Cherry Hinton Stakes), as well as Royal Anthem, were all guided by Stevens to pattern-race victories. Glorious Goodwood also, however, brought the news that he would be leaving Stoute and heading back to the States again at the end of August to take up a five-year contract with the Thoroughbred Corporation, less of a shock than it might have been seeing that Kieren Fallon had so recently become available as a suitable replacement. Stevens ended his stay in Britain, as he began it, with a winner. In the United States, Anees (in the Juvenile) gave him a seventh success at the Breeders' Cup meeting, to go with three Kentucky Derby triumphs and 4,512 victories in all before he announced his retirement from the saddle in December because of irreparable damage inflicted by arthritis on his right knee.

But by the end of 2000, Stevens was back riding again, winning the Preakness and Belmont Stakes in 2001 on Point Given in the colours of Royal Anthem's owners the Thoroughbred Corporation. Another career-break followed, during which he played the role of jockey George Woolf in the film *Seabiscuit*, before a surprise return to Europe in 2004 in a link-up with another top stable, this time that of Andre Fabre. That too, however, proved a short-lived venture, and Stevens announced his retirement again late in 2005. A further twist came in 2013, when he made yet another comeback, aged fifty, winning the Preakness Stakes for a third time, on Oxbow, as well as riding a winner at Ascot's Shergar Cup meeting and landing the Breeders' Cup Classic for the first time aboard Mucho Macho Man.

Despite Dylan Thomas winning the King George and Arc in 2007, there was a better horse in Europe that year in the Fabre-trained five-year-old **Manduro** (135) who put up the best effort of the season when beating Dylan Thomas and the subsequent Eclipse winner Notnowcato in the Prince of Wales's Stakes at Royal Ascot. The much-improved Manduro, who had begun his career in Germany, went through the season unbeaten in five starts, earning rare praise from his trainer:

> When a trainer describes a horse as the best he has trained, the identity of the trainer is every bit as important as that of the horse, maybe even more so. When the trainer is Andre Fabre, in his twenty-first consecutive season as France's champion trainer, and with nearly two hundred horses in his care each year, owned by a selection of the world's top owners, he has more candidates to choose from than most. Unlike some trainers whose assessments of their

horses can sound suspiciously like a sales pitch or advertising material for a future stallion career, Fabre is not given to handing out such accolades lightly. It was only in 2006, as the opening lines of the essay on Shirocco highlighted, that the trainer expressed his reluctance to compare that horse with the stable's other top older middle-distance performer Hurricane Run. That the trainer's opinions on his horses, or any subject for that matter, are available to the British media, be it in newspapers or on television, is perhaps taken too much for granted, because, on the other side of the Channel, much to the frustration of French racing journalists, Fabre has a long-standing policy of not communicating with the media. This results in the bizarre situation of the French media having to report second-hand information gleaned from their British colleagues, rather than from the trainer himself. For example, readers of *Paris Turf* found out two days after readers of the *Racing Post* that Fabre considered Manduro the best horse he had trained.

'It is like comparing me with Naomi Campbell' Fabre had said when asked to compare his two leading older contenders for the 2006 Arc—both of whom ended up being beaten by their three-year-old stablemate Rail Link.

Like Shirocco the year before (both were sons of Monsun and owned by Baron Georg von Ullmann), Manduro completed his Arc preparation with a win in the Prix Foy, a crucial test where Manduro was concerned as it was his first try over the Arc distance; his previous race had been the Prix Jacques le Marois over a mile. It appeared Manduro had come through his trial with flying colours but within hours he was found to have sustained a fracture to his off-hind:

> Manduro's win in the Prix Foy may have gone some way at least to answering unequivocally the question about his effectiveness at a mile and a half but the fact that he never ran again posed others. How would he have fared in the Arc itself? There's little doubt that the Arc would have been a sterner test of stamina than the Foy, given that in general it was the staying types who came to the fore. The Foy second and third finished only seventh and ninth in the Arc, beaten considerably further by the winner Dylan Thomas than they had been by Manduro. On the other hand, the fact that Manduro had given a sound beating to Dylan Thomas, albeit at a shorter trip, at Royal Ascot in the summer must have left Manduro's connections thinking what might have been. Andre Fabre has proved a master at preparing horses for the Arc using the established trials; all six of his three-year-old winners of the race contested the Prix Niel beforehand (Peintre Celebre the only one not to win the Niel, though an unlucky loser), while Fabre's other Arc winner, four-year-old Subotica, finished second in the Foy beforehand. It seems more than likely that whatever Manduro showed in the Foy, he could have been expected to be more fully tuned up for the Arc itself, in which maybe he would have given a public performance to back up his trainer's assessment of him as the best he has trained. But that's speculation, and Manduro achieved enough in reality without having to dwell too much on

what else he might have done. He was a top-class racehorse, in our experience the best to come out of Germany, ahead of the 1975 Arc winner Star Appeal (rated 133), whose career began in Ireland. Manduro's record of finishing out of the first three only once, when fourth, speaks for itself, and, while better at a mile and a quarter than a mile, and probably capable of proving as good at a mile and a half, he was given the opportunity to show rare versatility in a top racehorse these days, winning important races at eight, nine, ten and twelve furlongs on ground ranging from soft to good to firm.

It's bad enough when a big race like the Arc is missing one of its star names due to injury. But what about when a sound horse, and one of Europe's best, is left on the sidelines through being deemed ineligible? The gelding **Cirrus des Aigles** (rated 135) highlighted the absurdity of the rules governing entry to Europe's biggest race, as *Racehorses of 2012* explained—with more than a hint of exasperation!

The main purpose of the Timeform Annuals is to give an informative and entertaining account of the achievements of all the thoroughbreds that race in Britain each year, providing a precise measure of each horse's merit (the Timeform rating) and a keen appreciation of its racing character. The essays on the best horses have also traditionally been used as a vehicle for presenting Timeform's views on some of racing's wider issues. Every topic of importance in racing has had an airing at some time or another in *Racehorses*, with Timeform's editorial opinion—always standing for the overall good of racing—often fuelling a wider debate which has led to change. Some of the arguments, though, have appeared time after time and fallen on deaf ears, one of them being that top championship races should always be open to the best horses, which means making geldings eligible for all events for which entires are eligible. It is the best part of fifty years since *Racehorses* started regularly advocating allowing geldings to run in the top weight-for-age events, as in North America and Australia where an open policy has long been the norm.

Some traditionalists regard the gelding operation as 'performance-enhancing', providing further grounds for excluding geldings from races which, it is claimed, exist for the purpose of selecting the best colts for breeding. The arguments are nonsensical. High-class colts regularly meet geldings in the North American triple crown races, but defeat, when it happens, doesn't damage their popularity with breeders. Why should it? The presence, when they come along, of high-class geldings in the top races increases competition and provides a stiffer test for the colts—as well as making for better entertainment (where would Europe's top sprints be without geldings?). As geldings are campaigned for longer, they can help to provide a guide to the respective merits of colts from different crops. The sooner geldings are allowed to contest all the top races open to entires, the better—though no-one should hold their breath!

The exclusion, through ineligibility, in the last two years of France's finest middle-distance performer Cirrus des Aigles from the greatest race in his own country—and the biggest in Europe—has benefited neither French racing nor the French breeding industry. For the second year running, the best colts in the line-up for the Prix de l'Arc de Triomphe were beaten by a filly, after being beaten by three fillies in 2011, while no French-trained colt finished within five lengths of the winner in either year. Cirrus des Aigles is a top-class racehorse, the highest-rated gelding in the history of the *Racehorses* series, sharing with the German-bred entire Manduro, who was unbeaten in five races as a five-year-old in 2007, the distinction of being the best horse, of any age or sex, trained in France since Montjeu.

Cirrus des Aigles' absence from the 2011 Arc was very much France's loss and Britain's gain because later in October he was the first winner of the Champion Stakes (for which geldings first became eligible in 1986) at its new home of Ascot on the inaugural British Champions' Day. Cirrus des Aigles accounted for So You Think and Snow Fairy, the three of them covered by little more than a length, but an occasion intended to showcase British racing at its best was soon overshadowed by more controversy, and this time it was Britain's Rules of Racing that came under fire:

> While Cirrus des Aigles benefited from the difference between Britain and France in allowing geldings to compete in Group 1 races, his jockey at Ascot, Christophe Soumillon, fell foul of the difference in the whip rules in the two countries. In line with changes which came into force only five days earlier, Soumillon was hit with a five-day ban and forfeited his share of the prize money, which came to £52,390. The Qipco-sponsored Champion Stakes was worth £737,230 to the winner and overtook the Derby as Britain's most valuable race. Soumillon's offence was that he used his whip six times inside the final furlong—once more than the number permitted under the new rules. An incensed Soumillon looked all set to appeal against the decision, but, before a hearing could take place, the British Horseracing Authority amended the rules again—retrospectively—and Soumillon received his percentage after all, though the resulting amendments to the new rules could not undo the initial damage to the image of British racing as it attempted to launch its new showcase meeting. Soumillon himself had only just returned from a fifteen-day ban imposed by the Longchamp stewards after he was found guilty of causing a fall in the last race on Arc trials day, ruling him out of the Arc meeting. Soumillon is no stranger to success at the top level, or to controversy for that matter, but for Cirrus des Aigles and his trainer, the Champion Stakes was very much a career highlight to date and it was regrettable that a brouhaha which, in Soumillon's words, 'shamed British racing' should have soured the occasion. Headlines generated by Soumillon's whip ban were a huge embarrassment to the sport, an 'own-goal' that could and should have been avoided.

By the time Cirrus des Aigles returned to Ascot twelve months later, he had won another three races; the Dubai Sheema Classic, the Prix Ganay (by eight lengths) and the Prix Dollar. In the last-named contest, his nine-length win represented much better form than that shown by the Arc principals twenty-fours later. His attempt to win a second Champion Stakes was thwarted by Frankel but his gallant second place took his earnings past the £4m mark:

Cirrus des Aigles was kept off the course over the summer when he developed a leg infection, after plans had been announced that he would run in the Grand Prix de Saint-Cloud (rather than the Prince of Wales's) and then in the King George VI and Queen Elizabeth Stakes. The King George was won by the previous year's Arc winner Danedream who just got the better of Nathaniel, winner of the previous year's King George and successful in the latest season in the Eclipse. Both of those were late absentees from the Arc (as was Snow Fairy) but Nathaniel was able to join Cirrus des Aigles in a memorable Champion Stakes less than a fortnight later. They provided a strong challenge on soft ground to 11/2-on shot Frankel on his final appearance before going to stud. The performance of Cirrus des Aigles in running Frankel to a length and three quarters, with the reliable Nathaniel two and a half lengths behind in third, was arguably better than the form of his victory over So You Think and Snow Fairy the previous year. Cirrus des Aigles finished closer to Frankel than any other horse all season.

The first running of the Champion Stakes at Ascot and a stirring finale as Cirrus des Aigles (centre) gets the better of So You Think

Yeats

STAYERS

Stayers

The last decade or so has seen something of a revival in fortunes for the once ailing staying division, with the most prestigious long-distance prize, the Gold Cup at Royal Ascot, thriving again. Yeats became the most successful Gold Cup horse of all time in 2009, as well as one of the most popular. His trainer Aidan O'Brien, along with Saeed bin Suroor, handler of another of the best Gold Cup winners of the modern era, Kayf Tara, have now joined the late Sir Henry Cecil with five wins in the race. The 'Cup' races have some of the longest histories of any in the calendar, but a new end-of-season highlight for stayers that remain in Europe in the autumn (resisting the ever-greater pull of the Melbourne Cup) is the Long Distance Cup at Ascot, a higher-profile replacement for the old Jockey Club Cup at Newmarket and culmination of the 'Long Distance' category of the British Champions Series, which also includes both the Gold Cup and the St Leger.

Dual winner **Kayf Tara** (rated 130) was the second of Saeed bin Suroor's four individual Gold Cup winners—Classic Cliche in 1996, Papineau in 2004 and Colour Vision in 2012 are the others—and he became the first horse since early in the nineteenth century to regain the top race for stayers when winning the 2000 renewal, in which he beat former Gold Cup winners Celeric and Enzeli, the previous year's Queen's Vase winner Endorsement and smart geldings Arctic Owl, Far Cry, San Sebastian and Persian Punch, who were all capable of mounting a serious challenge for the stayers' title in an average year. 'The best Cup horse since the golden days of Sagaro, Le Moss and Ardross' was the verdict on Kayf Tara in *Racehorses of 2000*.

The late-developing Kayf Tara won his first Gold Cup (in 1998) as a four-year-old on just his fifth start and his eight pattern victories also included two Irish St Legers, the Goodwood Cup, the Yorkshire Cup, the Prix Vicomtesse Vigier and the Prix Kergorlay. Kayf Tara was also favourite for the Melbourne Cup in 1999—he'd bypassed the challenge the previous year because of perceived immaturity—but injury forced him to miss the race which his stable-companion Central Park came within half a length of winning.

That Kayf Tara won his second Gold Cup despite not having to reproduce the pick of his best form was testament to his top-class ability, but his dominance in the staying ranks at the time is perhaps better illustrated by this extract from his essay in *Racehorses of 1999*:

> Kayf Tara got back on the winning trail in the Goodwood Cup, a race in which he had finished fifth the previous year. He obliterated one myth here, since the ground was firmer than at Ascot. Admittedly, Kayf Tara didn't move well

to post, but he came back in tremendous fashion, edging closer to the pace, set by Seignorial, a mile out and sprinting clear once asked to quicken under three furlongs from home. Having gone eight lengths ahead, Kayf Tara was eased before winning by an official margin of four lengths over Three Cheers. With the intention of going for a repeat success in the Irish St Leger, Kayf Tara was aimed at the Prix Kergorlay rather than the Doncaster Cup; the Deauville race comes a couple of weeks earlier. Opposed by four rivals on soft going, including Invermark and Yorkshire Cup second Largesse—there was only one French contender—Kayf Tara had new tactics applied, making all and quickening away once shaken up in the straight to beat Invermark easily by five lengths.

Since being opened to older horses in 1983 the Jefferson Smurfit Memorial Irish St Leger has been won by five three-year-olds, with none successful in the 'nineties. Not that many have even contested the race lately, with twenty-four runners out of a total of seventy-seven from 1990 to 1998, and only two have started favourite, Patricia in 1991 and Key Change in 1996. Just one from the classic crop, rank outsider Genghis Khan, took on Kayf Tara and three other older horses in the latest renewal. The other older horses were: Silver Patriarch, the 1997 St Leger victor recently successful in the Geoffrey Freer Stakes; Enzeli, who hadn't run since winning the Gold Cup; and Yavana's Pace, winner of two listed races and the September Stakes in the current season. Kayf Tara started at 2/1-on and never gave his backers a moment's worry, travelling easily as Genghis Khan made the running, going on half a mile out and galloping on much too strongly for Yavana's Pace. He won by eight lengths, with Silver Patriarch and Enzeli running below form in third and fourth. This was the best performance by Kayf Tara all year and one which placed him in a select band of three horses to have won the race twice—Vintage Crop did so in 1993 and 1994, and Oscar Schindler in 1996 and 1997.

Like Kayf Tara, **Vinnie Roe** (rated 128) was Timeform's best stayer for three successive seasons. In 2004 Vinnie Roe won his fourth consecutive Irish St Leger, and he then ran the race of his life when second under top weight in the Melbourne Cup, having finished fourth in the race two years earlier (he was also eighth in the 2005 renewal on his final career start). Vinnie Roe missed the Gold Cup in both 2003 (when saved for an autumn campaign) and 2004 (due to concerns over a muscular injury and the prevailing firm ground), but he showed he was effective at the two and a half mile trip when placed in the renewals either side, including when finishing a neck second to Royal Rebel in 2002.

The game, genuine and consistent Vinnie Roe, whose career was masterminded by Dermot Weld, is the only horse to have won the Irish St Leger as a three-year-old since the 'eighties. His CV also included a win in the 2001 Prix Royal-Oak, as well as a fifth-place finish in the 2003 Prix de l'Arc de Triomphe. Vinnie Roe's record in the Irish St Leger earned him what was then a unique place in the history of the European pattern as *Racehorses of 2004* explained:

There was no shortage of rivals standing in the way of a fourth success, the thirteen-strong line-up for the latest Irish Field St Leger the biggest since the same number went to post in 1988. The previous year's St Leger winner Brian Boru was the only other in the field with a European Group 1 victory to his name, though Vinnie Roe's stable-companion Media Puzzle had won the Melbourne Cup, a Group 1 event notwithstanding that it is a handicap (disparagingly nicknamed in some quarters the 'Australian Cesarewitch'). Vinnie Roe and Brian Boru started joint favourites at the Curragh at 7/2, with the smart British-trained pair Orange Touch (9/2) and Lonsdale Cup winner First Charter (5/1) the only others at shorter than 10/1. Orange Touch set a true gallop, heading a group of four including Vinnie Roe and First Charter, who were clear of the remainder for much of the race. Travelling smoothly all the way, Vinnie Roe was sent to the front over a furlong out and won comfortably by two and a half lengths from the staying-on Brian Boru, who never looked like troubling him. Vinnie Roe's jockey Pat Smullen, who has partnered him in all his races except one, picked up his whip only to wave it in celebration in the last fifty yards. First Charter finished a further half length behind Brian Boru in third, Orange Touch weakening into eighth. Sagaro won three Gold Cups at Royal Ascot in the 'seventies, but Vinnie Roe is the only horse to win the same European Group 1 event four years running since a European-wide pattern system came into existence in 1971 (Marsyas won four successive Prix du Cadrans between 1944 and 1947).

Since then, fellow stayer Yeats (who features below) and Goldikova (winner of a fourth Prix Rothschild in 2011) have equalled Vinnie Roe's feat in a European Group 1, while Dermot Weld subsequently won a first Gold Cup with Rite of Passage in 2010 (also winner of the Long Distance Cup two years later) and a seventh Irish St Leger with Voleuse de Coeurs in 2013.

Vinnie Roe was third when **Westerner** (rated 130) won the Gold Cup (run at York) in 2005. Westerner's best performance may have come when he was runner-up to Hurricane Run in the 2005 Prix de l'Arc de Triomphe, but he was a high-class stayer, and his toughness, reliability and consistency saw him win eleven races, including five Group 1s, from twenty-eight starts over four full seasons. Westerner was the best stayer in France for three years in a row and the best in Europe as a six-year-old, when his victory in the Gold Cup took his record in leading staying races since his length-and-a-half defeat in the previous year's renewal of that race to six wins from as many starts. His career highlight is detailed in this extract from his essay in *Racehorses of 2005*:

> Westerner had little to prove over long distances when the season started, the only blot on his record being his failure to win the Gold Cup—he had already won the Prix du Cadran and Prix Royal-Oak twice but had been beaten by Papineau at Royal Ascot in 2004. Westerner arrived at York for the latest Gold Cup with easy wins behind him in the Prix de Barbeville and Prix Vicomtesse Vigier at Longchamp, the latter unchallenged by five lengths from Allez Olive;

on each occasion Westerner's turn of foot was used to full effect. He was sent off 7/4 favourite against sixteen rivals in the Gold Cup, a line-up which equalled the record number of runners for the race set when Enzeli won in 1999. It was the ninth year in a row that the event had been contested by a field in double figures—in comparison, the Prix du Cadran has managed this only three times in the same period—and the quality of the contenders seemed to confirm the Gold Cup's supremacy among international weight-for-age races for stayers. They included quadruple Irish St Leger victor Vinnie Roe, runner-up in the 2002 Gold Cup; Papineau and the 2003 winner Mr Dinos; pattern winners earlier in the season in the shape of Fight Your Corner (Henry II Stakes) and Franklins Gardens (Yorkshire Cup); and Darasim and Jardines Lookout, in the frame in previous renewals. York racecourse had had to make some alterations to its track, creating an extension to accommodate the long-distance races at the transferred Royal meeting, but the Gold Cup gallop did not look strong enough to make the race a real test of stamina and Westerner, together with Vinnie Roe, was never far away. Confidently ridden by Olivier Peslier in a manner reminiscent of the most recent French-trained winner of the race, Sagaro under Lester Piggott in the mid-'seventies, Westerner came to challenge Distinction over a furlong out, soon nosed ahead and did not have to be hard ridden to get the better of his rival cleverly by a neck, the pair five lengths clear of Vinnie Roe.

In terms of prestigious achievement, the Aidan O'Brien-trained **Yeats** (rated 128) takes the plaudits, having written his own chapter in racing history by winning a record four consecutive Gold Cups. Yeats raced for seven seasons (he was the subject of an essay in *Racehorses* each of those years), his career totalling twenty-six starts and fifteen wins, seven of them Group 1s, and he earned in excess of £1.3m. 'Yeats was, in short, a giant who will be virtually impossible to replace on the track', as *Racehorses of 2009* eulogised.

Like Kayf Tara and Westerner, and many other top stayers down the years, Yeats had a useful turn of speed and was no dyed-in-the-wool plodder; one-time ante-post favourite for the Derby, he was a Group 1 winner over a mile and a half (in the 2005 Coronation Cup) before his attentions were turned to the staying game. Yeats acted on any going but was probably at his very best on firmer than good—his Gold Cups were won on such ground, and by an aggregate winning distance of fourteen lengths—for all that his action was powerful and round, like many by Sadler's Wells (also the sire of Kayf Tara). Yeats also won the Goodwood Cup in 2006 and 2008, the Irish St Leger in 2007 and the Prix Royal-Oak in 2008.

It cannot be said that Yeats was the best stayer in the history of the sport but, when he was on top form, none of his rivals could hold a candle to him, as his essay in *Racehorses of 2009* highlighted:

> The nine runners who took on Yeats (in the Gold Cup) were hardly in the same league judged on their credentials. They were headed by the first two in the Henry II Stakes, Geordieland (who had chased home Yeats in the 2007 and 2008 Gold Cups) and Patkai (who had landed the Sagaro Stakes

The first step on the road to history - Yeats slams his rivals in the 2006 Gold Cup

on his reappearance). Saeed bin Suroor fielded three for Godolphin: Veracity, successful in the Jockey Club Cup and third to Yeats in the Prix Royal-Oak in 2008; Sagara, who hadn't won for more than two years; and Dubai Sheema Classic winner Eastern Anthem, who was unproven at the trip. Great Voltigeur Stakes winner Centennial was also unproven at the distance and the two others were Hindu Kush, successful in the Saval Beg Stakes after finishing second in the Vintage Crop Stakes, and Washington Irving, fourth in the Yorkshire Cup last time, both of them former stable-companions of Yeats. The good to firm going was much more suitable for Yeats than the going had been when only sixth on his reappearance at Navan and the betting suggested he was back to his best. After starting the day as 9/4 favourite, he was finally sent off at 6/4 (he started 7/1 in 2006, 13/8-on in 2007 and 11/8 in 2008). The tactics employed on Yeats in the Gold Cup varied little from year to year—he was ridden for stamina, racing quite close up before challenging for the lead over two furlongs out and making the best of his way home from there. Murtagh rode a cracking race on him in the latest edition, waiting in fourth as Hindu Kush led from Veracity at a relatively moderate gallop. Veracity took over with half a mile to go, but Yeats was soon challenging him. With three furlongs left, both Patkai and Geordieland were somewhat hemmed in on the rail. When Veracity went wrong—he had to be put down after fracturing a cannon bone—Murtagh used Yeats's useful turn of foot to send him all of four lengths clear with two furlongs to go. It was a winning lead. Patkai had got clear soon after entering the straight and stayed on gamely but he never looked like getting to Yeats, while Geordieland made some headway to chase the first two but found nothing more from a furlong out. At the line, to the delight of the Royal Ascot

crowd (though not the bookmakers, who claimed to have lost a scarcely believable £10m on the race nationwide), Yeats was the winner by three and a half lengths, with Geordieland fifteen lengths further back. After the winner had received his deserved rapturous reception, O'Brien was quite revealing in expressing how he felt about the record. 'I've never felt such pressure for any race before, this horse was the only time. I was so sick this morning as I really believed this couldn't happen. History is very hard to change, we knew we had a wonderful horse but usually fairytales don't come true. You dream and dream and dream, we were in this position and we never would be again.' To put the achievement into perspective, Yeats had broken Sagaro's record of three Gold Cup victories from 1975 to 1977 and, among out-and-out stayers, he had equalled Marsyas's record of four Prix du Cadrans from 1944 to 1947; Vinnie Roe won four successive Irish St Legers between 2001 and 2004 and, in America, Kelso notched five successive Jockey Club Gold Cups over two miles from 1960 to 1964. Yeats matched Triptych in notching at least one Group 1 race five years in a row, though John Henry (1980 to 1984) and Sunline (1998 to 2002) had also achieved the feat in the States and Australia and New Zealand respectively. Yeats was also only the second eight-year-old to win the Gold Cup.

Thanks to Sadler's Wells, Yeats has been by no means Ballydoyle's only good stayer of the Aidan O'Brien era. Among the great sire's sons or grandsons, four have won St Legers for the stable, Leading Light in 2013 being the most recent after Milan, Brian Boru and Scorpion. Another, Septimus (rated 129), despite being a contemporary of Yeats, recorded the top staying performances of both 2007 (Doncaster Cup) and 2008 (Irish St Leger). The ill-fated Age of Aquarius failed to make it five Gold Cups in a row for O'Brien but showed high-class form when runner-up in 2010 (he broke down in the Goodwood Cup next time and died of colic later that year), while former top-class middle-distance performer Fame And Glory stepped up in trip to go one better for the yard in the Gold Cup in 2011, also winning the Long Distance Cup later that season.

Gloria de Campeao (rail) wins the first running of the Dubai World Cup at Meydan

GLOBE-TROTTERS

Globetrotters

International competition, the quest to find the world's best, is integral to most sports and has been for a long time. Some of those events and rivalries date from well before the jet age transformed travelling around the world. The first modern Olympic Games, for example, which took place in Athens in 1896, whilst largely a European affair, was contested by a team from the United States. Nineteen years earlier, the first Test match had taken place, in Melbourne, between England and Australia. But even by 1930, when the first football World Cup was held in Uruguay, international travel was still not advanced enough to encourage competition between nations on different continents. With entry by invitation rather than qualification, no European teams were entered for the tournament by the original deadline and it was only after intervention by FIFA president Jules Rimet that four European teams were encouraged to undertake the two-week sea voyage to South America to compete. Three of those teams—France, Belgium and Romania—all travelled together on the same ship, along with Rimet, the tournament's three European referees and the trophy. With the logistics of transporting racehorses around the globe more difficult still, perhaps it is hardly surprising that horse racing long lagged behind other sports in bringing together the best competitors from different countries and continents on a regular basis. Notable early exceptions were the match at Belmont Park in 1923 between Derby winner Papyrus and Kentucky Derby winner Zev, and the ultimately ill-fated trip nine years later that took Australian champion Phar Lap to Mexico, a venture covered in more detail later in this chapter.

But by the beginning of the twenty-first century, horse racing was making rapid strides as an international sport. An attempt to combine some of the world's most valuable races into a global series, along the lines of motor racing's Formula 1 Grand Prix, began in 1999. Sheikh Mohammed's Godolphin operation, created with the very purpose of aiming at the world's top prizes, had more resources than most for a challenge on this scale, and turned out to have an ideal candidate in the five-year-old **Daylami** (rated 138) who was already a Group or Grade 1 winner in four countries.

> In Daylami, the inaugural Emirates World Series Racing Championship found a horse worthy of its ambition. The concept of a world champion in racing, which had seemed decidedly grandiose, not to say remote, when the series was announced, does not now seem so unrealistic. Daylami ran on three continents and in five different countries in 1999, taking part in four World Series races and winning three of them. He left one of the season's most striking images with

the unrestrained zest with which he sprinted clear in the King George VI and Queen Elizabeth Stakes at Ascot—then he did it again in the Irish Champion Stakes and the Breeders' Cup Turf. Last year's essay on Daylami discussed the strength of the latest Godolphin team and asked the question 'What odds Godolphin having the first "World Champion"?' If odds were available, those who snapped them up would have been delighted at the Maktoum family's efforts, as, in addition to the best that they could muster from Europe, the latest Godolphin team was supplemented by arrivals from Argentina and the United States. Daylami himself had been a most conspicuous purchase after the 1997 season, from the Aga Khan. In his colours, Daylami had won the Poule d'Essai des Poulains and registered three other Group 1 placings over a mile as a three-year-old. At four he added victories in the Tattersalls Gold Cup, the Eclipse and the Man o'War Stakes, along with fourth place in the King George and third in the Champion Stakes.

The nine-race series had been due to get under way with the King George in July and end with the Dubai World Cup in March 2000, but this scheme was fine-tuned shortly before the King George so that the competition would now bear some resemblance to a conventional calendar season and end with the Hong Kong Cup in December. Points for the Dubai World Cup were therefore awarded retrospectively. The Emirates World Series, framed around the structure of the world's top middle-distance races, required that a horse would necessarily have to travel outside its own country to win the championship and thereby earn a bonus of $1m. In between Dubai and Hong Kong, the series took in top events in Britain (for the King George), Ireland (Irish Champion Stakes), Canada (Canadian International), Australia (Cox Plate), the United States (Breeders' Cup Classic and Breeders' Cup Turf) and Japan (Japan Cup).

Inevitably, given the scope of such a championship, there were going to be criticisms of its format. Races on turf outnumber those on dirt by seven to two; sprinters, milers and stayers are not catered for at all and Australasian connections could no doubt point to the fact that the Cox Plate is the only contest in the Series in their part of the world. The intended addition of the Prix de l'Arc de Triomphe, Grosser Preis von Baden and Arlington Million to the Series in 2000 only serves to reinforce the image of essentially a northern hemisphere middle-distance turf championship. The organisers could also be criticised for taking the easy option when it came to the issue of medication, deciding that each country's local rules should apply to the individual races rather than adopting a blanket drug-free policy. Few will be surprised to see a Godolphin horse top of the Series rankings but connections with considerably fewer resources deserve credit for taking up foreign challenges, notably those concerned with Fruits of Love and the Hong Kong-trained Indigenous. Encouraging the best horses to be campaigned against each other worldwide is the most important benefit the Series has brought. The individual races, aided by the enhanced competition for them which the world series should bring, remain more important than the rankings which cannot, in all honesty, fairly represent the relative merits of the horses concerned, and more important also than conferring the title of 'world champion'.

Daylami won the Coronation Cup in addition to his World Series victories in the King George (by five lengths), the Irish Champion Stakes (by nine) and the Breeders' Cup Turf, run that year at Gulfstream, in which he became the first European-trained winner of a Breeders' Cup race in Florida where so many had failed before him. 'Instead of the Emirates World Series finding a horse worthy of it' concluded *Racehorses of 1999*, 'it is much nearer the truth to say that Daylami found a title which was worthy of him. Whether this series can regularly come up with truly international champions of similar credibility remains to be seen, but Daylami was a racehorse who deserved almost any plaudit.'

Godolphin soon found Daylami's successor in the form of Fantastic Light (rated 134) whose win in the Hong Kong Cup clinched him the World Series in 2000 and whose victories in the Irish Champion Stakes (over Galileo) and Breeders' Cup Turf the following year enabled him to retain the title. Fantastic Light's Breeders' Cup win at Belmont also made him the first horse in British racing history to pass the £4m mark in total prize-money, taking him past the previous British record holder Singspiel. The last of Godolphin's three World Series winners was the quirky Grandera (rated 129), successful in 2002 thanks to wins in the Singapore Airlines International Cup, the Prince of Wales's Stakes at Royal Ascot and, like his stable's other two World Series winners, the Irish Champion Stakes. Add in an outing in Dubai early in the year, two visits to Hong Kong and one to Australia, and it is easy to see why Grandera's owners summed him up as 'the equine manifestation of the Godolphin ethos.'

Interest declined in the World Series in due course but the lure of glittering foreign prizes has remained strong. Godolphin is a case apart, perhaps, but for most British-based stables, the financial rewards are the main incentive for campaigning a horse abroad. This was summed up neatly by the trainer of one of the most successful globetrotters **Presvis** (rated 126):

> 'You race in Britain for prestige and abroad for money.' Whilst trainer Luca Cumani's quote in an interview in the latest season might have been a generalisation—as well as a veiled criticism of British prize money levels—it is hard to imagine how Presvis, the best horse in his yard at present, would have earned anything like his 2009 haul of £2m by staying at home. As a five-year-old gelding, Presvis had no future stud career for his connections to consider, so rather than seeking prestige in top ten-furlong contests in Britain, such as the Eclipse, the International and the Champion Stakes (winning all three wouldn't have earned Presvis half the money he picked up on his travels), Presvis was aimed instead at much more valuable targets in Dubai, Hong Kong and Singapore. Cumani has long been alive to the potential rewards to be had from campaigning good horses internationally. He was the first British-based trainer to win the Arlington Million, with Tolomeo in 1983. In the modern era, it is easy to take successes in America for granted, but, in those days, before

A second Group 1 success for the globetrotting Presvis in the Dubai Duty Free

the advent of the Breeders' Cup, the Arlington Million was the world's richest race and Tolomeo's success was the first by a British-trained horse in top company in North America for well over a decade. A Breeders' Cup win for Cumani's stable came when Barathea took the Mile in 1994, and more recently the stable has exploited other opportunities in the expanding international programme. Alkaased won the 2005 Japan Cup for Cumani and he has come the closest yet of any British-based trainer to landing Australia's richest race the Melbourne Cup, Bauer being beaten a nose in 2008, a year after stable-companion Purple Moon filled the runner-up spot in the same race. Cumani's earnings on foreign soil in 2009 were £2,626,018, according to figures produced by the International Racing Bureau using the 'official' exchange rate; only Saeed bin Suroor (£3,361,108) and Sir Michael Stoute (£3,295,452) won more in a year when British-trained horses picked up £24,574,470 on their travels, smashing the previous record set in 2006 after a significant fall in the value of sterling as a result of the 2008 banking crisis.

Presvis won two races in Dubai that season, as well as the Queen Elizabeth II Cup in Hong Kong, and was placed in the Dubai Duty Free, the International Cup in Singapore and the Hong Kong Cup. Further wins in Dubai in the next two seasons, notably the Dubai Duty Free in 2011, took Presvis past the £4m mark in earnings and close to Fantastic Light's record. It wasn't long, though, before another Newmarket-trained horse raised the bar following her own string of successes abroad. The unlikely record holder was **Snow Fairy** (rated 128) who had been bought back on her breeder's behalf for just €1,800 when failing to find a buyer as a yearling. Already an Oaks and Irish Oaks winner, her three-year-old season ended with a lucrative trip to the Far East:

> The first prize for the Queen Elizabeth II Commemorative Cup for fillies and mares over one mile three furlongs at Kyoto in Japan in November, including Japanese Racing Association bonuses triggered by Snow Fairy's Oaks victories, amounted to a staggering £1,400,772 (the first prize itself was £715,100). This was more than twice the money Snow Fairy would have competed for—against Midday among others—if she had been aimed instead at the Breeders' Cup Filly & Mare Turf at Churchill Downs. In contrast to the saturation coverage of the Breeders' Cup by British racing's trade daily the Racing Post, Snow Fairy's triumph was seemingly almost overlooked. It was the third biggest haul won by a British-trained horse anywhere in 2010—behind only the prizes won by Dar Re Mi in the Dubai Sheema Classic and Workforce in the Prix de l'Arc de Triomphe—but the story was relegated to page twelve, a somewhat surprising sense of news values. Snow Fairy was one of only four three-year-olds in a field of eighteen, but the members of the classic generation also included the Japanese fillies' triple crown winner Apapane—racing in the colours made famous by Deep Impact—and Saint Emilion, who had dead-heated with Apapane in the Japanese Oaks. The patiently-ridden Snow Fairy quickened really well in the home straight, kept to the inside rail as the runners fanned out across the course, to win by four lengths from the five-year-old Meisho Beluga, who was fresh from a victory over the 2009 Japan Cup runner-up Oken Bruce Lee. Apapane was a further three quarters of a length away in third.

> With only two weeks between the Queen Elizabeth II Commemorative Cup and the Japan Cup, Snow Fairy's connections decided she needed a longer break before being pitched in against colts again, choosing instead to wait for the Cathay Pacific Hong Kong Cup (first prize £934,426) at Sha Tin in mid-December. Snow Fairy made a really good impression again, becoming only the second three-year-old to win the Hong Kong Cup (after another filly, Ouija Board's contemporary Alexander Goldrun, in 2004). Eight of the thirteen runners were from Europe, three from Britain and five from France (those including the previous year's winner Vision d'Etat, the Prix du Jockey Club runner-up Planteur and the very smart older filly Stacelita). Still nearly last approaching the home turn, Snow Fairy—who started favourite at 7/2—accelerated magnificently in the straight to come storming home down the outside. She hit the front well inside the final furlong to win by a neck and a length and a quarter from the

locally-trained pair Irian and Packing Winner who had filled the first two places in the previous month's Group 2 Jockey Club Cup over the course and distance. With the field finishing bunched, and only about five lengths separating Snow Fairy from Irian's stablemate and second favourite Collection in last, the form was no better than smart. That wouldn't have been of much concern to Snow Fairy's connections, however, who could reflect on an amazing campaign in which Snow Fairy won four Group 1s, including two classics, and earned the equivalent of £2,865,990 (converting overseas prize money and the Japanese bonus at the exchange rates prevailing at the time). Not bad for a filly nobody wanted as a yearling!

'Can lightning strike twice?' asked *Racehorses* that season, a reference to Ouija Board (rated 125), who had also won the Oaks and Irish Oaks for Snow Fairy's trainer Ed Dunlop in 2003 before embarking on a globetrotting career of her own which netted her the Hong Kong Vase, two editions of the Breeders' Cup Filly & Mare Turf and placings in the Arc and Japan Cup, her earnings a then record for a filly or mare trained in Britain. The answer was an emphatic 'yes'. Despite being badly bitten by insects whilst in quarantine, Snow Fairy won the Queen Elizabeth II Commemorative Cup again the following year

Another major win in the Far East for Snow Fairy (yellow cap),
this time in the Hong Kong Cup at Sha Tin

(after picking up plenty of place money, including when third in the Prix de l'Arc de Triomphe and Champion Stakes), and she successfully returned from injury as a five-year-old, with a win in the Irish Champion Stakes taking Snow Fairy's career earnings to a final total £4,688,487. A further setback prevented her from bidding to break the £5m barrier later that autumn, and the decision was taken to retire Snow Fairy in 2013.

British trainers might think nothing of campaigning their best horses abroad but their American counterparts have traditionally been less prepared to venture beyond their own shores. Good prize money at home is one major factor, but that became less of an excuse with the creation of the Dubai World Cup in 1999. The world's richest race has been enough to tempt a succession of America's best dirt performers halfway round the world, starting with Cigar's victory in that inaugural contest through to Kentucky Derby winner Animal Kingdom's success in 2013. One of the best American-trained World Cup winners was US champion **Curlin** (rated 134) who later in 2008 went on to break Cigar's record as the leading US-trained money earner. Curlin's essay, however, began with an all-too-regular theme in *Racehorses* where American racing is concerned and another factor in restricting American ventures abroad. The drugs issue, specifically the use of steroids in this case, was re-ignited following remarks by Richard Dutrow Jr, trainer of that year's Preakness Stakes winner Big Brown (and a couple of other winners on the Dubai World Cup card), that he 'routinely' (and legally, under the existing legislation) administered such medication.

'You can always count on Americans to do the right thing—after they've tried everything else' (Winston Churchill). Ambitions to promote racing as a global sport—with uniform philosophies and rules—cannot be fulfilled without the full co-operation of American racing. First and foremost, there must be a willingness on the part of America to come into line with other major racing nations by banning drug use, the only way to give the potential global audience full confidence in the honesty of the sport . . .

Leading owner-breeder Jess Jackson, whose Stonestreet Stables' colours were carried in the latest season by the world's best dirt performer Curlin (two erstwhile members of a wider ownership group stood trial for fraud in the latest season), was among the biggest supporters of reform. Curlin's victories in the Preakness Stakes and the Breeders' Cup Classic as a three-year-old earned him the titles of champion three-year-old and Horse of The Year, and Jackson was keen to show off Curlin on the world stage as a four-year-old 'both for the horse's legacy and to plant the US flag.' American horses running at the Dubai World Cup meeting over the years—and there have been plenty—have had to comply with strict rules on doping. Their good record provides evidence to counter the growing mistrust over recent years of American performances. Curlin had raced on steroids in America but that stopped in January as he was prepared for the world's richest race, the Dubai World Cup (for which he was warmed up in a handicap—off a mark of 129—over the course and distance at Nad Al Sheba at the end of February, having little trouble brushing aside five rivals who were all out of the weights).

Dubai World Cup night featured three victories for American-trained horses, Curlin joined by Diamond Stripes in the Godolphin Mile and Benny The Bull in the Golden Shaheen, the big sprint, both for Richard Dutrow. Dutrow wasn't in Dubai, having stayed behind to supervise Big Brown's preparation for the same weekend's Florida Derby which he won by five lengths to retain his unbeaten record and become a warm favourite for the Kentucky Derby. Curlin enjoyed a wide-margin victory too, becoming the fourth Breeders' Cup Classic winner to take the following year's Dubai World Cup when beating the previous year's UAE 2000 Guineas and Derby winner Asiatic Boy by seven and three quarter lengths, a record winning margin for the race. Curlin was one of four American-trained runners in the line-up of twelve, the others, Well Armed, A. P. Arrow and Great Hunter, finishing third, fourth and fifth.

Well Armed, incidentally, went on to break Curlin's record when winning by fourteen lengths a year later, but he would also go down as the final Dubai World Cup winner at Nad Al Sheba. The creation of the World Cup was just the first of a series of steps that have made the growth of racing in Dubai the most significant development to take place on the international racing scene in the last twenty years. Next came the strengthening of the supporting card on World Cup night. By 2002, three of those races, the Dubai Sheema Classic, Dubai Duty Free and Dubai Golden Shaheen all carried Group 1 status for the first time. In 2004, the $21m Dubai International Racing Carnival was inaugurated, aimed at attracting foreign stables to compete over the nine weeks leading up to World Cup night. As well as Britain, the likes of India, Turkey, Saudi Arabia and Macau were all represented, but if any country had its international profile heightened by that first Carnival, and subsequent ones, then it is South Africa, largely due to successes from the Mike de Kock stable. On the eve of the 2007 Dubai World Cup, plans were unexpectedly unveiled for the creation of a brand new racecourse to replace Nad Al Sheba. Its spectacular successor Meydan, where the synthetic surface tapeta replaced Nad Al Sheba's dirt, was up and running for the 2010 Dubai World Cup which was decided by the most valuable photo-finish in racing history. With total prize-money for the race increased to $10m, the verdict, by a nose, went to Gloria de Campeao, who, bred in Brazil, owned by a Swede and trained in France, fully embodied the cosmopolitan nature of racing in Dubai.

The Dubai Carnival in the early months of the year filled what was previously the only remaining quiet spell in the international racing calendar in the northern hemisphere. Traditionally, it is the autumn that has been the focus of attention for international campaigns when Europe, North America and Japan stage their end-of-season championship races in an increasingly congested calendar from September onwards. Since its inception in 1984, the Breeders' Cup meeting has dominated European ambition in America, though whether that is sufficient to justify the 'World Championships' tag appended to the meeting's name is open to question. Successes for British-trained horses in the early years of the Breeders' Cup were all the sweeter for being few and far between. Much has changed since *Favourite Racehorses* stated: 'Every year, the Press whips us up into a nationalistic fervour, and usually there has been just disappointment.' For a start, the fixture is now a two-day affair offering twice as many horses the chance to become a Breeders' Cup winner than in the days of the original seven-race programme. British successes could be counted on one hand when *Favourite Racehorses* was published, comprising only Pebbles (1985 Turf), Sheikh Albadou (1991 Sprint), Barathea (1994 Mile) and Pilsudski (1996 Turf). Success has come much more readily since, British stables winning four Breeders' Cup races in 2008 alone (the first year the races traditionally run on dirt were run on a synthetic surface, Pro-Ride) when the meeting was held at Santa Anita, a significant haul as the essay on Classic winner **Raven's Pass** (rated 133), who beat Ireland's Henrythenavigator into second, explained:

> 'The British are coming'. Paul Revere's legendary ride from Boston to Lexington, warning of the approaching British army, was evoked at the 1982 Oscars ceremony by writer Colin Welland when the British film *Chariots of Fire*, about the 1924 Olympics, won four Oscars. The winners of Britain's nineteen golds at the latest Olympics, the biggest number since the London Olympics a hundred years earlier, naturally enough dominated the end-of-year sports awards, the BBC Sports Personality being cyclist Chris Hoy, the first Briton to win three golds since swimmer Henry Taylor at the 1908 Games (Taylor, an Oldham cotton mill worker, who trained in the local canal and boating lake, died penniless and virtually forgotten). The Breeders' Cup, conceived in 1984 from an idea for a 'Thoroughbred Olympics', has never really lived up to its ideal—it is staged

Raven's Pass becomes the first British-trained winner of the Breeders' Cup Classic

now under the title of the 'World Championships'—but British-trained runners played their part in a memorable year for British sporting success, enjoying an unprecedented haul of four races at the twenty-fifth renewal to move ahead of the French as the most successful of the overseas contestants at the Breeders' Cup.

Since its inception, the Breeders' Cup has dominated European ambition in America. Pebbles opened the British account in 1985 and Royal Academy became the first Irish-trained winner in 1990, but, for many years, the French fared considerably better than their British and Irish counterparts, as they had done previously in the Washington DC International, introduced in 1952, and the most important American target for European-based horses in the era before the Breeders' Cup. The importance of the American market in an increasingly globalised thoroughbred breeding business continues to sustain British and Irish interest, though the latest Breeders' Cup Mile winner Goldikova and the Fabre-trained Turf Sprint also-ran Only Answer have been the only French-trained challengers in the last two years. French-trained Arcangues, who was trained by Fabre and started at 133/1 in 1993, had the distinction of being the only European winner of the Breeders' Cup Classic, North America's richest race, until the latest season when British-trained Raven's Pass became the second. The victory of Raven's Pass at Santa Anita wasn't, it must be said, entirely British, since he was American-bred, owned by Arabs (who bought him from Americans) and ridden by an Italian, but his success will mean that 'British' challengers for the Breeders' Cup Classic—traditionally the preserve of America's top horses—ought to be given more consideration when the Breeders' Cup returns for the second year running to Santa Anita in 2009.

Much of the French success at the Breeders' Cup has come in the Mile, starting with Last Tycoon in 1986 before Miesque became the first dual winner of a Breeders' Cup race when landing the next two renewals under Freddie Head. As a trainer, Head returned to the meeting more than twenty years later with a mare who topped even Miesque's Breeders' Cup record when winning her third Mile, at Churchill Downs, in 2010:

Goldikova's third successive victory in the Breeders' Cup Mile was a singular feat in itself—nine others have gained two wins in the same Breeders' Cup race (three doing so in the Mile)—but her victory also reinforced the fact that, even at five, Goldikova was still the best miler around. She gave one of the finest performances of her career, having to come from a little further back than usual, as she had had to do in 2009. Settled in mid-division from a wide draw, and around five lengths off the leaders at halfway, Goldikova produced blistering acceleration when brought to challenge on the outside in the short Churchill Downs straight, needing only a couple of slaps with the whip, after taking the lead, to win readily by a length and three quarters from Gio Ponti. The Usual Q T reversed Woodbine Mile form with Court Vision, the pair close up in third (a neck behind Gio Ponti) and fifth, split by the strong-finishing

Goldikova creates history - becoming the first horse to win three Breeders' Cup races

Paco Boy, with front-running Sidney's Candy sixth and Proviso seventh. In truth, though, Goldikova looked a class apart from her rivals in the latest Breeders' Cup Mile, fulfilling her trainer's pre-race assessment that she was coming into her third Breeders' Cup Mile in even better shape than in the two previous years. 'She is extraordinary, she has everything, tremendous nerves, great speed and she always has another gear,' said Head afterwards. 'Miesque was much more difficult, tense and nervous, and Goldikova is easier to ride, though it isn't really fair to compare them on ability. Miesque was a brilliant two-year-old and three-year-old, while Goldikova took a longer time coming. They can get lazier as they get older, but she just loves galloping and is always the same.' As if to complete her image as a paragon, Goldikova was even cured of a tendency to be mulish at the stalls, giving no trouble before any of her races in the latest season after her reappearance.

The latest chapter in the remarkable career of Goldikova, who remains in training as a six-year-old, saw her become the first racehorse trained in Europe to win twelve Group/Grade 1 races since the European pattern system was instituted in 1971 (adopted in similar form two years later in North America), and also the first in the twenty-seven-year history of the Breeders' Cup meeting to win there three times. Goldikova has now won thirteen pattern races in all—she also won the Group 3 Prix Chloe as a three-year-old—which puts her level at the top of that particular list, among European-trained horses, with Brigadier Gerard, Ardross, German-trained Acatenango and Persian Punch. Goldikova's total earnings—which so far stand at £3,690,023 (at prevailing exchange rates)—are still some way short of the earnings record (7,304,580 dollars) set for a filly or mare in North America by Zenyatta. Six-year-old Zenyatta's pursuit of a twentieth successive victory, in the latest Breeders' Cup Classic, inevitably overshadowed Goldikova's bid for a third Breeders' Cup Mile. Zenyatta was undefeated until just failing to catch Blame in the latest Classic, thirteen of her victories having come in Grade 1 events (surpassing the North American record for a filly or mare held by Bayakoa, who won twelve in 1989 and 1990). Zenyatta's achievements attracted adulation in America though they were undermined by some on the grounds that, except for her two appearances in the Breeders' Cup Classic (she won that race in 2009, after winning the Breeders' Cup Ladies' Classic in 2008), she was kept to races for her own sex, some of them very uncompetitive it has to be said. Others pointed to the fact that Zenyatta did nearly all her racing in California on synthetic surfaces, running only three times on traditional dirt. A much vaunted $5m showdown with Rachel Alexandra, who as a three-year-old had beaten Zenyatta to the Horse of the Year title, did not come off, Rachel Alexandra beaten at 20/1-on by one of Zenyatta's stablemates in a preparatory race for the proposed clash on dirt in the Apple Blossom Invitational in April (Zenyatta won that race, which had a much reduced prize, to equal the benchmark unbeaten sequence for a Flat champion in North America or Europe since World War II, shared at sixteen by Citation, Ribot and Cigar). Zenyatta was voted North America's Horse of the Year in the coveted 2010 Eclipse Awards, after being runner-up in the two previous years, and Goldikova retained her title as champion female turf performer, emulating Ouija Board who also won that title twice.

Goldikova (rated 133) finished third in her attempt to win a fourth Breeders' Cup Mile in 2011 before being retired as the highest-earning racemare in European history, a record broken subsequently by Snow Fairy. Further Group 1 wins in Goldikova's final season in the Prix d'Ispahan (for the second time) and the Prix Rothschild (in which she became only the third horse to win the same European Group 1 four years in succession since the pattern was introduced in 1971) took Goldikova's tally of top-flight successes to fifteen, her record at home and in the Breeders' Cup 'securing her place among the most illustrious fillies and mares in turf history.'

For all their success in the Mile, it is the Turf in which European-trained horses have fared best. Between Daylami's win in 1999 and St Nicholas Abbey's in 2011, only two renewals were won outright by American horses. The US-trained Johar had to share the spoils in 2003 with the previous season's winner High Chaparral, the latter becoming the first dual winner of the race, a double also completed by Conduit in 2008 and 2009.

Success on a more regular basis at the Breeders' Cup means that achieving a win at the meeting, it seems, is not quite the achievement it once was for a European-trained horse, all the more so given that some of the more recently-created Breeders' Cup races do not carry the same prestige as the races that formed the original programme. The issue of raceday medication, principally the widespread use of the anti-bleeding drug lasix, is another that takes much of the gloss off the meeting from a European standpoint (though it has to be said most European trainers feel obliged to take a 'when in Rome ...' approach to medication with their runners at the Breeders' Cup), attempts at reform seeming to take one step back for every one taken forward. Another positive move, on welfare grounds, that has stalled is the replacement of traditional dirt tracks with less demanding synthetic surfaces; drainage problems were purportedly the reason for Santa Anita ultimately reverting to dirt at the end of 2010. The postscript to the extract from the essay on Raven's Pass was that the Henry Cecil-trained Twice Over ran a good third to Zenyatta in the following season's Breeders' Cup Classic on Pro-Ride.

Another reason for the Breeders' Cup having lost some of its attraction from a European point of view is that, as alluded to previously, there are plenty of big-money alternatives nowadays in the international calendar towards the end of the year. Having gradually opened up all its top races to foreign horses, Japan has more to offer than just the Japan Cup, as Snow Fairy proved. Also in the Far East, European-trained horses have enjoyed plenty of success at Hong Kong's International meeting in December, or, in what looks an overt challenge to the Breeders' Cup, 'The Turf World Championships' as the meeting is now branded.

And then there is the Melbourne Cup, a race whose international profile has changed out of all recognition since the end of the twentieth century. Unlike the Breeders' Cup, the Japan Cup and the Hong Kong races, the Melbourne Cup has a long history—it celebrated its 150th running in 2010—but from being simply 'the race that stops a nation', it has become a race that other nations will now travel halfway round the world to win, putting it right up with more modern creations on the globetrotter's 'must win' list. The Dermot Weld-trained Vintage Crop was a ground-breaking winner of the Melbourne Cup in 1993, though it took a while for the prediction that his 'success looks sure to help to promote another phase in the internationalisation of racing' to be proved correct. In the meantime, Weld repeated the feat nine years later with **Media Puzzle** (rated 117):

> When Captain Scott finally reached the South Pole in January 1912, he found that Amundsen had already beaten him to be the first man to reach it. Without wishing to disparage Scott's achievement in any way, various European trainers are going to know how Scott felt, if, on winning one of the top prizes halfway round the world, they find the inscription 'trained by D. K. Weld, Ireland' already on the trophy. For Dermot Weld, Antarctica is the only continent out of bounds for his racehorses; he harbours an ambition to train a winner in Africa one day, having already been successful in Europe, America, Asia and Australasia. In 1990, Weld became the first and (despite Godolphin's and Coolmore's attempts to win a Kentucky Derby) so far only European-based trainer to win an American triple crown race when Go And Go won the Belmont Stakes. A year later 33/1-shot Additional Risk paved the way for European challenges at Hong Kong's

International meeting when winning the Hong Kong Invitation Bowl. But it was Vintage Crop's win in the Melbourne Cup in 1993, the first in Australia's most valuable race by a horse trained outside Australasia, which probably ranks as Weld's greatest international success.

There have been annual attempts by European-based stables to emulate Vintage Crop but none succeeded—until the latest season when Weld was back again, this time with Media Puzzle. What made his second success all the more praiseworthy was that Weld has made only selective challenges for the Melbourne Cup. Vintage Crop returned to Flemington twice after his win, finishing seventh (accompanied by stable-companion Cliveden Gail who was well beaten) and then third, but, until Media Puzzle and Vinnie Roe contested the latest Melbourne Cup, the stable had not had a runner in the race since 1995. 'Pick and choose your races. Like the Indians, you have to go in, attack, and get out. I do that pretty well, learning when to attack and when not to. I don't fight every battle; I choose my battlegrounds.' That was how Weld summed up his philosophy of raiding international prizes, one which contrasts with Godolphin's approach, for example, which has seen them send eight horses for the Melbourne Cup in the last five runnings.

Europe's next success—in that 150th Melbourne Cup—came from the French horse Americain (rated 129) whose trainer, Alain de Royer Dupre, like Dermot Weld, was no stranger to breaking new ground abroad. Beforehand, however, there was plenty of confidence in a local favourite who subsequently made a name for himself in the northern hemisphere too.

Americain, Shocking and Descarado were all prominent in the betting for the big race, but there was only one horse Australian punters wanted to know on Cup day itself at Flemington. Trained by 'Cups King' Bart Cummings, seeking his thirteenth win in the Melbourne Cup, So You Think had won three Group 1 races in as many weeks during October, including a second consecutive Cox Plate and, just a week later, the Mackinnon Stakes, which was run only three days before the Melbourne Cup. So You Think had shown top-class form, though the fact that he had never raced at much beyond a mile and a quarter failed to deter those who made him a 2/1-shot, even after heavy rain turned the going soft. So You Think looked like becoming the shortest-priced Melbourne Cup winner since odds-on Phar Lap in 1930 when hitting the front a furlong and a half out, after moving up easily from the home turn, but after pulling hard for much of the race he had no more to give when Mosse produced the patiently-ridden Americain to go clear inside the last half furlong. Mosse had the luxury of being able to blow a kiss to the crowd approaching the winning post, something which promptly landed him with a A$300 fine as Australian rules forbid celebratory gestures before the line. Americain had two and three quarter lengths to spare, with the lightly-weighted second favourite Maluckyday (who had gained automatic entry when winning the Lexus Stakes just three days earlier) depriving So You Think of second by half a length, with the veteran Zipping finishing fourth for a third time.

Trainer Alain de Royer Dupre has an outstanding domestic record as his totals in the French classics show, now having won six Prix de Dianes, five Prix du Jockey Clubs, four Poule d'Essai des Pouliches and three Poule d'Essai des Poulains, as well as recording two wins in the Prix de l'Arc de Triomphe with Dalakhani and Zarkava. But as an international pioneer he made his mark as long ago as 1984, becoming the first European trainer to saddle a Breeders' Cup winner when Lashkari caused an upset in the inaugural Breeders' Cup Turf. More recently, he has also struck twice at Hong Kong's International meeting, firstly when Pride followed up her Champion Stakes victory in the 2006 Hong Kong Cup. On his way back from Australia, Americain attempted to give the stable a second successive win in the Hong Kong Vase after Daryakana in 2009 but a steadily-run mile and a half was never going to play to Americain's strengths and he could only stay on for third behind the more enterprisingly-ridden winner Mastery. Americain wasn't discredited, though, especially as he was reported to have been struck into behind.

A year later, and the changing face of the Melbourne Cup was underlined by a second French-trained winner hot on the heels of the first in a field which featured plenty of names familiar in Europe. In his year, Vintage Crop had been one of just two runners from the northern hemisphere in a line-up of mainly Australasian-bred horses . . .

The latest Emirates-sponsored Melbourne Cup had a very different look. Dunaden became the second consecutive French-trained winner following Americain's success twelve months earlier, but what was most striking about the latest edition was not so much another European-trained winner, but the overwhelming northern hemisphere influence on the field. In addition to the French-trained pair (Americain was in the field again, running even better on form than the year before, carrying top weight into fourth), there were nine British-trained runners, among them Red Cadeaux (beaten a nose into second), Manighar, Lost In The Moment and Fox Hunt (fifth, sixth and seventh respectively). With six-figure prizes for the next four home behind the winner, and more than £80,000 for each of the finishers from sixth to tenth, even finishing down the field can make the trip Down Under a worthwhile venture for a European horse. An even more striking statistic was that only six of the twenty-three runners had been bred in Australia or New Zealand and begun their careers there. It is a paradox that Australia's most valuable race is a two-mile event, considering that the country's breeding industry has all but turned its back on producing stayers in favour of breeding sprinters—how successful that has been is demonstrated regularly to a wider audience nowadays at Royal Ascot and in Hong Kong. If Australian owners want to win their country's most famous race, they are having to turn to the northern hemisphere, and to Europe in particular, to find horses with stamina. Although still trained in France, the 2010 winner Americain had been purchased by Australians with that very aim. Of the ten horses who finished in the prize money in the latest Melbourne Cup, only eighth-placed Niwot was bred in Australia. The ex-German colt Lucas Cranach fared best of the imports in third, while more familiar names to British racegoers among the 'ex-pats' included the 2010 Derby runner-up At First Sight and the former Sir Michael Stoute-trained Gordon Richards Stakes winner Glass Harmonium. Even legendary trainer Bart Cummings, winner of twelve Melbourne Cups, is following the trend and was represented in the latest running by an ex-German horse, Illo.

Dunaden (rated 130) went on to succeed where Americain had failed the year before by following up in the Hong Kong Vase, and proved better than ever when making a successful return to Australia a year later to win the Caulfield Cup. French-trained he might have been, but it was the nationality of Dunaden's owner which has proven to be of far greater significance. Dunaden carried the colours of Pearl Bloodstock, one of the racing operations of Sheikh Fahad Al Thani of Qatar. 'In twenty years' time there should be a big statue of Dunaden in honour of the horse that brought Qatari interest in racing to Britain' claimed the owner's racing manager David Redvers in an interview in 2013. 'The rest of the Qatari royal family saw what happened and wanted to get involved . . . It showed them they were able to compete on the world stage.' Qatar might not (yet, at least) be a major racing centre in the same sense as near neighbour Dubai, but with large-scale investments through both ownership and sponsorship (including the British Champions Series and the Arc meeting), the Gulf state is already exerting considerable influence in Europe.

Meanwhile, Britain is still seeking a first Melbourne Cup winner. Jakkalberry, third in 2012, became yet another to be placed—behind Green Moon and Fiorente who were both formerly trained in Britain. As far as both permanent exports and flying visits are concerned, it is not all one-way traffic between Europe and Australia. So You Think, who went on to win another five Group 1 contests in Britain and Ireland for Aidan O'Brien, was following in the footsteps of the 2008 Queen Anne Stakes winner Haradasun and high-class sprinter Starspangledbanner as successful recruits to Ballydoyle from Australia. That trio, all Royal Ascot winners, made permanent moves to the northern hemisphere, but the Royal meeting's big sprints have also been the target for Australian-trained visitors since the start of the twenty-first century. Black Caviar, who is treated in depth elsewhere, has been the most celebrated of those, but it was **Choisir** (rated 126) who set the ball rolling in spectacular style in 2003:

> He had just three races in Britain, spread over little more than three weeks, and saw not much more than three minutes action, but few overseas-trained horses can have made so great an impression in such a short stay as the Australian sprinter Choisir. There have been better foreign visitors, and he wasn't the season's champion sprinter, but when the time came for his stallion career, the promoters had no shortage of advertising material. Choisir's victory in the King's Stand Stakes made him the first Australian-trained horse to win

*Choisir proves more than a match for some of Europe's best sprinters
in the King's Stand Stakes, the first leg of his historic Royal Ascot double*

in Britain, and when he won Royal Ascot's other big sprint, the Golden Jubilee Stakes, four days later, he earned himself another entry in the record books.

Royal Ascot has long drawn Irish and French runners but, until recently, has never been deliberately promoted as an international meeting in the same way as more recent creations such as the Dubai World Cup and the Hong Kong International meeting. Unlike those events, Royal Ascot is not reliant on top foreign horses taking on the locals to make the occasion, but with championship events over a range of distances there is considerable potential for the Royal meeting to become a major international festival. The Ascot authority will reap the rewards of its drive to draw competitors from all over the world, particularly once the racecourse's redevelopment has been completed. Choisir's successes made the headlines but he was just one of several runners from outside Europe who contributed to what must have been the most cosmopolitan Royal Ascot so far. Apart from Choisir, other competitors from outside Europe included: the American sprinter Morluc, twice runner-up in the Hong Kong Sprint; one of Hong Kong's leading sprinters Firebolt; the South African-trained UAE 2000 Guineas/Derby winner Victory Moon; and the Dubai-trained UAE Oaks runner-up Desert Glow.

Choisir certainly stood out in the preliminaries for the King's Stand in terms of physique, even in a field of top sprinters. He made an immediate impression once the race was under way as well. Equipped with a white bridle and black eyeshields or 'pacifiers', Choisir was soon going strongly in the lead near the stand rail with Hong Kong's Firebolt the only one able to go with him through the early stages. Approaching the last two furlongs, Firebolt had been seen off, and Choisir had the race sewn up when quickening clear against the stand rail over a furlong out. The significance of what Choisir was about to accomplish was not lost on BBC TV's Australian-born commentator Jim McGrath whose impartiality momentarily went out of the commentary box window with the words 'the Aussie's gonna do it!' as Choisir drew clear. Feeling the strain close home, Choisir had a length to spare over the strong-finishing Acclamation, who had been checked over a furlong out, with Oasis Dream third and Dominica, also making her reappearance, fourth.

That win in the King's Stand came as a 25/1 outsider, but Choisir was the 13/2 second favourite when following up four days later over the extra furlong of the Golden Jubilee, running out a game half-length winner from favourite Airwave. It had been twenty years since a horse had won two races in a week at Royal Ascot, the Irish mare Stanerra winning the Prince of Wales's Stakes and Hardwicke Stakes in 1983. Choisir had one more outing in Britain before being retired to stud, finishing second to Oasis Dream in the July Cup. His own racing career might have been over, but he opened the door to a succession of similar ventures.

As a promoter of Australian racing abroad, Choisir's achievements drew comparisons with those of Australia's horse of the twentieth century Phar Lap. The winner of thirty-seven of his fifty-one races, fourteen of them on the trot as a four-year-old (including the Melbourne Cup under 9-12), the New Zealand-bred Phar Lap gained his most famous victory on his first venture abroad—and in what turned out to be his final race—in the Agua Caliente Handicap at Tijuana in Mexico in 1932. Overcoming a heel injury and a lack of experience on dirt, not to mention being shipped across the Pacific to San Francisco and a four-hundred-mile road journey across the Mexican border, Phar Lap won the 50,000-dollar race, worth more than £10,000 at the prevailing rate of exchange. Phar Lap had been due to continue his career in North America, but within a fortnight of his win he was dead, seemingly as a result of 'his picking some poisonous vegetation' as the *Bloodstock Breeders' Review* phrased it. 'The death of Phar Lap was regarded almost as a national calamity,' it went on. 'The magnificent career of this exceptional racehorse ended at its zenith. He has left behind him an immortal reputation, and was universally regarded as the greatest racehorse ever bred in Australia [sic], and, in fact must have been one of the world's best racehorses.

Ascot's redevelopment meant the transfer of the Royal meeting to York in 2005 when Cape of Good Hope made his own piece of history by becoming the first horse trained in Hong Kong to win in Britain when successful in the Golden Jubilee Stakes. Cape of Good Hope thereby took an unassailable lead in the inaugural Global Sprint Challenge, a series linking some of the world's biggest sprints, similar in concept to the short-lived Emirates World Series, but one that has endured. Indeed, the incorporation of Royal Ascot's two Group 1 sprints into the series (the July Cup was added later) resulted in a big boost in prize money for both races (sprinters had long been poor relations to their middle-distance counterparts) so that now the Diamond Jubilee Stakes, as the Golden Jubilee became in 2012, is one of the most valuable races of the Royal meeting. Back at Royal Ascot, a further trio of high-class Australian sprinters carried off the King's Stand before the end of the first decade of the twenty-first century; Takeover Target in 2006, Miss Andretti in 2007 and Scenic Blast in 2009. Of the three, **Takeover Target** (rated 128) became an annual visitor to Royal Ascot. He made three attempts to emulate Choisir's double in all, finishing third in the Golden Jubilee after winning the King's Stand in 2006 and then making the frame in both races in each of the next two years, finishing runner-up in the Golden Jubilee in 2007 and in the King's Stand in 2008. Not bad for a horse with humble beginnings whose trainer was used to making rather shorter journeys in his other job:

> Combined with driving his taxi, Joe Janiak (also part-owner of the horse with his sons) has always had a very small-scale training operation, one which had yielded only around a hundred winners in the course of thirty years or so. Takeover Target was typical of the horses he had operated with, bought as an unraced four-year-old with knee problems for just A$1,250 (about £500). But Takeover Target made remarkable progress once put into training and was unbeaten in seven starts in 2004, starting with a maiden at his local track of Queanbeyan and completing the sequence at Wagga Wagga, Kensington, Rosehill, Gosford, Grafton and Flemington, his final win that year coming in the Group 1 Salinger Stakes. Takeover Target ended the following year with wins in a Group 3 and a listed race at Doomben before embarking on his international campaign in 2006.

If the jet age led to a great leap forward in making horse racing an international sport by facilitating travel, then the digital age has transformed the ease with which information about horses in different parts of the world can be transmitted. The point is made in Black Caviar's essay that the internet had done plenty to publicise her exploits to a worldwide audience well beyond Australia, whetting the appetite all the more for her appearance at Royal Ascot, well before she actually set foot in Britain. Computer technology also played its part in the campaign of another Australian sprinter successful in Britain in 2012, **Ortensia** (rated 123), who made up for defeat at Royal Ascot by winning the King George Stakes at Goodwood and the Nunthorpe Stakes at York.

> Information derived from sectional timing can be valuable in the training of racehorses, as well as in analysing their performances in races, and is just one example of technology being used in the training of horses which would formerly have been applied only to training human athletes. Such technology means that the trainer does not need to be there during the horse's training. Ortensia was a good example, with Paul Messara able to 'train' remotely from Australia while the mare was at Newmarket over the summer. Ortensia had a stable assistant with her at Newmarket, but additional information on Ortensia's regime, which could then be downloaded by the trainer in Australia, came from a saddle blanket equipped with GPS, to measure the speed and distance

of her workouts, and a heart-rate monitor to check on her fitness. 'It's almost as good as being there,' Messara claimed. 'Being able to email photographs, video footage [Ortensia's work rider was also equipped with a helmet-cam], as well as receiving comprehensive training reviews each day allows us to monitor the mare's well-being and exercise without being in the UK.'

'If and when an edition of *Favourite Racehorses* is published covering a future period in Timeform's history, perhaps the compilers will need to be as familiar with Japanese pedigrees as they had to be with American ones for this edition.' The closing remarks in *Favourite Racehorses* weren't far wrong. The rise of Dubai might be the biggest change on the international racing scene in recent decades, but Japan's transformation from a wholly self-contained racing country to a world power in breeding and racing has been almost as sudden and far-reaching. That change has come on two fronts. As well as lifting restrictions on foreign-trained horses in its top races, Japan has sent out its own globetrotters with successful results. In 2006 Delta Blues and Pop Rock finished first and second in the Melbourne Cup, while another Japanese one-two came from Victoire Pisa and Transcend in the 2011 Dubai World Cup. However, it is Europe that has been the main focus of Japanese ambitions abroad, with the Prix de l'Arc de Triomphe the most coveted prize of all. The foundations for Japanese raids on the Arc were laid at Deauville in the summer of 1998 when Seeking The Pearl's win in the Prix Maurice de Gheest was swiftly followed by **Taiki Shuttle** (rated 125) emulating her in the Prix Jacques le Marois:

> Added interest was given to the 1966 Grand National by the participation of the Japanese horse Fujino-O, a 100/1 shot who completed a circuit before refusing at the Chair. Until the latest season, Japanese runners competing overseas had been looked on with curiosity as much as anything else, due to the rarity of such ventures, the closed-door policy of Japanese racing and, it has to be said, a lack of success abroad. But things are changing quickly. The victories of Seeking The Pearl and Taiki Shuttle in Group 1 events on successive Sundays at Deauville in August were a sudden indication that from now on Japanese challengers in top races around the world will need to be taken very much more seriously, particularly as Japanese racing is taking steps to integrate with the rest of the world. Midnight Bet's win at 42/1 in the Hong Kong International Cup late in the year only serves to underline the point.

> Taiki Shuttle was fortunate to contest a Jacques le Marois lacking an outstanding European miler, but it took a high-class effort to defeat a line-up which included the Sussex Stakes first and third Among Men and Lend A Hand, the Lockinge winner Cape Cross, the d'Astarte winner Miss Berbere, the leading older miler in Germany, Waky Nao, and the smart French colt Marathon. Taiki Shuttle beat them with little fuss. Always handy near the stand rail, Taiki Shuttle headed the front-running Cape Cross inside the last and just needed to be ridden out by his forty-nine-year-old rider Yukio Okabe to hold the late challenge of Among Men by half a length, with Cape Cross a short head away third. There were some chaotic post-race scenes involving Taiki Shuttle's supporters and the media entourage

which had followed the horse's every move since his arrival in France. Some of them even wanted their winning pari-mutuel tickets photocopied as souvenirs! The pari-mutuel had apparently come close to a breakdown beforehand after one Japanese punter had record-breaking bets involving Taiki Shuttle totalling two million francs, which resulted in his odds crashing to 10/1-on at one point! It took an hour for the dividends on the Jacques le Marois to be returned, Taiki Shuttle's starting price finally settling at 10/3-on.

That wasn't to be the last time the pari-mutuel was overwhelmed by support for a Japanese horse, but, more immediately, those two Group 1 wins at Deauville were followed two years later by Agnes World's July Cup victory in 2000, the first by a Japanese horse in Britain. Agnes World had also won the Prix de l'Abbaye the previous autumn, his victory at Longchamp providing some consolation for compatriot El Condor Pasa's narrow defeat in the Prix de l'Arc de Triomphe later that afternoon. Already the winner of the Grand Prix de Saint-Cloud and Prix Foy in France that season, the four-year-old **El Condor Pasa** (rated 136) looked the chief rival to outstanding three-year-old Montjeu.

In the week before the race El Condor Pasa was reported to have worked superbly, and he was a firm second choice in the market behind the coupled pairing of Montjeu and his pacemaker Genghis Khan. The heavy ground was unlike any El Condor Pasa had encountered—although he had won on soft in Japan, his best form was on firmer, including the Japan Cup on firm. Over a mile and a half front-running tactics require courage, confidence in the stamina of one's own mount and considerable judgement of pace. El Condor Pasa's jockey Masayoshi Ebina was not inexperienced, having partnered over seven hundred and fifty winners, but the way he went about his business once the stalls opened left most observers bemused. Genghis Khan couldn't get to the front as El Condor Pasa soon took a three-length advantage and maintained a scorching gallop, having no trouble with the ground and racing with plenty of zest. If the other jockeys thought El Condor Pasa would come back to them, they were in for a major disappointment. Tiger Hill had a futile crack at him half a mile out, and with two furlongs left El Condor Pasa, extending his lead to some four lengths, had seen off just about all his rivals, who were under severe pressure and getting nowhere. The one he hadn't broken was Montjeu, who had got clear of the pack and was bearing down relentlessly on the leader. El Condor Pasa didn't stop at all, and increased his margin over the rest of the field in the closing stages, but for all his courage he simply had no answer to Montjeu, surrendering the lead in the final fifty yards and going down by half a length. It takes two to make a cracking race—Grundy and Bustino in the 1975 King George VI and Queen Elizabeth Stakes, for example—and the part El Condor Pasa, and his jockey, played in making the Arc the race of the season can easily be underestimated. They were magnificent, and it was astonishing that Ebina's front-running ride came in for some criticism after the race from the colt's connections, one of whom said: 'I can't say I'm happy—we did not plan to do that'. Some people are never satisfied, because to our eyes Ebina's ride was one of the best of the season in Europe. His tactics enabled his mount to come closer to beating an outstanding colt than anyone could have predicted.

El Condor Pasa remains the highest-rated Japanese horse since the *Racehorses* annuals began listing ratings of Japan's best horses in its 'Top Horses Abroad' section in 1997. But not far behind him is **Deep Impact** (rated 134), Japan's 2006 Arc challenger, who brought a towering reputation to Longchamp with him (after just one defeat in eleven races), along with a fan club thousands strong, his popularity aided by the superstar status of his regular rider Yutaka Take.

Yutaka Take had won fifteen jockeys' titles in Japan and in 2005 rode more than two hundred winners for the third consecutive year—he was champion again in 2006 with 178 winners. Take also partnered Japan's very first winner in Europe, Seeking The Pearl, in the 1998 Prix Maurice de Gheest, and he rode regularly in France in both 2001 and 2002. But, for all that, it's fair to say that Take enjoys a less exalted reputation in Britain, though that is essentially the result of one ride, when he received bad press for his handling of the leading British contender in the 1994 Arc, White Muzzle. Apparently going against instructions to have his mount handily placed, Take brought White Muzzle with a strong late run from the rear which resulted in a never-nearer sixth. Take's only ride in the Arc since then, third on Sagacity in 2001, had brought no adverse comment. Take's popularity with Japanese fans was a factor in what the French media called 'Impact mania' which hit Longchamp on Arc day. Two thousand Japanese racegoers had swelled the crowd when El Condor Pasa contested the Arc, but the Japanese contingent was reckoned to be about three times as large this time, the Arc day crowd of 60,400 (boosted by the usual influx of British visitors) reported to be the largest attendance at Longchamp for some time. That figure looks less impressive when compared to the 137,601 racegoers who had packed into Kyoto to see Deep Impact complete the triple crown the previous year, more than ten thousand of whom had slept outside the track overnight to guarantee entry! Many of Deep Impact's fans made their presence felt with flags and banners, some of them dressed in his owner's colours of black, blue and yellow, while near-hysteria broke out every time the horse, his rider or his trainer were shown on the screens around the course during the preliminaries. The French authorities had anticipated the influx of Japanese supporters to some extent, providing a help desk and dedicated betting windows, but these were soon overwhelmed. In addition to those who had made the trip to Longchamp, sixteen per cent of the Japanese population was reported to have watched the Arc on television despite the race taking place in the early hours in Japan.

'Impact mania' really made its presence felt on the pari-mutuel. British bookmakers had struggled to find a clear favourite for the Arc, with Deep Impact vying for the position with the two main Andre Fabre-trained contenders Hurricane Run and Shirocco. The nature of pool betting meant there was no

Orfevre looked likely to give the Japanese a long-awaited win in the Arc but was thwarted by the rallying Solemia (white cap)

such indecision on the pari-mutuel. On Arc day, a total of €4.8 million was bet at the meeting as a whole on course (representing a fifty-five per cent increase on the turnover the year before), but bets on Deep Impact accounted for around a third of that total. The weight of money for Deep Impact was described in the British media as a 'gamble', though perhaps 'unanimous support' would have been a more accurate description of what took place; it was certainly not a gamble of the old-fashioned variety, as British punters would understand it. For a while, it looked as though Deep Impact might start at his usual Japanese odds of 10/1-on. There was incredulity from the British bookmakers' representatives at Longchamp that Deep Impact's supporters should be queuing up to back him at such odds, but they were missing the point. Many of the bets were token ones at the minimum stake, the pari-mutuel tickets to be kept as souvenirs rather than cashed in. In the end, Deep Impact was sent off at 2/1-on (compared to the British industry odds of 9/4), resulting in his rivals going off at much longer odds on the pari-mutuel than with the bookmakers in Britain, most notably Rail Link, an 8/1 chance on industry returns who paid nearly 24/1 on the pari-mutuel.

All those win bet tickets went uncashed, with Deep Impact managing only third place behind Rail Link and Pride. Worse followed when Deep Impact was disqualified after testing positive for a prohibited substance (as a result of accidental contamination), though he retired to stud with his reputation back home as high as ever following two more wins, in the Japan Cup and Arima Kinen. A good deal less fanfare accompanied Nakayama Festa's Arc challenge in 2010 when he ran Derby winner Workforce to a head, but Japanese expectations were ramped up again when **Orfevre** (rated 130) started favourite in 2012. Unlike Deep Impact, Orfevre had the benefit of a prep race in France, while having the services of a French-based jockey in Christophe Soumillon was another cause for optimism. That confidence looked well placed, but . . .

> Surely this time! When Orfevre quickened down the outside of the field and swept into the lead a furlong and a half out in the Prix de l'Arc de Triomphe, the long wait for Japan's first winner of Europe's top prize looked about to end. When Orfevre then went a couple of lengths clear of his hard-ridden rivals entering the final furlong, the race looked as good as over. Any celebrations on Orfevre's behalf proved premature, however. In a classic case of defeat being snatched from the jaws of victory, the closing stages of the Arc were agonising for Orfevre's many supporters (as well as carrying the hopes of a nation, he was also favourite on the pari-mutuel). Almost as soon as he hit the front, Orfevre began to hang right and, despite Christophe Soumillon's attempts to straighten him up by using the whip, he ended up against the rail with half a furlong to run. Orfevre was still a couple of lengths ahead but began to idle and then compounded matters by colliding with the rail just yards from the line, by which time he had already been headed. Orfevre was beaten a neck by the filly Solemia, who was receiving 3 lb and whom Orfevre had seemingly left for dead when quickening earlier in the straight. What was particularly galling, as his trainer observed, was that Orfevre actually ran on again after the line when Soumillon stopped riding. He was clearly much the best horse in the race and should have won.

Hopes of a Japanese victory were higher still when Orfevre, sent off favourite again but at an even shorter price, returned for the Arc twelve months later, this time accompanied by his three-year-old compatriot Kizuna. The pair were successful in their respective trials three weeks beforehand, but Orfevre had to settle for second again, beaten on merit this time, by the brilliant French filly Treve, with Kizuna back in fourth.

SPRINTER SACRE

A Timeform Publication

Sprinter Sacre

A horse that dominates his contemporaries, one who beats his rivals hollow and is clearly the best around, automatically invites comparison with champions of the past. Being indisputably the best in a particular year or season is one thing, but it's natural to ask of a horse who has established himself as much the best among those around him, where does he fit in the wider scheme of things? Such horses, of course, do not come along very often. On the Flat, Sea-Bird in the 'sixties set the standard against which subsequent champions were long measured. It was not until Frankel emerged nearly fifty years later that one of them finally surpassed Sea-Bird's Timeform rating. Sea-Bird was about a stone better than what might be termed a 'good' winner of the Derby, which put him in a different league to most horses, but he was by no means out on his own when judged against some of the other very best Flat champions of the Timeform era.

Modern-day steeplechasers, it could be argued, face a still taller order than their Flat counterparts—what looks an insurmountable task, in fact—measuring up to jumping's all-time great. Arkle's career coincided with Sea-Bird's on the Flat; he won the second of his three Cheltenham Gold Cups in 1965, the same year as Sea-Bird's three-year-old season. But with the notable exception of his own stable-companion and contemporary Flyingbolt who was rated just 2 lb behind him (Arkle's highest Timeform Black Book rating was 212, Flyingbolt's 210), no chaser has ever come close to reaching the same level. Not that that has prevented a number of other chasers being talked of as 'the next Arkle'. Kauto Star had come closer than any horse since the 'sixties, his rating of 191 matching that of Mill House, the 1963 Gold Cup winner and Arkle's chief rival. The pair met for the final time in the Gallaher Gold Cup at Sandown in November 1965, a handicap in which Mill House received 16 lb from Arkle who carried 12-7. The following extract appeared in *Favourite Racehorses*, quoting the editor of the magazine *The Racing Week* (which was published by Timeform in the 'sixties), and gives some idea of the gulf that separated 'a great horse' from 'an even greater one'.

> One day someone, I hope, will write a book about Arkle, and on the first page I suggest they make the emphatic statement that he is the best horse that ever jumped fences. For ammunition to defend this declaration they need look no further than last Saturday's Gallaher Gold Cup, in which Arkle reached a height of achievement few people could have thought possible. He faced his most difficult task to date, and overcame it by the truly amazing distance of twenty

lengths, and in a course record time. It is incredible that even now, after almost three years at the top, Arkle is getting better . . . Just how much weight Mill House will need to receive from Arkle to give him an equal chance is a teaser I am glad to leave to those who get paid for working that sort of thing out.'

Rated 192p at the end of his second unbeaten season over fences, Sprinter Sacre is better placed than any chaser to reach heights not seen since the era of Arkle and Flyingbolt. Both of those greats are recalled in Sprinter Sacre's essay from *Chasers & Hurdlers 2012/13*, most of which is reproduced here:

'There'll never be another Arkle.' Or will there? Fifty years after Arkle made his first appearance on an English racecourse, jumping fences for the first time in public in the Honeybourne Chase at Cheltenham, Sprinter Sacre continued the process of carving out his own legend with a stunning victory in the Sportingbet Tingle Creek Chase at Sandown. Sprinter Sacre was never remotely at full stretch as he strolled home by fifteen lengths, a description that could also be given to his fourteen-length victory in the Victor Chandler Chase, the second Grade 1 open two-mile chase of the season, his nineteen-length victory in the Sportingbet Queen Mother Champion Chase and his easy success against the Ryanair Chase winner Cue Card and Ireland's highest-rated chaser Flemenstar in the John Smith's Melling Chase over two and a half miles. Sprinter Sacre's fifth Grade 1 success of the campaign in the boylesports.com Champion Chase at Punchestown, which stretched his unbeaten record over fences to ten, didn't quite turn into the familiar lap of honour. He had to be kept up to his work to beat the Queen Mother Champion Chase runner-up Sizing Europe—a top-class performer in his own right—by five and a half lengths, a victory which earned Sprinter Sacre the distinction of becoming the first since Istabraq in 1999 to win in the same season at the Cheltenham, Aintree and Punchestown festivals. Sprinter Sacre's Timeform rating is the highest recorded over jumps in the *Chasers & Hurdlers* era—shading that achieved by Kauto Star—and there is the prospect of even better to come (which is why the Timeform small 'p' remains attached to his rating). Arkle and his great contemporary Flyingbolt are the only horses to have earned a Timeform rating of over 200, a mark that Sprinter Sacre could probably achieve in the right circumstances. The imposing Sprinter Sacre is a magnificent sight in full flow, his ground-devouring stride and often spectacular jumping making it look easy to him. He has everything needed to become one of the most popular jumpers of all time and a fine ambassador for the sport.

Arkle's name will never be forgotten. When the *Racing Post* polled its readers in 2004—four decades after Arkle was in his prime (and before Kauto Star)—Arkle was voted racing's all-time favourite horse. Jumpers filled the first four places in the poll, with Desert Orchid, Red Rum and Istabraq next. Arkle's standing in the public's eyes owed as much to his sustained success, winning big races—including major handicaps under very big weights—over a number of seasons, as it did to his extraordinary innate ability. Arkle won three Cheltenham Gold Cups, for example, while Desert Orchid won four King George VI Chases, Red Rum three Grand Nationals and Istabraq three Champion Hurdles. Scaling the mountain again and again, breaking the mould, counts in the public mind when it comes to measuring 'greatness', as illustrated by the fact that Flyingbolt, rated within 2 lb of Arkle at his peak, didn't even feature in the top hundred in the Racing Post poll. Flyingbolt was plagued with injuries and illnesses of one sort or another—including contracting the blood disease brucellosis—and didn't show his true form again after a brilliant second season over fences in 1965/6, the season that Arkle won his third Cheltenham Gold Cup. The two years younger Flyingbolt had won all his five races as a novice chaser, including a none too impressive success in the Cotswold Chase (now the Arkle) at Cheltenham, in which he was reported to have been doped. Flyingbolt suffered his first defeat under National Hunt rules on his reappearance the next season, carrying 12-7 and finishing fourth in a handicap over hurdles at Phoenix Park.

Back over fences, Flyingbolt won three times before the turn of the year, taking the Carey's Cottage Chase at Gowran, the richly-endowed 'Black and White' Gold Cup at Ascot (by fifteen lengths) and putting up a scintillating display to win the Massey-Ferguson Gold Cup (as Cheltenham's big December handicap was then known). Flyingbolt carried 12-6 in the Massey-Ferguson, conceding lumps of weight all round, in the mud, and he put lengths between himself and his rivals when taking up the running three fences out before going on to a fifteen-length victory. It was back to Gowran in January, with an equally outstanding performance in another major handicap, the Thyestes Chase, in which Flyingbolt beat the top-class mare Height o'Fashion (received 28 lb) by a distance. Flyingbolt appeared on successive days at the Cheltenham Festival, running away with the Two-Mile Champion Chase—then run on the Tuesday—by fifteen lengths before going on to finish third in the Champion Hurdle. Seven-year-old Flyingbolt went on to make it six out of six for the season over fences when winning the Irish Grand National (then run over three and a quarter miles). He carried 12-7 and produced a performance that showed that he was almost as good as his stablemate Arkle at his best, giving a 42-lb beating to runner-up Height o'Fashion (Timeform 168+) and a 53-lb beating to the third Splash, who had won the race the year before under 10-13, after which he was rated 157 by Timeform. That pair had filled the same placings behind Arkle when he won the Leopardstown Chase under 12-7 the previous month, coming out 43 lb and 55 lb inferior at the weights. Very few of Arkle's or Flyingbolt's contemporaries could be set to carry more than 10-0 against their 12-7 in handicaps, and Height o' Fashion carried 9-7 at Leopardstown and 9-9 at Fairyhouse, with Splash carrying 9-7 in both races. Arkle and Flyingbolt were in different ownership and, although trainer Tom Dreaper kept them apart and they never met in racecourse competition, the 1965/66 season ended with the prospect that Flyingbolt's owners might insist on a Gold Cup challenge the next season. However, illness and injury, which confounds so many hopes and expectations in steeplechasing, intervened and Arkle never raced again after fracturing a bone in his hoof in the next season's King George VI Chase, while Flyingbolt was ruled out for the rest of that season after disappointing on his reappearance (tests eventually revealing brucellosis). Flyingbolt's subsequent appearances were limited and he never regained his best form, his career gradually petering out, though he was not retired until he was twelve—he managed just one more win, from thirteen starts, and was trained latterly in Britain (by Ken Oliver and then by Roddy Armytage). Would the history of steeplechasing have been different if Flyingbolt's second appearance at the 1966 National Hunt meeting had come against Arkle in the Gold Cup—for which Flyingbolt would have had a further twenty-four hours to recuperate—rather than in the Champion Hurdle? Both horses were at the peak of their powers and, on the form-book at least, there wouldn't have been much between them.

The two-mile chasers still tend to be overshadowed in the public consciousness by their staying counterparts, though the difference was more pronounced in Flyingbolt's day (there wasn't even a championship race for the top two-mile chasers at the National Hunt meeting until 1959). That, and the fact that some of the gloss was taken off Flyingbolt's finest achievements by later performances, were probably the main reasons that he never received the full credit he deserved. He was also most unfortunate to have been overshadowed in 1965/66 by Arkle who won all five of his starts, the Gallaher Gold Cup at Sandown (by twenty lengths in a record time that still stands), a second Hennessy Gold Cup at Newbury (by fifteen lengths, carrying 12-7), the King George VI Chase by a distance, the Leopardstown Chase, and the Cheltenham Gold Cup by thirty lengths. In any other year, Flyingbolt's brilliant performances would have earned him the wider recognition he was entitled to as one of the greats. Arkle was sent off at 10/1-on in the Gold Cup and Flyingbolt at 5/1-on in the Two Mile Champion Chase, the shortest-priced favourites in the history of those two races. Sprinter Sacre's ten-race unbeaten run in steeplechases is one short of Flyingbolt's at the end of his second season over fences and jumping's followers must hope that Sprinter Sacre goes on to become a lasting marvel and keeps his form to secure a place for all time in the steeplechasing pantheon.

Most winners of the Two-Mile (now Queen Mother) Champion Chase are specialists at the distance, though Flyingbolt was an outstanding performer over the Cheltenham Gold Cup distance too, and his near-contemporary Fortria, also Dreaper-trained, won successive Champion Chases and then twice finished runner-up in the Gold Cup. The winner of the 1971 Champion Chase, Crisp, went on to put up the best post-war Grand National performance—in handicapping terms—by any horse when runner-up to Red Rum in 1973, conceding him 23 lb. More recently, One Man won the 1998 Queen Mother

Champion Chase after two successes in the King George VI Chase. The very versatile Desert Orchid didn't win the Champion Chase but was twice placed in the race and, among his many accomplishments, was concurrently the best two-mile chaser and the best staying chaser for three successive years between 1988/89 and 1990/91, his wins in that period including the Cheltenham Gold Cup and the Irish Grand National (over three and a half miles), as well as three of his four King George VI Chases. Desert Orchid's two-mile titles were earned with brilliant weight-carrying performances in the Tingle Creek and the Victor Chandler, both of which were still run as handicaps in Desert Orchid's day. Kauto Star was also Timeform's top-rated two-mile chaser, thanks to a second straight win in the Tingle Creek, during the season when he claimed his first wins in the King George VI Chase and Cheltenham Gold Cup. He had been an early faller when favourite for the Champion Chase the previous season.

Sprinter Sacre is on a completely different level from his own contemporaries and a Gold Cup victory would help to spread his name beyond the confines of the racing world and cement his legacy. His horizons have already been broadened beyond the top two-mile chases by connections running him in the Melling Chase over two and a half at Aintree. The Henderson stable does already house two Gold Cup winners in reigning champion Bobs Worth and the 2011 winner Long Run, who finished third in the latest running, but Sprinter Sacre's pedigree has staying influences in it and he has already shown that he is not purely and simply a two-miler. Sprinter Sacre will be untouchable if it is decided to confine him to the two-mile division, but he gives the distinct impression that anything is possible with him and he would start a short-priced favourite for the Gold Cup (he was promoted to ante-post favourite for the next King George VI Chase after winning the Melling). Sprinter Sacre's jockey Barry Geraghty has warned that journalists 'might have to mint some new superlatives' for Sprinter Sacre. They certainly would if he were to create history by becoming the first to win a Queen Mother Champion Chase and a Cheltenham Gold Cup.

Barry Geraghty described his experience on Sprinter Sacre in the Arkle Challenge Trophy, the highlight of a brilliant first campaign over fences, as the first time he had ever schooled a horse round to win a championship race at the Cheltenham Festival. Perhaps Geraghty should be allowed a little poetic licence when it comes to a horse as good as Sprinter Sacre, whose Arkle performance put him ahead of the rest of only a handful of novice chasers who have recorded a rating of more than 170 in *Chasers & Hurdlers* history. Sprinter Sacre quickly put the Arkle result in little doubt once Geraghty allowed him to stride on down the hill. He sauntered home, only coming under minimal pressure once over the last to shake off Cue Card, winning by seven lengths and twenty-two from Cue Card and Menorah (subsequent big-race winners Al Ferof and Blackstairmountain were further back in fourth and fifth). A sparkling display in the Game Spirit Chase on his only outing outside novice

*Another typically impressive display from Sprinter Sacre
in the Game Spirit Chase at Newbury*

company and a thrilling exhibition of bold jumping in the Maghull Novices' at Aintree were among the other highlights in an unblemished first season over fences. There was another bold and spectacular two-miler among the season's novices that Sprinter Sacre had not met, the runaway Celebration Chase winner Sanctuaire. Sanctuaire's performance at Sandown was as dominant a display as any seen all season and there was plenty of interest in the meeting of the pair over the same course on their seasonal reappearance in the Sportingbet Tingle Creek Chase in early-December—Sprinter Sacre had missed a planned preparatory run in a valuable minor event at Cheltenham because of heavy going the previous month.

The seven-runner Tingle Creek, which attracted a crowd of 10,532 (500 up on the previous year), was billed in the media as a match—Sprinter Sacre started at 11/4-on, Sanctuaire at 11/4 against—but it proved very one-sided. Sanctuaire was quite unable to stretch Sprinter Sacre who took over on the bridle three out after his rival had set a scorching pace, in a clear lead for much of the way.

Sprinter Sacre coasted home, never in any danger in the home straight, to win by fifteen lengths from 25/1-shot Kumbeshwar who took second after the last from the beaten Sanctuaire. The second and third took on Sprinter Sacre again in the Victor Chandler Chase (registered as the Clarence House) which was transferred to Cheltenham's trials meeting after Ascot's January meeting was lost to snow. Cheltenham's meeting was saved after an impressive triumph by the course's management and staff over the elements (snow had to be cleared from the course before the frost covers could be lifted, with contingency plans—not needed in the end—put in place to run the meeting a day later than scheduled if the course couldn't be made ready in time). Sprinter Sacre's victory at 5/1-on in the Victor Chandler, in front of a crowd of 18,208, was another cakewalk as he drew clear on the bridle from three out. The rank outsider Mad Moose, who made much of the running after being gifted a huge lead at the start, finished fourteen lengths behind Sprinter Sacre in second, with Somersby, the winner of the race at its usual venue the previous year, a further two and a quarter behind in third. Waiting tactics were tried with Sanctuaire, who had paid the price in the Tingle Creek for carrying the fight to Sprinter Sacre, but had then won the Desert Orchid Chase at Kempton from Kumbeshwar. Sanctuaire ended up being beaten further under very testing conditions in the Victor Chandler than he had in the Tingle Creek, though he did repeat his Desert Orchid form with Kumbeshwar as the pair trailed home a well-beaten fourth and fifth. The Victor Chandler didn't reveal much new about Sprinter Sacre beyond proof of his ability to cope with heavy going. Typically, he jumped well and travelled strongly, winning with any amount in hand and looking to have the Queen Mother Champion Chase very much at his mercy.

The Queen Mother Champion Chase helped to attract a near-record second-day crowd of 52,854 to the Festival for a race that looked something of a formality for Sprinter Sacre who started at 4/1-on, the shortest-priced favourite for any race at the Festival since 1966. At least the presence of the most consistent Sizing Europe, an Arkle winner who had been first and second in the last two runnings of the Queen Mother, meant that the magnitude of the winner's show-stopping performance could not be underestimated. There had been only seventeen entries for the Queen Mother Champion Chase when the race closed in January—they also included the 2012 winner Finian's Rainbow and the novice Simonsig from the Henderson stable—and Sizing Europe was the only one of four Irish-trained challengers (who had also included Flemenstar) to stand his ground. Sizing Europe had been beaten only once in his eight previous races, that being his narrow (and arguably unlucky) Champion Chase second twelve months earlier when the last fence had to be bypassed and Sizing Europe was tightened up a little by Finian's Rainbow as they manoeuvred round it. Also in the line-up again for the latest running was Wishfull Thinking, whose fall at the relevant fence first time round had resulted in injuries to his jockey, and to a photographer, as Wishfull Thinking slid under the running rail

The home turn in the Queen Mother Champion Chase - the rest have already cried enough as Sprinter Sacre quickens impressively

after falling (the double running rail was arguably too close to the line of the fence and was realigned in the latest season to provide a 'lay-by' on the left hand side of the fence). After his fall, the enigmatic Wishfull Thinking had gone on to finish second to Finian's Rainbow in the Melling Chase at Aintree and had won two of his four races in the latest season, his most recent success coming in the Game Spirit Chase at Newbury, a traditional warm-up for the Champion Chase. Sanctuaire and Somersby were also in the field of seven which included the supplemented Mail de Bievre, a bold-jumping front runner who had shaped quite well in the Denman Chase (over three miles) on his return from a seventeen-month absence with leg trouble (he had won three times at Auteuil in 2009/10).

Mail de Bievre made the running for a long way at Cheltenham but Sprinter Sacre and Sizing Europe—also the last horse before Sprinter Sacre to win both an Arkle and a Champion Chase—soon had the race to themselves after they pressed on together at the fourth from home. Sprinter Sacre made a mistake there but both had been jumping fluently, though Sprinter Sacre perhaps hadn't been quite so measured as he can be. Sprinter Sacre took the advantage from Sizing Europe, with no visible encouragement from his rider, after jumping the third last and quickened away effortlessly rounding the home turn and facing up to the last two fences. Sizing Europe lost his footing and stumbled approaching the final bend but Sprinter Sacre had already taken his measure by then and drew clear to win by nineteen lengths, the winning distance arbitrary considering that Sprinter Sacre was barely off a tight rein and his rider spent the last hundred yards patting him down the neck. It may not have been the widest winning margin at the Festival—Salsify won the Foxhunter by twenty—but it was by far the most imperious performance of the week, and the most complete triumph in the Queen Mother Champion Chase since Master Minded's stunning first victory—as a five-year-old—in 2008. On the form-book, Sprinter Sacre's performance, with Wishfull Thinking and Sanctuaire completing the frame beaten a further six lengths, and three lengths, was superior to Master Minded's, though the manner of Master Minded's win—also by nineteen lengths from a previous winner of the race (Voy Por Ustedes)—certainly bears comparison with that of Sprinter Sacre.

The exploits of Master Minded, along with the other outstanding winners of the race in recent times, Moscow Flyer and Azertyuiop, are recounted in the next chapter. Back in the 'sixties, Dunkirk hacked up by twenty lengths in the Champion Chase and was rated 186 by Timeform, the third highest rating (behind Flyingbolt and Sprinter Sacre) achieved by any winner in fifty-four runnings of the race (had he not been killed in a fall in the 1965 King George VI Chase that Arkle won, Dunkirk would have been defending his two-mile title against Flyingbolt in the 1966 running).

…Sprinter Sacre's trainer Nicky Henderson had stopped short of acknowledging Sprinter Sacre as the best horse he has trained—'He must be getting very close,' he had said after the Tingle Creek—but he was almost speechless after the Queen Mother Champion Chase, saying he had endured the worst five minutes of his life and had 'nearly needed the doctor and a cardiac machine.' 'You'd have to say he's the best I've trained now, he is nearly the perfect racehorse, he just finds it so ridiculously easy,' said Henderson. Barry Geraghty equalled the record five winners in the race of Flyingbolt's jockey Pat Taaffe and he said that it was 'the ease and grace' with which Sprinter Sacre did things that set him apart from the other Queen Mother Champion Chase winners that he had ridden, including Moscow Flyer. 'He has a big stride but is also athletic, so well balanced, and I have never ridden a horse that can do it the way he does,' Geraghty said. Geraghty had been reluctant after the Tingle Creek to say that Sprinter Sacre was better than Moscow Flyer—'Moscow Flyer's Tingle Creek is the best race I have ridden in, because that race involved two other really outstanding two-milers in Azertyuiop and Well Chief [beaten a length and a half and a short head by Moscow Flyer in a thriller at Sandown].'

Straight after the latest Tingle Creek, Nicky Henderson had said that Sprinter Sacre would go for the Victor Chandler 'and quite possibly nothing else before Cheltenham, with a view to running at Aintree or Punchestown afterwards.' There were just over three weeks between the Queen Mother Champion Chase and the Melling Chase in the latest season, and just over two and a half between the Melling Chase and the Champion Chase at Punchestown and Sprinter Sacre eventually ran in all three.

Cue Card, runner-up to Sprinter Sacre in the Arkle the previous year, was directed to the Ryanair Chase at the latest Cheltenham Festival, rather than the Queen Mother Champion Chase. 'We could have finished second, but it's all about being first,' his trainer Colin Tizzard had said. Cue Card won the Ryanair in fine style and the form was franked by the victory in the Aintree Bowl of Ryanair runner-up First Lieutenant. That came twenty-four hours before Cue Card renewed rivalry with Sprinter Sacre in front of a crowd of 45,390 (the first sub-50,000 attendance for 'ladies day' in seven years) in the Melling Chase. The race also attracted the highest-rated chaser in Ireland, Flemenstar, and Sprinter Sacre's stablemate Finian's Rainbow who had missed the latest Cheltenham Festival, because of concerns over soft going, after landing the Champion Chase/Melling Chase double twelve months earlier. Master Minded's aura took a significant early knock when Voy Por Ustedes reversed Cheltenham placings with him in the 2008 Melling—Master Minded capitulated in alarming fashion after a mistake two out—but there was never any hint that a similar fate would befall Sprinter Sacre, who passed his stiffest test to date (both in terms of his stamina and the strength of the opposition) just as effortlessly as all his previous tests over fences. It bears repeating that the Melling was the best race of the season (at least in terms of quality) and it was run at a terrific gallop too, with the four principals proving far too strong for that proven graded performer For Non Stop who was struggling as early as halfway—the only other runner Mad Moose refused to race. Flemenstar and Finian's Rainbow were the first to crack as Cue Card pressed on three out, but Sprinter Sacre soon had matters under control once produced to challenge at the next, simply toying with Cue Card (who ran a fine race in his own right). The unextended Sprinter Sacre, who again had stacks in hand, was four and a half lengths clear of Cue Card come the line, with a further nineteen lengths back to third-placed Flemenstar.

Sprinter Sacre romped home from highly credible challengers at both Cheltenham and Aintree, but he had to work harder than usual to maintain his unbeaten record over fences in the five-runner Champion Chase at Punchestown where a record first-day crowd of 18,607 (up by over 4,000 on the previous year) turned up to see him. Sprinter Sacre received a splendid reception after beating Sizing Europe by five and a half lengths, Geraghty saying he couldn't remember 'anything like it since Desert Orchid won the Irish National when I was nine or ten.' Sprinter Sacre typically jumped well, as did front-running Sizing Europe who recorded his best performance of the season and kept on very gamely after Sprinter Sacre joined him at the second last, with Sizing Europe's very smart stablemate Days Hotel filling third place at the line, thirty-three lengths further behind.

A trademark bold leap from Sprinter Sacre as he maintains his 100% record over fences in the Champion Chase at Punchestown

The rangy Sprinter Sacre is a commanding individual who stands over seventeen hands and would be difficult to fault in the show-ring. He really filled the eye in the paddock before the Queen Mother Champion Chase, well muscled up with his coat gleaming, and very much on his toes, clearly trained to the minute and a credit to Seven Barrows where his home work is said to be spectacular. 'He is something of a show-off and the main job sometimes is harnessing his exuberance,' his trainer says. 'Along with Simonsig, he's as good a young horse in his work as I've had, quite frightening to watch.' Sprinter Sacre can, however, be 'a grumpy old sod' when he is in his box and is stabled away from the main yard to help to keep him relaxed (he also wears ear plugs on big-race days to shut out the noise of the crowd). The story of how Sprinter Sacre first arrived in Britain as an unraced three-year-old has been widely recounted. He was part of an 'all-in' job lot of twenty or so horses bought by bloodstock agent David Minton for €300,000 from French owner Robert Fougedoire who was dispersing his stock because of illness (the same batch turned out to include those useful Twiston-Davies-trained staying chasers in the latest season, Tour des Champs and Viking Blond, among others). Sprinter Sacre made his debut for Nicky Henderson as a four-year-old in bumpers—winning both his starts and looking an exciting prospect—and he took very well to hurdling the next season, though he was beaten twice in four outings, on the second occasion when third to Al Ferof in the Supreme Novices' at Cheltenham, a performance which apparently prompted the operation he had that summer to improve his breathing before being sent chasing.

. . . The memories of brilliant performances, even from the fairly recent past, inevitably fade over time, but Sprinter Sacre has made the sort of breathtaking start to his steeplechasing career that will hopefully help to lift him alongside such legends as Golden Miller, Arkle, Red Rum, Desert Orchid and Kauto Star in the public's mind. Towering over his contemporaries, both in stature and performance, Sprinter Sacre is in every way a thrilling steeplechaser to watch and, still only seven, he could potentially grace the sport for several more years. Nothing, though, should be taken for granted given the extent to which injury, illness and loss of form decimate the ranks of the top jumpers each season. A pertinent example of this is the Henderson-trained Spirit Son whom Geraghty plumped for instead of Sprinter Sacre when they filled the minor placings in the 2011 Supreme Novices' Hurdle. Spirit Son went on to thump Cue Card by thirteen lengths, with future Champion Hurdle winner Rock On Ruby a further eight lengths back, at Aintree on his only subsequent outing but has sadly since been retired due to serious injury. Therefore, the advice to jumping devotees is to enjoy Sprinter Sacre while you can. It might be a long time before his like is seen again.

Master Minded

TWO-MILE CHASERS

Modern Greats

A Timeform Publication

Two-Mile Chasers

The Cheltenham Gold Cup is the steeplechase with the most prestige in the calendar and the Grand National the richest prize over fences, as well as being the only jumps race that really matters as far as a large percentage of the public is concerned. As a result, the exploits of staying chasers tend to overshadow the achievements of those who excel at shorter trips, but anyone who has watched Sprinter Sacre over the last couple of seasons would find it hard to deny that the sight of a top two-miler in full flow over fences is one of the greatest spectacles steeplechasing has to offer. Sprinter Sacre is the latest, and now the greatest, of the two-milers to rank among the best chasers of the *Chasers & Hurdlers* era. Badsworth Boy (rated 179), the only horse to date to win three Queen Mother Champion Chases (1983 to 1985), set the standard for the two-mile chasers for much of the last two decades of the twentieth century, though several went close to matching him. Pearlyman, Barnbrook Again, Katabatic, Remittance Man, Viking Flagship, Klairon Davis, Martha's Son, One Man and Flagship Uberalles all recorded ratings in the 170s, as well as each being Champion Chase winners at least once. All bar Barnbrook Again were also the best two-mile chasers in *Chasers & Hurdlers* in at least one season; his stable-companion Desert Orchid (placed in both of Pearlyman's Champion Chases) had better form over two miles in both seasons that Barnbrook Again won the Champion Chase. Desert Orchid wasn't a specialist two-miler, of course, while One Man had shown his very best form over longer distances prior to winning the Champion Chase in 1998.

But the first decade of the twenty-first century featured a trio of outstanding two-mile chasers who each bettered Badsworth Boy's rating. As novices, Moscow Flyer, Azertyuiop and Well Chief won successive editions of the Arkle at the Cheltenham Festival from 2002 to 2004 before their rivalry reached its peak in a memorable 2004/05 season during which they dominated the season's top two-mile chases. The three came from very different backgrounds. Moscow Flyer, bred in Ireland where he was also trained by Jessica Harrington, had traditional jumping roots, and had already proved top class over hurdles. He twice won races in which the triple Champion Hurdle winner Istabraq fell and would have beaten him in any case on the first of those occasions. French import Azertyuiop, trained by Paul Nicholls, had himself shown smart form over hurdles before going chasing, while Well Chief had been useful on the Flat in his native Germany before finishing second in the Triumph Hurdle in his first season with Martin Pipe.

The Arkle was one of five wins for **Moscow Flyer** as a novice, three of them Grade 1 contests, but whilst winning all his completed starts, he also fell twice, including on his chasing debut. In the Arkle, though, his jumping was immaculate and included 'a spectacular leap at the ditch at the top of the hill' before 'galloping on with great zest to defeat Seebald by four lengths.' Moscow Flyer was rated 159p after his first season over fences; only Bobsline, rated 161p in 1984, had earned a higher rating among Arkle winners of the previous twenty-five years. Not surprisingly, the Tingle Creek and Champion Chase were named as Moscow Flyer's main targets in the next season. 'That plan doubtless will be applauded by British racegoers' concluded his essay in *Chasers & Hurdlers 2001/02*, 'though possibly not by the connections of such established two-mile stars as Flagship Uberalles, Cenkos and Edredon Bleu, who will certainly have to look to their laurels, if, as seems probable, Moscow Flyer maintains his progress.'

So it proved, though Moscow Flyer's second season over fences had its ups and downs as well:

> To deal with Moscow Flyer's 'downs' first, they were as different as chalk and cheese, though both involved his failing to complete the course. In the Tingle Creek Chase at Sandown in December, he started second favourite and was in touch when colliding with favourite Flagship Uberalles after the latter stumbled in front of him at the fifth, giving Moscow Flyer's jockey no prospect of staying in the saddle. Whilst Sandown was entirely excusable, Moscow Flyer's departure two out in the BMW Chase at Punchestown in May takes much more explaining. After taking up the running approaching four out, Moscow Flyer jumped that fence like a stag but then promptly went through the top of the second last and unseated Barry Geraghty. Geraghty claimed the horse took off too soon and 'paddled' the fence, though it looked very much as if he hardly took off at all. Such lapses are nothing new with Moscow Flyer—he had already done it at Punchestown two starts earlier. Blinkers might be worth considering as they often sharpen a horse up, but the most reliable safeguard for Moscow Flyer is likely to be continued alertness on the part of his jockey.

The positives outweighed the negatives, however, and Moscow Flyer duly proved himself the best two-mile chaser in training in 2002/03, his unbeaten record in completed starts over fences still intact and his rating now 170p.

> Moscow Flyer's record on his other starts was flawless, leaving him with a tally of nine wins from as many completed starts over fences. He had three races in Ireland before the Champion Chase, all on testing going and all at long odds on, as befitted a horse who had put up one of the best performances in the Arkle when defeating Seebald. . .

This succession of straightforward, some might say soft, races came to an end at Cheltenham. Moscow Flyer had been 4/1 favourite for the Queen Mother Champion Chase at the start of the season and was backed from 5/2 to 7/4 on the day, opposed by all the best two-mile chasers available. There were two of the old guard, Edredon Bleu and Flagship Uberalles, who had won the race in 2000 and 2002 respectively. The former had won three of his four starts in the current season, but two of those were in uncompetitive events, while Flagship Uberalles had not reproduced his Cheltenham form. The other members of the younger brigade were Arkle Trophy runner-up Seebald and Kadarann, winner last time out of the Game Spirit Chase in which he beat another contender, third favourite Cenkos, winner of the Tingle Creek. Second favourite Tiutchev had landed the Ascot Chase, Native Upmanship, runner-up in 2002, had been on the mark in a Grade 1 and a Grade 2 in Ireland and Latalomne, a faller when prominent two out the previous year, tried his luck again. The other runners were Florida Pearl, out of form and hardly likely to be suited by the distance, and Geos, winner of a weak renewal of the Castleford Chase. Held up as Edredon Bleu and Latalomne set a good pace followed by Cenkos, Moscow Flyer made a mistake four out but continued to travel well and was poised to take over in front when Seebald and Latalomne came a cropper independently at the second last. Neither faller was going so well as the favourite but their departure finished the race as a spectacle and Moscow Flyer was just kept up to his work to defeat the staying-on Native Upmanship by seven lengths, with Cenkos three lengths further back. In all probability the winner is better than he needed to show here, which is why a 'p' is retained on his rating.

Twenty-four hours before Moscow Flyer landed the Champion Chase, **Azertyuiop** announced himself as a serious threat to the reigning champion when putting up a breathtaking display to win the Arkle by eleven lengths. It was Azertyuiop's fourth win from as many starts over fences and it earned him the same rating as Moscow Flyer twelve months earlier, 159p.

Any winner of the Arkle Trophy has a hard act to follow given the achievements of those who have landed the race in the last fifteen years—between them, Waterloo Boy, Remittance Man, Klairon Davis, Flagship Uberalles, Tiutchev and Moscow Flyer have picked up seventeen Grade 1 races, including four Champion Chases. The latest winner Azertyuiop is a magnificent prospect and there is every reason to expect him to add his name to that list and, quite possibly, become another Champion Chase winner. Exuding a style and confidence reminiscent of Remittance Man in particular, he put up a performance at the Festival that was the equal of any at the meeting for sheer exhilaration, and very similar in merit to Moscow Flyer's in the race the previous year. Azertyuiop's style of racing, jumping with elan and lying close up or making the running, is in the best tradition of two-mile chasing, but an ability to quicken provides another valuable weapon in his armoury. Granted normal improvement Azertyuiop will ensure that Moscow Flyer does not have things

Moscow Flyer on the way to his first win in the Tingle Creek,
as well as a first decision over Azertyuiop (red star on cap)

all his own way in championship races. Any clashes between them should be worth going a long way to see, especially as the Irish horse has a contrasting style, doing best when held up.

The stage was thus set for two potentially fascinating clashes between Moscow Flyer and Azertyuiop in the 2003/04 season. Both chasers ended the campaign with outstanding ratings, Moscow Flyer on 183 and Azertyuiop on 182. But neither meeting between the two was entirely satisfactory in determining their relative merits. First came the Tingle Creek at Sandown in December for which Azertyuiop had had a less than ideal preparation; he was reckoned by his trainer to be 'twelve kilos heavy' after only getting as far as the first fence in the Haldon Gold Cup at Exeter on his reappearance. There had been no such problems for Moscow Flyer on his return:

> After a summer's rest, Moscow Flyer returned to action in the Ballymore Homes Fortria Chase at Navan in early-November. Usually held up over fences, Moscow Flyer made the running for a change and quickened after the third last to land the odds from three opponents. Moscow Flyer had previously shown a tendency to idle when in front for too long, but his performance at Navan gave

connections more options (Moscow Flyer had never been far away in his hurdle races and had dictated the pace when winning his first Grade 1, the Royal Bond at Fairyhouse). Moscow Flyer's next outing provided a mouth-watering clash with the latest Arkle winner Azertyuiop, who had given a breathtaking display at Cheltenham, matching Moscow Flyer's form in the race. Azertyuiop looked a magnificent prospect and started second favourite at 2/1 behind 6/4-shot Moscow Flyer in the William Hill-Tingle Creek Trophy at Sandown in December. Taking a good hold, Moscow Flyer tracked the leader Cenkos, who was seeking a second successive win in the race, until going on at the ninth of the thirteen fences. The expected stiff challenge from Azertyuiop never really materialised, Moscow Flyer having the race in safe keeping soon after quickening into the lead. Just kept up to his work after the last, Moscow Flyer came home four lengths in front of the strongly-ridden Azertyuiop, with third-placed Flagship Uberalles a further seven lengths back and another of the previous season's leading novices Le Roi Miguel fourth, and Cenkos fifth.

Moscow Flyer bettered his Queen Mother Champion Chase form by 7 lb on the bare result of the Tingle Creek. But the tempo of the race didn't really pick up until the runners were going down the far side (the time for the first third of the race was two seconds slower than for the preceding Grade 2 novice chase over the same distance won by Thisthatandtother). Moscow Flyer and Azertyuiop were still going away from the others as the post was reached and were value on the day—in our view at least—for a fair bit more than the distance they managed to put between themselves and the rest of the Tingle Creek field.

The rematch in the following spring's Champion Chase brought Moscow Flyer and Azertyuiop together on a more even footing. Moscow Flyer had completed a straightforward task when winning the Paddy Power Dial-A-Bet Chase at Leopardstown's Christmas fixture for the second year running, while Azertyuiop had likewise been untroubled to land the odds in the Game Spirit Chase after putting up an outstanding performance to be narrowly beaten under top weight in the Victor Chandler Chase at Ascot. The latter race is worth returning to, but first Cheltenham:

The second clash between Azertyuiop and Moscow Flyer in the Queen Mother Champion Chase promised to be one of the highlights—potentially the highlight—of the Festival meeting. Moscow Flyer was seen out only once between Sandown and Cheltenham—when landing the odds from Native Scout at Leopardstown at Christmas—while Azertyuiop followed up his Victor Chandler performance with a straightforward twelve-length victory from another stable-companion Armaturk in the Queen Mother Memorial Fund Game Spirit Chase at Newbury in February. Moscow Flyer started at 6/5-on at Cheltenham, with Azertyuiop at 15/8 and 14/1 bar in a thoroughly representative field of eight. The big clash failed to materialise, Moscow Flyer parting company with his rider four from home and leaving Azertyuiop to come home nine lengths ahead of the 2002 winner Flagship Uberalles (beaten two lengths

*Azertyuiop on his way to a nine-length success in the
Queen Mother Champion Chase; Moscow Flyer
had parted company with his rider four out*

further than he had been at Sandown), with another ex-Arkle winner Tiutchev a length and a half further away in third and Cenkos, third in the two previous runnings, a creditable fourth. Azertyuiop's performance was one of the best in the race in recent times. He produced a breathtaking round of jumping, going on at the seventh of the twelve fences and quickening magnificently round the turn into the final straight before running on in fine style all the way to the line. It was a major anti-climax that Moscow Flyer failed to complete, leaving the question of which was the better of two outstanding two-mile chasers still unsettled, for the time being at least. If there is anything between Moscow Flyer and Azertyuiop, it surely cannot be much. Among Champion Chase winners of Timeform's experience, only two have earned higher ratings than Moscow Flyer and Azertyuiop. They are Flyingbolt and the 1965 winner, the exhilarating Dunkirk who, in an all-too-short career, also carried 12-7 to victory in the Mackeson Gold Cup, then run over two miles and a few yards.

Arkle's stable-companion Flyingbolt, along with Desert Orchid, had cause to be mentioned earlier in Azertyuiop's essay that year in connection with the Victor Chandler

(then a handicap rather than the level-weights contest it is today), that race, rather than the Champion Chase, being the one that earned Azertyuiop his rating just behind Moscow Flyer that season.

The big handicaps offer more potential than weight-for-age championship events for finding out just how good the top horses are. Desert Orchid, for example, earned his Timeform rating of 187 not on any of his appearances in the King George VI Chase (which he won four times), nor in winning the Cheltenham Gold Cup, but in the Racing Post Handicap at Kempton in February 1990 in which, under a penalty and carrying 12-3, he won by eight lengths, putting up the finest performance seen over jumps since the halcyon days of Arkle, Flyingbolt and Mill House. Arkle's performances conceding lumps of weight in handicaps such as the Leopardstown Chase, the Hennessy and the Whitbread showed far better than his level-weights Gold Cup-winning performances what he was capable of. Likewise, Flyingbolt, whose career was dogged by illness and injury, showed when winning the Massey Ferguson Gold Cup (under 12-6 by fifteen lengths) and the Irish Grand National (carrying 12-7) that he was almost as good at his best as Arkle. An objective study of the form-book put those two performances ahead of Flyingbolt's form when running away with the Champion Two-Mile Chase at the Cheltenham Festival in the same season.

Azertyuiop was the latest winner of the Queen Mother Champion Chase, as the two-mile championship has come to be known. He won in the style of an outstanding chaser, jumping well and drawing clear in tremendous fashion, but the form he showed was 10 lb below his season's best. Azertyuiop's performance in the Victor Chandler Chase at Ascot in January was the one that earned him his Timeform rating of 182 and, as such, deserves pride of place in a review of his campaign. Azertyuiop didn't win the Victor Chandler, the best two-mile handicap of the season, but in going down by a neck to Isio, to whom he was conceding 19 lb, he put up—by our reckoning at least—the equal best performance (with Carvill's Hill's breathtaking display in the 1991 Welsh National) seen in a handicap over jumps since Desert Orchid's in the Racing Post. Desert Orchid put up several other really outstanding weight-carrying efforts in handicaps—including victories in the Whitbread and the Irish Grand National—and he underlined his versatility by continuing to give brilliant performances at two miles, at which distance he was regarded as a specialist for long enough. In the same season he completed the King George VI Chase/Gold Cup double, he also won the Tingle Creek (then a handicap) by twelve lengths, conceding between 20 lb and 28 lb to four rivals, and the inaugural running of the Victor Chandler, pushed to the limit by the very smart Panto Prince, who was in receipt of 22 lb. Desert Orchid prevailed by a head at Ascot in a driving finish after a tremendous duel with Panto Prince from the home turn, and the latest Victor Chandler also produced an epic.

With 7/2 favourite Azertyuiop carrying top weight of 11-10 at Ascot, only three of the thirteen runners—the others being the previous year's winner Young Devereaux (10-7) and Isio (10-5)—were set to run off their correct marks. Isio had finished third to Azertyuiop in the Arkle Trophy at Cheltenham the previous season and had a 19 lb pull for twelve lengths. Azertyuiop and Isio stretched clear of the Victor Chandler field in the home straight and, in a stirring duel, with very little in it from the second last, the pair produced good jumps at the final fence and answered their riders' every call on the flat. Azertyuiop nosed ahead briefly before just giving best in a pulsating finish, the first two nine lengths clear of third-placed Got One Too who had a further four to spare over fourth-placed Native Scout, an improving Irish handicapper who had finished a good second to Moscow Flyer in a Grade 2 event at Leopardstown on his most recent start. The in-form Hot Shots, 11 lb out of the weights, came fifth. Six of the Victor Chandler runners won next time out, including four of the first five home, and the form looked as solid by the end of the season as it did at the time. If there was another horse in training remotely capable of giving Isio a 19-lb beating over two miles, it could only have been Moscow Flyer. When Moscow Flyer and Isio met later in the season, however, it was at level weights in the Melling Chase over two and a half miles at Aintree where Moscow Flyer, with his ears pricked, beat Isio by six lengths. Immediately after the Victor Chandler, incidentally, Isio was quoted at only 14/1 for the Champion Chase in a market headed by defending champion Moscow Flyer and Azertyuiop.

There was so much discussion in the latest season of the pros and cons of running top-class horses under big weights in handicaps that it is worth recording the view of Azertyuiop's trainer after the Victor Chandler. 'Last year he had soft races and learned little, he was always winning on the bridle. He will have learned more from this than any other race he has had over fences.'

Moscow Flyer's blunder in the Champion Chase only added to his earlier history of jumping lapses—'much has been said and written on the subject of his jumping but, though fallible, he is mostly fast and accurate' stated *Chasers & Hurdlers*—but it was the last time in his career that he would fail to complete. That was just as well, perhaps, because Moscow Flyer's essay that season had begun by expressing some concern about his jumping errors tarnishing his otherwise superb record.

Badsworth Boy won his first sixteen completed steeplechases. The brilliant Moscow Flyer has now won his first completed fourteen but, if he's not careful, he will be joining Badsworth Boy as one of those champions whose reputation for making calamitous jumping mistakes was in danger at times of overshadowing his outstanding merit.

Moscow Flyer added two more Grade 1 wins to his tally by the end of the 2003/04 campaign, earning Timeform's Champion Jumper award (ahead of Azertyuiop and Best Mate who won his third Cheltenham Gold Cup that season), the first specialist two-mile chaser to be so honoured since Badsworth Boy in 1982/83.

Azertyuiop wasn't seen out again after Cheltenham but Moscow Flyer went on to contest Grade 1 events, as planned (hence his break after Christmas), at both Aintree and Punchestown. He atoned somewhat for his Cheltenham lapse when recording two more impressive victories, firstly in the Martell Cognac Melling Chase over two and half miles. Moscow Flyer settled better than at Cheltenham and jumped well, apart from getting a little too close to the fifth. He went on to win by six lengths after a duel from the third last with the top-class Isio, Moscow Flyer asserting himself between the last two fences and going away on the run-in. Moscow Flyer passed the post ears pricked, with Native Upmanship, winner of the race in the two previous years, a further thirteen lengths behind Isio in third. Back at two miles for the Betdaq.com Champion Chase at Punchestown, shortly after the end of the British season, Moscow Flyer didn't need to run anywhere near his best in a field lacking a British-trained challenger. Leading four out and soon quickening clear, he was always in control and found more than enough, when shaken up, to hold off Rathgar Beau and Strong Run by two lengths and six.

'Two-mile chasers don't always get the recognition they deserve but, in Moscow Flyer and Azertyuiop, the sport currently has two of the best it has ever seen and should celebrate them while it can' opined *Chasers & Hurdlers* 2003/04. The good news was that the rivalry between Moscow Flyer and Azertyuiop endured for another season, but what was less easy to foresee at the end of the 2003/04 campaign was that a third party, the latest Arkle winner **Well Chief**, would be up to rubbing shoulders with his two predecessors. Well Chief (rated 150p) won all three of his starts in novice chases, the Arkle being only his second outing over fences. He followed up in the Maghull Novices' Chase at Aintree and was entitled to improve further given his lack of experience over fences, but the Arkle field wasn't a vintage one and he hadn't even been the best horse at the weights; as a five-year-old he had received weight from runner-up Kicking King, who finished just a length behind. Unlike Moscow Flyer and Azertyuiop who had always looked the part for chasing, the angular Well Chief lacked size and substance, though that was now largely academic given the above-average ability he had already shown as a novice.

By the end of the following season the now eleven-year-old Moscow Flyer had his highest annual rating of 184+, ahead of Azertyuiop and Well Chief (three and five years his junior respectively) on 182, a rating also matched by the Gold Cup winner Kicking King. A quartet of chasers this good in the same season remains a unique occurrence in the *Chasers & Hurdlers* era, and while the likes of Kauto Star and then Sprinter Sacre have come along since to supersede him, Moscow Flyer's status as the very best among some other outstanding contemporaries entitles him to a place among the 'modern greats' at the very least.

'In the 'sixties, I was one of the best players around. You have your moment of glory and then it fades. Mind you, they'll never say that about Muhammad Ali!' BBC golfing commentator Peter Alliss displayed his appreciation of the universal truth that all but the legendary sporting heroes eventually fade from the public consciousness. It is rare for sporting fame to endure much beyond its natural span, as it will with Muhammad Ali, or has, to close followers of Alliss' own sport, with such as Harry Vardon, Bobby Jones and Arnold Palmer. Easter Hero, Golden Miller, Arkle, Red Rum and Desert Orchid are among steeplechasers in a similar category. Theirs is the nearest to immortality that a racehorse can achieve. Brilliant performers, however, even of the recent past, are sometimes forgotten and only time will tell whether Moscow Flyer and his three superb contemporaries among the chasers of 2004/05, Azertyuiop, Kicking King and Well Chief, will achieve legendary status. In terms of ability, they deserve to be remembered, as does a season which is unique in the era of *Chasers & Hurdlers* in featuring four horses rated above 180. The best of the quartet, Moscow Flyer, is Timeform's Champion Jumper and highest-rated chaser for the second year running. He is a phenomenon among steeplechasers, winner of nineteen of his twenty completed starts over fences. But for the fact that two-milers do not always get the recognition they deserve, Moscow Flyer would be assured of a place among the all-time greats. On form, only Desert Orchid has stronger claims to that overused mantle 'the greatest steeplechaser since Arkle'.

For those jumping devotees who tend to assume that the glories of the past supersede those of the present, the Timeform view of Moscow Flyer's exalted status may come as a surprise. It will certainly surprise general sports enthusiasts for whom Cheltenham Gold Cup winners and Grand National winners are the be-all and end-all of steeplechasing. Desert Orchid's sparkling career, which included a record four wins in the King George VI Chase, featured numerous performances superior, on form, to his hard-fought victory in the 1989 Cheltenham Gold Cup, yet his duel in the mud with Yahoo was voted the 'greatest race of all time' in a *Racing Post* poll in the latest season (Red Rum's Grand National victory over Crisp came second, Grundy's battle with Bustino in the King George VI and Queen Elizabeth Stakes third). The widespread lament for Best Mate's enforced absence from the latest Gold Cup was further clear evidence of the race's hold on the public imagination. Had a similar fate befallen Moscow Flyer before the Queen Mother Champion Chase, the news would almost certainly have been confined to the racing pages.

It would be trite to reiterate the reasons usually given by those who say it is impossible to compare sporting figures from different eras. One most often used, though, is the difficulty of assessing the quality of the opposition faced by respective protagonists from different generations. There should never be any such reservation about the quality of opposition faced by Moscow Flyer. Like Moscow Flyer himself, Azertyuiop and Well Chief are among the top dozen chasers seen over any distance since the *Chasers & Hurdlers* series began thirty years ago. Using Timeform ratings from the Timeform Black Book series between 1962/63 and 1974/75, and ratings compiled on the Timeform scale by Randall and Morris for *A Century of Champions*, it is possible to arrive at an authoritative list of the top chasers since the beginning of the twentieth century. Moscow Flyer, Azertyuiop and Well Chief all make the top twenty (as do Kicking King and, at his peak, Best Mate).

Moscow Flyer, Azertyuiop and Well Chief all met in the 2005 Champion Chase for what was billed as the highlight of the Festival, though anything they served up at Cheltenham was going to struggle to match the 'epic encounter' between the three of them in front of packed stands for the Tingle Creek earlier in the season:

The clash of Moscow Flyer, Azertyuiop and Well Chief in the latest Queen Mother Champion Chase—'the race of the Festival'—would have been even more of a marketing man's dream had it not already taken place at Sandown back in December. Moscow Flyer and Azertyuiop, each an outstanding winner of the Queen Mother Champion Chase, had met twice the previous season, Moscow Flyer beating Azertyuiop convincingly in the Tingle Creek but parting company with his rider at Cheltenham and leaving Azertyuiop to come home a nine-length winner of the Queen Mother Champion Chase, giving one of the best performances in the race in recent times. The question of which was the better looked likely to be settled in the latest William Hill-Tingle Creek, the mid-season championship for the two-milers. Azertyuiop had warmed up for Sandown with a tip-top performance—winning by five lengths under top weight—in the Haldon Gold Cup at Exeter (a limited handicap in which he had slipped and unseated his rider at the first the year before). Moscow Flyer arrived

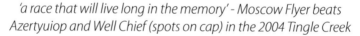

*'a race that will live long in the memory' - Moscow Flyer beats
Azertyuiop and Well Chief (spots on cap) in the 2004 Tingle Creek*

Modern Greats

at Sandown, as he had twelve months earlier, with a straightforward victory under his belt at odds on in the Ballymore Properties Fortria Chase at Navan in November (he won by twenty-five lengths after the last-fence departure of closest challenger Rathgar Beau). The betting public sided with the younger Azertyuiop at Sandown, the market going 6/5-on Azertyuiop, 2/1 Moscow Flyer, with the previous year's Arkle winner Well Chief at 6/1, Azertyuiop's stable-companion Cenkos at 25/1 and 80/1 bar in a field of seven. The race, which carried prize money down to sixth, was reopened after only the four named were originally entered. In a concession to Channel 4's schedule, Sandown dropped the parade stipulated in the conditions, a spectacle popular with racegoers involving the runners being led past the stands before being allowed to canter down.

And so to a race that will live long in the memory of the crowd, at 16,300 one of the biggest in Sandown's history and said to be larger than for any all-jumping card at the course. What was billed as a 'head-to-head' in the Tingle Creek turned into a three-way battle, Well Chief managing to bridge the considerable gap from leading novice to championship contender with a much improved performance which saw him right in contention turning for home. Azertyuiop's jockey had made the first move in the Champion Chase, but he decided to stalk Moscow Flyer in the Tingle Creek, the latter taking over from the front-running Cenkos four out. As in the previous year, Moscow Flyer was never going to be beaten once he established himself in front, especially after being much more fluent than Azertyuiop at the third last. Moscow Flyer produced excellent jumps at the last two fences for good measure and went on to win by a length and a half and a short head, giving the impression he could have found more had it been required. Azertyuiop briefly lost second to Well Chief at the last before rallying on the flat, the first three twenty-five lengths clear of fourth-placed Cenkos in a race that wasn't run at a particularly searching gallop. There was some criticism of Azertyuiop's rider for not harrying Moscow Flyer earlier, but there was no doubt that the best horse on the day had won. Moscow Flyer was simply superb, the first three all putting up performances of outstanding merit in an epic encounter that proved to be the race of the season.

Although he'd come off worst of the three main contenders in the Tingle Creek, Well Chief was the revelation of the race in just his fifth start over fences. But was he flattered to finish that close to Moscow Flyer and Azertyuiop? Not a bit of it.

The 'big two' among the two-mile chasers were now definitely the 'big three', anyone doubting the form of the Tingle Creek having only to wait until Well Chief's next completed outing for conclusive proof that, along with Moscow Flyer and Azertyuiop, he ranks among the best two-mile chasers that the sport has ever seen. The latest running of the Victor Chandler Chase was transferred to Cheltenham's end-of-January fixture because of Ascot's redevelopment. The presence of Well Chief, carrying 11-10, meant that half the field was out of the handicap proper. Well Chief's weight equated to a BHB handicap mark of 176, 8 lb higher than that allotted to Azertyuiop when he was just touched off by Isio in the race the previous year, and 2 lb higher than that allotted to Azertyuiop when winning the Haldon Gold Cup at Exeter on his reappearance. Well Chief himself had been beaten in a handicap (off a BHB mark of 153) on his reappearance, though he all but got up against Armaturk (who was conceding him 1 lb) after being dropped out in last and still having plenty to do two out. When he lined up for the Victor Chandler, Well Chief, who fell four out when seemingly going well in the rescheduled Castleford Chase at Wetherby, was without a win since landing the Arkle/Maghull double in the spring. Easy to back in the Victor Chandler at 5/1, Well Chief came close to repeating the form he showed when a close third in the Tingle Creek, jumping soundly, moving up to lead two out and quickening decisively. His performance in beating Thisthatandtother by a length and three quarters, conceding the runner-up 20 lb, wasn't quite of the calibre—at least the way we looked at the form—of Azertyuiop's cracking effort in the race the previous year, though it was the best handicap performance seen in the 2004/05 season, marginally better than Azertyuiop's at Exeter.

Like Well Chief, Moscow Flyer and Azertyuiop were also successful again before the three of them reconvened at Cheltenham where this time it was Azertyuiop whose jumping, unusually for him, let him down.

There was a field of eight for the Queen Mother Champion Chase, Moscow Flyer (6/4), Azertyuiop (2/1) and Well Chief (7/2) standing out. The progressive Oneway, unbeaten in five handicaps in the current season, and Central House, winner of the Grade 1 Dial-A-Bet Chase at Christmas in the absence of Moscow Flyer and beaten only once in his last four outings, started at 16/1 and 25/1 respectively, with Venn Ottery (fifth in the race the year before) at 50/1 and Azertyuiop's stable-companions Kadarann and Cenkos (in the frame in the last three editions) at 100/1. One of jumping's most endearing qualities is that its stars tend to be around for longer than their counterparts on the Flat. Although the top jumpers return season after season, however, only Royal Relief had regained the two-mile championship at Cheltenham since it was first run in 1959. He won the Champion Chase as an eight-year-old and, after coming second at nine, won it for a second time at the age of ten (Royal Relief made eight appearances in the race in all, also finishing second on two other occasions and third once). Ten is towards the top of the age range for a Champion Chase winner, but Skymas was eleven when he won in 1976 and Moscow Flyer emulated him when producing another magnificent display in the latest edition. Unfortunately, for the second year running, an eagerly-anticipated close duel between Moscow Flyer and Azertyuiop at Cheltenham did not materialise, Azertyuiop's winning chance effectively ended by a bad mistake at the water, the sixth fence. Moscow Flyer travelled strongly just behind the leaders Central House and Kadarann from the start, jumping well except for getting in close four from home (the fence at which he departed the previous year). Leading at the third last, Moscow Flyer was chased all the way from that point by Well Chief, always looking in command and winning by two lengths, with Azertyuiop (subsequently found to have pulled muscles in his abdomen) thirteen lengths behind Well Chief in third and seven lengths ahead of fourth-placed Oneway. Moscow Flyer, mobbed by well-wishers and euphoric Irish racegoers waving the country's tricolour, received a stirring ovation on his return to the unsaddling enclosure where his jockey Barry Geraghty executed a Frankie Dettori-style flying dismount. The celebrations must have gone on well into the night, none presumably more enthusiastic than those at Seven Barrows where Moscow Flyer's trainer was a house guest of Nicky Henderson, whose stable had two winners on the same card.

Once again, Moscow Flyer's campaign ended with visits to Aintree and Punchestown but back in Ireland his old jumping flaws resurfaced, contributing to his first defeat in twenty completed starts over fences.

Moscow Flyer extended his unbeaten record in races completed over fences to nineteen with a second successive victory in Aintree's two-and-a-half-mile Melling Chase. Moscow Flyer turned the six-runner event into an exhibition, hardly turning a hair in landing the odds by sixteen lengths from Le Roi Miguel. Moscow Flyer misjudged the second fence in the Melling, getting in a shade too close, but it was the only semblance of a mistake that he made. The days when perceived flaws in Moscow Flyer's jumping technique were a hot topic of conversation seemed to be behind him. The Melling was his seventh successive victory since the last hiccup at the 2004 Cheltenham Festival. 'It has taken six years but he has finally got there,' joked Moscow Flyer's trainer after the Melling. 'Barry said he is becoming a nice ride and you can settle him. He was always travelling and jumping superbly.' Mrs Harrington spoke too soon. The Kerrygold Champion Chase at Punchestown, shortly after the end of the British season, was billed as another lap of honour for Moscow Flyer who started at 4/1-on in a field of seven which did not include an overseas challenger. Moscow Flyer would not settle in the race, despite a sound pace, and, in front four out, looked like being strongly pressed by Rathgar Beau even before making a monumental blunder at the second last, the same fence at which he had unseated Geraghty in the race two years previously, at a time when lapses in his jumping were in danger of becoming a little too common. Moscow Flyer stayed on his feet in the latest renewal, after handing the advantage to Rathgar Beau, and he rallied gamely from the last to be beaten only a short head. The judge took longer examining the photo-finish print—the result was very close to being a dead-heat—than the race itself had taken. Because of the width of the chase course, Punchestown does not have 'mirror image' facilities for photo finishes, and it isn't altogether clear from the official print that Moscow Flyer was beaten.

Modern Greats

Even Homer nods - the mistake two out in the Champion Chase at Punchestown which contributes to Moscow Flyer's first defeat in twenty completed starts over fences

As for Well Chief and Azertyuiop, they had clashed again three days earlier on the final day of the season in Britain, turned out as the 'big guns' for their respective stables in what developed into an all-out battle for the trainers' championship which went right to the wire.

> Well Chief and Azertyuiop met for the fourth time in the Betfred Celebration Chase at Sandown on the last day of the season. The entire field of nine was made up of runners trained by Martin Pipe and by Paul Nicholls whose battle for the trainers' championship was a feature of the last few weeks of the season. Well Chief's owner admitted that, but for the close finish to the trainers' title, Well Chief might not have been pressed into action at Sandown. However, reports passed on through Channel 4's *Morning Line* programme that Well Chief had been confined to his box for four days were categorically denied. Perhaps because of the reports, Well Chief was sent off at 9/4, with Azertyuiop the 11/10 favourite. Next in the betting at 10/1 were Contraband, the latest winner of the Arkle in the Johnson colours, and Le Roi Miguel, runner-up to Moscow Flyer in the Melling Chase at Aintree. The two highest-rated chasers trained in Britain dominated the Celebration Chase, Well Chief drawing level at two apiece in their personal battle when beating Azertyuiop, who reportedly suffered a bad overreach and faces a lengthy absence, by four lengths, with Contraband a further ten behind in third. Well Chief jumped better than he had in the Game Spirit and was ridden clear up the hill after mastering Azertyuiop between the last two fences.

Well Chief's victory finally put the title out of Paul Nicholls' reach. Incidentally, as well as saddling five runners in the Celebration Chase, Martin Pipe ran seven horses in the Betfred Gold Cup and the same number in the opening handicap hurdle on Sandown's card (after declaring ten!), one of whom, Commercial Flyer, was making his third start in as many days. That proved to be the last of Martin Pipe's record fifteen trainers' championships; he retired a year later, handing over to his son David, while Paul Nicholls went on to take the title in the next seven seasons.

Nicholls was unable to call on Azertyuiop, however, who failed to recover fully from the injury he sustained in the Celebration Chase and was eventually retired in the autumn of 2006. In an abrupt end to the era of these three outstanding chasers Well Chief failed to recapture his very best form in what proved a stop-start career thereafter, while in the 2005/06 season 'old age seemed not so much to creep up on Moscow Flyer as to overwhelm him'. He was beaten at odds on in his two usual races in Ireland, the Fortria and the Dial-A-Bet (he missed the Tingle Creek with a lung infection), and made what proved to be his final appearance in the Champion Chase the following spring:

> In the end, the decision to retire Moscow Flyer virtually took itself, an announcement made just minutes after he had finished fifth of the six finishers in the latest Champion Chase. But up to that point, with the weight of his magnificent record behind him, it was difficult for most of those who had anything to do with Moscow Flyer—be it his connections or supporters, or even those who had to write about him—to bow to the inevitable and accept that an outstanding career was drawing to a close . . .

> Moscow Flyer was the senior runner in what was his fourth Champion Chase, and he was attempting to become only the second twelve-year-old winner after Skymas in 1977. Although hampered when Kauto Star fell early on, Moscow Flyer was beaten on merit, outpaced when it mattered and ridden out to pass the post nearly a dozen lengths behind the winner Newmill. Denied a final rapturous return to the unsaddling enclosure, despite the efforts of his rider to get him in the frame, Moscow Flyer had at least been given what turned out to be a valedictory round of applause as he circled the parade ring beforehand.

Barry Geraghty partnered Moscow Flyer in all bar two of his races over hurdles and fences and to twenty-five of his twenty-six wins, thirteen of which came at Grade 1 level. Moscow Flyer would have been the horse of a lifetime in the career of most jockeys, though Geraghty's subsequent association with Sprinter Sacre requires some diplomacy on the part of the rider when inevitably asked to compare them.

Moscow Flyer actually competed one more time, winning a charity Flat race at the 2007 Punchestown Festival ridden by Jessica Harrington's teenage daughter Kate. Now at the Irish National Stud, Moscow Flyer has served as an equine ambassador for the Irish Horse Welfare Trust in his retirement.

The junior member of the trio, Well Chief went on to contest three more Champion Chases for David Pipe. Well Chief started the even-money favourite for his next appearance in the race in 2007, having made a sparkling comeback from almost two years off the track in the Game Spirit Chase at Newbury after heat had been detected in a foreleg following his win at Sandown. However, Well Chief got no further than the second fence at Cheltenham and then failed to stay when odds on for the Melling Chase at Aintree, finishing third to Monet's Garden. Still only eight years old, Well Chief earned a rating of 167+ that season, putting him above the eventual Champion Chase winner Voy Por Ustedes (163). Another absence of almost two years followed before Well Chief contested the Champion Chase again, though this time he went straight to Cheltenham without a preparatory run, finishing an excellent seven lengths second to the previous year's outstanding winner Master Minded. That effort ensured Well Chief kept his rating of 167+, but in a five-race campaign in 2009/10 it became clear he was no longer the force of old. Even so, he made a winning return in the Connaught Chase at Cheltenham (beating a below-par Master Minded into third) that season before bowing out in the

Champion Chase, his sixth appearance at the Cheltenham Festival, when last of the seven finishers behind Big Zeb.

It was **Master Minded**, another French recruit to Paul Nicholls' stable from Guillaume Macaire, as Azertyuiop had been, who emerged as the best two-mile chaser between the Moscow Flyer era and Sprinter Sacre. While Moscow Flyer had stiff competition from his fellow two-milers, Master Minded had to share the limelight with some top-notch stable-companions, as *Chasers & Hurdlers 2007/08* explained:

It was almost like 1983 all over again. Twenty-four hours before an extraordinary collective performance by the members of one stable in the Cheltenham Gold Cup, another from the same yard put up the season's outstanding display of individual brilliance over two miles in the Queen Mother Champion Chase. Twenty-five years ago, the Michael Dickinson-trained Badsworth Boy set a new record when winning the two-mile championship by a distance, though for all the merit of his individual performance (he was Timeform's Champion Jumper that season, rated 179, 2 lb higher than the Gold Cup winner), it was the history-making achievement of his stable-companions that made the biggest impression. The Dickinson team, led by Bregawn, took the first five places in the next day's Gold Cup, an achievement which understandably took precedence in the public mind. History may not have been made at the latest Cheltenham Festival, but Master Minded ran out the easiest and most impressive winner of the Champion Chase since Badsworth Boy, while his trainer Paul Nicholls' feat of saddling the first three in the following day's Gold Cup is the closest anyone has come to Dickinson's record.

It would have been inconceivable right up until the latest Champion Chase that any horse would come close to stealing the limelight from his stable's two main Gold Cup contenders, Denman and Kauto Star, whose clash had been so keenly awaited all season. However, the BHA now have Master Minded as the highest-rated chaser in training, his mark of 186 in the Anglo-Irish Classifications of 2007/08 some 4 lb higher than Denman and 7 lb higher than Kauto Star. This is the reverse, incidentally, of how Timeform currently ranks the trio—Kauto Star 182, Denman 180p and Master Minded 179. Whatever the pecking order, there is no question that all three are outstanding chasers and Master Minded fully deserves to be bracketed with his higher profile stable companions. Coincidentally, his Timeform rating of 179 is exactly the same as that achieved by Badsworth Boy after his first Cheltenham win.

By our reckoning, Moscow Flyer put up an even better effort than Badsworth Boy when winning the second of his Champion Chases as an eleven-year-old in 2005 from two other outstanding two-milers, Well Chief and Azertyuiop. At least until Master Minded came along in the latest season, the standard of the best two-mile chasers in recent seasons had been less exceptional, the Champion Chase being won in the years since Moscow Flyer by Newmill and Voy Por Ustedes. That pair were in the field again for the latest Champion Chase, sponsored by Seasons Holidays, Newmill having deteriorated considerably since his success two years earlier, but the reliable Voy Por Ustedes clearly as good as ever.

A wide-margin win is not, of course, necessarily the sign of a good horse—plenty of horses of no more than average ability win ordinary races over jumps day in day out by a long way. However, the competitive nature of races at Cheltenham means that a surprisingly small number of races at the Festival in the twenty-five years since Badsworth Boy have been won by more than the nineteen lengths which Master Minded had to spare over Voy Por Ustedes. For Master Minded to win by that margin, over the minimum trip, in conditions which were not especially testing, and in a championship race against the best available opposition, was clearly the performance of a horse well above normal Champion Chase-winning standard. For the record, the only Festival winners since Badsworth Boy to score by a 'distance' were the 1995 National Hunt Chase winner Front Line and the 1999 Royal & SunAlliance Chase winner Looks Like Trouble. Rushing Wild (runner-up in the following year's Gold Cup) took the 1992 Foxhunter by twenty-five lengths, while twenty lengths was the winning margin for Northern Bay (who was left clear at the last) in the 1985 National Hunt Chase, Gainsay in the 1987 Ritz Club Chase (the only handicap to be won by that far), Fantus in the 1995 Foxhunter and Ventana Canyon in the 1996 Arkle.

Just as impressive as Master Minded's margin of victory was the manner of his win. By the top of the hill, Voy Por Ustedes looked the only possible danger to Master Minded as their six rivals were either beating a retreat or unable to go with the leading pair who had both been held up initially off the strong early pace. Third favourite Tamarinbleu had already dropped away by that stage, having seemed to resent being taken on for the lead by Schindlers Hunt, who was still holding on to third at the time, but about to pay for going off too quickly. Master Minded's stable-companion Twist Magic, who had looked Nicholls' chief hope for the race for much of the season, looked nothing like so well as Master Minded in the preliminaries, and was already beaten, having been held up, along with Newmill and Fair Along, while Ireland's chief hope Mansony had been pulled up at the fifth after trailing. Turning down the hill, Master Minded was still travelling very strongly in front with Voy Por Ustedes nudged along to keep in touch on his outer as they drew clear. Going to two out, Voy Por Ustedes came firmly under the whip and was soon left behind, Master Minded drawing right away round the turn, meeting the last fence spot-on and Ruby Walsh enjoying the luxury of being able to pat him down the neck well before they crossed the line. Voy Por Ustedes was himself sixteen lengths clear of the remainder in second, Fair Along picking off tiring rivals for third, with Schindlers Hunt fourth, Newmill fifth, Twist Magic only sixth and Tamarinbleu last to finish.

…it was rather ironic that Voy Por Ustedes should be denied a second Champion Chase by a younger rival as he had himself been only the second six-year-old to win it and looked set to have youth on his side for another season or two. As has already been said, Master Minded was an outstanding winner by any standards, though his achievements were made all the more extraordinary as he was a five-year-old. No horse of his age had ever even contested the Champion Chase since its inception in 1959. Earlier in the twentieth century, Master Minded would have been considered less of a rarity. The five-year-old Lutteur III won the Grand National in 1909 (the last of his age to do so) and fifteen years later the inaugural Cheltenham Gold Cup went to the five-year-old Red Splash, the first of three to win the race (including the great Golden Miller). But five-year-olds are no longer able to run in the Grand National and no horse of that age has contested the Gold Cup since World War II, although the race is still open to them. It was not until the influx of young French-bred jumpers into Britain in the last few decades that running five-year-olds over fences became common practice again, though, for the most part, their success has naturally enough been restricted to novice events. In France, on the other hand, where horses can start running over fences from the autumn of their three-year-old season, and where their four-year-old season is effectively the French equivalent of being a novice chaser in Britain, they are considered more or less fully-fledged chasers as five-year-olds—three have won the Grand Steeple-Chase de Paris in the last twenty years. A winner twice over fences at Auteuil as a four-year-old, Master Minded was ineligible for novice chases in Britain.

. . . What made Master Minded's win at Cheltenham even more noteworthy was that he was taking on his elders at level weights within a year of the BHA finally amending the weight-for-age scale for chasers. Master Minded was a ridiculously easy winner of the race as it was, but had he been getting weight from his rivals as well, it would surely have been the last nail in the coffin of an over-generous weight allowance which five-year-olds did not need. There couldn't have been a better or more timely example than Master Minded to prove the point.

Master Minded was sent to Aintree after Cheltenham but suffered a shock reverse (at 5/2-on) in the Melling Chase, beaten eighteen lengths by Voy Por Ustedes. Most observers, as well as Ruby Walsh, blamed lack of stamina over the two and a half mile trip, though *Chasers & Hurdlers* concluded that a 'temporary physical problem looked a more likely explanation' following a mistake at the second last. Incidentally, Badsworth Boy was also beaten at short odds at Aintree after winning at Cheltenham in 1983, taking a crashing fall at the last when already a long way behind eventual winner Artifice in the two-mile limited handicap chase.

'For most chasers his age, it would be expected that Master Minded's best days would be ahead of him' concluded his essay that season, 'but, whatever he achieves from now on, he has already proven himself to be an exceptional chaser.' Master Minded never put up a performance quite as spectacular as his 2008 Champion Chase victory again but in his second season in Britain he enjoyed an unbeaten campaign, landing the odds in the Tingle Creek, the Victor Chandler and the Champion Chases at both Cheltenham and Punchestown. His best performance came in the Victor Chandler (in its second running as a Grade 1 contest) when beating Petit Robin by sixteen lengths. The same rival was only nine lengths back in third at Cheltenham when Well Chief chased Master Minded home but 'those churlish enough to criticise Master Minded's performance should perhaps bear in mind the post-race comments of his trainer. 'We didn't set out to win by twenty lengths,' said Nicholls. 'If we look after him he'll stay at the top of the game for a few years yet."

Master Minded became the eleventh horse to win the Queen Mother Champion Chase at least twice and the first since Viking Flagship in 1994 and 1995 to win two consecutive editions. His 2009/10 campaign therefore held the promise of his joining Badsworth Boy as a three-time winner. Come the day, he was odds on to do so, but only after overcoming injury earlier in the season.

> Master Minded began his latest campaign—after the summer break—with a record of only one defeat in his last eight races, by Voy Por Ustedes in the Melling Chase over two and a half miles at Aintree on his last start of 2007/08. But that soon became two defeats in nine. Conceding 10 lb all round to five opponents in the newly-instituted Connaught Chase at Cheltenham's Open meeting in November, Master Minded was clearly not himself, hanging right for much of the race, when only third behind Well Chief and Mahogany Blaze. Scans after the Connaught Chase revealed the likely cause of Master Minded's display, a fractured rib. Master Minded missed his intended appearance in the Tingle Creek at Sandown which was won in his absence by stable-mate Twist Magic who also went on to win the Victor Chandler at Ascot in January. Master Minded meanwhile took exercise only on the mechanical walker until the New Year. He was off the course for three months all told, returning to action— after consideration had been given to going straight to Cheltenham—in the totepool Game Spirit Chase at Newbury in mid-February where, coincidentally, one of his four opponents was the smart Fix The Rib, who started third favourite behind Master Minded (odds on) and Voy Por Ustedes. Except for a lapse at the final fence, where both he and his rider did very well to survive a monumental blunder, Master Minded seemed back to his old self. Always moving well until that last-fence howler, and giving a vintage display of fluent jumping, Master Minded scarcely came off the bridle to win by thirteen lengths and a length and a quarter from Mahogany Blaze and Fix The Rib, with Voy Por Ustedes only fourth.
>
> With his rib—and his reputation—apparently repaired, Master Minded 'worked brilliantly', according to his trainer, with Kauto Star at home the week before Cheltenham. 'He's back to where he was two years ago,' announced Paul Nicholls who must have gone to Cheltenham with very high hopes of a fifth

victory in the Queen Mother Champion Chase in which he also saddled Twist Magic. Things went wrong for Twist Magic from a very early stage, starting when he bolted on the way to post, and he was already under pressure when blundering four out before eventually being pulled up. Even worse, Master Minded didn't travel with his usual zest and he too was in trouble some way out, no match on the day for the Irish-trained pair Big Zeb and Forpadydeplasterer, and even losing third to Kalahari King near the finish. A gloomy Nicholls made no excuses at the time. 'He has won two but might never win another, the mare has had numerous foals and none of them trained on and I've always had it at the back of my mind that it might happen to him,' he said afterwards. 'Something might come to light but I bet it doesn't.' The other thing Nicholls did consider at the time was the state of the going at Cheltenham. It was good, the same as returned for the Game Spirit, but Master Minded hadn't encountered anything firmer than good to soft before those two races and was reportedly found to be suffering from sore knees after Cheltenham which makes it possible that he does ideally need more give in the ground, as Nicholls has always maintained. After further investigation, Master Minded underwent an operation in the summer to help his breathing.

Master Minded was given another crack at winning the Champion Chase for a third time in 2011 only to let down favourite-backers again; he was already beaten when making a monumental blunder two out, after which he wasn't persevered with. That, though, was the only disappointment of a resurgent campaign which resulted in Master Minded's rating going back up to 175, one bettered that season only by the King George and Gold Cup winner Long Run. This was also the campaign in which Master Minded's attentions were once again turned, successfully this time, to races beyond two miles.

The prediction was made in *Chasers & Hurdlers 2009/10* that rekindling the career of Master Minded might hold the key to whether Paul Nicholls claimed a sixth successive trainers' championship in the latest season. In the event, Master Minded enjoyed a splendid campaign, earning £220,902, more than any other inmate at Manor Farm Stables with the exception of the hurdler Big Buck's who was the stable's top earner for the second year running. The prize money earned by Master Minded, who won four of his five starts, certainly helped to keep the mounting challenge from Seven Barrows at bay for another year in the closest finish to the trainers' championship in any of the six years that Manor Farm Stables has headed the table. With stable stalwarts Kauto Star and Denman reaching the veteran stage, even more will be expected of three-years-younger Master Minded in the next season when he has been pencilled in as a possible successor to the same owner's Kauto Star as the stable's principal hope for the King George VI Chase. Master Minded will probably have to face Long Run at Kempton, the new young star from Seven Barrows having upstaged Kauto Star in the latest King George and then won the Cheltenham Gold Cup from Denman and Kauto Star. Master Minded's most impressive victory in the Melling Chase—only his second outing in three years at much further than two miles—

A nine-length win in the Melling Chase at Aintree, Master Minded's eighth and final Grade 1 success

confirmed not only that he is back very close to his top-class best, but also that he is, after all, equally effective in top company at two and a half miles.

Master Minded's reappearance at Ascot was over two miles three furlongs and he saw the trip out well, jumping superbly and still on the bridle when his main rival, the previous year's winner Albertas Run, who had gone on to take the Ryanair Chase and Melling Chase, took a crashing fall at the third last. Master Minded won by sixteen lengths from Imsingingtheblues, his victory clearly opening up the option of campaigning him over further. But the Queen Mother Champion Chase remained the target after Master Minded's victories in the Tingle Creek [run at Cheltenham after Sandown's meeting was abandoned], by eight lengths from Petit Robin, jumping well again and always travelling smoothly, and in a strong renewal of the Victor Chandler. Master Minded jumped fluently and moved well from the start in the Victor Chandler, but he held on only by a short head from the strong-finishing Somersby after appearing in full control; Tony McCoy, who rode Master Minded at Ascot, blamed himself for going for home from too far out in a strongly-run race, though Paul Nicholls thought he might not have had the horse quite at his best. Master Minded's victory in the Tingle Creek was his stable's sixth in a row (and eighth in all) in the race, Kauto Star and the ill-fated Twist Magic having also won it twice; and Master Minded's win in the Victor Chandler was his stable's third in a row, Twist Magic having won the edition between Master Minded's two appearances in the race . . .

Two of those who finished ahead of Master Minded in the Champion Chase at Cheltenham, fifth-placed Somersby and sixth-placed French Opera, were also in the line-up for the John Smith's Melling Chase at Aintree a little over three weeks later, when the first two in the Ryanair Chase, Albertas Run and Kalahari King, were also aimed at a competitive renewal, the latter pair heading the betting at 11/4 and 9/2 respectively, ahead of Somersby (5/1) and Master Minded (11/2). Master Minded, who clearly had the best form and looked overpriced, proved far too good for his rivals, ridden with supreme confidence by Walsh and leading on the bridle between the last two before running out a very comfortable nine-length winner from Albertas Run, with Somersby half a length away third. It was Master Minded's third Grade 1 victory of the season and his seventh in such company in the three seasons since that epic first victory, at the age of five, in the Queen Mother Champion Chase, a performance of such brilliance that it has tended—somewhat unfairly—to overshadow his subsequent record in top company.

Master Minded began the next season still aged only eight, though it was his fifth consecutive campaign at the highest level in Britain. It was also to be his last. Master Minded duly stepped up to three miles for the King George VI Chase, but alongside, rather than instead of, the same connections' Kauto Star. The stable-companions had won their last starts before Kempton on the same day in November. Ruby Walsh had opted to partner Kauto Star in the Betfair Chase at Haydock leaving Daryl Jacob to take the ride on Master Minded in the Amlin 1965 Chase at Ascot which he won for the second time, showing top-class form again with a three-length victory over Somersby. 'Jacob was on board once again in the King George, but there was no happy ending this time. As Kauto Star and Walsh were recording their fifth win in the race, Jacob was dismounting from Master Minded after he was pulled up out of contention between the last two fences.' Having suffered a serious tendon injury, prompt action, firstly by his jockey in pulling him up immediately, and then by the veterinary team, both on-course and subsequently in Newmarket, enabled Master Minded to be saved, though his racing career was over. *Chasers & Hurdlers* of the same season summed up his career:

> One career-defining race will forever overshadow all others in any valedictory for Master Minded, who sustained a serious injury in the King George VI Chase at Kempton on Boxing Day and seems unlikely to race again. That race, of course, is the 2008 Queen Mother Champion Chase in which Master Minded put up one of the most impressive performances in Cheltenham Festival history when beating the 2007 winner Voy Por Ustedes by nineteen lengths. Only five years old at the time- the youngest horse to win the championship event—Master Minded seemed sure to go on to dominate the two-mile chasing division for many years to come. It could be argued that Master Minded didn't manage to live up to the highest expectations entertained for him, though he won ten more races over the next four seasons, seven of them Grade 1 events. Another Champion Chase was annexed in 2009 and he won the Tingle Creek Chase twice, the Victor Chandler Chase twice, the Melling Chase and, on his only visit to Ireland, the Punchestown Champion Chase. Some anti-climax!

*Stable companions
Kauto Star and Denman*

STAYING
CHASERS

Staying Chasers

By the end of the twentieth century, the number of horses to have won the Cheltenham Gold Cup more than once could still be counted on one hand. The five to have done so were spread over a period of forty years or so, the most recent among them being L'Escargot, Gold Cup winner in 1970 and 1971. L'Escargot went on to win the Grand National in 1975, when denying Red Rum a third successive win after being placed behind him in the two previous editions, making L'Escargot the last horse to have won both of steeplechasing's two most sought-after prizes. The greatest Gold Cup winner of them all, Arkle, recorded three wins in the 'sixties, though was still in his prime, aged nine, when breaking down in the 1966 King George VI Chase and could feasibly have added to his haul at Cheltenham. Another Irish-trained chaser, Cottage Rake, completed a hat-trick of Gold Cup wins in 1950, while the first dual winner Easter Hero (1929 and 1930) and five-time winner Golden Miller (1932 to 1936) were the two best Gold Cup winners between the wars when the Gold Cup was still in its infancy and the Grand National (which Golden Miller also won in 1934) was still much the most prestigious prize over fences.

Some of the very best chasers have won the Cheltenham Gold Cup more than once, but the number of Gold Cups won is not, of course, a measure of a chaser's greatness. There have been a number of Gold Cup winners better than L'Escargot, for example, to have won the race just once. But the exploit of winning chasing's blue riband twice or more is a feat rare enough to ensure a special place in the history of the sport. After more than thirty years had passed since L'Escargot, another successful defence of the Gold Cup title looked long overdue, and the 2002 Cheltenham Gold Cup winner **Best Mate** (rated 173 that season) looked a better candidate than most to add his name to the list of dual winners, as outlined in *Chasers & Hurdlers* of the same year:

> Fatalistic students of statistics will probably dismiss Best Mate's prospects of winning a second successive Cheltenham Gold Cup. It is now thirty-one years since a Gold Cup winner successfully defended his or her crown and

the record of those who have attempted the feat since L'Escargot achieved it provides plenty of food for thought. The full list, given in the essay on Looks Like Trouble in *Chasers & Hurdlers 2000/01*, illustrates vividly the ever-present risks to top jumpers of injury, illness or loss of form, or combinations of the three. Logic, however, dictates that Best Mate's prospects should not be judged on the subsequent performances of previous Gold Cup winners, but rather on the evidence provided by the horse himself and by his form. Best Mate's performance at Cheltenham is rated a little behind that recorded by the 2000 winner Looks Like Trouble, but it puts him on a par with most of the other Gold Cup winners of the previous decade or so. Further encouragement can be drawn from the fact that there may be improvement to come from Best Mate, given his age—only six other seven-year-olds have won the race since L'Escargot—and his relative lack of experience as a steeplechaser. The Gold Cup was only Best Mate's seventh steeplechase, making him the least experienced winner of the race since Dawn Run succeeded in 1986 on only her fifth outing over fences. Garrison Savannah and Mr Mulligan won the Gold Cup on their eighth appearance in a chase, though that didn't stand them in particularly good stead for the following year, both falling victim to injury before the Festival. Dawn Run, incidentally, was killed in action the same year as her triumph. Let's hope that nothing befalls Best Mate and that he lines up fit and well at the next Cheltenham Festival. If he does so—and there is a long way to go—this genuine and consistent performer, a good, accurate jumper of fences and a straightforward ride, looks to have the credentials to join Easter Hero, Golden Miller, Cottage Rake and Arkle, as well as L'Escargot, and become only the sixth horse to win the Gold Cup more than once.

The arrival on the chasing scene of Best Mate was one of the bright spots in a 2000/01 season which coincided with the wettest twelve months since records began and also had to contend with the effects of a serious outbreak of foot and mouth disease. One of the casualties of the latter was the Cheltenham Festival, plans to rearrange the fixture in April eventually abandoned after a case nearby put the racecourse within a foot and mouth exclusion zone. Best Mate was being aimed at the Arkle Trophy and (with Irish challengers ruled out because of travel restrictions) he would have started odds on. He was unbeaten in three novice events, at Exeter, Cheltenham (November Novices' Chase) and Sandown (Scilly Isles Novices' Chase), looking hugely promising and being saddled, as have a long line of potential champions over the years, with tiresome comparisons with the legendary Arkle. Best Mate was somewhat surprisingly put back over hurdles for his final race of 2000/01 and, starting favourite, was beaten fourteen lengths by Barton in the two-and-a-half-mile Aintree Hurdle. The Maghull Novices' Chase had seemed a natural target for Best Mate but connections evidently regarded the Aintree two-mile chase course as too sharp for him.

Best Mate was an easy winner of his first start outside novice company in the Haldon Gold Cup at Exeter on his reappearance and there was no disgrace in losing his unbeaten record over fences in another handicap when attempting to give 20 lb to the smart Wahiba Sands in the First National Gold Cup at Ascot. On the contrary, 'the evidence of the First National Gold Cup confirmed that Best Mate was headed for the top of the chasing tree and he looked a very worthy contender for the King George VI Chase.' Best Mate ended up being beaten three quarters of a length by Florida Pearl in the Kempton showpiece under Tony McCoy, standing in for his regular jockey Jim Culloty who was injured. McCoy was given instructions to ride a waiting race on Best Mate's first attempt at three miles but was convinced afterwards that he would have won if making his challenge sooner. Any lingering doubts over his stamina were soon put to bed at Cheltenham:

> Best Mate wasn't seen out between the King George and the Tote Cheltenham Gold Cup and he arrived at the Festival with the question of his stamina for the Gold Cup not fully resolved by his performance at Kempton. With a field of eighteen and plenty of runners who often race up with the pace, Cheltenham looked sure to expose any chinks in Best Mate's armour, though he was still

Best Mate jumps the last on his way to winning his first Gold Cup

sent off at shorter odds than Florida Pearl (a well-beaten fourth when hot favourite for the Irish Hennessy in the interim). With pre-season ante-post favourite First Gold sidelined for the season after the King George, Looks Like Trouble started favourite at 9/2 in the most open-looking Gold Cup for years. Bacchanal, an impressive winner of the AON Chase at Newbury since the King George, was next in the betting at 6/1, followed by Best Mate at 7/1, Florida Pearl and Thomas Pink Gold Cup winner Shooting Light at 10/1, and Behrajan at 11/1. Alexander Banquet, winner of the Hennessy Gold Cup at Leopardstown by a length and a half from Behrajan, started at 12/1, along with Marlborough and Foxchapel King.

Looks Like Trouble had shown plenty of zest when making all in the John Bull Chase at Wincanton on his comeback after a fourteen-month absence with a serious tendon injury (he wouldn't have been able to defend his crown had the 2001 Festival taken place). He was soon at the head of affairs, initially racing and jumping with plenty of enthusiasm, harried for much of the way by twelve-year-old See More Business, the 1999 Gold Cup winner who had seemed not quite the force of old and started at 40/1. Looks Like Trouble tended to jump and edge right as the race progressed and, weakening after being headed three out, was found afterwards to have broken down. There were other big disappointments in the race, including the four who had contested the Hennessy on barely raceable ground, Alexander Banquet (never moving or jumping well), Behrajan (eventually pulled up after being let down by his jumping, later found to have thrown a splint), Florida Pearl (gradually dropping away after four out and found to have a lung infection) and 33/1-shot Sackville. Shooting Light was pulled up lame at halfway and Bacchanal, whose jumping wasn't good enough, had faded by the time See More Business took the lead from Looks Like Trouble under pressure, with Best Mate, jumping well just off the pace for most of the race, now looming up full of running with 25/1-shot Commanche Court, without a win for nearly two years, also having worked his way steadily into contention. The Gold Cup was between the three of them as Best Mate momentarily looked short of room on the inside after rounding the home turn to face up to the second last where Commanche Court made a mistake. Best Mate was in front soon after jumping that fence and Culloty kept him up to his work and drove him out up the final climb to the winning post to hold off the rallying Commanche Court, cutting perceptibly into the winner's lead as the line was reached, by a length and three quarters. Commanche Court pulled eight lengths clear of third-placed See More Business, with the patiently-ridden Marlborough a further six lengths back in fourth, and the never-nearer What's Up Boys another five away, fifth of thirteen finishers in a truly-run race that firmly quashed any doubts about Best Mate's stamina. While Florida Pearl, who had only Bacchanal and Looks Like Trouble behind him at Cheltenham, went on to restore his reputation and put himself back in the limelight with fine victories in the Martell Cup at Aintree and the Punchestown Heineken Gold Cup, Best Mate was put away for the season after the Gold Cup.

Best Mate duly came back twelve months later to successfully defend his crown, producing an even better performance:

> Nothing had the slightest chance with him as soon as he was sent effortlessly into the lead after three out . . . Best Mate passed the post ten lengths in front of runner-up Truckers Tavern, a margin of victory bettered only twice in the Gold Cup since Arkle won by a record-breaking thirty in 1966.

Incidentally, that ten-length winning margin has been surpassed only once in the race since, in 2009 by Kauto Star, more of whom later. Prior to Cheltenham, Best Mate had gone one better than the year before in the King George (under McCoy again, Culloty suspended this time) so became the sixth horse to win the two most important weight-for-age chases in the British calendar in the same season. Now rated 182, Best Mate was 10 lb clear of the next-best chaser in training according to Timeform ratings at the end of the season, but a much more contentious issue was how he measured up against the greats of the past.

> Henry Ford's popularly-remembered *Chicago Tribune* quote that 'History is more or less bunk' seems apt when applied to the welter of historical, statistical information published on horse-racing nowadays, particularly before big races at showpiece meetings. Ages and weights carried by previous winners, the races they had run in, the record of the top stables in the particular races or at the meeting, the position in the betting market of previous winners—the list goes on. Such facts may be of interest but the prominence they are sometimes given can create an impression that such statistics are a more fruitful avenue for research for a punter than a study of the ability of the individual runners, and how they might be suited by the prevailing conditions. Statistics are a poor substitute for form study. More horses win races because their form said they had a good chance at the weights than for any other reason. An unfortunate by-product of preoccupation with statistics is that when, in popular parlance, a horse 'defies the stats' it tends to earn a reputation out of proportion to the actual form-value of its performance.

> Take the Cheltenham Gold Cup, for example. Until the latest season, no horse had won the race in successive years since L'Escargot in 1970 and 1971, statistical analysis illustrating, according to some, that, because of the often-gruelling nature of the race, 'Gold Cup winners are never the same again', a well-worn view which has tended to be proffered before each renewal in which the previous year's winner has taken part. The portents for the winner of the same season's King George VI Chase have also been regarded as anything but good, eleven of its winners having failed in the same season's Gold Cup since Desert Orchid completed the double in 1988/89, the only one to do so since Arkle. And then there were statistics showing the Gold Cup to be a 'bogey' race for favourites, the shorter the odds the worse the prospects apparently, the last

eleven horses to start at 7/4 or shorter in the Gold Cup having been beaten. Not surprisingly, 'history' was portrayed as being stacked against 13/8-favourite Best Mate, winner not only of the previous year's Gold Cup but also of the current season's King George VI Chase. On a glorious spring day and on near-perfect going, Best Mate won his second Gold Cup in imperious style, as the form-book said he should, under a copybook ride from Jim Culloty, waited with and jumping flawlessly and economically before cruising into the lead on the bridle after three out and quickening clear from the last.

Best Mate's performance confirmed that he is a class apart from his contemporaries among the staying chasers, at least when conditions place the emphasis on speed. He was deserving of a good proportion of the praise he received afterwards, but to place him above Desert Orchid and some of the other champions of the last thirty years or so—let alone ahead of Arkle—was hardly justified on any rational appreciation of the actual performance. Almost everything written afterwards began with the fact that Best Mate had become the first to win successive Gold Cups for thirty-two years, closely followed in some reports by the fact that he had also become the first since Desert Orchid to win the King George VI Chase and the Gold Cup in the same season. More than one reviewer stated that Best Mate had 'overcome' or 'defied' history. 'Best is better than Arkle', 'Best Mate's Gold strike ranks him with Arkle', 'The best of all time? History beckons for Gold Cup hero' provide just a flavour of the exaggerated headlines in the national dailies. The *Independent* correspondent wrote 'If Arkle's memory is secure in the mists of time . . . it cannot any longer be said to be without challenge' and a specialist writer in the *Daily Telegraph* offered the view that 'To mention another horse in the same breath as Arkle was blasphemy. We may not have found his better but yesterday perhaps we found his equal in Best Mate.' The chief sports writer of the *Daily Express* thought that Best Mate had provided enough glory 'to last a whole year', just as well since the horse's connections announced almost immediately that he would not be seen out again and would have a similarly truncated campaign in 2003/04, his principal targets the King George and the Gold Cup.

As it happened, Best Mate missed the King George (which was won by the same connections' Edredon Bleu) in favour of the Ericsson Chase at Leopardstown, but he was back at Cheltenham in the spring bidding for a third Gold Cup:

And so the expected came to pass: Best Mate kept his date with destiny and joined Golden Miller, Cottage Rake and Arkle as a three-time winner of the Cheltenham Gold Cup. Such is his superiority among the current crop of staying chasers and, touch wood, so strong is his constitution that he may yet surpass Cottage Rake and Arkle in winning a fourth Gold Cup or even join Golden Miller in winning a fifth. After his latest success in March, Best Mate was quoted at no longer than 5/2 to win again in 2005 and at just 12/1 to win both then and in 2006. 'Immortal' screamed the front page of the next day's *Racing Post*, a word which can, of course, often be heard followed by invisible. How appropriate. Best Mate was, frustratingly, notable by his absence for much of the season and wasn't required to show himself any better than he had in either of his previous Gold Cup campaigns. He was seen in action just twice in the first part of the winter, not at all between Christmas and the Festival and was back in cotton wool even before the last torn-up betting ticket had been swept up at Prestbury Park. Best Mate's latest Gold Cup, all told a substandard affair, at least had the novelty of being in the balance until very late in the race. His best performance of the season came in the Ericsson Chase at Leopardstown at Christmas, when he put up a display which has had no equal by a chaser in Ireland for at least a decade. Best Mate also suffered a rare defeat, just his third in thirteen starts over fences, when going down to Jair du Cochet on his reappearance in the Peterborough Chase at Huntingdon.

Chasers & Hurdlers remarked that 'three wins in the Cheltenham Gold Cup has to qualify as one of the great equine achievements', but it had to be said too that Best Mate's third Gold Cup was anything but a vintage edition. That, though, didn't make it any less compelling as a spectacle:

The 2004 Cheltenham Gold Cup was a thrilling race, run at a generally searching gallop. Harbour Pilot and First Gold were well away and, after the former hit the second fence, First Gold set the pace. The field was soon quite well spread out and by the top of the hill first time, with First Gold clear, Irish Hussar was already off the bridle, Alexander Banquet well behind and Beef Or Salmon also well off the pace. Best Mate had settled comfortably in fifth and was again jumping like clockwork. As First Gold was briefly given a breather, the field closed up passing the winning post with a circuit to go, but he soon stretched again, leaving Irish Hussar and Truckers Tavern toiling. Keen Leader was the next to feel the pinch, after a mistake at the third ditch, and Therealbandit folded soon after. By four out, only four mattered: First Gold, still leading but now narrowly, Harbour Pilot, the improving Sir Rembrandt and Best Mate. At that stage it looked more a question of how far Best Mate might win by, but as the quartet came down the hill another question, which hadn't often sprung to mind in Best Mate's Gold Cup runs, came up. Might he, perhaps, after all be beaten? At the third last Best Mate was tucked in on the rails and turning for home the situation was beginning to look critical, as he was hemmed in by Paul Carberry on Harbour Pilot. Culloty managed to extricate Best Mate and he quickened to lead two out as First Gold dropped away. Even then victory wasn't looking secured. Harbour Pilot continued to press and still held every chance at the last, while on the flat Sir Rembrandt rallied wide. At the line, Best Mate was all out to hold Sir Rembrandt by half a length with Harbour Pilot a length and a quarter further back in third. Beef Or Salmon, who had been eight lengths down and flat out three out, closed all too late, in fourth, with First Gold fifth and a distance back to the remaining three finishers.

The aftermath of Gold Cup win number three for Best Mate

The Cheltenham Gold Cup was the third and final race of Best Mate's campaign in each of the three seasons in which he won the race. 'It is impossible not to be impressed by the way Henrietta Knight, with husband Terry Biddlecombe, has produced Best Mate spot on for each of his Gold Cup appearances' conceded *Chasers & Hurdlers*. But, as hinted at above, the 'cotton wool' treatment he received left Best Mate's connections open to plenty of criticism too in the same pages. Looking ahead to Best Mate's proposed programme in the next season, the annual asked 'What will a campaign, even if completed without blemish, of a customised race at Exeter, the successor to the Ericsson and a fourth Cheltenham Gold Cup prove unless another chaser of Best Mate's ability emerges among his rivals?'

Ten years on, light campaigns for Gold Cup winners have become the norm (the 2013 winner Bobs Worth, for example, was seen out only once before Cheltenham and not at all afterwards) which means that criticism of that policy has tended to become attenuated, even if it remains as regrettable now as it was in Best Mate's day that the best chasers are not seen out more often.

In the longer term, though, Best Mate's infrequent appearances begged another question. Did his achievements earn him the sort of following that they deserved?

> Anyone who has seen Desert Orchid on his many public appearances since he was retired, or remembers the affection felt for Red Rum in similar circumstances, will know the warmth with which the true greats of the sport are regarded. Will cheers ring out quite so resoundingly down the years for Best Mate?

A burst blood vessel on the gallops prior to what would have been an attempt at his fourth Gold Cup reduced Best Mate's usual three-race campaign to just the two starts in 2004/05, a short-head win in what was 'effectively a glorified schooling session' in a specially arranged race at Exeter and then a comprehensive defeat by Beef Or Salmon at Leopardstown in the Lexus Chase, as the Ericsson had now become. In Best Mate's absence from Cheltenham, the Gold Cup had gone to an outstanding young chaser in Kicking King (rated 182) who had put up his best effort of the season when winning the King George VI Chase. Best Mate now had a serious rival, and the 2005/06 season held out the promise of meetings between them in the new Betfair Chase at Haydock, the King George and the Gold Cup, a prospect looked forward to in *Chasers & Hurdlers*:

> This all raises the tantalising prospect of three clashes between Best Mate and Kicking King. Tantalising, for after five seasons and fifteen races over fences, it is still not clear quite how good Best Mate is. Best Mate and Kicking King may well be the two best three-mile chasers since Desert Orchid. Tantalus, of course, never got hold of the fruit, but it is profoundly to be hoped that one of the three races at least will show just how good this pair of top-notch chasers really are.

It wasn't long into the next season before hopes of any meeting, let alone three, between the pair were dashed for good. Kicking King won his second King George (run at Sandown) but without being near his best and missed the remainder of the season with a tendon injury. As for Best Mate, who had by now 'become the nation's most popular horse', the question posed earlier about whether he'd really won a place in the public's affections seemed to have been answered in the affirmative. 'Only Red Rum and Desert Orchid have enjoyed greater celebrity among British-trained horses in the last thirty-five years.' Unlike that pair, however, who were able to maintain a high public profile once their racing days were over, Best Mate wasn't so fortunate.

There is always the danger of an excess of sentimentality whenever the sport loses one of its favourites. All credit therefore to trainer Henrietta Knight for the realistic and dignified way she coped in an interview on *At The Races* within an hour of the demise of Best Mate. The three-times Cheltenham Gold Cup winner collapsed near the final fence as he was trotting back after being pulled up on his reappearance at Exeter in November. 'When you train horses you have to expect anything can happen . . . it's just one of those tragedies,' Knight began. 'We feel very honoured to have had a horse like him to train, he put my yard on the map and was just a wonderful horse . . .'

...With Kicking King not in the same form in the latest season and the Gold Cup field nothing out of the ordinary, Best Mate would have had a clear chance of a fourth win in chasing's blue riband event if he had made it to Cheltenham fully fit and in his best form. As it was, Festival racegoers had to make do with a bronze statue of the big, rangy chaser which was unveiled on the opening day of the four-day meeting and will stand as a lasting memorial, making Best Mate the fourth Gold Cup winner (after Golden Miller, Arkle and Dawn Run) to be remembered in such a way at Cheltenham. The course also became Best Mate's final resting place, his ashes scattered near the winning post in a ceremony commemorated with a plaque.

In the same season that steeplechasing lost Best Mate, another chaser whose exploits were to prove great enough to warrant his being immortalised in the form of a statue by the end of his career was just beginning to make a name for himself—even if nobody seemed quite sure how to pronounce it. **Kauto Star** started out as a two-miler, winning the Tingle Creek at Sandown in 2005/06 and falling early on when favourite for the Champion Chase on his final outing of that campaign. It was the following season, however, that Kauto Star quickly established himself as not just the best chaser in training, but the joint-best since Desert Orchid according to Timeform ratings. By winning the Tingle Creek again (from subsequent Champion Chase winner Voy Por Ustedes) and finishing the season with a win in the Cheltenham Gold Cup, Kauto Star went close to matching Desert Orchid in terms of versatility too. Kauto Star joined Best Mate among only five horses to have gone unbeaten through a Cheltenham Gold Cup-winning season since Arkle in 1965/66, as well as emulating both Best Mate and Kicking King by winning the King George and Gold Cup in the same season. Kauto Star was seen out six times in all ('he desperately needs more experience' his trainer Paul Nicholls had said at the start of the season), and his record seasonal prize-money total was supplemented by other earnings as detailed in the Introduction to *Chasers & Hurdlers 2006/07*:

> Jumping is now doing more to market itself, the Order of Merit series born out of the suggestion in the Racecourse Holdings Trust blueprint for a '£500,000 Grand Prix series' for the top hurdlers and chasers who would earn points on a sliding scale based on performances in designated races. The points-based Racing UK Order of Merit lived up to its name in the latest season when its first prize of £200,000 went to the best chaser around, Kauto Star, with the second

prize of £175,000 collected by the horse who finished runner-up to him in both the King George VI Chase and the Cheltenham Gold Cup, Exotic Dancer . . . Kauto Star's Timeform rating of 184+ is the joint highest (with Moscow Flyer) achieved by a jumper since Desert Orchid. Only three-times Gold Cup winner Best Mate has consistently earned wider recognition outside the confines of the sport in the period since Desert Orchid but Kauto Star could be on the way to making a similarly big name for himself. In the latest season, he put up the best performances at two miles, two and a half and at around three miles, versatility almost on a par with that shown by Desert Orchid (whose stamina stretched to win a Whitbread and an Irish Grand National). Kauto Star's prize-money earnings of £607,263 were a record seasonal total for a jumper trained in Britain and Ireland. He also became the first horse to land the Betfair Million, a bonus of £1m put up by the Betfair Chase sponsors if the winner goes on to success in the King George (or the Lexus at Leopardstown) and the Cheltenham Gold Cup.

There was still the possibility of another big pay out after Kauto Star had landed the first two legs of the Betfair Million again in 2007/08, gaining only a narrow verdict over old rival Exotic Dancer in the Betfair Chase but having him back in third when winning the King George for the second time, 'virtually without coming off the bridle.' However, it was already clear by this stage that Kauto Star would not have the limelight entirely to himself that season, not even in the confines of his own stable. Next-door neighbour **Denman** had kept his unbeaten record over fences with an outstanding display of his own carrying 11-12 in the Hennessy Gold Cup at Newbury on his reappearance:

Unbeaten in five novice chases the previous season, including the Royal & SunAlliance at Cheltenham, and well above average for the season's leading novice, Denman was hardly let in lightly on his handicap debut in the Hennessy and didn't even start favourite, that position going to the Royal & SunAlliance runner-up Snowy Morning, 18 lb better off with Denman for a ten-length beating at Cheltenham. In common with the Gold Cup, Denman was spurned by the national tipsters, the only one for Denman out of sixteen selections in that day's Racing Post coming from the paper's West Country correspondent. The essay on Denman in *Chasers & Hurdlers 2006/07* had outlined the story of Arkle and Flyingbolt—the two highest-rated horses in Timeform's history—being housed concurrently in the same stable. Kauto Star and Denman were in adjacent boxes at Manor Farm Stables, though there didn't seem to be much doubt in the trainer's mind as to which was number one. Paul Nicholls said before the latest Gold Cup that he was convinced that Kauto Star 'is not only the best horse I've ever had, but the best I am ever likely to train, and so I still can't bring myself to believe that the horse in the box next door to him is going to turn out even better than the champion.' Denman's trainer reported before his reappearance in the Hennessy that 'he is still eight to ten kilograms above his ideal racing weight and he faces a mammoth task'. Nonetheless, Denman overcame the apparent lack of a preparatory race in stunning style, having missed the Charlie Hall at Wetherby in early-November because of unsuitably firmish conditions. In the original handicap for the Hennessy, Kauto Star was allotted top weight of 11-12, with Exotic Dancer on 11-5 and Denman and Neptune Collonges on 10-8. Denman's performance in a good quality and highly competitive eighteen-runner Hennessy narrowed the gap considerably between him and Kauto Star and was one of the best in the race's long history; with the notable exception of Burrough Hill Lad's victory under 12-0 in 1984, it was probably the best since Arkle's day. Denman went to the front with a long way to go. Taking a good hold, he made most from the eighth and proceeded to run the opposition into the ground. Most of his rivals were already toiling when Sam Thomas (standing in for the injured Ruby Walsh) went for home in earnest on Denman from five out. In complete command from a long way out, the relentless Denman won easily by eleven lengths and eight from Dream Alliance (received 19 lb) and Character Building (received 26 lb), with Madison du Berlais fourth and Knowhere fifth (Snowy Morning fell at the seventh).

With Denman still unbeaten after two more runs (in the Lexus at Leopardstown and the AON back at Newbury) and Kauto Star warming up successfully in the Ascot Chase, the scene was set at Cheltenham for a duel in the Gold Cup between these 'two paragons of steeplechasing.'

Oh ye of little faith, wherefore didst thou doubt? Steeplechasing's biggest clash in years—between the outstanding stable-companions Kauto Star and Denman—really caught the public imagination and seemed to divide opinion almost equally on the long road to Cheltenham. For much of the season, as the pair successfully negotiated their respective stepping-stones to the Cheltenham Festival, the bookmakers found it hard to separate them in the Gold Cup ante-post betting, with defending champion Kauto Star mostly just having the edge. At the start of Cheltenham week, one of the big four, Coral, bet 11/10 each of two and, as the Gold Cup drew nearer and rain continued, some layers were forecasting that Denman might start favourite. Come the day, however, after all the arguments had been put and all the professional opinion listened to (including the trainer's 'Denman has a mountain to climb to beat Kauto'), Denman found himself almost deserted by the racing media (the *Daily Telegraph* was able to trumpet the next day that J. A. McGrath was the only national newspaper racing correspondent to select Denman). The strong body of opinion that Denman's stamina and sound jumping would decide a war of attrition seemed to have melted away by that stage. With the going good to soft, the perception suddenly appeared to be that Denman was facing a task almost akin to St Peter's being asked to walk on water. He drifted to 9/4 on the day as Kauto Star was supported down to 11/10-on.

The general consensus was that Kauto Star would not be inconvenienced by the conditions and would have too much speed for Denman who would make the running and be 'a sitting duck' for his rival. The 1964 Gold Cup, which also featured a clash of two Titans, Arkle and the easy 1963 winner Mill House, was the race most widely referred to in the build-up and Mill House had led for most of the way, putting in a splendid round of jumping, only for Arkle to quicken past him between the last two fences and win by five lengths for the first of his three victories in the race. 'Races of the century' come round more frequently than the definition should allow. *The Times* used the term in anticipation of the Mill House and Arkle race, writing that 'not since Golden Miller met Thomond in 1935 has the Gold Cup raised such an exhilarating prospect.' The hope that Kauto Star and Denman—whose ten rivals included the previous year's runner-up Exotic Dancer—would jump the last together in a stirring battle (as Golden Miller and Thomond had done) was not realised as Denman meted out a merciless drubbing to an underperforming Kauto Star, a fine champion made to look fairly ordinary by championship standards on this occasion. A race talked about for months may not have quite delivered everything expected of it, but Denman nonetheless still recorded the best Gold Cup performance in over a decade, jumping into the lead at the eleventh of the twenty-two fences and galloping on relentlessly, stretching his lead to a dozen lengths at the second last before winning by seven from Kauto Star with another stable-companion Neptune Collonges (who'd led until halfway) a short head away in third, highlighting the dominance of the Nicholls stable in jump racing in the latest season. Denman didn't run after the Gold Cup and Kauto Star was again below his best when narrowly beaten by Our Vic in the totesport Bowl Chase at Aintree after making a bad mistake when clear two out. However, Neptune Collonges and fourth-placed Halcon Genelardais (nine lengths behind Neptune Collonges at Cheltenham) both upheld the Gold Cup form afterwards, the former impressively winning the Punchestown Gold Cup for the second year running and the latter finishing a good second, conceding lumps of weight away all round, in the Scottish Grand National.

The Cheltenham Gold Cup clash—before which the trainer and both sets of owners co-operated admirably with the media in the build-up—was widely portrayed as the classic head-to-head between two versions of jumping's ideal horse, the modern top-class, versatile chaser with speed against the big, long-striding stayer who gallops his rivals into submission. Nicknames given to Denman, who is over seventeen hands, included 'the tank', 'the bulldozer', 'the battleship', and even 'the monster', and his trainer explained that it required so much work to get him fully fit ('I sometimes work him the day before he runs') that he is a very difficult horse to train. Kauto Star, by contrast, is more straightforward at home. 'You couldn't find two more different horses. Kauto Star is more relaxed with each season, needs half the work of Denman and does everything so easily,' said Nicholls. In so far as the comparisons with Arkle and Mill House went, Denman was very reminiscent of Mill House, both conforming to that oft-used description 'real old-fashioned type'.

Denman at the last in the 2008 Gold Cup, leading home a 1,2,3
for trainer Paul Nicholls

Once he was out in front in the Gold Cup, Denman was an exhilarating sight, making the race a true test and jumping splendidly, his rider able to afford the luxury of a long look round at the end of the back straight. Denman brushed through four out and the third last, though, by that time, the game was up for Kauto Star who failed to jump with his usual fluency once the pace quickened and came under the whip after hitting the top of the fourth last. Kauto Star made hard work of getting past Neptune Collonges, who stuck to his guns admirably after Denman deprived him of his early lead and almost got back up for second place on the stiff climb after the last. Denman seemed to tire himself in the straight—his advantage reduced to seven lengths at the line—though Thomas maintained afterwards that Denman was idling and would have found more if he had been challenged. Incidentally, Denman was entitled to be tired after his race-winning move on the final circuit—he clocked a quicker time (by well over a second) between the fourth last and second last than the principals in the two-mile Grand Annual Chase later that afternoon!

Neptune Collonges was to step out from the shadow of his outstanding stablemates by winning the Grand National some four years later, but more immediately, the Gold Cup result might have suggested that the still-unbeaten Denman (now rated 180p) had the brighter future of the pair of eight-year-olds, even if Kauto Star (182 in 2007/08) did have an apparent off-day in the Gold Cup. Not that the latter's owner saw it that way.

'I've heard it said that we'll be going for the Ryanair Chase next year, but that's rubbish. We'll be taking on Denman again in the Gold Cup and on better going I'm confident that, even over the Gold Cup distance, we'll win.' The fighting talk is from Kauto Star's owner Clive Smith. The view of Denman's part-owner Harry Findlay was that the Gold Cup drubbing suffered by Kauto Star 'will have absolutely blown his head off.' 'If I owned another top horse, I wouldn't go near Denman. Who will want to take him on?' was the ebullient Findlay's post-race assessment.

But Denman had a far from ideal preparation for the 2009 Gold Cup whereas Kauto Star enjoyed another outstanding campaign, one spoiled only by his unseating when looking likely to land a third Betfair Chase. 'It has taken a while but there surely cannot be anyone left who would deny Kauto Star his place among the very best jumpers in history, in terms of overall achievement perhaps ranked behind only Arkle, Golden Miller and Desert Orchid' concluded *Chasers & Hurdlers*. Successful in the Champion Chase at Down Royal on his reappearance, Kauto Star won a third King George after his mishap at Haydock, becoming just the third horse after Wayward Lad and Desert Orchid to win the race at least three times. A significant achievement, but so too was Kauto Star's second Gold Cup, making him the first horse in the eighty-five-year history of the race to regain the prize. 'His victory at Cheltenham, was, without much doubt, the best performance in the Gold Cup since the days of Arkle himself.'

Despite winning a third King George in such good fashion, Kauto Star was still only second favourite for the Gold Cup immediately after Kempton. Denman, whose return was delayed by treatment for an irregular heartbeat, remained at the head of the market with their stable-companion Neptune Collonges, third in 2008, a close third favourite, holding that position even after a fall in the Lexus at Leopardstown two days after the King George, that race going to Exotic Dancer. With Kauto Star's preparation focussed on the Gold Cup, the next major change in the ante-post market came when Denman finally returned. With his intended preparatory outing in the AON Chase lost to the weather, a hastily-arranged Levy Board Chase was staged as a replacement at Kempton, ironically over the same course and distance as the King George. Denman went down to a surprising defeat on testing ground, comprehensively beaten by Madison du Berlais, the Hennessy winner at Newbury. Kauto Star replaced Denman at the head of the Gold Cup ante-post market and remained there until Gold Cup day itself . . .

In contrast to the previous year, when Denman forced the pace from a long way out, the Gold Cup was run at a much more even tempo. Neptune Collonges, Snoopy Loopy and Madison du Berlais led the field away from a rather ragged start (though not one that was to the detriment of any of the runners), with Kauto Star, on the rail, and Denman sharing fourth, Exotic Dancer dropped right out last. Kauto Star jumped in much more assured fashion than he had twelve months earlier and was travelling supremely well as a result. After a circuit, only

2009 Gold Cup - Kauto Star turns the tables on Denman and becomes the first Gold Cup winner to regain his crown after losing it

Halcon Generlardais, soon to be pulled up, was out of contention. Going away from the stands for the final time, as Snoopy Loopy and Madison du Berlais lost their places, Kauto Star and Denman moved up to track Neptune Collonges but plenty were still in contention as the race built towards its climax. By the final ditch, six from home, Albertas Run and Roll Along, both being ridden along, were giving chase to the Nicholls trio, with Barbers Shop and Exotic Dancer, under a very patient McCoy, creeping closer. On the descent from four out, the first three began to stretch those behind, both Kauto Star and Denman looking poised to go past the under-pressure Neptune Collonges. Immediately after jumping three out, Kauto Star, still being matched stride for stride by Denman, eased into the lead and for a brief moment an epic duel looked a possibility. However, Denman had no answer to Kauto Star's turn of foot and, soon clear, Kauto Star jumped the last two fences as well as he had jumped the twenty previous ones and was ridden out on the run-in to score by thirteen lengths from Denman. Exotic Dancer, who never really got to the leaders, came third, placed in the race for the second time at what would be his final attempt to get the better of Kauto Star.

In terms of the merit of the Gold Cup form overall, it is rare in the modern era for an edition of this race to produce form with such a water-tight look to it. There were no honest plodders close up, no Sir Rembrandts or Harbour Pilots whose reserves of stamina enabled them to run above the balance of their form. Nor is there an 'imposter', a gatecrasher at the 'A' list party, in the mould of Turpin Green in Kauto Star's first Gold Cup. That race, not truly run and a relative test of speed, clearly represents less solid form than the latest running . . .

Denman had played his part in making the 2009 Gold Cup such a solid race in the form-book, but his comprehensive defeat by Kauto Star left him trailing in the ratings that season (171+ to Kauto Star's 184), and, as well as the Gold Cup, Timeform's Horse of the Year title was another accolade he had to hand back to his stable-companion:

That Denman would be beaten on all of his starts in the latest season (he fell in the totesport Bowl at Aintree on his final outing) is a prospect that would have been greeted with incredulity had it been proffered following his demolition of a below-par Kauto Star in the 2008 Cheltenham Gold Cup, Denman's ninth win in nine starts over fences.

Denman bounced back the following autumn, however, and in what was to prove a vintage season in the staying chase division, Denman set the bar high on his return at Newbury for the Hennessy once again.

Denman suffered no long-term damage from his Aintree fall and, when resuming work ahead of his bid for a second win in the Hennessy Gold Cup, was reported to be in much better form than the previous autumn, delighting his trainer in a racecourse gallop at Exeter. As when successful two years earlier, Denman carried top weight of 11-12 at Newbury, though this time he was competing from a BHA mark of 174, compared to 161 in 2007. As a result of his campaign in 2008/09, Denman's BHA mark had come down from the 182 (3 lb higher than Kauto Star at the time) he had been allocated in the Anglo-Irish Classifications of 2007/08, though he still had to give a minimum of 12 lb to his eighteen rivals, six of whom were out of the handicap. Despite his troubles in the interim, and the fact that the Nicholls stable fielded another strong candidate, What A Friend (carrying 10-4), Denman was sent off favourite at 11/4. Apart from What A Friend, another second-season chaser Killyglen and the Gold Cup seventh Barbers Shop were Denman's closest rivals according to the betting, while the remainder of the field included another former Hennessy winner, State of Play, the Grand National winner Mon Mome, and the 2006 Cheltenham Gold Cup winner War of Attrition, no longer the force of old and contesting his first handicap, on 10-6.

Whilst lacking the dominance of his 2007 victory, when he had the race won from a long way out in much more testing conditions, Denman's second success in the Hennessy again owed plenty to his assured jumping and resolute galloping. His resolution served him well at the finish but, back at the start, he had needed plenty of rousting by Ruby Walsh to get away on terms on the outside of the field and take up a prominent pitch jumping the first. Denman is, by all accounts, prone to laziness at home and, though he has never failed to jump off in a race, no chances are taken on racedays when he is accompanied at the start by the trainer's assistant. Once under way in the latest Hennessy, Denman soon settled on the heels of the leaders Joe Lively and Niche Market, briefly taking the lead over the water passing the stands for the first time. Going down the back straight on the second circuit, Denman asserted and went on again, for good this time. A bold jump at the cross fence by Denman put daylight between himself and Barbers Shop, who had emerged as his closest pursuer, and, while the latter closed again seemingly going well on Denman's inner four out (the first in the straight), another fine leap from Denman saw him off. Niche Market was still in contention at that stage too, but it was stable-companion What A Friend who was to prove the only real threat. Denman briefly looked to have a fight on his hands going to the last when What A Friend drew upsides under Sam Thomas (who had partnered Denman to victory in 2007), but, with his stable-companion hanging fire, Denman showed much the greater resolution when driven out on the run-in to win by three and a half lengths. There was a similar gap back to the Irish National winner Niche Market who, racing from 3 lb out of the weights, pipped Barbers Shop for third, with the others finishing at long intervals behind those in the frame.

Six of the last seven Hennessy Gold Cups have now been won by horses carrying 11-0 or more; Trabolgan also carried 11-12 in 2005 though, with him, that corresponded to a BHA mark of only 151. Denman's two victories are the best performances in the race since Burrough Hill Lad's win under 12-0 in 1984, that horse the last Hennessy winner before Denman to have won a Cheltenham Gold Cup as well. Not long before Burrough Hill Lad, in 1982, the Hennessy winner Bregawn went on to win at Cheltenham in the spring, but all the other horses to have won both races achieved the feat early in the Hennessy's history. Between them, the Cheltenham Gold Cup winners Mandarin, Kerstin, Mill House and Arkle won six of the first nine runnings of the Hennessy Gold Cup after the race was inaugurated in 1957. Mill House, who won under 12-0 in 1963 (with Arkle third under 11-9), and Arkle, who defied 12-7 in the next two runnings (Mill House fourth under 12-4 in 1964) are the only other horses, apart from Burrough Hill Lad, to have carried more weight to victory in a Hennessy than Denman. He is in very good company then, joining an exclusive club along with Mandarin and Arkle as the only dual winners of the Hennessy.

What would Kauto Star have to do to better Denman's Hennessy performance? The answer came in breathtaking fashion at Kempton a month later, when once again the spirit of Arkle was conjured up.

History, wrote the eighteenth century Italian philosopher Giambattista Vico, repeats itself. Vico's work was largely neglected in his own lifetime and he lived a spartan academic existence, the corridor from his hovel too narrow to take his

*Kauto Star wins his fourth King George VI Chase by
a distance, evoking memories of Arkle*

coffin which had to be passed through a window. Vico's theory of the cyclical nature of history has, however, subsequently gained ground. He portrayed the story of humanity and society as one of progressive development, but without ever reaching perfection, progress interrupted from time to time by a return to earlier conditions. When Kauto Star crushed his rivals by a distance in the latest King George VI Chase at Kempton on Boxing Day, he was repeating the achievement of Arkle in the same race forty-four years earlier. Captain Christy won the King George by an official thirty lengths in 1975 from Bula (who started 6/4 favourite for the Cheltenham Gold Cup three months later!) but only Arkle and Kauto Star have won by 'a distance', officially the widest margin that can be recorded between two horses as they cross the finishing line. 'A distance' was originally returned when the margin between two horses was too great to be measured, but things have moved on and, since 1997, the turf authorities in Britain have used conversions of time lapses, rather than visually judged margins, to decide the distances between horses. The time lapse between Kauto Star and runner-up Madison du Berlais was approximately eight seconds, converting on the scale used by the BHA handicappers—amended most recently in June 2008—to thirty-six lengths (the same distance as measured by Timeform, using a similar approach), though the official returns credited the margin as a distance ('a distance still stands in the rules of racing for anything greater than 30 lengths...' said senior racecourse judge Nick Bostock).

The achievements of Arkle over fences were remarkable and he has achieved legendary—almost mythical—status, tiresome references to him sometimes dogging the careers of the great steeplechasers who have come afterwards. Commentators on the sport have seemed to denigrate some top-class chasers simply because they were not Arkle, while, at the same time, the emergence of a chaser who might be 'the new Arkle' has on occasions been greeted as if by an explorer who had just found a fresh footprint of the Abominable Snowman. Why has steeplechasing's Arkle complex lasted for so long? Why, when Kauto Star invokes comparisons with Arkle, for example, do some grope around for evidence to prove that Arkle's brilliance was exaggerated? The answers to both questions are far from clear, but the fact that the questions can be raised at all is a telling testament to Arkle's standing in the pantheon of steeplechasing greats. His name still resonates over forty years after his career was ended at the age of nine by a fractured bone in his off-fore foot, incurred before he was caught close home by Dormant in the 1966 King George VI Chase, one of only four defeats in twenty-six starts over fences.

Some direct comparisons between Kauto Star and Arkle are possible with the King George and the Cheltenham Gold Cup, but there aren't many other grounds on which they can be made because Kauto Star has not had enough opportunities to try to emulate Arkle's weight-carrying feats in handicaps (he has only run in three handicaps, losing two of them). Arkle's three Cheltenham Gold Cup wins were achieved by five lengths, twenty lengths and thirty lengths (the first two from Mill House). Kauto Star's two Gold Cup wins have been gained by two and a half lengths and by thirteen lengths and his three previous King George VI Chase wins had been by eight lengths, eleven lengths and eight lengths respectively. Kauto Star has also won the Tingle Creek Chase twice and the Betfair Chase three times in his superb haul of thirteen Grade 1 wins. Kauto Star's prodigious victory in the latest King George VI Chase set the seal on his claims to be regarded as the best steeplechaser since the days of Arkle and his great contemporaries Flyingbolt and Mill House. Kauto Star's Timeform rating of 191 actually puts him joint third with Mill House on the all-time list, behind Arkle (212) and Flyingbolt (210), and ahead of Easter Hero (190), Golden Miller (188) and Desert Orchid (187). The ratings on the Timeform scale for Easter Hero and Golden Miller, who both raced in the pre-Timeform era, were compiled by Randall and Morris for *A Century of Champions* which was produced in conjunction with Timeform to celebrate the millennium . . .

Apart from the winning margin, there was another similarity between Arkle's King George and Kauto Star's in the latest season. Arkle's King George nearly did not take place at all, the meeting being the only one to survive that year in a Boxing Day programme decimated by frost, whilst Kauto Star's was saved (despite similarly inclement weather), by the increasingly familiar modern-day use of frost blankets covering the whole course in the build-up to the big day. The twelve rivals who took on Kauto Star were headed by the previous season's Ryanair Chase winner Imperial Commander who had stamped himself a tip-top chaser when making Kauto Star pull out all the stops to claim his third win in the Betfair Chase at Haydock in November. The Betfair was run at championship pace and came down to a duel between Kauto Star and the boldly-ridden Imperial Commander, who had the race to themselves from some way out. Kauto Star was just in front after three out, where Imperial Commander surrendered the advantage after getting in too close, but the pair were locked together over the last two fences and virtually inseparable to the naked eye as they passed the post, Imperial Commander having looked as if he might just shade the verdict until collared again right on the line. Most racegoers seemed surprised when the photo-finish went to Kauto Star (who traded at odds against on Betfair on the photo), the margin of victory the minimum of a nose. Third-placed Madison du Berlais was beaten twenty-four lengths and Imperial Commander's performance seemed to set the scene for further close encounters with Kauto Star, both sets of connections claiming their horses would come on for the run at Haydock. Imperial Commander had finished a well-beaten sixth to Kauto Star in the previous season's King George, at a time when his trainer Nigel Twiston-Davies' horses were badly out of form, but he started second favourite at 13/2 in the latest edition, with the Charlie Hall Chase and Peterborough Chase winner Deep Purple next at 17/2. Only two others started at shorter than 25/1, the 10/1-shot Madison du Berlais and 14/1-shot Barbers Shop (seventh to Kauto Star in the Gold Cup back in March and fourth in the Hennessy, receiving 18 lb from Denman, on his reappearance).

Imperial Commander's King George prospects were compromised as early as the second fence, where he made a bad mistake, nearly unseating his rider, as his stablemate Ollie Magern, a rank outsider, and 25/1-shot Nacarat set a searching gallop. Kauto Star had no difficulty lying up once the pace began to tell—unlike the struggling Albertas Run and Our Vic who had finished runners-up in the last two editions—and his jumping remained supremely accomplished. Sauntering clear in the home straight after joining Nacarat full of running at the fourth last, and crossing the line seemingly with plenty left, Kauto Star produced the most masterly and, in terms of form, the best performance of his already glittering career, his display, in all its aspects, near-perfect and one which will be recalled for as long as the King George continues to be run. The runner-up was Madison du Berlais, who as well as finishing third in the Betfair had won the previous season's Hennessy and two other good races in which he lowered the colours of Denman. Denman's absence from the King George field, after his brilliant win in the Hennessy, was the only thing that detracted from the representativeness of the Kempton race. Third in the King George was Barbers Shop who chased Kauto Star from the third last, only to be caught on the run-in and be beaten a length for second. The rallying Nacarat, whose bold jumping had all bar the winner in trouble from over four out, was still pressing for second when making a mistake at the last but eventually finished a further three and a half lengths behind Barbers Shop. There was another twenty-three lengths back to fifth-placed Imperial Commander, beaten over sixty lengths by Kauto Star in the race for the second year running. Albertas Run came sixth and Our Vic eighth, while Deep Purple was pulled up, reportedly having bled.

The Kempton racecourse executive and the sponsors of the King George, William Hill, played their part in anticipation of an historic occasion by having 12,000 cardboard handbills in Kauto Star's colours distributed beforehand among a near sell-out crowd of 22,000 carrying the words 'I'm 4 Kauto'. Kauto Star's jockey Ruby Walsh entered into the spirit of things by flinging his gloves, goggles and whip into the crowd lining the rails as he made his way back, while Kauto Star himself entered the winner's enclosure to a rousing reception worthy of his performance. Already the third horse to win the King George three times—Wayward Lad won in 1982, 1983 and 1985—Kauto Star matched Desert Orchid's four wins, though 'Dessie' didn't win his in four successive years, being beaten by the French-trained outsider Nupsala in the year after his first win before winning the next three. Desert Orchid won his fourth King George at the age of eleven, and Wayward Lad won his third at ten, the age that Kauto Star will be if he lines up at Kempton again in the next season to attempt a fifth King George win. His fourth win attracted a terrestrial TV audience of 1.1m, 200,000 up on the previous year, while the latest King George was also run as the fifth race on the card, later than its traditional position, to fit in with Channel 4's scheduling and also to build up the anticipation.

And talking of building up anticipation . . .

Kauto Star v Denman: The Decider. So-called two-horse races have a habit of failing to live up to their billing and of providing a story different from the one widely anticipated. The third meeting of 'the big shots', stablemates Kauto Star and Denman, was supposed to produce the headlines after the latest totesport Cheltenham Gold Cup. A public relations campaign orchestrated by British racing's new promotional body Racing for Change, and aimed at a wider audience beyond the racing pages, concentrated on the pair to the exclusion of the other Gold Cup contenders. Presenting steeplechasing's blue riband event as a head-to-head between Kauto Star and Denman, who each had a decision over the other in the Cheltenham Gold Cup, was perceived as the best way of stirring the imagination of a potential new audience for the sport. The promotion included the use of a touring 'battle bus', the distribution of partisan rosettes and scarves and a photo shoot featuring heavyweight boxing champion David Haye (a film was also used interposing racing shots of Denman and Kauto Star with scenes from the celebrated Benn/Eubank boxing match twenty years earlier). The pre-race publicity was hailed as 'a brilliant job' by Racing for Change, which praised the co-operation and involvement of the connections of both Kauto Star and Denman in the build-up. 'If you added up the column inches as to how much publicity Kauto Star, Denman and Cheltenham received and the TV airtime [BBC Breakfast and GMTV both promoted the story in the run-up to the race], you'd be looking at many millions of pounds,' said one of the directors of Racing for Change. Gold Cup day was a sell-out as usual at Cheltenham, with a crowd of 67,716, and the Channel 4 audience for the race was measured at 1.9m (24% terrestrial TV audience share), just below the 2m (26%) for Denman's win over Kauto Star in 2008, which is the highest since Channel 4 took over the Festival coverage in 1995 (the averages for the Gold Cup since then have been around 1.4m and just over 20%).

Kauto Star was sent off the 11/8-on favourite for the 2010 Gold Cup ahead of Denman at 4/1, the latter suffering something of a setback to his prospects when blundering and unseating in the AON Chase at Newbury on his only outing between the Hennessy and Cheltenham. Kauto Star wasn't seen out between the King George and the Gold Cup, and neither was Imperial Commander, next in the betting on 7/1.

Carruthers, Denman, Imperial Commander, Kauto Star and Cooldine made up the leading group in the first half of the Gold Cup in which the pace gradually got stronger, after being a little steadier than anticipated in the early stages. By the time Denman joined Carruthers at the front towards the end of the first circuit it was clear that the latest Gold Cup was going to prove a true test, one worthy of the quality of the field. Kauto Star, though, had made a very bad mistake at the eighth and the writing looked on the wall for him when he was receiving reminders and being niggled along on the approach to the final open ditch, six from home. Denman stepped up the pace again on the downhill run towards the fourth last, where the rallying Kauto Star took a horrible-looking fall when still a fairly close fifth. Imperial Commander and Cooldine had moved into second and third respectively at the third last, Carruthers, who made a mistake there, and the improving Calgary Bay being the only others still in contention. Imperial Commander, travelling well throughout and impressing with his jumping, was clearly moving better than Denman straightening up for home and soon got on top after taking over at the second last. He was ridden out from the last to win by seven lengths from Denman who kept up his splendid record of never finishing out of the first two at the Festival, his third successive appearance in the Gold Cup following a second in the Royal & SunAlliance Hurdle and victory in the RSA Chase on his two earlier appearances (Kauto Star, also in the first two in three Gold Cups, has now fallen twice at the Festival, having come down at the third in the Queen Mother Champion Chase on the first of his five appearances). Imperial Commander and Denman drew a long way clear in the closing stages, the winner putting up almost as good a performance as Kauto Star had done twelve months earlier, one which deserves to be ranked among the best in the Gold Cup's history.

Imperial Commander's Gold Cup victory belonged in the same bracket as Denman's Hennessy win, if not quite up with Kauto Star's imperious display in the King George. Kauto Star headed the ratings of 2009/10 with a new career-best of 191, ahead of Imperial Commander on 182 and Denman, better than ever in the Hennessy, on 181. Yet each of them ended the season with performances far less impressive than their annual ratings. Kauto Star was cantered back apparently unharmed after his heavy fall in the Gold Cup but took some time to recover and was retired for the season. Imperial Commander was turned out again for the totesport Bowl at Aintree but he too ended his campaign with a non-completion, jumping badly before finally unseating his rider. Denman clearly wasn't in the same form after Cheltenham either when beaten in the Punchestown Gold Cup, never looking comfortable on the right-handed track.

Kauto Star and Denman were to turn eleven in the next season, the more lightly-raced Imperial Commander a year their junior, so there was plenty of scope for a challenger to emerge from the ranks of younger chasers. The one to do so was **Long Run** whose best effort as a novice in 2009/10 had come on his British debut, still aged four, when routing his field in the Feltham Novices' Chase over the same course and distance, and on the same day, that Kauto Star won his fourth King George. Long Run had finished third in the Paddy Power Gold Cup on his reappearance, while Kauto Star had repeated his 2008 win at Down Royal with a workmanlike success. In Kauto Star's absence from the Betfair Chase, Imperial Commander gained compensation for his narrow defeat at Haydock twelve months earlier before an infected cut ruled him out of the King George; he was fit again by the time the King George was staged three weeks later than scheduled after the Boxing Day jumping programme had been wiped out by the weather but the race wasn't re-opened. In any case, the sixtieth running of the King George VI Chase was principally about Kauto Star's attempt to win the race for a record fifth time and he started at a shorter price to do so than in any of his four previous appearances.

> Kauto Star was cheered on his way down to the start but his legion of supporters had precious little to cheer about in the race itself. Kauto Star was well below form on the day, the writing on the wall a long way from home. Long Run never looked like being caught after beginning to assert three out, by which stage Kauto Star was already flat out to try to keep up with him. A shocking blunder at the second last, where Kauto Star and his jockey Tony McCoy did well to keep their partnership intact, put paid to any hopes of a rally and Long Run, whose jumping was much more fluent than it had been on his two visits to Cheltenham, stayed on strongly to win by twelve lengths, with Riverside Theatre giving his stable a one, two, and a weary Kauto Star finishing a further seven lengths behind in third, with Nacarat repeating his fourth after he had again ensured a good gallop and seen off the majority of his rivals before his efforts took their toll. Albertas Run and Forpadydeplasterer were among three who were pulled up.

If Long Run's beating of Kauto Star in the King George was the first indication of a changing of the guard, then he could have hardly have faced a stiffer task in the Gold Cup in a bid to confirm it. As well as Kauto Star, Denman (third in the latest Hennessy, carrying top weight of 11-12 again) and Imperial Commander were also in the line-up again as past winners. The race itself, fittingly for the centenary of the Cheltenham Festival, or 'National Hunt meeting', as it used to be known, 'produced a vintage contest that deserves to rank with some of the great Cheltenham Gold Cups.'

In a truly-run race for the latest Gold Cup the cream rose to the top. At the fourth last, Kauto Star, Imperial Commander and Denman were all prominent, with Long Run just behind. The three Gold Cup winners had all jumped well, Kauto Star and Imperial Commander also taking the eye with their obvious exuberance, though it hadn't been quite such plain sailing for Long Run who had one or two 'do-or-die moments', as his rider put it afterwards, and made a few mistakes, including at the tenth and twelfth. Imperial Commander was the first of the principals to crack, fading after blundering at the fourth last where Long Run wasn't fully fluent either. Kauto Star and Denman were at the head of the field jumping the third last where Denman took a narrow lead, and the pair threatened to pull away rounding the bend on the run to two out, the race looking for two hundred yards or so as if it might deliver the head-to-head encounter between them that had been billed the previous year.

Long Run might briefly have seemed booked for third place, but any such impression proved illusory. He soon began to produce extra under pressure and came to join Denman and Kauto Star on their outside at the second last.

Two out in a vintage renewal of the Gold Cup in 2011; eventual winner Long Run (far side) making headway on Denman and Kauto Star

Long Run took over in the lead approaching the final fence and drew clear up the steep climb to the finish, seeing the trip out really well, ridden out to win by seven lengths from Denman, who stuck to his task to finish second in the Gold Cup for the third year running since his victory over Kauto Star in 2008 (he hasn't finished out of the first two in six appearances at the Festival). Kauto Star didn't keep on so well as the first two, tiring on the run-in and just holding on for third, four lengths behind Denman, bringing his Gold Cup record to two wins and two places in five attempts (like Denman he was making his sixth successive Festival appearance). What A Friend, blinkered for the first time, ran on to finish only a nose behind Kauto Star in fourth, giving Manor Farm Stables second, third and fourth (the stable's fourth runner Neptune Collonges, contesting his fourth Gold Cup, came eighth). Midnight Chase finished a creditable fifth, after setting a sound pace until Kauto Star deprived him of the lead with a circuit to go, while Imperial Commander (who broke a blood vessel) and Kempes were both pulled up, as was China Rock who jumped soundly and was prominent for a long way.

The victory of Long Run, the youngest to triumph in the race since Mill House in 1963, illustrated that the sport can still provide rare moments that serve to remind racegoers of the Corinthian spirit of jump racing in days gone by. Although he was professionally trained, Long Run's win was essentially a great family triumph, owner Robert Waley-Cohen (who takes over as chairman of Cheltenham in the next season) and most of the rest of his family cheering home his son Sam, whose saddle bears the initials of brother Tom who died at just twenty from cancer. Mr Sam Waley-Cohen became the first amateur rider to win the Gold Cup since Mr Jim Wilson thirty years earlier on another family-owned but professionally trained chaser Little Owl.

Long Run was now rated 184, while all three former Gold Cup winners he beat at Cheltenham, whilst still capable of top-class form, were below their very best career ratings. Imperial Commander was off with a leg injury for the best part of two years after the 2011 Gold Cup, while Denman wasn't seen out again; he remained in training ahead of a planned return in the Lexus Chase but a tendon injury beforehand prompted his retirement. There were calls in some quarters for Kauto Star to be retired after his defeat in the 2010/11 King George, and again, with more justification perhaps, after being pulled up when odds on for the Punchestown Gold Cup seven weeks after Cheltenham. Even Clive Smith had spoken of Kauto Star in the past tense—'he has been a wonderful horse . . . he's been terrific'—after his third to Long Run at the Festival. But Kauto Star was back for a seventh season in the top flight in the autumn of 2011.

It has become a sporting cliche that the ability to come back from defeat marks a great champion. If it is true, then Kauto Star enhanced his reputation in his latest campaign and the comeback story that unfolded will feature strongly in the legend that is passed down. Any idea that Kauto Star might resume his reign as king of the steeplechasers after slipping right down the rankings in

2010/11 must have seemed fanciful to all but his most optimistic supporters. Even those closest to Kauto Star had their doubts, illustrated by the fact that it was decided to have Kauto Star fully tuned up ahead of his reappearance in the Betfair Chase at Haydock in November, a race in which he squared up to Long Run for a third time. Kauto Star was attempting a fourth win in the Betfair, before which trainer Paul Nicholls announced that Kauto Star was 'fitter than I have ever had him at this stage of the season . . . Long Run [making his seasonal debut] might not be cherry ripe, but there will be no excuses from our side, if Kauto Star runs moderately then I suspect he will be retired.'

Kauto Star started at 6/1 (the longest odds for any race he contested for Paul Nicholls), with Long Run the 6/5 favourite:

'Kauto Star's odds at Haydock reflected the general feeling that he was on the decline, and perhaps very close to being pensioned off. His display in the race was a revelation, showing that, even in the autumn of his career, he was anything but a back number. Kauto Star comprehensively despatched his five opponents at Haydock, not to mention his critics, forcing the pace (different tactics to usual) and jumping impeccably before seeing off the gritty challenge of Long Run in the home straight to beat him, going away on the run-in, by eight lengths . . .'

Long Run was expected to be more fully tuned up at Kempton and started favourite again for the King George in which Kauto Star's connections were also represented by Master Minded. The latter was pulled up with a serious tendon injury but Kauto Star was already making the best of his way home by then . . .

Kauto Star was in front before halfway and began to stretch the field after the twelfth of the eighteen fences. His faultless jumping was again an asset and he was four or five lengths clear approaching the third last, still moving fluently while Long Run couldn't quite match his jumping and was beginning to struggle to keep up. Kauto Star maintained the gallop in the home straight and always had the measure of Long Run who was, nonetheless, closing strongly towards the finish. Kauto Star held him off by a length and a quarter to become the first horse to win the King George VI Chase five times, surpassing the record he had previously shared with Desert Orchid . . .

Acknowledging the significance of the victory, Walsh paraded Kauto Star back in front of the ecstatic near sell-out Kempton crowd of 22,000 (the Channel 4 audience peaked at 1.5m) before returning to the winner's enclosure. There wasn't much doubt that Kauto Star was a different horse to the previous season and was right back to something like his best. 'He has looked fantastic this season and seems better in himself. Last year he bled here and was out on his feet at the end, but he's come in this time and is not even having a blow,' said his trainer afterwards. 'He can't have been right last year and, in hindsight, I think it might have taken him last season to get over that horrific fall in Imperial Commander's Gold Cup.'

Applause also greeted Kauto Star's next outing in the Cheltenham Gold Cup but not to welcome him back to the winner's enclosure. 'As the course announcer relayed the news that Kauto Star was being pulled up approaching the tenth fence, the crowd reacted with spontaneous applause, similar to the sympathetic reaction ten years earlier when Istabraq was pulled up after just two flights while attempting a fourth Champion Hurdle victory.' That had been Istabraq's final race, and, as many in the crowd must have suspected at the time, the 2012 Gold Cup proved to be Kauto Star's swansong, though he wasn't officially retired until the following October. His statue was unveiled at Haydock the following month on the day stable-companion Silviniaco Conti won the Betfair Chase. Kauto Star was rated 179 in his final season (1lb ahead of Long Run), making him Timeform's best staying chaser for the fifth time in six seasons.

Long Run was only third to Synchronised in that Gold Cup (Kauto Star's sixth participation in the race, one behind The Dikler's record, had been prefaced by a bad fall in a schooling session) and filled the same position behind stable-companion Bobs Worth in 2013 after winning the King George for a second time.

Only time will tell if the current crop of chasers are able to sustain, in Kauto Star's absence, what had been hailed as a 'golden age of steeplechasing'. 'It is hard to imagine a jumps season without Kauto Star' remarked *Chasers & Hurdlers* in his final essay before going on to list his sixteen Grade 1 victories gained over seven consecutive seasons. The essay on Silviniaco Conti also summarised the bare statistics of Kauto Star's remarkable career.

> His career spanned ten seasons, the last eight of them in Britain when he earned £2,233,093 in race prize money (his career total exceeded £2.3m including earnings as a juvenile hurdler in France). Kauto Star's £1m bonus for landing the Betfair Million (by completing the Betfair, King George and Gold Cup treble in the 2006/07 season), and the £400,000 he earned through heading the BHA's short-lived Order of Merit table in 2006/07 and 2007/08, took his total earnings while trained in Britain to £3,633,093, easily a record for a British- or Irish-based jumper and one that will stand for a long time.

What proved to be Kauto Star's final essay in *Chasers & Hurdlers in 2011/12* recorded that it had been the eighth devoted to him (one short of the number that chronicled Desert Orchid's career, another chaser 'whose longevity contributed to his making a name for himself beyond the normal boundaries of the sport') and that those essays had totalled more than 25,000 words. But as time passes and Kauto Star's status changes from a 'modern' to an historical great, many more words are sure to be written about him, just as they have been about great chasers of the past such as Golden Miller, Arkle, Red Rum and Desert Orchid long after their own lifetimes.

Istabraq

CHAMPION HURDLERS

A Timeform Publication

Champion Hurdlers

Chasers & Hurdlers—jumping's equivalent of the *Racehorses annuals*—was first published covering the 1975/76 season, around halfway through a period that has since become known as 'the golden age of hurdling'. *Favourite Racehorses* used that very title for its chapter devoted to the best hurdlers, several of whom competed against each other regularly over a number of seasons from the mid-'seventies onwards. Hurdlers dominated *Chasers & Hurdlers'* 'Horse of the Year' title in the annual's first five seasons; Night Nurse (who remains Timeform's highest rated hurdler on 182) won the accolade twice, as did his successor, another outstanding hurdler Monksfield, while Sea Pigeon was Timeform's Champion Jumper in the 1979/80 season. Monksfield, Sea Pigeon and Night Nurse filled the first three places in the 1978 Champion Hurdle; Night Nurse had won the two previous editions (with Monksfield runner-up in 1977). Monksfield went on to win it again in 1979 (beating Sea Pigeon into second), while Sea Pigeon had his turn in 1980 (Monksfield second again) and 1981. Bird's Nest was another tip-top, if unreliable, hurdler of the same era who was placed in two (second to Night Nurse in 1976 and third to Sea Pigeon in 1980) of the five Champion Hurdles he contested, while the outstanding novice Golden Cygnet, killed in a fall in the 1978 Scottish Champion Hurdle when looking likely to beat both Night Nurse and Sea Pigeon, also takes high rank among the best hurdlers of the *Chasers & Hurdlers* era.

It was to be the best part of twenty years before another hurdler came along who showed form to rival the likes of Night Nurse and Monksfield. **Istabraq** made his first appearance in a Timeform annual in *Racehorses of 2004*, showing promise when mid-division in a two-year-old maiden at Doncaster for trainer John Gosden in the colours of Hamdan Al Maktoum. He made into a fairly useful performer the following season, winning twice, but without living up to his pedigree. By Sadler's Wells and a close relative to the 1984 Derby winner Secreto, Istabraq was sold for 38,000 guineas at the Newmarket July Sales in 1996. The purchaser was Gosden's former assistant John Durkan who knew Istabraq 'inside out' but, tragically, died from leukaemia before his own training career could get under way. Istabraq thus remained in the care of Aidan O'Brien who oversaw his novice season during which he won his last five races after being beaten a head on his hurdling debut. Istabraq, in the colours of J. P. McManus, was the 'Irish banker' at the 1997 Festival and duly landed some big bets in the Royal SunAlliance Novices' Hurdle:

> Attempts to stifle some of the usual excesses of the celebrating crowd by keeping unauthorised celebrators from the winner's enclosure resulted in the racecourse manager attempting to evict the winning trainer who was not wearing the correct badge. The former was later said to be 'anxious' about the prospect of an Irish victory in the Gold Cup. That result went well for him and, of course, very little since seems to have gone wrong for Aidan O'Brien. Mistaken identity cannot be something that he now has to contend with very often. The twenty-seven-year-old has been champion jumps trainer in Ireland in every year that he's had a licence and took his amazing success story into new territory in the latest Flat season when winning both the Irish One Thousand and Two Thousand Guineas and the Irish Derby.

Aidan O'Brien was to continue to prove a hard man to keep out of the Cheltenham winner's enclosure thanks to Istabraq. Twelve months later, Istabraq returned for the Champion Hurdle and was once again the subject of good support, sent off the 3/1 favourite in a field of eighteen:

> 'Roofer required. Apply Cheltenham racecourse.' The pithy message carried in Ladbrokes' press advertising the day after the Champion Hurdle summed up a splendid St Patrick's Day for the Irish at the Festival meeting. French Ballerina, in the opening Citroen Supreme Novices' Hurdle, and Istabraq, in the Smurfit Champion Hurdle, completed a notable first-day double before a record Tuesday crowd of 44,356. Istabraq's victory the previous year in the Royal SunAlliance Novices' Hurdle had landed some of the biggest bets at the Festival and, unbeaten in the interim, he started favourite to give the Irish their first victory in the Champion Hurdle since Dawn Run fourteen years earlier. Owned by the legendary heavyweight punter J. P. McManus, who warned 'It's easier to make them favourite than make them win,' Istabraq had gained a tremendous following and it seemed all Ireland expected him to deliver the goods again.

Much of that expectation had been fuelled by some unusually bullish words from his trainer. 'He is a better horse than he was this last time year, much quicker and stronger', O'Brien had reported beforehand, '. . . obviously, in the Champion Hurdle everything has to go right, there's not much room for making mistakes, but I expect Istabraq to destroy them.'

> 'Destroy them' Istabraq duly did. In a Champion Hurdle field distinguished more by quantity than quality—there hadn't been a bigger field since Morley Street's year—Istabraq moved to the front three out before producing a telling burst of acceleration rounding the home turn. The Champion Hurdle became a procession in the home straight, Istabraq drawing twelve lengths clear under

hands and heels to deafening cheers from the stands. Istabraq was coasting as the line was reached and is probably a bit better than we are able to rate him on the bare result. His stable-companion Theatreworld, who had given much more like his true running when winning twice since a laboured sixth in the AIG Europe Champion Hurdle, came from well back to fill the runner's-up spot for the second year in succession . . .

Istabraq's spectacular victory equalled the widest winning margin in the history of the Champion Hurdle, that of Insurance back in 1932 when the race was nowhere near so important (the County Hurdle was worth more, for example). There have been two eight-length winners in the past fifty years, Bula and Comedy of Errors in the 'seventies, and, since then, Sea Pigeon (on the occasion of his first win) and For Auction have won by seven, a margin of victory subsequently achieved by See You Then when gaining two of his three victories. The historical parallels are mentioned for interest only. Winning a championship race by a record margin doesn't automatically stamp the winner as a great horse. Istabraq may well go on to prove himself one of the great champions—he must have excellent prospects of successfully defending his title in the next season—but he cannot yet be rated one, not the way we read the form-book. Comedy of Errors (Timeform-rated 178), Bula (176)—who won thirteen successive races over hurdles—and Sea Pigeon (175) are among the leading dozen hurdlers in Timeform's experience. All beat stronger fields on the day in the Champion Hurdle than Istabraq, and built up impressive records over a number of seasons, something which can also be said, to a lesser degree, of lightly-raced three-times winner See You Then (173). For Auction (174) was a surprise winner who never repeated the form, but he was very impressive on the day in beating a high-class field headed by Broadsword, Ekbalco and Pollardstown, all championship-standard performers in their own right. As in the previous season, the two-mile hurdling scene in the latest one suffered from a shortage of top horses—Istabraq, Dato Star (judged on his Haydock win) and Pridwell excepted—and most of Istabraq's opponents at Cheltenham could hitherto be regarded as good-class handicappers at best. That said, Istabraq, whose performance earned him the title Timeform Champion Jumper, could hardly have beaten the field that was turned out against him any more impressively and, as already stated, probably had a bit more in hand than the winning margin. Istabraq's chances of challenging Bula's sequence—having already matched the ten straight victories achieved by two other Timeform top-rated hurdlers Night Nurse (182) and Lanzarote (177)—were ended on his only subsequent start. Pridwell, vastly more reliable and resolute in the main than in previous seasons, fought back under an inspired ride by Tony McCoy to pip Istabraq by a head in the Martell Aintree Hurdle. Istabraq has won on going ranging from heavy to good to firm but the Aintree Hurdle was run in desperately testing conditions—strikingly different to those at Cheltenham—

and no lengthy post-mortem into Istabraq's defeat is necessary. Let's hope he trains on well and enriches the jumping scene for many more years to come.

Istabraq was rated 172+ in *Chasers & Hurdlers* 1997/98 and after an unbeaten campaign in 1998/99 saw his rating rise to 177+, he 'took a further step towards securing himself an exalted place in racing history.'

Istabraq's aura of invincibility—he had run up a winning sequence of ten since losing by a head on his hurdling debut—was dented by his narrow defeat in the Aintree Hurdle. But his reputation was fully restored in the latest season when he never looked like being beaten on any of his starts. Istabraq's programme followed the same path as the previous year, building up firstly to the AIG Europe Champion Hurdle at Leopardstown . . .

If Istabraq's performance in 1998 fell some way short of Champion Hurdle-winning standard (he jumped with less fluency than usual and was ridden out to hold off the novice His Song), the style of his victory in the latest edition ensured that he would start long odds on at Cheltenham. Meeting his main market rival for the Cheltenham championship, the strapping British-trained French Holly, Istabraq won in breathtaking fashion, in the process making a second Champion Hurdle victory look as near a formality as it was possible to be. Always moving supremely well and giving a faultless display of jumping, Istabraq toyed with French Holly, his rider Charlie Swan coolly easing him into the lead going to the last. Swan barely moved a muscle on the flat, cheekily keeping French Holly at bay by a length, like some latter-day Piggott at his most impudent. As in his preceding races, Istabraq's display was the acme of economy. How much he had in hand only Swan knew for certain, but no good judge watching from the stands could have been measuring it in inches.

Sent off the shortest-priced Champion Hurdle favourite for forty-five years, Istabraq was less impressive when landing odds of 9/4-on at Cheltenham from stable-companion Theatreworld again, but in what was 'a near-carbon copy of the closing stages of the AIG Europe Champion Hurdle', he beat French Holly (third at Cheltenham) by a hard-held length once more when following up in the Aintree Hurdle. Istabraq's best performance of the season, however, came in the inaugural running of the Shell Champion Hurdle at Punchestown, thereby completing a hat-trick of wins at the three big spring festivals, a feat not matched until Sprinter Sacre did the same over fences in 2013.

Istabraq has become an ideal vehicle for followers of the maxim 'Better a short-priced winner than a long-priced loser.' Another polished display in the Shell Champion Hurdle at Punchestown—where he started odds on, as in all his other races in the latest season—took his career record over hurdles to seventeen wins from nineteen outings. Once again, those who took the odds—4/1-on this time—never had a moment's anxiety. He won in fine style, recording arguably his best effort in terms of form, by three and a half lengths and five from Decoupage and another horse who developed into a high-class hurdler in the latest season, the most genuine Limestone Lad. Limestone Lad's rider set out to stretch the field but Istabraq and Decoupage (tracking the winner throughout) closed up after the fourth last and always had Limestone Lad in their sights. Istabraq took the lead before the final flight and quickened away with minimum assistance from Swan, again winning with any amount in hand. Little wonder that the connections of Decoupage and Limestone Lad intend sending their horses novice chasing in the next season. That said, judged on his performance at Punchestown, the most progressive Decoupage would be in prime position to take over at the top of the hurdling tree if anything were to befall Istabraq. It was, perhaps, fitting that Istabraq, whose achievements had already assured him of all the Horse of the Year awards going, should have produced his best performance in front of his home crowd at Punchestown.

As it happened, Limestone Lad was kept over hurdles the next season and inflicted a shock defeat on Istabraq who started 7/1-on for the Hatton's Grace Hurdle at Fairyhouse in November. Istabraq had easily beaten Limestone Lad again in the John James McManus Memorial Hurdle at Tipperary beforehand, but over two and a half miles in the Hatton's Grace on soft ground, he found the front-running Limestone Lad a very

2000 Champion Hurdle - Istabraq joins Blue Royal at the last and goes on to join the illustrious list of triple Champion Hurdle winners

different proposition, attempting to give him 5 lb as well as an enormous start. Hatton's Grace (1949-51), incidentally, had been the first horse to win the Champion Hurdle three times; Sir Ken (1952-54) soon emulated him, and so too, in due course, did Persian War (1968-70) and See You Then (1985-87). Istabraq duly joined that illustrious list too, though only after a last-minute scare when a trickle of blood was detected coming from one of his nostrils in the Cheltenham stables the evening before the race.

Just prior to the news of Istabraq's nosebleed, with uncanny timing, two of the biggest Irish bookmakers had grabbed themselves some publicity by declaring that they were paying out ante-post bets on Istabraq before the race was run. Even with the pre-race scare, the course bookmakers opened up at 5/2-on, which would have equalled the shortest-ever price in a Champion Hurdle, that of Sir Ken in 1953. Istabraq, who started at 9/4-on in 1999, was eventually sent off at 15/8-on, with a £75,000 to £150,000 among the recorded wagers. 'I think every single horse in the race is a potential danger,' O'Brien had stated. This was polite, and yes, another runner could fall in front of him, but in terms of all known form Istabraq appeared to face no serious rivals. The only hurdler that might have been capable of giving Istabraq a good race over two miles in the last five years, let alone the latest season, is Dato Star, a runaway winner at Haydock one day before the latest AIG Europe, but he needs good to soft going or softer to produce his best and, after a ludicrous interlude a fortnight before the Festival when it was reported that the going might actually become heavy, the now-customary sound surface duly prevailed. Indeed, as a course record in the Arkle soon revealed, ground conditions were on the firm side of good. Apart from Dato Star, ten others took on Istabraq and the paucity of this opposition can be gauged from the fact that the morning favourite in that betting without Istabraq was the novice Stage Affair, whom Istabraq had beaten so comprehensively last time out . . .

The possibility that Istabraq had suffered a more than superficial injury the day before, combined with Charlie Swan saving his challenge rather later than in 1998 or 1999, made for a slightly more suspenseful race. Two of Istabraq's eleven rivals, however, failed to even take up the gauntlet. Most immediately there was Balla Sola who effectively refused to race, but also declining to put his best foot forward was Theatreworld, who set off behind, as usual, but this time decided to remain there. In hindsight, Theatreworld's failure to finish second was the only slight surprise. Make A Stand set a strong pace; Istabraq won with ease. The others who grabbed some share of the glory up front were Katarino who had his say when Make A Stand wilted turning down the hill, and then Blue Royal who went on at the third last. Two out was where Istabraq had taken over for his first two Champion Hurdle triumphs, but this time he had just moved through into third. Swan was playing much more of a waiting game, holding him up in mid-division and on the inside throughout, and in total, eight of the runners were still thereabouts at the second last. The moment of doubt for the crowd came when Istabraq was shaken up for half a dozen strides in order to go past Katarino on the inside into second, but, greeted by a roar from the grandstand, the champion came back on the bridle entering the straight. Whereas he had taken the last flight six lengths clear in both the previous two years, this time he still had one rival to dispense with but, with the pair of them two lengths ahead of the rest, Istabraq touched down just in front of Blue Royal at the final hurdle and quickly raced clear, four lengths ahead at the line from Hors La Loi III who just caught Blue Royal for second with Ashley Park in fourth.

The Champion Hurdle was Istabraq's final start of the 1999/2000 season—he'd gained revenge on Limestone Lad when easily winning a third AIG Europe Champion Hurdle at Leopardstown beforehand—and his rating, which now stood at 180, had only ever been bettered over hurdles by Night Nurse. 'Istabraq's dominance of his own generation is now so assured, and of such duration' claimed *Chasers & Hurdlers*, 'that the issue is no longer one of judging his ability against his contemporaries.' That Istabraq was head and shoulders above his rivals was plain for all to see, though quantifying that superiority was a harder task.

In the majority of his races, though, Istabraq has shown just how misleading winning distances can be as a measure of superiority. In the four consecutive years that Istabraq has been to the Cheltenham Festival—an achievement in itself—the closest he has come to losing was the length which separated him from Mighty Moss in the 1997 Royal SunAlliance Novices' Hurdle. In those days with Istabraq a length meant a length—Istabraq was not value for any more against Mighty Moss—but since then the official margins and traditional methods of measuring a horse's superiority have been stretched and mocked by Istabraq to such an extent that they have almost lost their meaning. In the plethora of races Istabraq has won over the last three seasons, a length could usually be converted into several times that distance, often ten or even fifteen. In three runnings of the Champion Hurdle, where it should not be possible for a horse to win with such ease, or advisable for his jockey to try to do so, Istabraq has nevertheless remained demonstrably in a class of his own. In addition to his aggregate margin of superiority in the Champion of nineteen and a half lengths, from the second last flight, over all three years, the aggregate moments in which victory has looked in the slightest doubt cannot be more than three or four seconds. Charlie Swan has delayed his retirement from race-riding to continue on board Istabraq, and this appears as good a preparation as any for an increasing number of hours spent in the armchair.

It was hard to see, barring some kind of physical problem, what could prevent Istabraq from becoming the first horse to win four Champion Hurdles. Indeed, there were rumours for a time about Istabraq's wellbeing after he had fallen when attempting to win the December Festival Hurdle at Leopardstown for a fourth time on his return the following season (he was already labouring in diabolical conditions when coming down at the final flight in a race won by Moscow Flyer), though those were scotched when his Cheltenham preparation was completed in good style with a fourth win in the AIG

Europe Champion Hurdle at the same track. But not only was there no fourth Champion Hurdle for Istabraq, there was no Champion Hurdle at all, nor even a Cheltenham Festival come to that.

> . . . the Cheltenham Festival was postponed for a month following a major outbreak of foot and mouth disease in Britain in late-February. Racing resumed in Britain, after a voluntary seven-day suspension in early-March, and the Festival at first looked set to go ahead as planned, though the Irish government, which had banned domestic racing as a precaution, took a hard line on Irish-trained horses travelling. Farcically, however, Cheltenham was caught out by new Ministry of Agriculture guidelines preventing racing if farm animals had grazed on racecourse property within the previous twenty-eight days. Though twenty-three offending sheep had been removed some time previously and Cheltenham could, quite legitimately within the guidelines, have staged the Festival by moving it forward two days to Thursday, Friday and Saturday, the decision was taken to postpone the whole meeting to mid-April. For a time, there was some optimism that Istabraq and other Irish challengers would be able to be sent over, perhaps on a 'one-way ticket'. There was even a rumoured sighting of Istabraq in an English stable! A confirmed case of foot and mouth right on the doorstep of Cheltenham racecourse at the end of March ended all speculation, and the rescheduled meeting was abandoned. What Cheltenham would have been like without the Irish horses (and quite a few of the humans as well) will never be known. There is no rule that says the Irish have to be present at Cheltenham, any more than there is a precept that the British have to be present at Punchestown, but the foot and mouth crisis paralysed parts of rural Britain, particularly Cumbria, Dumfries and Galloway and parts of Devon, and, with Dantean images of pyres of farm animals filling the television news bulletins, the decision to press ahead with the Cheltenham Festival had already aroused considerable opposition within racing and among the rural community.

Istabraq's only other outing in the 2000/01 season ended in a another final-flight fall, one which cost him victory this time and from which he was lucky to emerge unscathed. It came in the Shell Champion Hurdle, transferred to Leopardstown following the abandonment of the Punchestown Festival. Once again, Moscow Flyer was the chief beneficiary, though the way Istabraq had cruised past him into the lead gave the clearest indication that season that he retained all his ability. But whether that ability was still intact by the time the 2002 Festival came round was another matter. Nonetheless, Istabraq, now aged ten, was sent off the 2/1 favourite to win another Champion Hurdle.

> There was no mighty roar after all for a fourth Champion Hurdle victory by Istabraq. Ireland's most popular jumper went out with a whimper in a race won by Hors La Loi III, clearly already struggling when pulled up after just two flights, following weeks of rumour, speculation and conflicting reports about his well-being. A tendon injury in a hock was believed by his trainer to have

been sustained either getting into his stride at the start or, more likely, when jumping the first flight, after which, according to Istabraq's jockey, the horse 'lost his action immediately'. Istabraq, who was dismounted, received a sympathetic round of applause, but there were those who felt that his abject performance showed that he should not even have been in the Champion Hurdle line-up. Restrictions in force because of the foot and mouth epidemic had prevented the Champion Hurdle being run in 2001 but Istabraq had given the clearest indication—to our eyes at least—that, in terms of merit, he retained all his ability. But he did end up on the deck on two of his three outings in 2000/01, which put a question mark for the first time over his jumping. He appeared only once in the latest season before Cheltenham, making rather heavy weather, after the early fall of main rival Liss A Paoraigh, of beating markedly inferior opposition in the Tote December Festival Hurdle at Leopardstown. Istabraq jumped well in the main but had to be shaken up to get on top of Bust Out after the final flight, winning by a head and raising doubts about whether, now rising ten, he might be past his prime.

Istabraq was retired as the winner of twenty-three of his twenty-six completed starts over hurdles and became the first British or Irish jumper to win over £1m in prize-money. Although he fell twice late in his career, fluent jumping was a hallmark of his performances, as was a fine turn of foot. He was beaten only twice (both times over two and a half miles) in twenty-three races between December 1996, in his novice season, and March 2000. It was to be a while before that sort of dominance by one horse was seen again in the top two-mile hurdles, but in the meantime, the Irish had plenty more Champion Hurdle victories to celebrate at Cheltenham.

With Hardy Eustace winning in 2004 and 2005, followed by successes for Brave Inca and Sublimity in the next two seasons, Irish-trained horses won four consecutive renewals of the Champion Hurdle, as well as taking the first five places in 2005 and the first four a year later. Hardy Eustace's trainer Dessie Hughes had ridden Monksfield to the second of that horse's Champion Hurdle wins. While none of the horses involved were in the same league as Monksfield and his contemporaries, the Irish hurdlers of the first decade of the twenty-first century enjoyed a similar period of sustained, and close, rivalry. Only necks separated Hardy Eustace, Harchibald and Brave Inca in the finish of the 2005 Champion Hurdle, while the AIG Europe Champion Hurdle at Leopardstown earlier in the season had been closer still, with Macs Joy coming out on top by a short head from Brave Inca, and Hardy Eustace a head back in third. Macs Joy and Hardy Eustace finished second and third respectively behind Brave Inca at Cheltenham in 2006, while Brave Inca was runner-up in the Champion Hurdle the following season to Sublimity, with Hardy Eustace in fourth.

Thrilling as it was, the 2005 Champion Hurdle wasn't a vintage edition and *Chasers & Hurdlers* speculated that 'it may end up being remembered as much for being a race Harchibald lost, as for being one which Hardy Eustace won' after Harchibald had been upsides on the bridle a hundred yards from the line. Harchibald's defeat resulted in

A controversial finish to the 2005 Champion Hurdle - halfway up the run-in and Harchibald and Paul Carberry are apparently cruising alongside the hard-ridden Hardy Eustace

plenty of criticism for his rider, Paul Carberry, though in the opinion of *Chasers & Hurdlers* 'whether Carberry's tactics contributed to his defeat, or whether all the blame attached to Harchibald himself, is virtually impossible to prove one way or the other, though, as we have said, Harchibald has a history of shirking it.' Whereas Hardy Eustace, Brave Inca and Macs Joy were all game and reliable performers, Harchibald was very much the joker of this particular pack, much as Bird's Nest had been among his peers. Harchibald received the Timeform 'squiggle' to alert subscribers to the fact that he was no reliable betting proposition, something that needed reiterating in his essay the following season too:

> Only two hurdlers in the history of *Chasers & Hurdlers* have been rated higher than Harchibald when allotted a squiggle, namely Bird's Nest (the best horse never to win the Champion Hurdle) and Morley Street (1991 Champion Hurdle winner and successful four times in the Aintree Hurdle). Naturally, connections of top performers tend to be defensive (and/or offended!) in the face of criticism of their charges. Mercy Rimell, for example, was very outspoken about Timeform's decision to add a squiggle to her former champion hurdler Gaye Brief in the mid-'eighties, whilst Josh Gifford is reputed to have thrown his 1982/83 annual into the fireplace after similar treatment had been meted out to his prolific high-class staying chaser Royal Judgement. Noel Meade has also taken exception to media criticism of Harchibald, who like the other quartet

mentioned has proved a marvellous servant to connections. It bears repeating, however, that failure to run on is a sign of unreliability and whether Harchibald's problem in this area is temperamental or physical is irrelevant when it comes to assessing his suitability as a betting proposition.

It wasn't until 2009 that Brave Inca, Hardy Eustace and Harchibald each contested the Champion Hurdle for the final time, though they were all veterans by then and none of them played a part in the finish. The most regrettable absentee from that year's Cheltenham Festival had been the leading novice hurdler **Hurricane Fly** who had comprehensively beaten Harchibald's stable-companion Go Native, subsequently winner of the Supreme Novices' at Cheltenham, at Leopardstown's Christmas meeting. That had been Hurricane Fly's fourth win from five starts over hurdles but a splint problem meant he wasn't seen out again that season. In fact, it was to be another two years before Hurricane Fly made his first appearance at Cheltenham after a sprained ligament had kept him off the track for much of the 2009/10 season.

Perhaps at last a true heir to Istabraq has emerged. Hurricane Fly, enjoying a more trouble-free campaign than in the two previous seasons and able to run at the Cheltenham Festival for the first time, won all five of his starts (culminating in the Champion Hurdle at Punchestown which took place after the end of the British season). All his wins were at Grade 1 level, the undoubted highlight his success in the Stan James Champion Hurdle in March. His victory over the previously unbeaten Peddlers Cross, with the subsequent Aintree Hurdle winner Oscar Whisky in third and the subsequent Grande Course de Haies winner Thousand Stars in fourth was—judged on the bare form—good enough to have won nearly all the most recent runnings of the race. Hurricane Fly's comprehensive victory in the Rabobank Champion Hurdle at Punchestown over Thousand Stars and the previous Champion Hurdle winner Binocular, who had been forced to miss Cheltenham in controversial circumstances, left no doubt that Hurricane Run was not only the best two-mile hurdler around at the moment, but also one of the best seen for years, rated behind three-times Champion Hurdle winner Istabraq at present but with Alderbrook the only other Champion Hurdle winner to earn a higher Timeform rating in the two decades since Morley Street, who was the highest-rated two-miler of his year at 174. It is no surprise that Hurricane Fly figures at short odds to follow up his victory at Cheltenham next March. Like the World Hurdle winner Big Buck's and the Cheltenham Gold Cup victor Long Run in their respective categories, he is the undisputed champion in his sphere, and the style of his successes in an unbeaten campaign at the highest level, that lasted longer and took in more races than the corresponding campaigns of Big Buck's (also unbeaten) and Long Run, combined to just tip the balance in Hurricane Fly's favour when it came to deciding the Timeform Horse of the Year . . .

Hurricane Fly might have been a grandson of Istabraq's sire Sadler's Wells, but beforehand there had apparently been a school of thought that his pedigree might have contained a weak link regarding his ability to come up the Cheltenham hill:

> There were some who feared whether Hurricane Fly would make it to Cheltenham, having missed the two previous Festivals, though, in the build-up this time, no news turned out to be good news. For some reason, however, momentum seemed to gather behind statistical analysis produced to show the poor record of the progeny of Montjeu, Hurricane Fly's sire, in races at Cheltenham, the theory that his stock were not effective on a track with such a stiff finish seeming to gain some credence. It was left to Hugh Taylor, of At The Races, to produce a further set of statistics which showed the excellent record of Montjeu's progeny at Towcester, a track with the stiffest finish in the country!

Hurricane Fly wrapped up the campaign by winning his second Rabobank Champion Hurdle at Punchestown and, rated 172, was cut to just 2/1 favourite for the 2012 Champion Hurdle. After a belated—but tremendously impressive—winning return in the Irish Champion Hurdle at Leopardstown nine months later, Hurricane Fly went to Cheltenham as the first odds-on favourite for the Champion Hurdle since Istabraq twelve years earlier.

> As defeats in championship races go, that of Hurricane Fly at odds on in the latest running of the Champion Hurdle at Cheltenham was one of the biggest upsets in recent years. Hurricane Fly was aiming to repeat his impressive victory of twelve months previously and was sent off at 6/4-on. That he managed only third, five and a half lengths behind the 11/1-chance Rock On Ruby, showed that Hurricane Fly was almost certainly not quite at his peak on the day, even though the tactics employed on him in the race weren't ideal—in hindsight—and he had seldom encountered in any of his previous starts over jumps anything like the true end-to-end gallop at which the latest Champion was run. The gallop was set by eventual runner-up Overturn, with the winner among those giving chase, while Hurricane Fly, as usual, was held up towards the rear, typically travelling strongly. Such tactics served Hurricane Fly well in 2011, when he won a slower-tempo Champion by a length and a quarter from Overturn's stablemate Peddlers Cross (Overturn was seventh that year), but in the latest edition it proved more difficult to get into the race from off the pace. Hurricane Fly was off the bridle before he reached a challenging position and, although he was still closing on the leaders on the long run to the last, the effort took its toll and he was making no further headway up the stiff climb to the finish.

The 2012 Champion Hurdle proved to be Hurricane Fly's only defeat in his last fourteen races to the end of the 2012/13 season. Whilst that deprived him of the chance to join Istabraq in the select group of Champion Hurdlers to have won the race three times (consecutively, at least), his subsequent win in the 2013 renewal made Hurricane Fly a still rarer Champion Hurdle winner—one who had lost his title and then regained it.

Hurricane Fly becomes the first since Comedy of Errors in 1975
to regain the Champion Hurdle crown

It is often said that staying at the top can be harder than actually getting there. All credit, then, to any champion who loses his crown and wins it back. The Champion Hurdle winner who relinquishes his title usually does so for good, with only Comedy of Errors having regained the trophy after losing it—until the latest season. Comedy of Errors first won the Champion Hurdle in 1973, was beaten the following year and then won the race again in 1975. Former Cheltenham Gold Cup winners have found it just as hard to regain past glories. Long Run became the latest to try—and fail—leaving Kauto Star as the only horse to have won back chasing's blue riband after losing it. The 2011 Champion Hurdle winner Hurricane Fly succeeded where many before him had failed since Comedy of Errors, winning the two-mile hurdling championship for the second time in the latest season after finishing only third when odds on for the race twelve months earlier.

It is rare for a Champion Hurdle winner not to bid for another win in the race, with the 1994 winner, the mare Flakey Dove, who was retired after suffering an injury the following year, the last Champion Hurdle winner not to contest the race again. Seven horses have now won the Champion Hurdle more than once since Comedy of Errors, Hurricane Fly adding his name to those of Night Nurse, Monksfield and Sea Pigeon (who won the next six renewals between them after Comedy of Errors), triple winner See You Then in the 'eighties, Istabraq who emulated him a decade or so later, and Hardy Eustace in 2004 and 2005. A slightly longer list of Champion Hurdle winners since Comedy of Errors have been beaten in the following year's renewal and then failed—miserably in most cases—in at least one further attempt to win the race again a second time. For Auction, Beech Road, Morley Street, Granville Again, Rooster Booster, Brave Inca and Sublimity all come into that category and, while only Morley Street and Granville Again failed to reach the frame twelve months after winning the race, all of those were without trace when making a further attempt . . .

Recapturing Champion Hurdle-winning form that has been lost is therefore beyond most winners of the race who, in addition, have to face new and often younger contenders who have emerged since they won the championship. For both Comedy of Errors and Hurricane Fly, however, failure to retain their Champion Hurdle titles was not an indication that their form was on the slide, or that others had improved past them, but were merely blips in records that were otherwise hard to fault. Comedy of Errors won four races in a row before his three-length defeat by Lanzarote in 1974 when it was noted that he did not look so well as usual and had sweated up—the Rimells were also critical of the ride given to him by Bill Smith. He went into the following year's race after a very similar programme, having won the 'Fighting Fifth' at Newcastle for the third year running, and also gained repeat victories in the Cheltenham Trial Hurdle (now the International) and the Sweeps Hurdle at Leopardstown, all of those victories achieved under Ken Whyte, who had taken over as stable jockey from Smith. Comedy of Errors and Lanzarote dominated the betting for the 1975 Champion Hurdle, with Comedy of Errors coming out on top this time and Lanzarote disappointing back in seventh . . .

Comedy of Errors and Lanzarote were rated 178 and 177 respectively at their best and belonged to the first half of the 'golden age of hurdling.' As for Hurricane Fly, he was rated 173 in 2012/13 as he had been the previous season. Beaten only once on Irish soil, Hurricane Fly's second Champion Hurdle win at Cheltenham had come between a third success in the Irish Champion at Leopardstown and a fourth in the Rabobank Champion Hurdle at Punchestown, and just as this book was going to press, a second success in the Morgiana Hurdle at Punchestown took his total of Grade 1 wins to seventeen, breaking the record set over jumps by Kauto Star. As his latest essay concluded, Hurricane Fly was now worthy of a place alongside Ireland's other outstanding two-mile hurdler of the modern era. 'The essay on Hurricane Fly in *Chasers & Hurdlers* 2010/11, the season of his first win in the Champion Hurdle, began with the suggestion 'that perhaps at last a true heir to Istabraq has emerged.' Few would deny Hurricane Fly that accolade now.'

Big Buck's

STAYING HURDLERS

A Timeform Publication

Staying Hurdlers

For much of its forty-one year history, the Stayers' Hurdle (renamed the World Hurdle in 2005) has traditionally been viewed as the poor relation among the Cheltenham Festival's major championship events, overshadowed in particular by the Champion Hurdle. In truth, for about three-quarters of this period the standard of runners was consistently lower than that for the Champion, as was illustrated by those to have run in both races, with most of them aimed at the longer event only when they were no longer contenders for the two-mile crown. All of that has changed in recent history, however, with Timeform's best staying hurdler having achieved a higher rating than its two-mile counterpart in ten out of the last twelve seasons. Pride of place amongst this group must go to the Paul Nicholls-trained **Big Buck's**, who simply hasn't looked back since connections opted to revert him to hurdles after jumping problems were beginning to blight his nascent chasing career. His rating of 176+ is the highest achieved at three miles or further over hurdles on British and Irish soil since the *Chasers & Hurdlers* series began in 1975/76, whilst Big Buck's made racing history with two notable feats in 2011/12—he became the first horse to win the World Hurdle four times and, on his very next start, he broke Sir Ken's long-standing record for the longest winning sequence over jumps (sixteen victories).

> The vice-like grip of Big Buck's on the staying hurdling division showed no immediate sign of being loosened as he strode imperiously through another unbeaten campaign. He took in five races, one more than in each of the two preceding seasons, and rarely looked troubled. If anything, the gap between him and his opponents is widening, with margins of five, eight, seven and nine lengths recorded for four of his victories. Only when gaining a fourth win in the Ladbrokes World Hurdle did Big Buck's face any sort of challenge to his hegemony, with the runner-up Voler La Vedette briefly looking to be going the better and becoming just the second horse since the 2009 Liverpool Hurdle to trade at odds-on in running against Big Buck's on Betfair, a measure of the

Big Buck's lands his fourth successive World Hurdle

manner in which he has dominated the opposition. The victory of Big Buck's in the latest Liverpool Hurdle at Aintree was his fourth successive one in that race too, following his third wins in the Long Distance Hurdle at Newbury and the Long Walk Hurdle, and his second in the Cleeve Hurdle at Cheltenham. The Aintree win was his seventeenth in succession in a run stretching back to January 1st 2009. It surpassed the long-standing record of sixteen over jumps in Britain set by triple Champion Hurdle winner Sir Ken in the early-'fifties, a period when hurdling was generally less competitive than it is nowadays (Sir Ken once started at as short as 33/1-on while building that sequence). With a splendid combination of ability, consistency and longevity, Big Buck's has truly proved himself the horse of a generation. In more recent times, only Istabraq and the top staying hurdler Baracouda—both of whom raced in the colours of J. P. McManus—have come close to such complete dominance. Following a second on his hurdling debut, Istabraq met with defeat only once on his next nineteen starts, when beaten a head by Pridwell (under an inspired Tony McCoy) in the 1998 Aintree Hurdle. French-trained Baracouda showed top-class form and proved almost invincible in the four seasons between 2000/01 and 2003/04, a sequence of ten straight victories ending when he was beaten by front-running Deano's Beeno (ridden by McCoy) when trying to win a third Long Walk Hurdle at Ascot in the 2002/03 season. Baracouda suffered only his second defeat in sixteen outings when going down to Iris's Gift in the following season's Stayers' Hurdle. Baracouda wasn't so good in 2004/05 but still won two of his three races, suffering his only defeat at the hands of Inglis Drever in what had been renamed the World Hurdle. That Big Buck's has created a jumping record, and run up a sequence with which only Istabraq's and Baracouda's stands comparison in recent times, reflects great credit on him and those who have guided his career. He is the deserved recipient of the Horse of The Year accolade in this Annual.

To examine first his durability and consistency, Big Buck's was last beaten over hurdles by Good Bye Simon in the Prix Alain du Breil at Auteuil in June 2007. He won three times in seven starts over fences after joining Paul Nicholls before he reverted to hurdling, in a handicap at Cheltenham. That was followed by wins in the Cleeve, the World Hurdle and the Liverpool Hurdle. In all, twenty-eight different opponents took on Big Buck's in those four races and several of them threatened him. In all, five traded at odds-on against him in running—the subsequent Grand National winner Don't Push It in the handicap, Punchestowns in the Cleeve, Punchestowns and Kasbah Bliss in the World Hurdle and Mighty Man at Aintree—but he saw them all off, displaying stamina and resolution in equal measures. The jumping technique of Big Buck's had appeared a frailty in his races over fences (when he unseated Sam Thomas at the last in the 2008 Hennessy it had a significant impact on both their careers) but his technique has proved well-nigh faultless over hurdles. Of his earliest opponents, Kasbah Bliss (who started odds-on for the 2009 World Hurdle) was driven away to the Flat, winning the Prix du Cadran in 2011, while Punchestowns was sent off to try his hand over fences, with some success though without living up to the highest expectations. In the next season, 2009/10, twenty-six individual opponents took on Big Buck's in his four races but none came particularly close to beating him, Time For Rupert pushing him closest when runner-up in the World Hurdle, unable to capitalise on a rare error by Big Buck's at the final flight. In 2010/11, Big Buck's was taken on by twenty-eight different rivals, only Grands Crus making much of an impact against him. In a muddling race for the World Hurdle, Grands Crus looked a big danger to Big Buck's as he came from a long way back to challenge. Any idea that he might have proved an even more dangerous opponent had the race been more strongly-run was scotched at Aintree where, in a truly-run race, Grands Crus was put firmly in his place. Like Punchestowns and Time For Rupert before him, Grands Crus didn't stick around to take on Big Buck's again, trying his luck over fences in the latest season, coincidentally starting favourite for the RSA Chase, as had both Punchestowns and Time For Rupert. All three ran below expectations in that race.

In the latest season, Big Buck's didn't have to be anywhere near his best to win the sportingbet Long Distance Hurdle at Newbury in November, landing odds of 8/1-on in a canter from five opponents. The odds were the shortest at which he has yet started and he hasn't been sent off at odds against in any race since his first World Hurdle. Big Buck's didn't have to run any better than in the Long Distance Hurdle to add the Long Walk Hurdle at Ascot the following month. Big Buck's faced six rivals, of whom Dynaste looked the most interesting. A fresh rival in the Grands Crus mould, Dynaste made the running in an attempt to wear out Big Buck's but the tactics didn't work, Big Buck's coming through to win with the same authority as at Newbury, his stablemate Five Dream, a 66/1-shot, finishing second, as he had in the Long Distance Hurdle. It was the first Long Walk Hurdle that Big Buck's had won at Ascot, the two previous runnings having been transferred to Newbury due to abandonments.

The intention was that Big Buck's would go straight to the World Hurdle, as he had in the two previous campaigns but the Cleeve Hurdle at Cheltenham was added. Dynaste again looked the main opponent in a field of six but, even under a better judged ride than at Ascot, Dynaste couldn't lay a finger on Big Buck's, even though he ran right up to his best. Big Buck's landed odds of 4/1-on by seven lengths, Dynaste beating the previous year's World Hurdle third Mourad by ten lengths for second. The way Big Buck's cut through the field and galloped home up the hill was remorseless and his performance, in terms of bare form, rates as one of his very best. While Newbury and Ascot had been cakewalks by comparison, merely showing his well-being, the Cleeve proved that Big Buck's was every bit as good as ever and sure to take all the beating in his fourth World Hurdle. Big Buck's faced ten opponents in the World Hurdle, two fewer than in 2011 and three fewer than in both 2010 and 2009. As in the two previous runnings, he was sent off at a shade of odds on, at 6/5-on this time, facing two fresh opponents, both of whom had contested the Champion Hurdle the previous year, the third and fourth from that race Oscar Whisky and Thousand Stars. In form terms, Oscar Whisky was as good a hurdler as Big Buck's had faced, on a par with Punchestowns and Grands Crus. If Oscar Whisky's stamina held, he looked sure to prove a worthy rival, while Thousand Stars had won the Grande Course de Haies d'Auteuil over twenty-five furlongs since running in the Champion Hurdle. Dynaste and a couple of improving younger hurdlers Smad Place and So Young were also in the World Hurdle line-up, along with old rivals Mourad and Five Dream. Five Dream, ridden fairly patiently previously to finish as highly as he could behind his stable companion, was this time used more in the role of a pacemaker, sharing the lead and ensuring there was no repeat of the previous year's dawdle, something which might play into the hands of Oscar Whisky and Thousand Stars. Sent on by Ruby Walsh turning down the hill after three out, Big Buck's was not the last on the bridle by any means but he responded with his usual gameness under pressure, seeing off Oscar Whisky, who patently failed to stay, and Thousand Stars before the mare Voler La Vedette was produced to make the final challenge. Despite wandering both ways, Big Buck's found more and drew away to win by a length and three quarters, with a further seven lengths back to the staying-on Smad Place in third. With several of his rivals failing to run to their best—among them Dynaste as well as Oscar Whisky and Thousand Stars—the latest World Hurdle might not have turned into so strong a renewal as it threatened to be but Big Buck's put up another top-class effort.

As with Istabraq, Big Buck's is so superior to most of his rivals that it is very rare that he is required to run right up to the limit of his ability. He mostly comes up against opponents who just aren't up to making a race of it with him at level weights. Sir Ken's winning run came to an end with defeat in a minor event at 7/1-on; Istabraq was 7/4-on when he was touched off by Pridwell at Aintree and Baracouda 11/4-on when beaten by Deano's Beeno at Ascot. It will surely be an upset of similar magnitude if, or when, Big Buck's has his sequence ended.

Sir Ken, a French-bred gelding like Big Buck's, is widely acknowledged as the finest hurdler of the era just after World War II—he won the Champion Hurdle in 1952, 1953 and 1954—and racked up his unbeaten sequence of sixteen wins during that reign. Jump racing may well be more competitive nowadays than it was then, yet there is still a feeling that even Big Buck's (who extended his unbeaten sequence to eighteen in 2012/13 before injury intervened) could be tested more fully—a return to chasing, the Gold Cup at Royal Ascot and the Grande Course de Haies d'Auteuil have all been mooted as possible targets for him. However, surely a clash with the Irish-trained mare **Quevega** (rated 164), another top-class staying hurdler whose own unbeaten record stretches back to March 2010, is the one that most jumping fans would clamour for? Quevega has been busy making her own piece of Cheltenham history in recent years, her fifth straight win in the David Nicholson Mares' Hurdle in 2013 making her only the second horse (following five-times Gold Cup winner Golden Miller) to win the same race that many times in the Festival's long history. From a ratings viewpoint, however, Quevega's four successive wins in the Grade 1 World Series Hurdle at Punchestown are a far more significant achievement and have long marked her out as the only viable challenger to Big Buck's, if only such a meeting could be arranged. *Chasers & Hurdlers* 2011/12 examined the prospect:

> The lightly-raced Quevega, at this stage seems unlikely ever to meet Big Buck's, though the prospect of a meeting between the pair remains tantalising. Another Irish mare Voler La Vedette momentarily threatened to push Big Buck's very close in the 2012 Ladbrokes World Hurdle, briefly trading at a shade of odds-on in running before going down by a length and three quarters. Voler La Vedette has lost all three of her encounters with Quevega and has never finished closer to her than the five and a half lengths which separated them in the latest ladbrokes.com World Series Hurdle at Punchestown in April in which they were first and second. Big Buck's versus Quevega—the two outstanding staying hurdlers of the moment—would be a head-to-head full of entertainment value, a 'battle of the sexes' fitting into Racing For Change's remit to promote events that 'broaden the appeal of the sport.' Dawn Run's famous match over two miles against Buck House, after the pair had won the Gold Cup and the Queen Mother Champion Chase respectively, attracted thousands of

new racegoers to the Punchestown Festival in 1986 when the enterprising Irish Racing Board contributed IR £10,000 of the IR £25,000 prize, the rest of the prize money coming in three equal portions from the connections of Buck House, from Coolmore which stood Dawn Run's sire Deep Run and from Punchestown racecourse. The size of the prize for the Buck House/Dawn Run match dwarfed the other races at the Punchestown Festival—the principal two-mile chase at the meeting at the time was a handicap and there was no Punchestown Gold Cup until 1999—and it was bigger than for any race at Aintree's Grand National meeting except the National itself.

There would appear to be an opportunity for either Aintree or Punchestown to tempt the respective connections of Quevega and Big Buck's, perhaps by offering to double the prize money for their staying championship if both horses line up. When Dawn Run met Buck House in their specially-arranged match, she did so at levels and started at 6/4-on before leading most of the way to beat him by two and a half lengths. Quevega would receive a 7 lb weight-for-sex allowance at both Aintree and Punchestown, the allowance raised from 5 lb to 7 lb in Ireland in the 2011/12 season.

The views of Ruby Walsh, the regular rider of the pair, on a prospective clash would certainly be interesting, though it remains to be seen if he continues to partner Big Buck's in 2013/14 following his decision to surrender his role as Paul Nicholls' stable jockey.

Regular riders weren't an issue for **Inglis Drever** (rated 169), who held the record for most wins in the World Hurdle until Big Buck's came along, his three Cheltenham victories all coming under different jockeys (Graham Lee in 2005, Paddy Brennan in 2007 and Denis O'Regan in 2008). Despite that, Inglis Drever wasn't an altogether straightforward ride and had a tendency to race a bit in snatches, though the fact he always showed tremendous battling qualities at the business end of the race ensured his popularity with racing fans. He was the early flagbearer for Newcastle-based software tycoon Graham Wylie, who was briefly dubbed as jump racing's answer to Chelsea owner Roman Abramovich following a string of big-money purchases upon entering the sport, along with his wife Andrea. Indeed, Inglis Drever was the Wylies' second-ever Cheltenham Festival runner (their first had been unplaced less than twenty-four hours earlier) when he narrowly failed to justify short-priced favouritism in the 2004 Royal SunAlliance Novices' Hurdle, finishing a rallying second to Fundamentalist after showing the first signs of the on-and-off-the-bridle racing style that would characterise his career later on.

A tilt at the Champion Hurdle was initially on the cards for Inglis Drever the following campaign, with connections racing him at around two miles on all four starts prior to the Festival—he warmed up with wins in the Champion Hurdle Trial at Haydock and Kingwell at Wincanton, having previously finished runner-up in both the Fighting Fifth at Newcastle and the Bula at Cheltenham. The decision to switch him to the longer race (when he became the Wylies' third winner of the 2005 Festival) was no doubt influenced by Inglis Drever's novice season, when he'd been campaigned solely at around two and

Denis O'Regan celebrates on board Inglis Drever after the gelding's third win in the World Hurdle

a half miles, but it should also be stressed that the World Hurdle doesn't represent quite the test of stamina it once did. Prior to 1993, the race was run straight after the Champion Hurdle on the Tuesday and took place on the Old Course at Cheltenham over a distance of three miles and a furlong, as opposed to its current home on the New Course over just three miles. The stopwatch suggests an even bigger discrepancy between the two tracks than merely one furlong, however. The last winner under the race's previous conditions was Nomadic Way in 1992, when he clocked a time of 6:33.93 on good ground, in what is widely considered to be one of the strongest ever renewals of the staying championship. Since its switch to later in the week on the New Course, the average winning time using the fourteen of the twenty runnings when the going was good, is 5:47.23—which clearly casts some doubts as to the accuracy of the advertised race distances in both examples.

Whatever the merits of the latter debate, it is a shame the World Hurdle is no longer staged on the Old Course as it is the better of the two hurdling tracks on offer at Cheltenham, though such a switch seems unlikely since the advent of the four-day Festival in 2005. There was one last hurrah for the race over the Old Course, though, as Inglis Drever completed his hat-trick of World Hurdle wins on the original track (albeit over the new trip of three miles) when the Festival became an impromptu three-day meeting again in 2008.

The abandonment of racing on the Wednesday of the Cheltenham Festival, when high winds raised safety concerns, resulted in mammoth cards being staged on the last two days. The rearranged ten-race card on the Thursday incorporated two of the meeting's biggest championship races, the Queen Mother Champion Chase and the Ladbrokes World Hurdle, the centrepieces nowadays of the second and third days respectively. With three other Grade 1s on the revised card (Royal & SunAlliance Chase, Ryanair Chase and Champion Bumper), there was plenty of competition for airtime and newsprint—both before and after! Master Minded's breathtaking victory in the Champion Chase—one of the most impressive performances ever seen at the Festival—

stole some of the thunder from a prodigious achievement by the season's leading hurdler Inglis Drever who became the first horse to win the staying hurdlers' championship at Cheltenham three times, one better than Crimson Embers, Galmoy and Baracouda, the first- and last-named very unlucky in their different ways not to end up as triple winners.

The latest World Hurdle was run at a sound pace, ensuring a proper test of stamina, and there were no real excuses for the beaten horses. In a field of seventeen, the form horses came to the fore, the first five home being the first five in the betting. Inglis Drever doesn't always fill the eye beforehand but he did on this occasion, looking in really good shape. Held up and jumping well, Inglis Drever began to make his effort approaching the third last, despite not having much room at that point, and responded well under pressure to reach the leaders entering the final straight. He battled on gamely after taking the lead early on the run-in from Kasbah Bliss whom he held by a length. Kasbah Bliss's rider Christophe Pieux picked up a three-day suspension for excessive use of the whip in the World Hurdle as the first two fought out a battle royal, clear of third-placed Kazal, who did best of the five Irish-trained challengers, finishing seven lengths behind Kasbah Bliss and four and a half ahead of fourth-placed Blazing Bailey, with his stable-companion My Way de Solzen, the 2006 winner, fifth. The only real disappointments were the poor running of the previous year's Spa winner Wichita Lineman and of dual Champion Hurdle winner Hardy Eustace for whom the well-run three miles seemed to be too stiff a test of stamina, though tests afterwards showed that his blood was wrong.

As that account of the 2008 World Hurdle reported, the stewards took a dim view of the performance by Christophe Pieux aboard Kasbah Bliss in the latter stages, though that pales into insignificance compared with some of the treatment that has been meted out to French-based jockeys on high-profile jumpers in Britain since the early-1990s. Polish-born Adam Kondrat bore the brunt of the early criticism following three successive defeats (including very narrow ones in both 1991 and 1992) aboard The Fellow in the Cheltenham Gold Cup before finally winning the 1994 renewal, but the real venom was reserved for trainer's son Thierry Doumen when he took over as stable jockey to his father Francois at the end of that decade. Costly reverses aboard First Gold at Newbury (beaten into second at 3/1-on) and Sandown (soft unseat when 13/8-on) in 2000/01 didn't exactly endear him to British punters, particularly as his mount had shown himself to be the best staying chaser around that season thanks to runaway wins in the King George at Kempton and the Martell Cup at Aintree—he'd have been a hot favourite for the Cheltenham Gold Cup had it not been lost to the foot-and-mouth outbreak which claimed that year's Festival. Another horse to suffer from the loss of that year's Festival was the outstanding novice **Baracouda** (rated 175), who would have taken all the beating in the Stayers' Hurdle and, unlike First Gold, did manage to win the one-off replacement race staged at Sandown's end-of-the-season meeting. It was Doumen's association with this gelding which drew most jingoistic criticism from the armchair jockeys, though he was to have the last laugh when Baracouda claimed his second Stayers' Hurdle crown in the truly vintage renewal of 2003.

'The French are wiser than they seem,' wrote Francis Bacon. 'And the Spaniards seem wiser than they are.' Some four hundred years later, and leaving the Spanish question for another day, weighing up the French is as hot an issue as ever and the Bacon view isn't one that everyone goes along with. On the world political stage, the spring of 2003 saw the United States and British governments fall out with the French, and more specifically President Jacques Chirac, over policy towards Iraq. One of Britain's newspapers took to portraying Chirac as a worm and, across the Atlantic, assorted expressions of disgust included a restaurateur pouring a thousand dollars worth of French wine down his toilet, french fries renamed as freedom fries and a fourteen-ton armoured vehicle in Las Vegas grinding its way over a pile of 'French goods' including their flag, Chirac's portrait, a Paris travel guide, Perrier water, yoghurt and a French loaf. Hollywood personalities threatened to boycott the Cannes Film Festival. It was all pretty much unprecedented. In racing, of course, the French issue is something that seems never to go away. World leaders have merely begun to sound like the British media or punter when they get their knives out for a French jockey.

There was, to our knowledge, no mashing of their portraits by armoured vehicles, but Thierry Doumen and Jacques Ricou certainly got plenty of stick in Britain during the latest season. They must be used to it. Doumen in particular seems to have criticism follow him around on this side of the Channel and during 2001/02 the signs were that he would never win the doubters round as criticism centred on his riding of Baracouda, on whom he was in the process of compiling the sport's most impressive current winning sequence. In all, when the latest season commenced, Baracouda had eleven wins from fifteen starts and was on a winning run of nine in a row. He was still a novice when he won the Long Walk Hurdle in December 2000 by fourteen lengths. The form he showed that day put him among the very best novice hurdlers in the history of *Chasers & Hurdlers*. Among other exploits the following season, he took the Long Walk again, this time by twenty-four lengths, and a high-quality renewal of the Stayers' Hurdle at Cheltenham, confirming himself the season's best hurdler and earning the Timeform accolade of Champion Jumper. The only disappointment was that he had not crossed swords with the outstanding Irish hurdler Limestone Lad, who was forced to miss the Festival because of injury. The pair had never met.

Baracouda's bid to make it ten wins in a row came in the Pricewaterhousecoopers Ascot Hurdle in November, immediately setting the tone for a season of burlesque achievement. He started 5/2-on against three opponents and what an extraordinary race it turned out to be. Two of the runners, Landing Light and Carlovent, ran nowhere near their best but 11/1-shot Mr Cool posed more than enough problems for Baracouda. A horse as good as Baracouda should not, all other things being equal, have any trouble beating Mr Cool—39 lb separated them in the 2001/2 Timeform ratings—but all other things weren't equal at Ascot as, in addition to giving Mr Cool 8 lb, Baracouda also conceded him a lead of forty lengths. This was not entirely an act of generosity on the part of Thierry Doumen, nor one of opportunism on the part of Mr Cool's jockey Tony McCoy, but after the field of four took some thirteen seconds to respond to the tapes having risen, Mr Cool found himself in a lead of fifteen lengths not long after he was the first to put himself forward. This advantage was soon extended into a massive lead which still comprised some forty lengths when the field took the seventh of the eleven hurdles. Second favourite Landing Light made no contribution to the pursuit, while Carlovent simply isn't good enough to overturn a deficit of such proportions against his stable companion. However, Baracouda and Carlovent had reduced the margin to twenty lengths rounding the final turn, and, leaving Carlovent behind, Baracouda was only eleven lengths down at the last. Only eleven lengths! Getting the distance down to those proportions was an achievement in itself but when, in the heavy ground, the leader negotiated that flight like a tired horse, honourable defeat for Baracouda was surprisingly no longer the only possibility. Baracouda didn't take the last a great deal better than the leader but he was staying on strongly and came with a wet sail to head Mr Cool just before the post. Never a moment's doubt. 'He's perfectly amazing,' reported Doumen. 'I was just waiting for Baracouda to tell me when to attack.' Five days earlier, at Navan for his second race of the season, Limestone Lad had his own big scare in justifying odds of 11/8-on in a four-runner race, just getting the upper hand with Ballyhampshire Boy when that rival fell at the last. Over distances short of their best though, the top hurdlers in France and Ireland had both again emerged victorious.

Baracouda won by a neck at Ascot—with thirty lengths back to Carlovent—but from much of the comment and media reports afterwards, you would have thought he had lost. The real thing was just around the corner. Once again, the betting indicated a cakewalk for Baracouda when he attempted a third successive victory in the Long Walk at Ascot just before Christmas. At 11/4-on, Baracouda again encountered heavy going, this time over an extended three miles and a furlong. With outsider Young American, in the same ownership, seemingly there only to ensure that something made the running at a true pace, there were only three serious rivals and they did not look nearly serious enough. Deano's Beeno, sent off at 14/1 behind Native Emperor and Brother Joe, had not shown anything like his best for well over a year. At his best, however, Deano's Beeno was some 30 lb better than Mr Cool and a worthy opponent for Baracouda at level weights. The point was well made when Baracouda set about trying to catch him in the latest Long Walk. With no messing about this time up front, but a pretty good idea surely of how Baracouda might be beaten, McCoy on Deano's Beeno managed to stretch his advantage to at least ten lengths on the run down to Swinley Bottom; crucially, third-placed Baracouda was not on the second horse's shoulder or anything near it, but another ten lengths back. A twenty-length disadvantage, even to Deano's Beeno, was something that Baracouda managed to eliminate, but on the run-in, having drawn upsides but never actually got his head in front, Baracouda's finishing effort expired and he went down by a length. It was widely believed that Deano's Beeno had been given too much rope. 'Doumen Gloom' proved highly popular among headline writers on both the tabloids and the broadsheets. For our part, Baracouda lost little in defeat against a rival who ran right up to his best under ideal conditions.

Winning on the best horse can lead to more praise than is deserved, losing on the best horse can gain more than its fair share of criticism, and few had any doubt that Baracouda was the best horse in the Long Walk. The best horse, but with flaws. If he had to be ridden like this, Baracouda was flawed indeed. 'Everything went all right,' reflected trainer Francois Doumen stoically. 'The only thing Thierry blamed himself for was that he actually came a bit too early. He should have left Deano's Beeno alone in front at the last and come to beat him after the last. There has been a bit of pressure on him not to leave it too late, and the criticisms that he is doing the wrong things maybe influenced Thierry to come a bit earlier than usual.' After Baracouda's previous race, in victory, the trainer commented 'Thierry has cold blood. If he had ridden the horse in a different way, he probably wouldn't have won. This horse needs to be relaxed and then he can use that lethal turn of foot.' Circumstances in these two Ascot races made these tactics hard to execute. Some observers also questioned Baracouda's stomach for the fight. In the Ascot Hurdle, there were several strides approaching the second last when he carried his head awkwardly. Baracouda's tendency to idle in front—strange as it may seem for a horse that won by twenty-four lengths only twelve months earlier—was longstanding and well known but was there also now a certain idleness well before the finish as well? Baracouda's demeanour when asked to go about his business in the Long Walk was hard to gauge. The course was shrouded in fog. But all would surely be laid bare when he was also required to go in pursuit of Limestone Lad in the Bonusprint Stayers' Hurdle at Cheltenham.

Catching Limestone Lad is a stern test of any horse's stamina and resolution but the Stayers' seemed likely to suit Baracouda a lot better than the two races at Ascot. Most importantly, Baracouda would not have to lead the chase himself, he could follow others as they did their share of the donkey work for a change. Whether Limestone Lad could indeed be passed though, however favourable the circumstances, remained to be seen. Ireland's most popular horse had been in excellent form, taking his tally to five for the season when easily seeing off Boss Doyle and Bannow Bay at the Leopardstown Christmas meeting, though he too went to Cheltenham after a defeat, a narrow one at the hands of Like-A-Butterfly back over two miles in the AIG Europe Champion Hurdle. There was no remaining talk, incidentally, that it might be a realistic proposition for Baracouda similarly to drop back in distance to replace the same owner's Istabraq in the Champion Hurdle. A good job too, because, even in the absence of the 2002 runner-up Bannow Bay, who had suffered a life-ending injury, the Stayers' once again promised to be a better quality race than the Champion and it would have been a great loss to the racing public if the first clash between the French and Irish champions, something which had been in the offing for at least two years, had again failed to materialise. With Limestone Lad at the age of eleven, there would not have been many future opportunities. As it was, Limestone Lad's participation was threatened at one stage by a bout of coughing, but he recovered in time to take his chance. There were nine runners apart from the 'big two' and they had mopped up a total of nine pattern races between them earlier in the season. The aforementioned Deano's Beeno was one, sent off at 25/1, reflecting his lack of form at Cheltenham, and there were three younger horses of considerable potential in unbeaten novice Iris's Gift, the Pipe-trained Classified, who looked set to improve for the step up in distance, and the reappearing Royal & SunAlliance Novices' Hurdle winner Galileo. Baracouda and Limestone Lad dominated both the build-up and the betting and were eventually sent off 9/4 co-favourites.

Baracouda and Limestone Lad were the very best that hurdling had to offer, both famous for taking their directly contrasting styles of running to the limits, the sport's most formidable front runner pitted against its most dramatic procrastinator. If horses can have charisma, this pair had it in abundance. It was easy to predict how the race might unfold and all the more thrilling to see as it came perfectly to fruitition. Limestone Lad duly set a strong pace that gradually stretched the field and had nearly all of his rivals off the bridle more than a mile from home, with Baracouda all the while creeping closer. Seventh commencing the final circuit, Baracouda was fourth (with only four still in contention) at the third last, around seven lengths off the lead, and he had moved into third at the second last, on the heels of the leaders. The prize was still up for grabs entering the straight, but with the major, unexpected addition that Iris's Gift was there as well—three outstanding stayers instead of two. At the final flight, all three were in the air together, with Baracouda holding a slight lead from Iris's Gift, and Limestone Lad three quarters of a length behind them. Baracouda had played his hand a bit earlier than expected but, having wrested the advantage, he never looked like relinquishing it and passed the post to the good by three quarters of a length. Limestone Lad was five lengths back in third, with Classified thirteen lengths behind him in fourth.

The decision to extend the Cheltenham Festival to four days hasn't been universally popular among racing purists, with many pointing out that the best horses are increasingly avoiding each other due to the meeting's new races (as in the case of Big Buck's and Quevega), but the 2003 Stayers' Hurdle provides one of the strongest arguments for the extra day, as that epic renewal really deserved to be centrepiece of the afternoon's action. As it was, the exploits of Baracouda and his two brave rivals got somewhat overshadowed by Best Mate's historic second win in the Cheltenham Gold Cup some forty minutes later—rather like the exhilarating dead-heat between Night Nurse and Monksfield (the former recording the highest-ever Timeform rating for a hurdler) at Aintree in 1977, which didn't receive the coverage it deserved at the time due to Red Rum's record-breaking third Grand National win being the next race on the card! Night Nurse was unable to maintain that superiority over his younger adversary when they renewed their rivalry the following spring, losing out to Monksfield at both Cheltenham and Aintree, and it was a similar story with Baracouda come the 2004 Festival, where he had to play second fiddle to **Iris's Gift** (rated 172), going down by a length and a half when sent off 11/8-on favourite to complete a hat-trick of wins in the race.

A hat-trick bid was never on the agenda for Iris's Gift, however, as he was already being touted as a live Cheltenham Gold Cup contender in the immediate aftermath of his Stayers' Hurdle win. Unfortunately, things didn't go to plan for Iris's Gift the following season, when he was initially sidelined with two hairline fractures of a cannon bone, whilst his stable endured a virus-ravaged campaign which saw it shut up shop completely for a brief period during the core winter months. The latter issue might well have been the main factor in why Iris's Gift never really fulfilled his potential as a chaser subsequently but, whatever the merits of that theory, it is worth noting that surprisingly few top-class staying hurdlers have made the grade over fences, as his essay in *Chasers & Hurdlers 2005/6* explained:

> Dawn Run is the only horse to achieve victory in both the Champion Hurdle and the Cheltenham Gold Cup. To reach the top at two miles over hurdles and at three and a quarter miles over fences calls for a degree of versatility that is found rarely. Dawn Run was, however, also a champion at around three miles over hurdles, winning France's most important hurdle race the Grande Course de Haies d'Auteuil over twenty-five furlongs. No horse has won Britain's most important long-distance hurdle the Stayers' [now the World Hurdle] and the Gold Cup, though Brown Lad and Dorans Pride both went on to be placed twice in the Gold Cup after winning the former race. Trainer Jonjo O'Neill, who rode Dawn Run in the Champion Hurdle and the Gold Cup, looked to have a potential steeplechasing star on his hands when Iris's Gift, a top-notch winner of the Stayers' Hurdle in 2004, was sent over fences. The big, workmanlike Iris's Gift possessed the physique, as well as the ability and the stamina, and his prospects looked excellent. Unfortunately, Iris's Gift's first campaign over fences was restricted to one run—last of five when pitched in at the deep end in the Grade 1 totesport Chase at Lingfield—and he did not begin his chasing career in earnest until the latest season. Dawn Run, who was also restricted to a single outing (a successful one) in her first season over fences, contested only four steeplechases in all before she lined up for the Gold Cup, still a virtual novice. Judged by the media attention given to Iris's Gift, it seemed that he was expected to achieve something similar.

Unfortunately, despite making a good start in novice company in 2005/06, winning three times, Iris's Gift's campaign ended in anti-climax, falling at Warwick following a second to Darkness in a Grade 2 novice at Newbury, and then running as if amiss in the Gold Cup. He was retired after failing to make much impact in two runs over fences the following season.

The other placed horse from that epic 2003 renewal of the Stayers' Hurdle, **Limestone Lad**, also tried his hand over fences (in 2000/01) without achieving the same sort of success. Four wins from six starts would be viewed as a highly satisfactory novice chasing campaign in most circumstances, particularly as he made the frame in Grade 1 company on the other two occasions, but Limestone Lad never fully convinced with his jumping over the larger obstacles and it wasn't the biggest surprise that connections opted to revert him to hurdles—indeed, he even notched up two hurdling wins during his one season of chasing. Such versatility in the face of a heavy workload became a trademark of Limestone Lad's career and he regularly defied convention, never more so than when (at the age of ten) he became Timeform's highest-rated two-mile hurdler in 2001/02, two seasons after he'd topped the Timeform standings in the staying ranks—in doing so becoming the only horse since Dawn Run and Gaye Brief in the 'eighties to head the Timeform rankings in both categories. Limestone Lad's peak Timeform rating of 177 came when he claimed the scalp of triple Champion Hurdle winner Istabraq in the aforementioned Hatton's Grace Hurdle at Fairyhouse in 1999, though that was over two and a half miles whereas his highest rating over staying trips was 172. It speaks volumes for Limestone Lad that he was still able to achieve the latter rating in the final season of his remarkable career and, fittingly, he signed off (at the age of eleven) with that brave third in the 2003 Stayers' Hurdle.

> Limestone Lad had a quiet season by his standards in 2002/3, appearing just seven times and going for periods of more than a month without a run! Limestone Lad's chief assets, very accurate jumping and the ability to set and maintain a relentless gallop, mean that the majority of the more exciting races he's been involved in have been when he's been beaten. The appearance of Limestone Lad's running his heart out is somehow more admirable when it isn't quite enough. It isn't only God who loves a trier. Limestone Lad's five victories in the latest season took his tally under National Hunt rules to thirty-five, a phenomenal total for any horse, Flat or jumps, top class or merely very durable. Indeed, very durable isn't automatically enough. Sonny Somers, for example, the last eighteen-year-old to win a race in Britain, had a fourteen-year career but managed a mere twenty-six successes. The remarkable Flying Ace gained fifty-nine victories in the 'eighties but only twenty-three came in hunter chases while the rest were gained in points. At a higher level, Limestone Lad's tally takes a lot of beating, probably the best horse with a better score being the great dual-purpose horse Sea Pigeon who won twenty-one times over hurdles and sixteen times on the Flat for a total of thirty-seven. Thirty-five is one more win than Desert Orchid managed in a career that stretched over ten seasons while the top French jumper Or Jack was another to amass

thirty-four victories (including two wins on the Flat). The best hurdler of all time Night Nurse, later good enough to finish second in the Cheltenham Gold Cup, managed thirty-two wins over jumps and when added to three wins on the Flat give him a career total matching Limestone Lad's. One other notable jumper to muster over thirty wins is Lochroe whose 1958 King George VI Chase win was one of thirty-two from sixty-one starts. For allcomers, the twentieth-century record belongs to Crudwell who gained fifty wins (including seven on the Flat) in a twelve-year career between 1949 and 1960. That total is surpassed by The Admiral, who raced in Ireland at the end of the nineteenth century. His tally of wins, variously reported at fifty-two or fifty-three, included the 1894 Irish National.

Limestone Lad wasn't the only top-notch staying hurdler of this era who regularly ground his rivals into submission with displays of relentless galloping from the front, though the similarities between him and **Deano's Beeno** (rated 175) very much end there. For one reason or another, Deano's Beeno was nowhere near so consistent nor durable as his Irish counterpart, but he was a formidable performer granted the right conditions (both in terms of ground and frame of mind!) and, like Limestone Lad, was still claiming big-race wins at the age of eleven. Because of his quirky nature, however, Deano's Beeno was sometimes underestimated, as *Chasers & Hurdlers 2002/03* argued:

'Will the real Deano's Beeno step forward please.' The Anglo-Irish Hurdle Classification for 2002/3, published in the Racing Calendar in May, ranked him only joint-ninth in the two-and-a-half-miles-plus category. Deano's Beeno is assessed at 154, 16 lb behind Stayers' Hurdle winner Baracouda who beat him into sixth place at Cheltenham. However, the pair also met in the Cantor Sport Long Walk Hurdle at Ascot in December, the form of which—astonishingly for a Grade 1 championship event—has been completely ignored by the BHB and Turf Club handicappers. Deano's Beeno inflicted the first defeat in eleven starts on Baracouda and is the only horse to beat him for the best part of three seasons. On any logical reading of the form-book, Deano's Beeno produced a top-class performance that day, one bettered over the distance during the season—by our reckoning—only by Baracouda, Iris's Gift and Limestone Lad, the three who filled the places in a vintage Stayers' Hurdle. Deano's Beeno has now contested three editions of the Stayers' Hurdle, finishing ninth and eighth on his two previous appearances, and has never finished closer than twenty-five lengths to the winner. It is wrong to judge him on those performances, however, and he is certainly slighted by his latest Classification assessment. For all his well-documented quirks and physical problems, Deano's Beeno is capable of top-class form on his day and proved himself still too good in the latest season for most of the leading staying hurdlers in training. In a busier campaign than usual, he also won two other graded events, the Rendlesham at Kempton in February and the Long Distance Hurdle at Ascot in April. Deano's Beeno is a tricky customer and can be unpredictable, and is not one to take a short price about as he showed when twice beaten at odds on in the

*Deano's Beeno holds off Baracouda at a foggy Ascot
in the 2002 Long Walk Hurdle*

latest season. Earlier in his career, regular jockey Tony McCoy gave a clue as to why Deano's Beeno's 1999/2000 campaign had turned into such an anti-climax. Pointing to his temple, McCoy said as he unsaddled after the gelding's reappearance win the following season: 'It's all up there, when you get him on a going day he'll beat anything, but when it's not a going day you know early.' Despite seeming difficult to keep sound in his first few seasons over hurdles, and reportedly having been hobdayed and had a tie-back operation to alleviate a wind infirmity before his 1999/00 campaign, Deano's Beeno's career has featured enough 'going days' to keep him near the top of the tree as a staying hurdler—there is no doubt that Deano's Beeno is an outstanding performer when on song.

Ironically, it was the quirkiness of Deano's Beeno, rather than the merit of his perfor–mances, which endeared him to the racing public (he even ended up with his own fan website!) and he became the star inmate at Greatwood's centre for the rehoming of racehorses upon his retirement in 2004, where he is still going strong today. Unfortunately, Inglis Drever succumbed to colic (aged just ten) less than a year after being retired through injury, but the likes of Baracouda and Limestone Lad have gone on to enjoy lengthy retirements at their owner's homes.

Don't Push It and Tony McCoy

GRAND NATIONAL

A Timeform Publication

Grand National

Purists may like to pretend otherwise, but there can be little doubt that the Grand National is the most important horserace so far as the British general public is concerned. Few sporting occasions in Britain capture the public imagination quite like the Aintree showpiece, which thoroughly deserves its reputation as the 'people's race'—an example of this came in 2013, when 8.9m viewers tuned into the first Channel 4-screened Grand National, compared to just 900,000 for the TV station's Royal Ascot debut two months later. Therefore, although the exploits of equine superstars such as Frankel and Sprinter Sacre may have raised the sport's profile in recent years, it is impossible to ignore the fact that the National remains the only event which truly makes an impact in non-racing circles. For example, three-times winner Red Rum is still the most popular answer if a man in the street is asked to name a famous racehorse, whilst one has to question whether Dick Francis's post-jockey career as a novelist, or even Bob Champion's long-running cancer charity, would have been anything like so successful without their high-profile National tales aboard Devon Loch and Aldaniti respectively. In addition, the Grand National is responsible for racing's only win in the main award of the BBC's prestigious Sports Personality of The Year during that show's fifty-eight year history, with Tony McCoy picking up the trophy in 2010 after finally breaking his duck in the race (at the fifteenth attempt) aboard **Don't Push It** earlier that year. McCoy is a sporting phenomenon who has smashed just about every statistical record during a remarkable career—he recently passed the 4000 winners mark and has been crowned champion jockey for every season since turning professional (eighteen times and counting)—yet it seems only this win mattered to the general public.

> Tony McCoy's victory on Don't Push It in the Grand National, a race recognised by the nation at large, was one of the great sporting moments of 2010. It eventually brought recognition for the record-breaking champion jockey when he won the BBC Sports Personality of the Year award in December. The richly deserved accolade—McCoy polled 293,152 votes, 42% of those cast

*Don't Push It jumps to the front at the last, ahead of the rallying
Black Apalachi and the weakening Big Fella Thanks*

by viewers—provided racing with its first winner of the prestigious individual award. Lester Piggott was part of the team award for triple crown winner Nijinsky in 1970 and Bob Champion and Aldaniti won the team award in 1981, but the best result in the individual category had been Frankie Dettori's third in 1996, the year of his 'Magnificent Seven' at Ascot, and McCoy's third in 2002 (Lester Piggott never finished higher than fourth). Although Tony McCoy and the twenty-six-times champion from the first half of the last century, Sir Gordon Richards, are from different branches of the sport, McCoy regards his greatest achievement as breaking Richards' fifty-five-year-old record of two hundred and sixty-nine wins in a season. McCoy achieved that during the period when his career was at its pinnacle, riding two hundred and eighty-nine in 2001/2 and going on to finish third in the BBC awards after not even making the final shortlist of six the previous year, when campaigns were run in the racing pages of the Sun and the Racing Post. The BBC and the voting public have sometimes resisted orchestrated campaigns but the sport's own public relations efforts undoubtedly helped in 2010. Cheltenham's big December handicap, for example, was renamed the Vote A.P. Gold Cup, one of numerous examples of race titles used to draw attention to McCoy's claims as part of Racing for Change's attempts, from the autumn onwards, to influence public opinion. McCoy's remarkable career features a string of riding records which have seen him transcend the sport like no jump jockey has ever done before (though he didn't make the final BBC shortlist either in the year that a blaze of publicity accompanied his reaching 3,000 winners). Though it was good to see McCoy recognised at last, it shouldn't be overlooked that his BBC Sports Personality award owed much to the enormous popularity of the Grand National. Without the victory of the admirable Don't Push It there would have been no award.

As that last sentence emphasises, the role of Don't Push It in this story is sometimes underplayed, as is the fact he put up one of the best Grand National-winning performances in post-war history with a Timeform rating of 162. In truth, the gelding had never quite fulfilled his potential after an excellent first season over fences, in which he was the only horse to run subsequent Cheltenham Gold Cup winner Denman close, and in which he was still in with a chance when falling two out in the Arkle Chase at Cheltenham. Suspect jumping and a rather highly-strung nature were possible reasons why his best form had been so sporadic in the intervening years, during which he'd also had his share of training problems—including 'a kissing spine and bad stifles' according to trainer Jonjo O'Neill. A dismal pulled-up effort in the Pertemps Final over hurdles at Cheltenham on his final outing before Aintree meant Don't Push It wasn't an obvious choice for McCoy's Grand National mount, particularly as he was one of four runners owned by the jockey's boss J. P. McManus—the others were stable-companion Can't Buy Time and the Irish-trained pair Arbor Supreme and King Johns Castle (who'd finished runner-up to Comply Or Die in 2008).

In the end, however, it came down to a choice between the O'Neill-trained pair Can't Buy Time, a faller in the previous year's race but successful at Cheltenham's New Year's Day fixture in the latest season, and Don't Push It. 'I jocked myself up for Can't Buy Time ten days before the race, but Jonjo was pretty persuasive that I should ride Don't Push It because he has more class and had the better chance of staying. It was more his decision than mine, he was adamant and for once I had the brains not to argue with him!' McCoy's record over the National fences is much better than some have given him credit for. He has won the Topham twice—in 1998 on Cyfor Malta, one of the easiest winners ever seen over the big fences, and in 2000 on Northern Starlight, one of the smallest ever to win over the National course—and he had been placed three times in the National itself before winning on Don't Push It. The big bookmakers certainly made a mistake in pricing up Don't Push It at a generally available 20/1 when betting shops opened up on Grand National morning. Apart from McCoy's first National ride—on 25/1-shot Chatam in 1995—none of the horses he has partnered in the race has started at longer than 16/1 (Blowing Wind when third in 2001) and ten of the fifteen have started at 10/1 or shorter. A public gamble on the day in 'the people's race' by the legion of McCoy fans—the money mostly for McCoy, rather than his horse—forced Don't Push It down to 10/1 joint favourite at the off, making him the sixth Grand National favourite or joint favourite ridden by McCoy. It soon became clear that the money wasn't misplaced. Don't Push It—'really enjoying himself', according to his rider afterwards—was the only one of the four McManus runners still in the race as the field passed the stands for the first time. King Johns Castle had refused to race, whilst both Can't Buy Time and Arbor Supreme had unseated their riders, Can't Buy Time at the Canal Turn when in mid-division and Arbor Supreme when towards the rear at the Chair. Thirty-one set off into the country for a second time and, with Conna Castle's exertions beginning to take their toll, Black Apalachi took over in front at the twentieth. Don't Push It had moved up to fifth behind Black Apalachi, Conna Castle, Hello Bud and Big Fella Thanks at second Becher's, the fence which accounted for Maljimar, who fell when making eye-catching headway, tracking Don't Push It. In contrast to the previous year, when a steady gallop resulted in sixteen still being tightly grouped crossing the Melling Road for the final time, the field for the latest National was much more strung out by the time the survivors joined the main racecourse with two to jump. Black Apalachi, Hello Bud, Don't Push It and Big Fella Thanks had built a healthy lead over the remainder of the survivors, the jockeys on the last-named pair seemingly yet to show their hand as the leaders ran towards the second last. Hello Bud began to fade after a mistake and Don't Push It was finally asked to assert himself at the last, soaring over the fence and landing running. Black Apalachi, whose jockey received a three-day ban for using his whip with excessive frequency from the last fence, stuck on very well as the first two pulled clear on the first part of the long run-in. He managed to hang on to Don't Push It's coat tails until rounding the elbow, after which Don't Push It, driven out by the irresistible McCoy, stretched his advantage to five lengths at the line. Big Fella Thanks found no extra from the last and was passed for third by State of Play who reached the frame for the second year running, staying on to finish twenty lengths behind Black Apalachi and three in front of Big Fella Thanks.

Stamina and jumping ability were tested to the full in the latest National in which the winning time of 9m 4.42sec was the fastest in the race since Rough Quest's 9m 0.74sec in 1996; the only other faster winning times before Don't Push It in the race's long history are Royal Athlete's 9m 3.94sec in 1995, Red Rum's 9m 1.9sec in 1973 and Mr Frisk's 8m 47.8sec in 1990 (at least eight in the National that year bettered Red Rum's time, illustrating the unseasonably firm going). The times have tended to get faster in the National as the course has been remodelled and the fences made easier. Lord Gyllene, Party Politics,

Bindaree and Papillon have also all recorded winning times under 9m 10sec since Mr Frisk (only Red Rum had done so before).

As Don't Push It crossed the line, the normally undemonstrative McCoy became as animated as he has ever been after a race, showing his obvious joy and relief by standing up in his stirrups while turning and waving his whip towards the grandstands where the crowd was in raptures. 'I have never had a reception like that after any race, not even at Cheltenham,' said McCoy afterwards. 'I've won a few other big races and I'm supposed to be a good jockey, so if I didn't win the National it was going to be a negative on my CV ... people who don't know much about horse racing know about the Grand National and, from a jockey's perspective, that's why it's important. At least I can think I have sort of done all right as a jockey now and my little girl Eve, who is two and a half, will be proud of me when she grows up.' Of Don't Push It, McCoy said that, once he had jumped Becher's on the first circuit, he wouldn't have swapped the horse for anything. 'A couple of times he made little mistakes, nothing serious, but he had totally adapted to the fences. He was on and off the bridle but every time I switched him out for a bit of daylight he picked up again. We'd gone a good gallop and his class got him there easily. It's a long way from turning into the straight here, so I was worried about going too early, but I thought on the way to two out that, unless I'm totally jinxed, I'd win.' Don't Push It's owner wasn't quite so emotional as his jockey—'I tend to come here more in hope than expectation, so for me to win the National is great, but to win it with Jonjo and AP makes it special.' The trainer expressed similar sentiments. 'To be honest I didn't expect him to win, I have had so much bad luck in the race that I never thought it would happen to me!' Both McCoy and O'Neill praised the commitment to the sport of J. P. McManus, whose presence, along with several other 'super rich' owners, has been a boon in recent times. 'He is the best supporter this game has ever had and ever will have,' said McCoy. 'I am very privileged that I rode a Grand National winner in these colours.'

Don't Push It returned twelve months later to finish an honourable third under top weight behind Ballabriggs—who shaved 3.34 seconds off the 2010 time to post the third quickest National in history—but the bad luck which had dogged Messrs McCoy, O'Neill and McManus prior to Don't Push It came back to haunt them in 2012, when their Cheltenham Gold Cup winner Synchronised was fatally injured in a freakish incident whilst running loose after a fall at first Becher's. The incident provided an eerie reminder of O'Neill's National woes during his riding days—the two-times champion jockey failed to complete on all eight of his National rides, his lowest moment undoubtedly coming when reigning Cheltenham Gold Cup winner Alverton (who was sent off 13/2 favourite) fell fatally at second Becher's in 1979. There has been ill-luck in the race for O'Neill as a trainer too, notably with the McManus-owned Clan Royal, who was placed twice but arguably should have won in both 2004 (jockey Liam Cooper dropped his whip five out and then steered an errant course on the run-in when runner-up to Amberleigh House) and in 2005 (carried out by loose horses at second Becher's when travelling strongly in front under McCoy). The misfortune didn't end with Synchronised in the 2012 renewal either, as the McManus-O'Neill second string Sunnyhillboy suffered a serious tendon injury (that required a 'touch and go' operation after the race) which arguably contributed to his being pipped on the line by Neptune Collonges, losing out by a nose in the closest National finish since 1938, when Battleship prevailed by a head in an era before the photo-finish. That grandstand finish in 2012, plus the tragic deaths of two horses (According To Pete was also fatally injured when brought down in another freakish incident at second Becher's), inevitably grabbed most of the post-race headlines, which resulted in the merit of the winner's performance being largely ignored—as had been the case, to some extent, when Don't Push It won two years earlier. **Neptune Collonges**, who was retired immediately after Aintree, was good enough at his peak to have won an average Cheltenham Gold Cup (he made the frame twice in that race) and became the highest-quality National winner since the great Red Rum.

> Neptune Collonges spent much of his career in the shadow of his outstanding stablemates Kauto Star and Denman, but, on his final mission at the age of eleven, he made a lasting impression of his own when putting up one of the best Grand National performances in Timeform's long experience. In his time, Neptune Collonges won the Punchestown Gold Cup twice and the Hennessy Gold Cup at Leopardstown, but he will be remembered very much longer for his thrilling, last-stride victory in the closest finish in Grand National history. Under 11-6, the highest weight carried to victory since Red Rum's era, off a BHA mark of 157 and conceding 15 lb to runner-up Sunnyhillboy, Neptune Collonges put up a performance that was almost the equal of any in his prime, and one that, strictly on form, has not been bettered by any Grand National winner since the Chasers & Hurdlers series began in 1975/6.

In truth, there had been signs early in the 2011/12 campaign that age might have been catching up with Neptune Collonges, who was turned down as being 'a bit too old' by stable jockey Ruby Walsh come Aintree (though, in the event, Walsh had to sit out the National anyway following a fall earlier in the afternoon). That said, the grey had made the frame under big weights in valuable staying handicap company on all three starts prior to the National and certainly held a much better chance on form than his starting price of 33/1 suggested, particularly as he was one of the beneficiaries from the BHA handicapper's current (dubious) policy of allotting lower handicap marks to some of the higher-weighted entries than they'd receive away from Aintree—Neptune Collonges ran off a mark 2 lb lower than he would have been allotted in a conventional handicap when the National weights came out in early-February (the difference had been 8 lb when entered twelve months earlier, though that hadn't been enough to tempt connections to run him at Aintree). Although he needed to be shaken up by Daryl Jacob when briefly looking like getting behind over the early fences, Neptune Collonges took well to his first experience of the National course and was part of a leading group of eight, covered by no more than half a dozen lengths, crossing the Melling Road for the final time.

The closest finish in National history as Neptune Collonges, the first grey winner for over fifty years, catches Sunnyhillboy on the line

Neptune Collonges remained in fifth, behind Seabass, Shakalakaboomboom, Sunnyhillboy and In Compliance, at the second last, and Seabass was still in front over the final fence until Sunnyhillboy took it up on the run-in. Mastering Seabass, Sunnyhillboy began to draw clear and was just over a length in front after passing the elbow, with a two- to three-length advantage over the staying-on Neptune Collonges in third. In an extraordinarily dramatic finish, Neptune Collonges passed Seabass inside the final furlong and then gradually began to close in on Sunnyhillboy whose rider Richie McLernon put his stick down in the closing stages, pushing out his mount with hands and heels after he felt him getting a little unbalanced. Sunnyhillboy and Neptune Collonges passed the post together and the verdict could have gone either way, though it looked as if Sunnyhillboy might have held on until the freeze-frame was shown. It still took the judge the best part of two minutes to announce the result of the official photo-finish (the result would have been a dead heat before the age of pixels). Neptune Collonges was in front for just one stride of the four and a half miles, but it was the one stride that mattered. The photo-finish showed that he had just got up to win by a nose, the smallest possible margin . . .

Neptune Collonges matched the Timeform rating (166) achieved by Red Rum after his second National win in 1974, when he also won the Scottish National—becoming the only horse to complete the Aintree-Ayr double in the same year. Even higher Timeform ratings have been posted in defeat on a handful of occasions since then, notably by dual runner-up Suny Bay (who ran to 171 when chasing home Earth Summit under twelve stone in 1998), whilst the top-class Irish chaser Hedgehunter's second place to Numbersixvalverde in 2006 also resulted in a rating of 166, 9 lb higher than when successful in 2005. The latter gelding is one of ten National winners since 2000 who tried to follow up twelve months later, with four others from that group making the frame too, Comply Or Die (runner-up in 2009) the closest to winning again other than Hedgehunter. If anything, all of this brings into sharper focus the remarkable Aintree record of Red Rum, who remains the last horse to claim back-to-back National wins in 1973 and 1974, and finished runner-up the next two years before winning again as a twelve-year-old in 1977, in doing so becoming the last top-weighted winner of the National (he was also top weight when winning in 1974). Of course, there is a danger that modern racing fans may view Red Rum in a similar light to the many cross-country specialists who've emerged over the past twenty years, yet cannot replicate that form over conventional fences. That simply wasn't the case with Red Rum during the bulk of his career—indeed, he was allotted the same rating as that season's Cheltenham Gold Cup winner Royal Frolic in the inaugural edition of *Chasers & Hurdlers* in 1975/76, and enjoyed plenty of success away from Aintree, as Hedgehunter's essay in *Chasers & Hurdlers 2005/06* explained:

> Just as Hedgehunter's best form in 2005/06 wasn't restricted to Aintree— he also finished a fine second in the Gold Cups at both Leopardstown and Cheltenham—it is often overlooked that Red Rum was similarly effective on park courses during the peak years of his career. Red Rum's highest Timeform rating was 166, after his performances in 1973/74 when he ran ten times, his six victories (he also won six races in 1972/73) including another top-class performance in the Scottish National, when he carried 11-13 including a 6-lb penalty for Aintree (Proud Tarquin, to whom Red Rum gave 20 lb and a four-length beating, went on to pass the post first, ahead of that season's Cheltenham Gold Cup runner-up The Dikler who gave him 24 lb, in the Whitbread a week later). That said, ratings derived from a study of the form-book have only a minor role in the Red Rum story. He owes his place among the immortals of the turf—and as a wider 'sporting superstar'—solely to the Grand National. His three victories were without precedent and his record of never being out of the first two in five successive editions reveals a degree of domination unmatched by any other horse in the history of the race, an achievement all the more meritorious given the quality of opposition he often

faced at Aintree (the trio who chased him home in 1973—Crisp, L'Escargot and Spanish Steps—had filled three of the first five places in the betting for the previous year's Cheltenham Gold Cup). *Chasers & Hurdlers* recounted after his third victory that Red Rum was 'the best Grand National horse for a very long time, perhaps for all time.' Few racehorses have ever achieved the popularity of Red Rum who became, in every sense, a National hero. He continued to carry out public engagements, including leading the traditional Grand National parade, until the age of thirty. More column inches were devoted to his death in October 1995 than the obituaries for novelist Sir Kingsley Amis and former prime minister Lord Home.

Such coverage of a deceased racehorse may seem like overkill, but it underlines Britain's reputation as a nation of animal lovers, something which can act as a blessing or curse so far as the Grand National is concerned. When things go well, the outpouring of goodwill dwarfs any negative voices about the sport—Red Rum's third Grand National win in 1977, for example, is regarded as one of the great events in steeplechasing history (Charlotte Brew also stole some headlines by becoming the first woman rider in National history), yet few recall that two horses (Winter Rain and Zeta's Son) were killed in the race. By contrast, thirty-four years later, two deaths in the 2011 renewal were all that dominated the following day's headlines, with much of the comment on winner **Ballabriggs** centred around his jockey Jason Maguire picking up a five-day ban for excessive use of the whip. It was a PR disaster on many fronts and protest groups such as Animal Aid had a field day, whilst the ever-increasing number of social media users had their say in the immediate aftermath of the race, which included some unfortunate TV camera angles—the stricken pair Ornais (covered by a tarpaulin) and Dooney's Gate (surrounded by screens) could be seen clearly by TV viewers as the field bypassed the fences they'd fallen at second time around, which was the first time in Grand National history that obstacles had been omitted in this manner (a move, ironically, brought in as a safety measure). It is no exaggeration to say that the fallout from the 2011 renewal placed the National in a very vulnerable position, in terms of public opinion at least, which led to a strong rebuttal in Ballabriggs' essay in that season's *Chasers & Hurdlers*:

> With Animal Aid and its supporters in the media hovering like vultures to pick over any bones left after the running of the race, every death nowadays has the potential to be a public relations disaster, for Aintree and for jump racing in general. 'Aintree day of horror', 'National carnage', and the familiar 'Is it time to stop killing horses in the name of sport?' give a flavour of the headlines after the latest National. Furthermore, newspapers are no longer the main vehicle through which campaigns can be organised and promoted. Any tiny network of attention-seeking complainers can fuel a commotion by posting a few incendiary comments on the internet, their random contributions to various mediums reaching a ready audience (including newspaper editors looking for easy headlines). Most of the new social media platforms deal not in argument but simply in opinion—opinion after opinion with no context and apparently no need for justification. Maddening as it may be for those who love the

Ballabriggs never stops responding as he gamely holds off Oscar Time;
2010 winner Don't Push It is a most creditable third

National, and appreciate the enormous effort that has been put in over the years to try to make it safer, the race will never be able to shake off the over-sensationalised charges of callousness and cruelty which are now ingrained and have dogged the race in the modern era.

In truth, Britain—and the world in general—needs to become a far better place before society seriously thinks about consigning the Grand National to history. Despite long-standing criticism and controversy down the years, the race has stood the test of time and is enjoying one of the most successful periods in its history. The Grand National has always been a risky and potentially deadly race—for both its equine and human participants—but there has never been any particular justification for its being singled out for special criticism. Steeplechasing, and hurdling for that matter, is a hazardous sport and, as with other hazardous sports, the dangers of serious injury are always present, as evidenced by the horrific fall suffered by young conditional Peter Toole in the Maghull Novices' Chase, the second race on the latest Grand

National card. Anyone who thinks that steeplechasing in particular can be made safe enough so that no horse or rider will suffer serious harm is deluded. That some racehorses will be killed in action is simply a fact of life. The sport recognises it openly, the British Horseracing Authority (which works closely with welfare organisations such as the RSPCA) publishing information about equine fatalities on its web site. There are currently four fatalities per thousand runners over jumps—0.4 per cent—and the average has decreased over the past few decades. All racecourse injuries and fatalities are investigated by the BHA and, thankfully, fewer serious injuries now come into the category of those that could and should have been prevented. The overwhelming majority of racehorses live to enjoy a pampered retirement as was evidenced in the latest season when ten previous National winners, all looking in great order, paraded before the race. They ranged from twenty-eight-year-old Miinnehoma, through Rough Quest, Lord Gyllene (still ridden out at twenty-three), Papillon, Red Marauder, Bindaree (now a competition horse), Amberleigh House, Hedgehunter and Numbersixvalverde (now does dressage) down to the youngest, fourteen-year-old Silver Birch. Two more recent winners, Comply Or Die and Don't Push It, were in the line-up again while the 2009 winner Mon Mome was also still in training, though he missed the latest edition after suffering a setback in late-January.

Ballabriggs was the first Grand National winner to be saddled by Donald McCain, though it is worth noting that he also played a huge part in the training of one of those previous winners parading before the race, namely 2004 hero **Amberleigh House**, when acting as assistant to his father Ginger before taking over the licence from him in 2006. The colourful Ginger McCain (pictured below), of course, earned his nickname of 'Mr Aintree' largely because of Red Rum's three wins, though Amberleigh House's dramatic success twenty-seven years later meant he joined Fred Rimell as the winningmost trainer in Grand National history. McCain Jnr has quickly established

himself as one of the most dominant trainers in the country, his string having swelled to nearly 200 horses in 2012/13 on the back of two successive top three finishes in the trainers' championship. All of this is a far cry from Ginger McCain's training career, the bulk of which took place from a small yard behind his used-car salesroom in a residential part of Southport, his horses famously doing much of their training on the beach. The McCain family had moved to Cheshire just over a decade before Amberleigh House joined the fold from Ireland, with the gelding (who also finished third in the 2003 National) doing plenty to disprove Ginger's reputation as a 'one-horse trainer'.

With Red Rum long departed (he is buried near the Aintree winning post), few, including perhaps the

Amberleigh House has leader Clan Royal in his sights at the last; 2005 winner and 2006 runner-up Hedgehunter appears held when falling

man himself, could have envisaged Ginger McCain's triumphing in the National for a fourth time. 'If the ground stays as it is and he gets the luck, he's nailed on to be in the first five, a clear run and he can be in the first three,' was how he summed up Amberleigh House's chances beforehand. Amberleigh House actually didn't enjoy the clearest of passages early on and was still ten lengths behind as the survivors crossed the Melling Road for the final time, and he was no closer to the three leaders at the second last where he jumped to the right. Clan Royal's rider, whose whip had flown out of his hand when his mount made a mistake five out, went for home in earnest from the second last. Clan Royal led over the last by two and a half lengths from Lord Atterbury; Hedgehunter fell when seemingly held in third while Amberleigh House had begun to close perceptibly as the leaders started to tire between the last two fences. Clan Royal's flashing tail was a sign of his distress and, desperately tired, he had to be wrenched to the right after blundering at the last and briefly

*Graham Lee celebrates one of the most dramatic National wins
in recent memory on Amberleigh House*

looking as if he might run off the course, seeming to be heading too straight for a time. The equally exhausted Lord Atterbury was kept to the straightest line for negotiating the elbow, diagonally from the last fence to the finishing rail that passes the Chair fence. The two leaders were locked together rounding the elbow as they began the final run to the line. Amberleigh House's rider reported afterwards that he had resisted an urge to try to go after the leaders any earlier—'There was a strong headwind in the straight and I thought they might come back'—but by the elbow the staying-on Amberleigh House was making up ground hand over fist and the gap had been reduced to two or three lengths. Though out on his feet, Clan Royal rallied gamely to get the better of Lord Atterbury, but the pair were seemingly going up and down on the spot relative to Amberleigh House who kept on relentlessly to deprive Clan Royal of the lead well inside the final furlong. Some drew comparisons afterwards with Red Rum's overhauling of the wandering and exhausted Crisp in 1973, but Crisp had been fifteen in front at the last and the horses involved in the finish of the latest National weren't in anything like the same league as Red Rum and Crisp. Amberleigh House passed the post three lengths in front of the luckless Clan Royal with Lord Atterbury two lengths away in third.

Amberleigh House's owner was locally-born vintner John Halewood, who died in 2011 but continues to have an association with the race following the news that ginger-beer maker Crabbie's (which is part of the Halewood International empire) will take over sponsorship of the Grand National from 2014, when prize money is set to reach £1m for the first time. Such lavish sponsorship deals have helped transform Aintree into one of Britain's premier National Hunt venues, so it is easy to forget that the course faced the very real threat of closure for most of the 1970s and early-1980s. Aintree was eventually saved when it passed into the hands of Racecourse Holdings Trust, a Jockey Club subsidiary, in May 1983 for £3.4m, a little more than the Walton Group had reportedly paid for the course in 1973—the year of the first National win for Red Rum, whose huge popularity played a significant role in saving the race during this fraught era. The Walton Group staged the Grand Nationals of 1974 and 1975 but did not excel at racecourse management—much increased admission charges in 1975 resulted in the smallest crowd in living memory, around 9,000 (compared to the 64,626 who attended in 2013!)—and they made an agreement with Ladbrokes who developed the Grand National meeting with flair from 1976 to 1982, abandoning Flat racing and designing an all-jumping programme to complement the Cheltenham Festival.

Social commentators would probably conclude it reveals plenty about the British psyche that the 'people's race' has been sponsored by alcohol manufacturers since 1984. Indeed, the fact that the National's tipple has gone from whisky (Seagram's) and cognac (Martell) to bitter (John Smith's beer) and ginger beer or cider (Crabbie's) during this period could also be viewed as a reflection of the general 'dumbing down' of society! Ginger McCain, who died in 2011 just two days short of his eighty-first birthday, would no doubt have accused the Aintree management of 'dumbing down' the Grand National too had he been around to witness the 2013 renewal won by **Auroras Encore**, which saw arguably the most significant changes to the race in its long history. A raft of new safety measures were introduced in the wake of back-to-back tragedies in 2011 and 2012 (when two horses died in each), including a slight reduction in race distance, levelling work at several fences, further modifications to the landing side of Becher's and an informal (much shorter) parade replacing the traditional one that was held in race-card order. The most fundamental change, however, was the traditional timber design of the famous Aintree fences being consigned to history in favour of more forgiving plastic replacements. Outwardly, the new fences looked identical to those they replaced but it soon became apparent that the Grand National had been changed, with all forty runners in the 2013 renewal still standing after seven fences—a situation unprecedented in the history of an event sometimes labelled 'the most perilous race on Earth'. Admittedly, a largely mundane and incident-free Grand National in 2013 came as a welcome relief (there was a huge on-course cheer when the whole field cleared first Becher's) after a couple of tough years, but there were some in racing who felt the changes had robbed the race of its usual magic:

The last—Auroras Encore takes over from Teaforthree, who survives a rare mistake thanks in part to the modified 'softer' fences

'The whole point of the National is that it should be exciting, but it didn't look that way to me any more,' was the reaction of seven-times champion jockey John Francome, a key Channel 4 commentator before walking away when a new team was put in place in the middle of the latest season. Francome described the 'new' National as 'just a long-distance steeplechase . . . it used to be a jumping test, but no longer . . . the jumping discipline has been taken out of the event and I hope they rename Becher's Brook, because there's no brook, no drop, and it's not the same fence. It's a travesty.' Although some of Francome's criticisms could be dismissed—his assertion that Red Rum (also a high-class performer away from Aintree) would have been lapped over the new fences was frankly ridiculous—the BHA and Aintree management would do well to ponder the points made by Francome. Perhaps the most important was that 'You needed a special type of horse to jump round Aintree, one that looked at the bigger fences and backed off them, but on Saturday they were going faster as they got closer to the jumps . . . going faster over these easier fences is a recipe for more injuries.' Francome's appeal for the fences to be built more solidly should at least be considered.

In truth, it is far too soon after just one edition of the Grand National using the new fence design to be drawing firm conclusions—be they positive or negative—about the modifications. Ironically, even if they do prove to be consistently safer than before, this could result in the first Canal Turn becoming an accident black spot. There has been a melee there in each of the last two Nationals (five departed in 2012 and three in 2013), with the above-average number of runners still standing at that point arguably a major factor. Congestion was certainly to blame in 1974 when thirty-eight runners were still standing at the first Canal Turn (as in 2013, Becher's was cleared safely on both circuits that year too) only for seven horses to be put out of the race in a concertina effect caused by fallers towards the head of the field. Two of the most infamous pile-ups in Grand National history also came at the first Canal Turn, though a loose horse was the principal cause of the mayhem in both 1928 and 2001, the latter renewal won by **Red Marauder** under rain-drenched conditions.

Aintree in a quagmire has produced some bizarre Grand National stories, not least that in 1920 when Irish-trained Troytown, rumoured to be carrying 'a substantial portion of the funds in the Sinn Fein war chest' and given a rousing reception after his victory, won in one of the slowest times in the history of the race, 10m 20.40sec, and there were only four other finishers. A sodden track the year after Troytown's victory saw four finishers, Shaun Spadah winning in 10m 26sec, the finishers each separated by a distance or more after three were remounted, including the owner/trainer-ridden favourite The Bore, third in Troytown's year, who looked like making a race of it when coming down at the second last and breaking his rider's collar bone, and fourth-placed Turkey Buzzard whose lady owner reportedly chastised her jockey with an umbrella in the paddock for continuing after the horse had fallen or unseated four times on the second circuit. Shaun Spadah's victory was a carbon copy of that by Glenside ten years earlier when the course was described as 'a perfect morass . . . one horse after another slid, slipped and was counted out . . . Glenside was so exhausted that he slowed almost to a walk on the run-in.' Glenside's winning time of 10m 35sec was the slowest of the century before Earth Summit's 10m 51.56sec in 1998. The Grand National probably came closest to being abandoned on account of ground conditions in 1955 when the event survived a series of course inspections, the last of them only two and a half hours before the race; parts of the course were waterlogged and the water jump, ironically, had to be omitted, while parts of the fence that is the thirteenth and the twenty-ninth were dolled off. Quare Times was credited with a time of 10m 20.60sec, the slowest of the century at up to that time since 100/1-shot Tipperary Tim's 10m 23.40sec in 1928. Tipperary Tim's heavy ground National featured an infamous pile-up, caused by Easter Hero landing on top of the fence at the first Canal Turn then falling back into the ditch (which was filled in before the next National). More than half the field was put out of the race in an incident widely recalled after the latest running when the riderless Paddy's Return caused chaos and the field was reduced by nearly a quarter at the same fence. The fence before the Canal Turn, the twenty-third on the second circuit, was the scene of an even more sensational occurrence in the forty-four runner National on good ground in 1967 when loose horses brought to a halt virtually all of the remaining runners by careering in front of the fence, only 100/1-shot

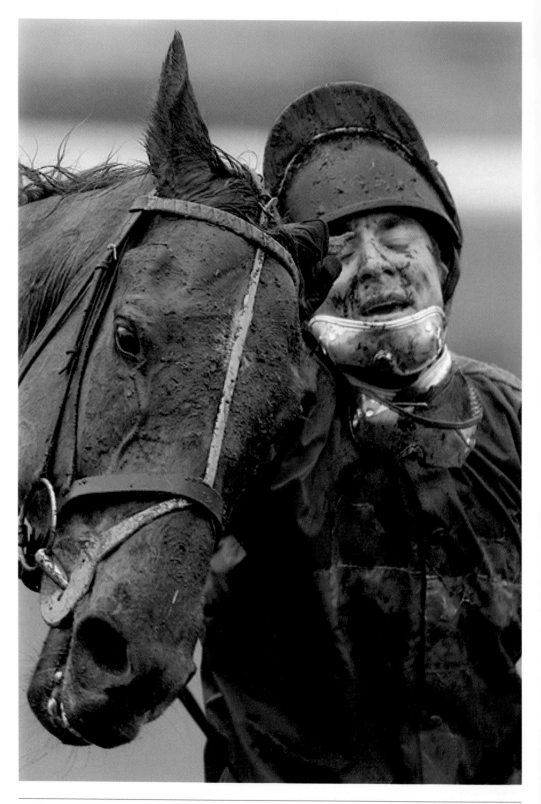

Foinavon, towards the rear as the field approached, managing to negotiate the fence at the first attempt. The victories of Glenside, Shaun Spadah, Tipperary Tim and Foinavon, famous as the only runners to complete the National course without mishap in their years (though in each case at least one other runner eventually completed), are a lasting reminder of the uncertainty that has often attached to the running of the National. Had it not been for the sure jumping of runner-up Smarty, the latest winner 33/1-shot Red Marauder would have joined that select group. The ground was even more testing than for the recent Nationals won by Miinnehoma and Earth Summit—or for the one won by Ben Nevis in the mudbath of 1980, the last time only four finished—and Red Marauder's time of 11m 00.06sec is the slowest since the reputed 11m 39sec taken by the 1883 winner Zoedone who beat the smallest field ever assembled for the race.

No Grand National has surely been run in conditions of such extreme meteorological misery or on going more taxing than the latest one, and the race, though extraordinarily dramatic, turned into a lottery, the one saving grace being that all forty runners and riders returned safely. A potential disaster was much easier to foretell than in Foinavon's year and the wide-ranging debate about whether the race should have been allowed to take place could so easily have turned, under different circumstances, into outrage in the media which would have been a public relations disaster. The winning jockey Richard Guest said he had never ridden on worse ground—'borderline . . . it was unraceable really'—and connections had apparently debated whether Red Marauder should be allowed to take his chance, eventually opting for Guest to 'showjump round because any horse that was left standing at the end would be in the money.' Red Marauder and Smarty were the only two horses left standing (though Blowing Wind and Papillon were remounted after being taken out by loose horses early on the final circuit) with fully ten fences still to jump, by which stage the Grand National was no longer a race but a battle for survival. In hindsight it was perhaps a blessing, given the atrocious conditions, that there weren't the normal number of survivors left by this stage, most of whom would have been flat out to keep up and struggling over the fences.

Debate raged in the racing pages afterwards as to whether the 2001 National should have been run in such deplorable ground, with many opining that there was undue pressure from the racing industry for the race to go ahead after several bleak months (including the abandonment of that year's Cheltenham Festival) caused by a foot-and-mouth outbreak. Fortunately, the viewing public of largely once-a-year punters seemed to lap it up, the chaotic scenes in 2001 merely adding to the rich folklore of the world's

Richard Guest looks more exhausted than Red Marauder
after winning the four-finisher National in 2001

greatest steeplechase, with incidents such as Devon Loch's infamous bellyflop in 1956 or the shambolic void race of 1993 arguably just as important as momentous feats of individual achievement in maintaining the National's extraordinary public appeal. Red Marauder's win also bolstered the public's perception of the National as a 'lottery', as did the 100/1 success of **Mon Mome** eight years later, though the latter's essay in that season's *Chasers & Hurdlers* was keen to downplay the validity of such a theory:

> The National's reputation as a lottery can be overstated. There have, for example, been only five 100/1 winners in the long history of the race. The tubed Tipperary Tim and Foinavon were among them, both genuine 'no-hopers' who owed their victories to circumstances. The main culprit for the mayhem in Tipperary Tim's year, Easter Hero, was actually one of the outstanding chasers of the first half of the twentieth century and, twelve months after his Canal Turn shenanigans, he started 9/1 favourite under top weight of 12-7 in the 1929 Grand National. That edition attracted a world record field of sixty-six and Easter Hero led nearly all the way, only for 100/1-shot Gregalach to deprive him of it between the last two fences and beat him by six lengths. Gregalach carried 11-4 in the 1929 National but his stable, which saddled five in the race, believed beforehand that it had better chances. Gregalach had won the Stanley Steeplechase over the National fences as a five-year-old two years earlier before missing the whole of the next season with injury. He hadn't won in five outings in the current campaign, though he had been runner-up four times, including in the valuable Brook Chase at Gatwick, before falling at Sandown on his last outing before Aintree. Gregalach went on to confirm himself a top-class chaser and he ran in five more Grand Nationals, in all of which he shouldered 12-0 or more. He finished second to former stable-companion Grakle in 1931 and was finally retired after coming seventh on his last National appearance as a twelve-year-old when he headed the weights on 12-7, followed by Thomond II (who had won the Becher Chase from Gregalach in November) on 12-4 and the winner Golden Miller (who had won his third successive Cheltenham Gold Cup) on 12-2.
>
> Reynoldstown is the only horse to win the National more than once in the twentieth century apart from Red Rum, though his second National victory in 1936 may well have produced another tubed 100/1 winner if front-running Davy Jones had not run out at the last when still holding every chance, his amateur rider Anthony Mildmay (Aintree's Mildmay course, opened in 1953, is named after him) losing his reins as the buckle slipped through the hasp when Davy Jones pecked on landing at the penultimate fence. There was no Grand National after 1940 until 1946 because of the curtailment of racing, but the immediate post-war years produced another 100/1 winner in Caughoo in 1947 and probably an unlucky loser the following year at the same odds, the strong-travelling Zahia, who was steered by her rider to the left of the final fence after joining the leader First of The Dandies. Zahia's rider thought the finish was on the inside of the water jump. Getting back to Caughoo, the 1946/7 season

Mon Mome (right) serves it up to Comply or Die - who is attempting to become the first winner in successive years since Red Rum in 1974 – at the final fence

was disrupted by the worst winter weather in living memory, resulting in the loss of sixty-seven fixtures and the main races at Cheltenham's National Hunt meeting being postponed until April. The Grand National meeting escaped by the skin of its teeth and a field of fifty-seven—the second largest in the history of the race—lined up for the big race. The severe winter resulted in all racing in Britain between January 21st and March 15th being lost, with the preparation of most Grand National contenders interrupted. Conditions were very heavy and looked set for an upset in the Grand National, which was staged on a Saturday for the first time in eighty-nine years at the request of the Government 'in the interests of British industry'. There was discussion about having to omit two of the fences on the main racecourse and, although all thirty fences were jumped in the end, the rain and heavy mist made it very difficult to follow the race out in the country. The 1946 Cheltenham Gold Cup winner Prince Regent, who had towered above his contemporaries in Ireland during the war years, shouldered top weight and started favourite for the second year running in the National, conceding between 19 lb and 35 lb to the fifty-six others. Among the other Irish-trained challengers was Caughoo, carrying 10-0, who had won the Ulster

National at Downpatrick in 1945 and 1946 and was making his first visit to England. He had finished down the field under 9-9 in the Leopardstown Chase in February on his final outing before the National, though he had at least been able to complete a full preparation for Aintree on the sands at Portmarnock, which could well have given him a fitness edge.

The Bloodstock Breeders' Review describes the field as being 'led over the water by the diminutive Lough Conn from Musical Lad, Kilnaglory, Klaxton, Tulyra and Bricett. There followed Prince Regent, jumping a little erratically, but going great guns, and "number 33" on the saddlecloth, which turned out to be a horse called Caughoo.' One horse came out of the mist at the Anchor Bridge turn, before the long run to the second last . . . 'It proved to be Caughoo, fortunately distinguished by a large white sheepskin noseband. Behind him, quite hopelessly behind, was the gallant Lough Conn, followed by Kami and the heavily-weighted Prince Regent. The last fence, a bit knocked about by now, but still more than formidable for a tired horse, stood between Caughoo and victory. But Caughoo took it like a tiger, very nearly pitching his rider over his head. This remarkable little horse proceeded to gallop along the straight as if he had gone a mile instead of the best part of four and a half miles. He passed the winning post as fresh as a daisy.' Lough Conn, finishing twenty lengths behind the winner, Kami and Prince Regent completed the frame. The vivid description of Caughoo's performance is interesting in the light of an unusual sequel which is said to have resulted in fisticuffs when, some time later, Lough Conn's jockey Daniel McCann accused winning jockey Eddie Dempsey of cheating in the National by pulling up Caughoo in the mist at the furthest point of the course from the stands and rejoining the field as it came round a second time. McCann reportedly went to his grave believing he was 'robbed' but the suggestion was totally unjustified [as was proven by photographs of Becher's on the first and second circuit, both reproduced in Chasers & Hurdlers 2008/09].

The latest 100/1-shot to win the Grand National was the seasoned Mon Mome whose victory probably has most in common with that of Gregalach, rather than those of Tipperary Tim, Caughoo and Foinavon. The Grand National by David Hoadley Munroe covered the history of the race up to 1931 and described Gregalach's starting price for the 1929 National as 'a real puzzle . . . one only had to look at him to realise that here was no doubtful horse. Somehow or other, it just didn't occur to anyone that he might figure prominently in that great field of sixty-six.'

It was a similar scenario with Mon Mome, whose win was celebrated by bookmakers as 'the best ever Grand National result'—though that tag has subsequently been used to describe the 66/1 success by Auroras Encore in 2013! Unlike Gregalach, Mon Mome had won already that winter, in a £57,000 handicap at Cheltenham no less, and had been sent off 9/2 favourite for the Welsh National at Chepstow (where he'd finished a well-held eighth following an uncharacteristic early blunder) just over three months before the Aintree showpiece. Dismal displays on his final two preparatory runs, however, had seen confidence in Mon Mome dwindle, including within his own yard—stable jockey Aidan Coleman turned down the ride in favour of stable-companion Stan (fell seventh), in the process following in the footsteps of Jason Maguire, who turned down the ride on 2007 winner Silver Birch to remain loyal to the Donald McCain-trained Idle Talk (unseated nineteenth), though gained compensation four years later aboard Ballabriggs.

> Mon Mome had looked in excellent shape at Chepstow over Christmas but didn't take the eye at Haydock (beaten forty-two lengths) or Uttoxeter (beaten fifty-seven lengths) where his lacklustre appearance and demeanour on both occasions was in keeping with his rather laboured performance. On the face of it, however, a horse who had started favourite for the same season's Welsh National should never have been 100/1 for the Grand National. Though he seemed out of form and was set to race off a BHA mark (148) 7 lb higher than in the previous year's National (when he'd finished tenth after being hampered at second Becher's), Mon Mome still had a better than average chance at the weights judged on the form of his Cheltenham win earlier in the season. Mon Mome underlined that in no uncertain manner, asserting early on the run-in and being clear by the elbow, forging further ahead on the run to the line to win impressively by twelve lengths from 2008 winner Comply Or Die, with second favourite My Will a further length and a quarter away in third.

Mon Mome and Auroras Encore were saddled by Venetia Williams and Sue Smith respectively, who joined Jenny Pitman as the only female trainers to have won the National. In contrast to those wins in 1983 and 1995 for the irrepressible Mrs Pitman, most of the post-race attention for the two recent female-trained winners centred on the winning jockeys instead, albeit unwittingly in both cases. Ryan Mania made the national news when he was airlifted to hospital with back and neck injuries (he was back in the saddle twelve days later) less than twenty-four hours after winning aboard Auroras Encore, the fact his injuries came in a fall over hurdles at Hexham underlining the fact that jump racing is a hazardous sport all year round, with the risks attached not restricted to just one day at Aintree in April. Fortunately, there were no injury concerns for Liam Treadwell in the aftermath of Mon Mome's win, though his pride took a dent when the usually sure-footed Clare Balding made a clumsy remark about his teeth in the post-race interview—the public fallout resulted in Treadwell being fitted with a £30,000 new set of teeth (free of charge), which is surely a longer-lasting and more practical prize than the Sports Personality of The Year award!

Merigo

READERS' CHOICE

A Timeform Publication

Readers' Choice

Whilst this publication is primarily concerned with the highest-rated horses of recent times, there are those who have captured the imagination in other ways, which is why, earlier in the year, readers were invited to nominate their favourite horses of the twenty-first century, along with a brief rationale behind their selections.

Federico Tesio, one of the most important racehorse breeders in history, once wrote: 'A horse gallops with his lungs, perseveres with his heart, and wins with his character'. All six horses featured in this section—a selection of the contributions we received—displayed plenty of 'heart' and character in their forays on the racecourse, many of them coming back year after year, often as good in their later years as in their supposed physical prime. The sextet were seemingly selected because of their durability, versatility and honesty, an impressive mix of attributes almost certain to create a strong bond between racehorse and racegoer . . .

The big and strong liver chestnut DENMAN (rated c181) might have sometimes failed to impress in appearance, but he rarely failed to make an impression on the track, with his trademark qualities of most assured jumping and never-say-die attitude enabling him to scale the heights as a top-class chaser. Steve Miller, a racehorse owner from London, explains why Denman, who in the autumn of 2013 overcame a life-threatening infection which saw him spend four and a half months in veterinary hospital, means so much to him . . .

"The great racehorses have defining qualities that single them out not just from the herd but from other great racehorses. If not the best in purist terms (in deference to the likes of Arkle and Sprinter Sacre), Denman was my favourite steeplechaser. I was mesmerised over six seasons by a racehorse that defied logic and confounded the sceptics.

Never out of the first two in six consecutive Cheltenham Festivals, he destroyed his field by 10 lengths in the 2007 RSA Chase, the same year his stablemate Kauto Star won his first Gold

---

Denman on his way to a second success in the Hennessy

Cup. When Denman beat Kauto Star in the 2008 Gold Cup he had won 14 of his 15 starts (including nine chases).

Although he was to win just once more—despite the not inconsequential achievement of finishing runner-up in no less than three more Gold Cups—that one time more is perhaps what typified his qualities the most and defined him for what he was.

Overcoming a heart condition in his 2008/09 season, he returned to Newbury for his second Hennessy. That day he did the impossible. He won this most exacting and competitive of handicaps, off a mark of 174 and carrying 11st 12lb. He didn't just win, but put his field to the sword in a brutal display of power and resilience. The Hennessy field of seasoned chasers fell away or pulled up due to the sheer ferocity of Denman's performance—stumbling around like newborn giraffes in his wake. He had been through the wringer and had beaten his opposition senseless. His trainer and connections were overjoyed, his rider, Ruby Walsh, dumbfounded. This defined the great horse for what he was—a magnificent, inspiring, relentless tank of a horse. A heavyweight champion among champions."

> *Chasers & Hurdlers 2010/11* said: "For all Denman's consistency in the Cheltenham Gold Cup, it is his gallant weight-carrying performances in the Hennessy Gold Cup—which have been among his very best career performances—that have gone a long way to his earning such popularity among racegoers and punters."

The strapping **MERIGO (rated c142)** perennially took a while to find his form, but come Ayr's meetings in March and April he was usually ready to produce his best. A thorough stayer who acted on a wide variety of ground, Merigo won five times at the Scottish course, and his sound jumping was a factor in both his Scottish Grand National wins. Merigo's fan club wasn't confined to Britain either, as this eulogy from Ollie O'Donoghue of the Dublin Racing Club proves . . .

"I can only sing the highest praise for Merigo. It is always a great feeling when you see a horse achieve something special, and this horse did.

His sire, Pistolet Bleu, died relatively young aged thirteen. Only two of his progeny have earned more on the track than Merigo, and one of them was a certain Sizing Europe. The man who eventually owned this gelding is a big supporter of the Scottish turf, Raymond Anderson Green. He was sent to the yard of Andrew Parker. The horse was sent handicapping early on in those green and yellow silks, often seen in northern racing. Not off the mark on his first few starts, Merigo eventually won in a Class 3 chase. What perhaps brought about this change in fortune was a new track, one that he would later shine on: Ayr. Timmy Murphy later won four times on Merigo—interestingly Ray Green is his father in law!

The horse will mostly be remembered for his participation in the Scottish Grand National. In just his third season, he got his first start in the race. Carrying bottom weight, he led from the twelfth and stayed on strongly. A special win for connections, but what was so special for the public was what he achieved two years later. He returned to Ayr the following season, but try as Timmy Murphy and Merigo might, the pair fell just short, beaten three quarters of a length by Beshabar. At eleven years old, he had his third and final start in the Scottish National, and this time he came up trumps, regaining his title. Getting up by a head, Merigo, with his distinctive white blaze, saw off the efforts of Ryan Mania on Auroras Encore. We know what happened to them.

His jockey paid Merigo the highest compliment: "He's a superstar". I would agree."

> Chasers & Hurdlers 2011/12 said: "There was little between them two out, but with Auroras Encore a length up again jumping the last it looked as though Merigo might have to settle for second again. But Merigo is as tough and game as they come and he rallied on Auroras Encore's inner to get his head in front near the line."

As with many horses in this section, longevity was a key part of the popularity of MISTER MCGOLDRICK (rated c161) who won his final race aged thirteen and was still racing a year later. Versatility was also a hallmark of workmanlike Mister McGoldrick, and he was effective at two miles to two and a half, on ground ranging from good to firm to heavy, ridden with restraint or ridden prominently. Richard Longley of Leeds, the horse's owner, pays his own tribute . . .

"A letter from a North Yorkshire veterinary practice in May 1999 advised this horse had a "severe skeletal problem" and would never make a racehorse. Undeterred, this horse did eventually race, but in late 2001, after moderate performances on the Flat, the advice given was to send him to the sales and if an offer of £500 was bid, then take the money and run. Hardly a credible profile, then, for a horse to be nominated for a "Modern Greats" award.

Fast forward ten years to Wetherby racecourse on Boxing Day 2011 when Jonjo Sanderson confessed to being "extremely privileged" to be able to honour the career of this "marvellous ambassador for National Hunt racing", as, just retired, he strode round the parade ring, then cantered in front of the main stand, to a tumultuous reception from the large crowd gathered to be part of this special occasion. His CV will forever show that he raced ninety-one times . . . seven times on the Flat, and eighty-four races under National Hunt rules, in which time he earned £372,366.

Mister McGoldrick turned out to be a very special racehorse.

The racing public in their thousands soon began to warm to his talent for attacking his fences, and throughout his career, in both victory and defeat, his increasingly adoring followers continued to marvel at his prodigious jumping and never-say-die attitude to racing. Everyone

---

came to love Mister McGoldrick, I've got the emails and letters to prove it, and this stalwart eventually had his big day at the Cheltenham Festival in 2008, a result which warmed the hearts of the press, TV presenters, and the vast majority of the National Hunt racing fraternity.

He was never going to win the Gold Cup, and history will tell that his overall performances fell just short of the very top drawer, but whatever he lacked, he always gave his best, and from such lowly beginnings, the fairy tale success story of Mister McGoldrick's racing career will be remembered for ever. Jonjo Sanderson was right. There could be no finer example for everything National Hunt racing stands for than Mister McG."

> *Chasers & Hurdlers 2007/08* said: "A bold jumper, he is a most enthusiastic, free-going sort, a credit to his connections and deservedly one of the most popular horses in training."

PERSIAN PUNCH (rated 124) couldn't fail to take the eye in both the paddock—he was a big, strong gelding—and on the track—he had a powerful, round action—and he was a very smart performer who was at his best at two miles and beyond. An admirably tough front runner, Persian Punch was a great credit to the David Elsworth stable, which had been responsible for another fans' favourite in Desert Orchid in the 1980s. Bill Jackson remembers Persian Punch fondly . . .

Persian Punch (left) and Royal Rebel battle out the finish in the 2004 Gold Cup

"*I can think of no other horse that has fired the imagination more than Persian Punch. The times I have watched that horse cut out most of the running then get passed by others and instead of giving in, this big-hearted horse would fight back and get his head in front again. One race he was in I had called my wife in and told her how I loved this horse which was about to run in a televised race, and we both sat and watched with tears streaming down our faces as he did his usual trick of leading, to be overtaken not by one but three or four horses, and then miraculously fighting back to win. What a marvellous horse who sadly passed away so young.*"

> *Racehorses of 2004* said: "The five previous essays in Racehorses on renowned battler Persian Punch contain numerous heart-stirring examples of his snatching victory from the jaws of defeat. Racing is unlikely to forget him in a hurry."

SAKHEE (rated 136) was a strong and good-topped horse who showed top-class form at ten and twelve furlongs, both at home and overseas. Sakhee acted on any going on turf and dirt, and his achievements as an older horse were all the more meritorious for he broke his knee in the Derby, an injury that didn't come to light until after his next run a month later. The genuine Sakhee struck a particular chord with Nick Pemberton from Malvern . . .

"My favourite racehorse of the modern era would be Sakhee whose achievements, particularly as a four-year-old in 2001, were quite simply unforgettable.

Sakhee had shown himself to be a colt of real quality for John Dunlop in his classic year. Having won two trials leading up to Epsom, he had looked the Derby winner two furlongs from home only to be reeled in close to the winning post by the brilliant Sinndar. A sensational finish to the race by two exceptional horses, who would both go on to win the Prix de l'Arc de Triomphe.

Injury curtailed his three-year-old season but Sakhee would be back the following year, this time in the blue of Godolphin. His demolition of high-quality fields in both the International Stakes at York and the Arc at Longchamp stamped him as an all-time great of the Turf. That agonizing defeat by a head in the Breeders' Cup Classic to the great US champion Tiznow, with Galileo trailing in behind on the unforgiving dirt, was both glorious and heartbreaking in equal measure.

In his relatively light career Sakhee produced some truly stunning performances. This magnificent bay colt possessed the qualities that are most laudable in a racehorse; he had the acceleration, stamina and all-round brilliance of a champion. In particular, that combination of natural talent and fighting spirit was irresistible. Sakhee was not unbeaten, but this takes nothing away from a wonderful career and the words of that great Olympian Eric Liddell seem apt: "In the dust of defeat as well as the laurels of victory there is a glory to be found if one has done his best."

Sakhee deservedly shares the official record for the longest winning distance in the Prix de l'Arc de Triomphe with Ribot and Sea-Bird. Illustrious company indeed."

> *Racehorses of 2001* said: "The genuine Sakhee is a strong, good-topped colt who carries plenty of condition and acts on any turf going, as well as on dirt . . . He has a splendid turn of foot which he is able to produce after being ridden up with the pace, making him all the more formidable."

Evergreen sprinter THE TATLING (rated 123) enjoyed his finest moment in terms of prestige when winning the King's Stand Stakes at Royal Ascot in 2004. However, as Robert James Peacock of Shipley points out, it was the final of The Tatling's 176 lifetime starts, during an illustrious career that began in 1999 and ended in 2011, that rubber-stamped his status as one of the most popular horses of the modern era . . .

The Tatling (number 9) winning the King's Stand in 2004

"A winner at Royal Ascot and Glorious Goodwood, and three times Nunthorpe runner-up, The Tatling held his head high in the ranks of early-21st century sprinters. Those achievements alone, however, would leave him a mere footnote in a book like this, a near-great, another vanquished foe of the peerless Oasis Dream. But The Tatling's career was to have an extended second act, less glamorous, but equally enthralling. Long after his contemporaries had retired, The Tatling was still to be found schlepping round Britain's racetracks for dwindling pots of prize money. We grew to love him, like we grew to love snooker's Steve Davis or football's Stanley Matthews, as an ageing star, raging against the dying of the light, battling on in ever decreasing circles, not for glory, but because of a deep love for the game. Every time his equally venerable trainer Milton Bradley planned to put him out to grass, he'd grump and want to return to the fray. When, aged 14, he entered the stalls for the final time, it was for a Class 6 Wolverhampton handicap, a world away from the Ascot paddock he once graced. The also-rans he lined up against weren't fit to walk in his hoofprints. Yet here he was, a lowly 16/1, unfancied for even this humbling last assignment. When he short-headed his way to victory, carrying with him a sentimental slab of my own cash, it was a victory not just for veteran trainer, veteran charge and my bank balance, but for the romance of the sport. Sure, Bradley and The Tatling were no Cecil and Frankel. There will be no films and books written about them. But for me their story was, in its own small way, equally poetic."

Racehorses of 2003 said: "The Tatling, a tough and consistent gelding, should continue to give a good account in top sprints in 2004, making another healthy contribution towards (his trainer Milton) Bradley's retirement fund, not that the trainer has given any hint that he is ready to call it a day just yet."

Kicking King

FROM THE CORRESPONDENTS

A Timeform Publication

From The Correspondents

The main chapters of this book are by and large concerned with the best horses of the past fifteen years or so, as defined by Timeform ratings. To spread the net a bit wider, figures from the racing media were invited to select a horse that has inspired them in recent times, starting with Timeform's Chief Correspondent, Jamie Lynch.

Jamie Lynch (Timeform Chief Correspondent) Frankel (147)

'It's not titles that honour men, but men that honour titles.'

Far be it from a Teesside University graduate to disagree with the father of modern political theory, Niccolò di Bernardo dei Machiavelli, but I think that a title can in fact be both an honour conferred and an honour earned, certainly when that title is Frankel. It may be the exception rather than the rule, but normal rules have never applied to Frankel, who specialised in the exceptional.

One horse, decorating two men, enrapturing a whole sport. The title honoured Bobby Frankel, and Sir Henry Cecil honoured the title. Life and death are one thread, the same line viewed from different sides. Rarely has that dictum resonated so much than with the Frankel story; the horse of a lifetime whose name and fame exalts lifetimes now passed, Frankel by name and Cecil by nurture. The embodiment of vitality, Frankel was a memorial to one and a running epitaph to the other, both illustrious trainers.

But the beauty of Frankel was that his reflective glory shone far beyond his direct honoraries. He was no private matter. By the time of his fourteenth and final race, in the 2012 Champion Stakes, Frankel was nationalised. In fact, he was internationalised. At the same time he was covering furlongs like no other horse, Frankel was covering miles like no other horse, over land and sea, galloping into the global consciousness as the legend spread.

True, a myth is easier escalated these days, networks making the world a smaller place, but also a more discerning place, and a legend is now nothing without content. Publicity isn't enough; matter is what matters. Frankel, though, scored highly on content, through his outstanding form. Content and form.

Ask any critic what constitutes art and they'll tell you two things: content and form. Was Frankel art? That's a debate for Machiavelli and co, but I would argue that, at times, Frankel was theatre, pure theatre, and always a virtuoso performance. The purpose of theatre is to entertain and inspire, unifying people in shared moments of heightened emotion and unforgettable drama. Frankel did that more prodigiously, and more regularly, than almost any other racehorse in history, and for that contribution alone he's a modern great. But it also helps when you're obscenely brilliant.

Frankel's phenomenal achievements on the track are covered and explained in full in his own section, so there's no need to dwell on any of his races, other than the Two Thousand Guineas when, for a ten-second period midway through that classic, the world made a little less sense. Horses simply weren't supposed to run like he did at Newmarket, so fast, so far ahead, so easily. Racegoers weren't supposed to be questioningly quiet, commentators weren't supposed to sound surprised, and Teesside graduates turned Timeform 'expert' race-readers certainly weren't supposed to mistake the mighty Frankel for the meek Rerouted, his presumed pacemaker.

On Timeform ratings, Frankel would go on to run several pounds better several times over, but the Guineas was the day the game changed, literally for Frankel and figuratively for racing. Frankel, at Newmarket, beat twelve horses, but above and beyond that he beat racing's received laws of logic and limit. He fought the laws and he always won.

Frankel was a winner because he was the best, and vice versa; and, at the risk of being carted away by the PC police, this is the point I have to remind you that there is something to be said for being the best. Once upon a time, being the best was a virtue and even an ambition. Not now, in *The X-Factor* age, when mediocrity is celebrated and taking part really does matter more than winning. One Direction took part in *The X-Factor*, Leon Jackson (who?) won it.

Even in this book it's happening! You'll read, if you haven't already, that 'Y' or 'Z' deserves to be a modern great because of an 'X' factor, a convenient attribute that isn't strictly talent-related, which is all well and good, but, traditionally, the best is said to be the highest quality of all. To be the best is the reason that writers write, that runners run, that singers sing, and that trainers train. Do you think that it would have been such a hit if Tina Turner had sung 'You're Simply Third Best', or that the Oscars would still have the same pulling power if the Academy Award was given to the fifth best motion picture, or that he'd have become a footballing legend if he'd been called George West?

The point is that there's a lot to be said for, and lot to admire in, being the best, and every now and then something comes along to gently reawaken our sleeping realisation, though Frankel just slapped us in the face. With a Timeform rating of 147, Modern Great barely does Frankel justice. Modern Greatest is closer to the mark, but Greatest Ever is the best fit; the BEST fit.

From The Correspondents

To be the best requires other contemporary greats by means of measurement, and, not that it was needed, nor that it seemed possible, it's remarkable how in 2013, while Frankel was busy—very busy, and very fertile—in his new endeavour as a stallion, his legend has been strengthened further still. Lest we forget Excelebration, who won two Group 1s at the end of 2012 after he'd been mercifully taken out of the Frankel firing line, but this year another five Group 1s have been won by Frankel fodder. St Nicholas Abbey was responsible for two of them, though it would surely have been more without his career-ending injury, while the thrilling 2013 Champion Stakes, arguably the race of the season, was fought out by Farhh and Cirrus des Aigles, two of the most luxurious toys Frankel ever played with.

Let's finish where we started, with Niccolò Machiavelli, and with honour. Machiavelli's grave site is unknown, but a cenotaph honouring him was built at the Church of Santa Croce, in Florence. The Latin legend reads: TANTO NOMINI NULLUM PAR ELOGIUM – For so great a name, no praise is adequate, and no words are equal to such a name. Sometimes actions speak louder than words, and Frankel's actions were about as perfect a tribute as could be made to honour the passing of the men who defined him and whom he defined, Bobby Frankel and Sir Henry Cecil. The legacy is immortal for Frankel, the best racehorse there has ever been.

Paul Haigh (racing journalist) Silent Witness (129)

There was no 'where-were-you-when?' moment. No JFK, John Lennon, Berlin Wall explosion, burned on your consciousness so you can remember every detail of where and when it happened.

Silent Witness snuck up gradually through information received, starting in a place called Hua Hin with Lawrence Wadey. We were talking about the upcoming Hong Kong International races and I started on about the British sprinters who, in my innocence— shows how long ago it was although really only November 2003—I still believed to be the equals, or more probably the superiors, of any in the world.

They'll have to be good to beat this one' said Lawrence, or words to that effect. 'If you can get evens anywhere you'd better get on'.

It would be almost the definitive example of understatement to say that Wadey is better at picking horses than I am. He'd paid for the trip after all out of one of the innumerable triple trios he'd won. And since there was something about the uncharacteristically quiet emphasis of his words I went straight to have a look at Betfair. This was before the memorandum of understanding that closed off Betfair betting on Hong Kong. The hotel (hotels play quite a big part in this story) wouldn't let you access the site because Marriott is a respectable chain and won't let you break Thai government interdictions. But somehow I found an internet café where they didn't give a damn and hoovered up all the 11/8 I could find. Almost as much as I'd lost on Dancing Brave at Santa Anita in 1986 in fact. Told Wadey. He said: 'Well done'.

At the time Silent Witness had won his first five races, only one of them Group class and that a Hong Kong Group 3 by no more than a nose from Planet Ruler. It took a major leap of faith to believe he could beat all three of Acclamation, The Trader and (don't laugh, he was very good once) The Tatling over the five furlongs which was then the trip of the Hong Kong Sprint.

His next run, though, in the Group 2 International Sprint Trial, over the same five, improved confidence considerably, or as they say, no end. He made all to beat Cheerful Fortune by two and a half lengths, with Firebolt a length and a quarter away in third and Cape of Good Hope, a horse who would later play a major if supporting role in his history, just behind in fourth. So did the time of 56.3 seconds. Did they really run sprints that fast? Maybe they start the clock late to make it look more impressive. And of course there's never any cut in the ground at Sha Tin. Never mind, now he was odds-on everywhere.

On December 14th, 2003 (yes of course I've looked up the exact date) came the moment of truth. The South Africans had one called National Currency they were very excited about, winner of nine out of 13, unbeaten in his last four. National Currency broke fast and went off in front with Silent Witness trailing him. At halfway the favourite moved up to him, then went past. Nothing flash. No urgency from the saddle. Just went past. It wouldn't be fair to say Hong Kong's new hero toyed with the South African. He just did what was necessary: simple routine. At the line he only had a length to spare but from halfway there had never been the slightest doubt. Acclamation, The Trader and The Tatling ran fifth, sixth and seventh, with another Brit, Deportivo (winner of six out of nine previously), last. National Currency ran only once more, winning the Al Shindagha Sprint over six at Nad Al Sheba by six and a half lengths in a field of 13.

From there on it was sailing, not plain but spectacular for the gelding known in Chinese as Ching Ying Dai Si, which translates appropriately as Elite Master. He won his next five, all except one Group 1s, and he won them with complete authority. Most of them, it seemed, with the supremely consistent Cape of Good Hope staring at his substantial rump from a distance of about two and a half lengths. Silent Witness was always ridden by Felix Coetzee who appeared to be getting money for letting out old rope. But then jockeys never get the credit they deserve for partnering authentic champions, do they? Ask Luke Nolen. Ask Tom Queally.

By the time a year later he'd repeated his victory in what is now recognised as the toughest sprint in the world to win, he was a national celebrity in what was then still often referred to as 'the former British colony of Hong Kong'. Bigger than any canto pop star. Bigger even than Jackie Chan.

Every time he ran, cheerleading teams clad in his owner's black and green silks (no it's not quite as astonishing as it sounds: the Hong Kong Jockey Club paid for the outfits) turned up en masse to give him raucous adulation. When they offered free Silent Witness baseball caps at Sha Tin station on a race day 10,000 people got caught in a stampede and many were injured. More so even than others, the Chinese seem to love an aura of invincibility. He became the symbol of Hong Kong's pride.

From The Correspondents

2004 was Silent Witness's year. By April 2005 he'd won fifteen on the trot and all the talk was of him surpassing the unbeaten record of the great Ribot (comparing oranges and apples of course, but no point in trying to tell that to the green and black hordes). One of the most attractive things about him was his effectively rags to riches legend, and that included his ancestry. His father was the virtually unknown El Moxie, a son of the American dirt star Conquistador Cielo who'd somehow found his way by a steady process of downward mobility to a small stud in rural Tasmania. When El Moxie aged 12 met a mare called Jade Tiara, something extraordinary happened. Bloodstock agent David Price saw the result and brought it to Hong Kong.

A side note: It was shortly after his second Hong Kong Sprint that Wadey set up an interview with Arthur Antonio ('Archie') da Silva. The three of us met for lunch. It was at the Peninsula in Kowloon, arguably the best hotel in the world. I bought myself a new sweater, thinking 'smart casual' (or 'smart causal' as the HKJC always typo-ed it in those days) would mitigate the normal shabby, imagining Archie holding court in the centre of a huge dining room with lunching acolytes examining him with respectful if envious awe. Instead they hid us in a corner behind some fronds with a string quartet playing between him and the common or garden members of the Peninsula clientele.

What the hell were they playing at? Didn't they realise this was the multi-millionaire lawyer and businessman—and, much more importantly, the owner of Hong Kong's most famous inhabitant/god. Actually they realised all too well. Archie is a very likeable man but quite . . . boisterous, and he likes swearing more than any man on earth. I have no problem with this. But Archie maybe tends to overdo it just a tad. Every second or third word is a profanity, and not delivered sotto voce either. So that's why they camouflaged us behind the palm fronds and put in the chamber music as a sound barrier. The resulting Racing Post article incidentally, in which I decided to quote him verbatim for authenticity, holds the record for the number of F words in a 1500 worder in any English language newspaper, and probably always will. Great if you're paid by the word of course.

One thing about the Peninsula lunch did bug me though. Did it at the time or was it with the wisdom of hindsight? 'And Tony ' (Cruz, his trainer) 'says he's going to be even better when he stretches him out to a mile!' bellowed Archie, adding in his usual stream of expletives.

Call it stupidity but I've always hated it when people ask undisputed champions to stretch out in trip. Cut back? No problem. But not stretch out. Frankel is the only example of justified confidence I can think of. But anyway . . . On APQEII Cup Day 2005 they stretched him out to seven furlongs. He won of course, but really not in a way that suggested he was howling for an extra furlong. A month later he went for the Champions Mile.

There is a peculiar sort of agony in seeing one of your heroes meet his match. Trepidation fills you beforehand, particularly when you feel he's being asked to do something he should never have been asked to attempt. I was in Singapore for the SIA Cup that day and everything else at Kranji just stopped as every eye turned to the TV from Hong

Kong. Silent Witness went off at 1/5 instead of his more usual 1/20, an ominous sign in itself.

His stablemate Bullish Luck was in those days a truly exceptional miler. Later in his career he went to Tokyo and won the Yasuda Kinen, a feat not many attempt in spite of the million quid on offer just because it's so damn difficult. Silent Witness dictated the pace as was his habit and until the last 50 yards it seemed sure he'd hang on, if without impressing. Then Bullish Luck and Gerald Mosse gradually, inexorably bore down on him, and at the line they were a nose in front. How the crowds gathered round screens in central Hong Kong took it I don't know. But I felt like going back to the hotel to weep.

A month or two later—trainers hate to admit they might have got it wrong—he went to Japan and finished third, albeit creditably, in the Yasuda Kinen. But the invincibility spell was broken even though he went back to Japan and six furlongs in October to bolt up in the Sprinters Stakes. Meanwhile Cape of Good Hope, Watson to his Holmes, won the Golden Jubilee. His trainer David Oughton said he'd had to run him to get away from the Silent Witness backside he'd had to watch eight times.

Sadly, that trip to Nakayama effectively finished Ching Ying Dai Si as a racehorse. While he was there he caught what has never been better described than as 'a mystery illness'. He did come back but he was never the 'Elite Master' again. He ran nine more times after his 'recovery' but never won again, his best effort being a four-and-a-quarter-length beating by Absolute Champion in the Hong Kong Sprint that should have belonged to him. Towards the end he reminded me of Elvis in his Vegas days. He was always a big horse, but when he'd won his first race he weighed 1164 pounds. When he won for the last time he was 100 pounds heavier. For his last race he was a pound shy of 1300.

All life ends in failure. Napoleon's whispered last words were 'Chief of the Army'. (No, mate. Not any more). But Silent Witness's story doesn't end in tragedy. He went to Living Legends in his native Australia. There, now 14, he shares the greenery with such as Better Loosen Up, Saintly, Sacred Kingdom and Bullish Luck. How he gets on with the last named is not recorded. What is recorded is that from Hong Kong and elsewhere pilgrims still come to gaze in awe and have their photos taken with him just as they did in the days when he was great.

Chris Cook (Racing Reporter of the year 2012) **Overdose (126+)**

They called him the Budapest Bullet but he never did find a Group 1 with his name on it. Overdose's talent was tricky to measure but it seemed immense, easily enough to win him one of the big sprint races. How on earth did the Hope of all Hungary fall short through the whole of a seven-season career?

The short answer is that he didn't; we all saw him win the Prix de l'Abbaye in 2008. But it doesn't count because the race was voided and re-run later that day without Overdose, an outcome which is still the cause of some seething resentment among the loyal.

If you don't remember this sorry stramash, having perhaps allowed the footling matter of Zarkava's Arc triumph that same afternoon to distract you, the replay can be found on YouTube. You can watch the race as it happened, with Fleeting Spirit trapped by a starting stall that failed to open, causing a flag-flapping official to signal a false start. Alas, he was seen and understood by only some of the jockeys and, woe of woes, Andreas Suborics aboard Overdose missed him completely.

Alternatively, YouTube allows you to watch that race in a split-screen with the 'real' Abbaye that took place four and a half hours later. In the void race, Overdose crosses to the stands-side rails and powers clear. Meanwhile, in the version that made it into the form book, Marchand d'Or picks off his rivals remorselessly.

The two appear to flash past their winning posts at exactly the same moment. In Hungary, I'm told, the general belief is that Overdose clocked the faster time, though Timeform recorded Marchand d'Or as being ahead by four hundredths of a second.

Can this be offered as proof that Overdose was among the very best sprinters in the world? More than half the field were being pulled up as Suborics urged him through the final furlong but it was by no means clear that they could have caught the leader in any case.

The French stewards' decision to restage the Abbaye was perhaps the most practical response, since postponing it for a week or more would have brought other problems, but it had the cringe-making effect of ruling out the contest's most exciting participant, the only runner from outside the major racing nations. It was almost certainly not a deliberately protectionist act but, to some of Overdose's Hungarian fans, it may have seemed that way.

One TV personality from Budapest went so far as to compare the stewards' ruling with the Treaty of Trianon, the post-war settlement of 1920 that cost Hungary two-thirds of her land and population. The Treaty was signed at Versailles, about 20 minutes' drive from Longchamp, a connection which did not go unnoticed.

For Zoltan Mikoczy, Overdose's affable, avuncular owner, losing the Abbaye was a distinct change of luck. To that point, he might have been regarded as among the most fortunate men in the game, because of the circumstances by which the colt dropped into his lap.

A successful steel trader who has become the dominant owner in Hungary, Mikoczy was visiting friends when attending Tattersalls' December sale in 2006. Having recently paid for four horses in his home country, he was under strict instructions from his wife not to buy any more and supposedly intended to comply.

It was, he later explained, only a momentary urge toward mischief that caused him to stick up his hand as a bay son of Starborough was led around the ring. The bidding had only reached 2,000 guineas; he was certain it would not stop there, remembering how impressed he had been when the sire made every yard of the running in the St James's Palace Stakes nine years before.

But no one else was interested and Mikoczy was stuck with a new acquisition. Nor was the low price a great disappointment to the British vendors, whose advisor had told them: 'Get rid of this horse, whatever happens'.

Off went Overdose to Dunakeszi, a town about 20km from Budapest which was apparently known, in the heyday of Hungarian racing, as 'Little Newmarket'. That heyday would be a very long time ago; 95% of the country's thoroughbreds were lost during World War II and it is now reduced to a single track, Kincsem Park, named after the great mare who went unbeaten in 54 races, including the Goodwood Cup in 1878 on her only visit to Britain.

Overdose began his own career with an unbeaten run that stretched to 14, his trainer, Sandor Ribarszki, recalling that he showed his ability almost as soon as he was put on the local gallops. Faced with six rivals for his debut in the June of his juvenile year, he hacked up at Kincsem by 18 lengths, an astonishing margin for a race over five furlongs on ground recorded as good.

To Bratislava he went and then Vienna, gradually widening his orbit to take in Baden-Baden and Hamburg after turning three, hammering all opponents in each city, never appearing at risk of defeat. That was the more remarkable because he was a poor traveller, fussing and fretting across central Europe.

When the time came to take him to Paris, Ribarszki sent him on his way fully six days before the event, knowing a smooth passage was unlikely. Sure enough, Overdose worked himself into such a stew that he was brought back to Dunakeszi and set out again the next day. Though he made it at the second attempt, he required an overnight stay near the German border.

Mikoczy could be entertaining on the subject of his star's quirks but I always hoped he was embroidering a little, or else that something was lost in translation, because he made Overdose sound a very odd horse indeed. Supposedly, he refused to travel in a full-sized box, preferring trailers of the kind normally used for riding school hacks rather than pattern-class racers. And, according to the owner, he hated to travel at less than 60mph, and would start pawing at the floor if the pace slackened too far below that mark.

Taking your prized animal in a trailer from Hungary to Haydock at 60mph is surely asking for trouble, but Overdose made that journey, in stages, in the spring of 2011. It was his long-awaited British debut and expectation was high, for all that he had been through injury problems and lost his unbeaten record.

Mikoczy made light of those issues. Yes, Overdose had actually altered the shape of one foot with the way he had responded and adapted to the pain of an abscess but it had been gradually reshaped and all was now normal again. The horse would wear stick-on shoes to prevent a repeat of the infection caused by a stray nail. And yes, he had faded into a tame seventh in Germany the previous year, but he had thrown that race before entering the stalls, boiling over so badly that the start was delayed by eight minutes.

But there were no such excuses available when Overdose again faded into seventh in Haydock's Temple Stakes. Age and various setbacks had taken a toll and he could not now be the same fireball that blazed unrewarded at Longchamp three years before.

Mikoczy reacted as if in mourning. His twenty-four guests dared not approach him as, for almost half an hour, he stared sombrely out over the Merseyside track.

'I believe the journey may have taken a lot more out of the horse than we thought,' he eventually told me. 'Pulborough [his base while in England] to Ascot is not far, so he has no more big journeys to make.'

And there may have been something in that, because Overdose was a thrilling fourth, beaten a length and a quarter, in the King's Stand Stakes the next month. There was just a second when it looked as though he might be about to seize the major prize his owner so craved for him, but he couldn't match the finishing speed of Prohibit or Star Witness.

Mikoczy admitted that Overdose would have been long retired if his Abbaye victory had stood. What the owner wanted was to get his horse a place at stud and he felt that required a Group 1 win.

He was still hoping to achieve it in April 2013, by which time Overdose was eight, even as he conceded that 'the structure around the hoof is not as great as it should be and he needs specialist treatment.' By August, Mikoczy was prepared to accept the inevitable and Overdose marked his retirement on September 1st, almost two years after his final race, by parading in front of thousands at Kincsem.

A place at stud in Germany remains a possibility, although Overdose's pedigree is not nearly so flashy as his turn of foot once was. He will not attract mares of quality and it will be a surprise if he can breed anything remotely as good as he was in his pomp.

How will we remember him? Long after the petty workings of racecourse officials have faded from the mind, the image of Overdose will remain, streaking across a field in Paris as those behind him give up and slow to a walk.

Donn McClean (racing journalist) Kicking King (182)

Standing in the unsaddling area at Cheltenham after the 2004 Arkle Trophy, Kicking King's trainer Tom Taaffe was asked quietly about plans for his gallant runner-up. Come back for the Champion Chase next year? The question was almost rhetorical.

'No,' said Taaffe with a smile. 'The Gold Cup.'

Second place at Cheltenham is a conflicted position: delight at having run so well flows against the emotion of the what-might-have-been tide. And the significance of a Kicking King victory would not have been lost on Tom Taaffe, son of Pat Taaffe, in the Cheltenham race named after Arkle on the 40th anniversary of the day that Himself went global by winning his first Gold Cup.

Yet Taaffe's demeanour as he welcomed his horse back in was one of contentment, not tension—delight that his horse had been good enough to go as close as he did, and happy that there was plenty more to come from the six-year-old as he grew in strength and experience.

Kicking King had been there before. Same place, same day, just rewind twelve months. In the 2003 Supreme Novices' Hurdle, Kicking King had also finished second behind compatriot Back In Front. And, just as in 2004, Taaffe was not despondent. To finish second in the Supreme Novices' with a horse who was built to jump fences, not hurdles, was an achievement which was to be celebrated, not lamented.

Kicking King reached a high level over hurdles. Never out of the first two in five runs over the smaller obstacles, he had finished second to mighty mare Solerina on his second run over hurdles, and he had beaten Central House (and it wasn't the last he saw of him) on his fourth. His Supreme Novices' Hurdle run was his swansong over timber before he went on to begin to fulfil his true destiny.

That said, his beginnings over fences were decidedly inauspicious. Pitched into the Grade 2 Craddockstown Novice Chase on his chasing bow at Punchestown in November 2003, the form book says that he finished fifth of eight, some twenty-three lengths behind the winner Anxious Moments.

But that doesn't tell the full story. Timeform's comment that he 'left the strong impression that the race was needed, jumping well taking a good hold and disputing the lead but one-paced 2 out' gets closer. He actually travelled and jumped superbly, gaining ground at every one of his obstacles, such was his fluency, and he looked by far the most likely winner before he just blew up after the third last fence.

His second run over fences was better, but also a little inconclusive. Stepped up to Grade 1 company for the Denny Gold Medal Novice Chase at Leopardstown that Christmas, he was clear at the second last fence when he jumped to his left and came down, leaving the way clear for old friend Central House to come home by a distance. Jockey Barry Geraghty said afterwards that his horse would have won by the length of the home straight if he had stood up.

The Old Vic gelding did gain his first victory over fences on his next attempt, bloodlessly, in a beginners' event at Punchestown two weeks later, and he went 2-1 up in his private series with Central House when he beat Dessie Hughes' horse in the Irish Arkle at Leopardstown at the end of January in what was to be his final run before his second behind the top-class Well Chief in the Arkle at the Festival.

He started his sophomore year over fences by beating Rathgar Beau in the National Lottery Agent Champion Chase at Gowran Park in October. 40/1 for the Gold Cup before the race, he was still 33/1 directly afterwards, and his defeat by Beef Or Salmon on unsuitably tacky ground in the James Nicholson Champion Chase at Down Royal on his subsequent run, his first attempt at three miles, actually caused more of a stir in the Gold Cup market. Victory in the John Durkan Chase at Punchestown, when he beat Rathgar Beau and Beef Or Salmon, booked him his ticket to Kempton on Boxing Day.

That King George was a hot King George. Azertyuiop, an Arkle and Champion Chase winner, had only just been beaten by Moscow Flyer in one of the best Tingle Creek Chases ever run (Well Chief third) three weeks previously, and was an intriguing contender stepped up to three miles. Christie's Foxhunter winner Kingscliff had won big handicap chases at Ascot and Cheltenham earlier that season—the former on half a rein—and was a genuine Gold Cup contender. Therealbandit, a prolific staying novice chaser the previous season, and considered good enough by trainer Martin Pipe to run in the Gold Cup as a freshman, had looked good in winning a handicap chase at Cheltenham three weeks previously. Yet Kicking King spread-eagled them all.

With Azertyuiop as his closest pursuer at the end of the back straight, Barry Geraghty decided that he would stretch on, to test the two-miler's stamina. As it turned out, Paul Nicholls' horse didn't have enough of it, and he wilted from the top of the home straight. Even so, although the race was long over as a contest by the time that Tom Taaffe's horse made his way down to the final fence, it wasn't without its final-act drama.

First there was that mistake at the last obstacle, when Kicking King seemed to put in three strides when one would have sufficed, and when a lesser horseman than Geraghty would have been out over the horse's head and probably over the inside rail as well. Then there was the sprawling Santa Claus on the run-in, and Kingscliff's surging finish, which would have got him home in front had Kicking King not had the energy to build his momentum back up from that shuddering final fence blunder. It was that ability that told you that he had every chance of staying the extra two and a half furlongs that he would have to stay if he was to win a Cheltenham Gold Cup.

There was a new staying chaser on the scene, a genuine threat to Best Mate's dominance. Kicking King was just six when he won the King George, about to turn seven. Triple Gold Cup hero Best Mate was nine, about to turn ten. There was a sense that we were on the cusp of two eras.

The build-up to the 2005 Gold Cup was not without its drama either, first act and final act, and all the acts in between. Just two weeks before the Gold Cup, Kicking King worked poorly in a gallop at Punchestown and scoped dirty afterwards. Gold Cup plans were in tatters, and the horse drifted to 999/1 on the betting exchanges.

Crucially, Taaffe decided not to put his horse on a course of antibiotics. To have done so would have ruled him out of the Gold Cup for certain, as the antibiotics would not have cleared his system by Gold Cup day. Instead, the trainer put him out in a field beside the entrance gate at Portree and kept a close eye on him.

A week later, as Taaffe drove out the gate of his yard, some stones jumped up under his car on the gravel driveway and startled the horse who stood in the field beside the gate, causing him to bolt. A sick horse wouldn't have bolted like that, thought the trainer, and just like that, the Gold Cup bid was back on.

But while it was on for Kicking King, it was off for others. In the swings-and-roundabouts world of National Hunt racing, on the day that Kicking King was ruled back in, Best Mate was ruled out. Then Kingscliff was ruled out, Rule Supreme was re-routed to the World Hurdle and Farmer Jack dropped dead on the gallops.

If Kicking King's first King George was a vintage renewal, it is fair to say that his Gold Cup wasn't. Sent off the 4/1 favourite on the day, and likely to have been shorter but for the pre-race scare, he tanked through the race for Geraghty, took it up on the run to the third last and, with only Take The Stand for company, jumped the last two fences well and stayed on gallantly all the way to the line to record a famous victory.

It was a significant victory on a number of levels. It was a first Gold Cup for Ireland since Imperial Call in 1996, and just a second since Dawn Run. It was Barry Geraghty's first as a rider, and Tom Taaffe's first as a trainer, forty-one years after Tom's dad Pat had won the first of his Gold Cups on Arkle, thirty-seven years after he won the last of his Gold Cups as a rider on Fort Leney, and thirty-one years after he won his only Gold Cup as a trainer with Captain Christy, who was trained just on the other side of the hedge from Portree.

Kicking King wasn't finished there though. He wasn't even finished for the season. He went on to Punchestown the following month and danced in in the Punchestown Gold Cup, registering his fifth win in an almost flawless six-race season, and his fourth Grade 1 win on the spin.

Defeat at the hands of new kid War of Attrition on his return in the 2005/06 season was no negative, nor was defeat in the Betfair Chase at Haydock on his next run, when a twisted shoe meant that you could easily put a line through his run. He went to Sandown that year as the warm favourite to land the King George again, and he duly did, for all that he was not as impressive as he had been at Kempton twelve months earlier.

We obviously didn't know it at the time, but that was to be Kicking King's final victory. A tendon injury suffered at Sandown that day saw him sit on the sidelines for over two years and, while he did make a return, he was simply unable to rekindle past glories.

As a Cheltenham Gold Cup and dual King George winner, Kicking King is part of an elite group in National Hunt racing. He now lives out his retirement at the Irish National Stud, where he—along with Moscow Flyer, Beef Or Salmon and Vintage Crop—is part of the stud's illustrious Living Legends team.

Hugh Taylor (pundit, At The Races) **Dubai Hills (102)**

The role of the specialist has expanded greatly in many sports worldwide over recent years. Baseball allows a designated hitter to replace the pitcher in the batting line-up, whilst the NFL not only has specialist kickers and punters, but also long snappers, whose sole role is to snap the ball back on special teams plays, the elite amongst them earning over £1m annually. In cricket, out-and-out sloggers with a dubious batting technique can now find themselves plying their trade at International/World Cup level thanks to the advent of the 20/20 game, whilst in top-flight football there is invariably a substitute goalkeeper on the bench nowadays.

Horseracing should be the natural home of the specialist given the huge amount of variables at play in the sport, and from a betting point of view, especially in this country, those variables (ground, distance, track type etc) have a major impact on results. However, in terms of race planning, commercialism tends to hold sway over altruism in respect of catering for specialists. Both the Breeders' Cup and the Cheltenham Festival have expanded their respective meetings, introducing new races over intermediate distances, or ones restricted to fillies or horses of a certain age, despite the fact that there hadn't hitherto appeared to be a huge band of horses that were missing these two top-class meetings due to lack of a suitable race. Other Festivals have followed suit. We even have a relatively valuable handicap restricted to greys, and again it surely exists solely because of the potential commercial appeal of such a race.

However, if you own a specialist in a less glamorous area that isn't seen as a money-spinner, the race programme won't necessarily expand to meet your needs. Dubai Hills is unquestionably a specialist; but his specialism is fibresand racing, and as we have only one fibresand track now (Southwell), and one that appears to have been designated for low-grade racing at that, he has ended up, like so many fibresand specialists before him, with nowhere to go.

A son of Dubai Destination, Dubai Hills' first three seasons appeared to establish him as an unremarkable low-grade northern sprint handicapper. Indeed, his first Southwell start, over six furlongs, saw him finish only a fair third. However, he showed enough for connections to persevere with him on the surface, and stepped up in trip, he proceeded over his next four starts to stamp himself as one of the most talented fibresand horses we have seen in this country in recent years. He won with complete authority on each occasion, and his second win in particular, when he recorded a big time figure despite being heavily eased throughout the final furlong, remains one of the most memorable performances we have seen on the surface.

The problem then became the same one eventually encountered by connections of every useful fibresand performer. His BHA rating went up to 95, and the number of 0-95 handicaps run at Southwell each year can be counted on the fingers of one hand (whilst the number of 0-100 handicaps can be counted on the thumb of one hand). With no suitable programme for him to aim at—the evidence suggests he is nothing like the same horse on polytrack—this most progressive performer, so exciting to watch on his favoured surface, was forced back onto turf, and to add insult to injury he was forced to race off his swollen all-weather rating. He did his best, finishing a creditable third in the 2011 Lincoln, and winning a little race at Redcar the following season, but it was generally a struggle until his mark dropped sufficiently to enable him to return to Southwell, where he promptly won two races in a row. He wasn't quite at his best when recording his sixth consecutive course win (off a mark of 92), giving the impression that, at the age of seven, he was understandably doing no more than what was required in front, but he still got the job done, before his revised mark and the paucity of fibresand opportunities saw him banished from Southwell, as if he were Good Hand caught sneaking in with the two-year-olds again.

How good was Dubai Hills on his favoured surface? It's hard to say, because he didn't race there between January 2011 and March 2013, at the stage of his career when he should have been at the peak of his powers. On the face of it, his form doesn't quite measure up to that of the likes of Hail The Chief and Gentleman's Deal, who earned

Timeform ratings of 116 and 114 on fibresand respectively (though Hail The Chief's efforts came at Wolverhampton before the switch to polytrack at that venue). However, Dubai Hills lacked the opportunities to progress on his favoured surface at a crucial time of his career—for instance, Gentleman's Deal won a mile handicap at Southwell off a mark of 100, but that race seems to have disappeared from the calendar.

Polytrack has staged a number of listed races in recent years which have brought together the most progressive regulars from the winter polytrack season with some classy Group 3/listed types from the turf. Generally the class turf horses have prevailed in the Winter Derby lately, the required Timeform rating of around 115 setting a tough standard. But we just don't know how the better fibresand horses would fare against horses of established class from turf (or polytrack), because they never meet.

Most ratings (including those of Timeform) suggest that the bare form of Dubai Hills' best Southwell efforts would leave him around 12lb short of Group Three level. But if there really are legions of animals, unraced on the surface, that could stride home three or four lengths ahead of him at level weights, it's a crying shame that we don't get to see them do just that. Other than the sanitized strolls of Galileo, Black Minnaloushe and Mozart round the track a dozen years ago in preparation for their Breeders' Cup dirt sorties, horses of established quality never set foot on fibresand.

The only potential outlet for Southwell specialists that have outgrown the limitations of the racing programme involves a journey across the Atlantic to race on dirt, but although that surface represents the nearest equivalent to fibresand, there are no guarantees that their UK success will be replicated in that very different racing environment. Hail The Chief managed to win the hugely valuable Grade 2 Hawthorn Gold Cup, but other exports have proved harder to place, and Dubai Hills' trainer Bryan Smart has stated that he has never had an offer for the horse from anyone with a US campaign in mind; Smart feels that the programme over there means buyers are looking for horses that have won no more than one race.

The ratings ceiling also has a small impact on the horses-in-training market in this country. Most major sales feature horses whose pedigrees suggest they might excel on fibresand, but there is little incentive for potential owners to buy anything with a rating of above, say, 70, as after winning a couple of races worth less than £5,000 to the winner the horse is likely to have no further options on the surface.

It's sad to say that Dubai Hills owes his place in this book as much to unfulfilled potential as to track achievements. But he's a poster child for a number of similarly talented horses on the surface, and with fibresand racing apparently growing in popularity—especially amongst punters, who relish the betting angles it provides and the minor impact played by luck in running compared to some of our other all-weather tracks—it would be nice to imagine that more opportunities will be created for the better specialists on the surface in the near future.

Richard Hoiles (racing commentator & broadcaster) **Dvinsky (95)**

'You want to know what true greatness is ? It's knowing when to get off.'

That line from a Stephen Sondheim musical has always resonated with me when hearing of the latest boxer, racing driver or even pop group announcing an ill-advised comeback. Yet from a horse racing perspective many of the 'greats' included in this book have arguably made their exits too early. The prospect of reaching the holy grail that is a career at stud and its commercial riches have led to many a premature departure.

No doubt such lofty aspirations were also held for Dvinsky when he lined up for his debut at York in August 2003. Having been knocked down to Demi O'Byrne for 200,000 euros at the Goffs October Yearling Sale the previous October, Dvinsky, who was under the care of Gerard Butler and sported the famous colours of leading owner Michael Tabor, made a promising start in finishing sixth, and the dream still seemed very much alive following a maiden win at Goodwood the following month, after which the colt was packed off to winter quarters with a Timeform rating of 90p.

Like with so many, however, that dream soon turned sour. Just 12 months after that maiden victory Dvinsky found himself in a claimer at Wolverhampton, where a breathing problem was the official reason given for another career low. No doubt his connections at the time, the Beetle and Wedge Partnership, were far from upset when a next-time-out fourth at a similar level resulted in him being claimed for £5,000 by Tony Carroll.

Fast forward to September 11th 2013, when after 231 starts Dvinsky finally decided it was time to 'get off'. Those races had yielded 19 victories and a total of 87 top three finishes. He had been partnered by over 40 jockeys, five of them Champions, had eight different trainers (though Paul Howling trained him for the majority of his career), run at 24 tracks, and on September 21st 2012 he broke Sharp Hat's all-time appearance record of 217 starts, carving himself a niche in racing history.

Regular-running sprinters are nothing new, as those who grew up with the exploits of the likes of Chaplin's Club and Glencroft will remember well. Both won nine handicaps in a single season, Chaplin's Club achieving the feat twice, and along with my personal favourites Densben and Rambling River were regular fixtures in virtually any northern sprint handicap. However, once the turf season drew to a close at Doncaster in November they were able to recharge their batteries and rest weary legs. Not so Dvinsky, who in a quite astonishing display of durability and resilience, was for a period of over six and a half years never absent from the race track for more than 44 days.

Of course the advent of all-weather racing in 1989 was the main reason he was able to achieve such a feat. The regularity of meetings and consistency of surface increased the opportunities available and as a result the all-weather immediately began to spawn its own course specialists. The likes of Suluk at Southwell and Rapporteur (in whose colours Dvinsky ran for several seasons) at Lingfield began to etch themselves into the consciousness of betting shop punters up and down the land, a fact which continues to the present day with the likes of Almaty Express at Wolverhampton and La Estrella on the fibresand at Southwell.

All-weather racing is much maligned, but often quite unfairly in my opinion. When it arrived late at racing's fixture feast all it found on offer was some curled-up pieces of old pizza and some dodgy-looking quiche. Such low-grade fare will nearly always have unpleasant consequences, and virtually all recent integrity cases have revolved around rides on the all-weather, muddying its name still further. However, this is often more of a reflection on the low grade nature of the racing on offer rather than the surface it is conducted on.

Mistakes were made, however. The failure to grasp the opportunity to implement sectional times and to capitalise on the fact that the lack of rail movements and greater consistency of the surface lends itself to a type of analysis which would have given the all-weather a unique selling point. Timeform's founder Phil Bull's whole ethos was founded on time-based evaluations, and it is to racing's great shame that it still does not deem the components of how those times are arrived at to be of sufficient worth to be provided to the racing public.

There are many positives for all-weather racing that are overlooked. It has been a key component in not just providing Flat jockeys with a living all year round, but has specifically enhanced the careers of those who battle hardest with the scales. For such pilots regular riding can be the difference between winning and losing such a fight, and the likes of George Baker and Adam Kirby readily spring to mind as riders whose careers might have floundered but for all-weather racing. It also provides valuable experience and rides for apprentices—Daniel Tudhope, Kirsty Milczarek and William Carson are amongst those that rode Dvinsky when they were still claiming an allowance—and, of course, all-weather racing is vital in avoiding long periods of no racing when winter flexes its icy grip. Indeed, Dvinsky himself appeared on Channel 4 in January 2013 when all turf racing, along with a good deal of the day's other major sport, was lost to the elements. Keeping racing in the shop window is crucial in the competitive era of media coverage and Premiership football domination.

All-weather surfaces themselves have also improved significantly from those early days, and it was on polytrack that Dvinsky truly found his niche. He won a total of 15 times on the surface, at all the tracks including Great Leighs, though it was Kempton, where he won on 10 occasions, that seemed to play to his strengths the most. Strangely he was never tried at Southwell, where it was felt the deeper fibresand surface would not suit.

On all other surfaces though, Dvinsky seemed bombproof. Having seen an initial handicapper's assessment of 90 wane to just 64, he operated in an amazingly narrow band for the majority of his career, including a period of three years and over 70 consecutive races where he ran between marks of 66 and 75. In ratings terms, Dvinsky was in his prime as a seven- and eight-year-old, despite already having well over 100 starts behind him by that point. Breaking out of the ceiling of 75, he gradually edged up with a string of consistent efforts which in January 2009 saw him win off a mark of 84. He also appeared in a listed race at Lingfield, the only time he ran in a class 1 race, finishing last at odds of 50-1.

Gradually he drifted back down the ratings but it would not be until 2013 that he would fall below 60 as age seemed to take its toll. Finally, with his enthusiasm seemingly on the wane, it was sensibly decided to draw stumps after an outing at Kempton in September of that year. His career earnings for those 19 wins and 68 places spread over ten years were just over £118,000, which is £30,000 less than for being third in the 2013 Derby.

So should Dvinksy be worthy of a place amongst the list of modern greats?

He has the lowest Timeform rating of any in this book (his highest recorded figure was 95 in 2009), yet surely greatness should not just be about the level of achievement. Some in life are fortunate enough to move in grand circles and on a stage where by winning a single feature race lasting just a couple of minutes, greatness is guaranteed. However, for others it is about chiselling out a living day in day out, about rewarding consistency and durability, and recognising the importance such horses play in the fabric of the wonderful sport that is horseracing. If that is the true barometer of greatness, then Dvinsky is up there with the very best.

Gary Crispe (Head of Timeform Australia)
Makybe Diva/Sunline (both 129)

When thinking of Modern Greats in Australia, attention nowadays gets focused on the brilliant unbeaten mare Black Caviar who captured the imagination of a generation with her breathtaking performances here and abroad. However, Australia has had other modern greats who risk being overlooked in the Black Caviar era, such as champion staying mare Makybe Diva and champion mile and middle-distance mare Sunline. Both reached a Timeform rating of 129 during their careers, and the racetrack deeds of both are worthy of closer examination.

The career of Black Caviar has been dealt with elsewhere but Makybe Diva's career is equally as enthralling, the only horse to win three Melbourne Cups (2003, 2004 and 2005) as well as several other feature Australian races.

It is significant that Makybe Diva was bred in the northern hemisphere as Australia's feature staying races are now dominated by horses from that part of the world. Whether intended or not, she has left a lasting legacy for stayers down under. As with many racing legends, Makybe Diva evolved from humble beginnings. Tugela, the dam of Makybe Diva, was purchased in foal to Desert King by owner Tony Santic's bloodstock agent for 60,000 guineas at the 1998 Tattersalls December Sale. Tugela gave birth to Makybe Diva at five minutes past midnight on 21st March 1999, and when she could not be sold (she failed to make the reserve), both Makybe Diva and Tugela were shipped to Australia in August 2000.

Sent to trainer David Hall, it was not until July 29th 2002 that Makybe Diva made her racecourse debut, in a lowly maiden at the Victoria country racetrack of Benalla, finishing fourth. She then went on a run of six straight wins, however, taking her from a maiden handicap at Wangaratta to a Group 2 win in the Queen Elizabeth Stakes over a mile and a half at Flemington. Makybe Diva returned briefly in the autumn of 2003 with two unplaced efforts before again being put aside for her 2003 spring Melbourne Cup campaign that commenced with a fourth at Caulfield over seven furlongs.

After three more lead-up races, that included a fourth in the Group 1 Caulfield Cup, Makybe Diva landed her first Melbourne Cup in November 2003, scoring by over a length from She's Archie and UK visitor Jardine's Lookout.

Makybe Diva's 2004 autumn campaign of six runs culminated with a Group 1 victory in the two-mile Sydney Cup, making her the first mare in history to take both the Melbourne and Sydney Cups in the same racing season (only the fourth horse overall to land the double) and the first since the mighty Carbine in 1890.

At this juncture David Hall was granted a licence to train in Hong Kong, so the mare was sent to one of Australia's leading trainers Lee Freedman. With Freedman at the helm for her Melbourne Cup defence in 2004, Makybe Diva reappeared in the Group 2 Memsie Stakes over seven furlongs, finishing fourth.

She again tackled the Caulfield Cup as the final lead-up to the Melbourne Cup, going down narrowly to Elvstroem after coming from third-last on the home turn in the eighteen-runner field. Regular rider Glen Boss was on board at Flemington for her historic second Melbourne Cup victory. Sent off a 2.6/1 favourite, and in driving rain, she won by the same margin as in 2003, defeating multiple Irish St Leger winner Vinnie Roe and Zazzman. In the process Makybe Diva set a new weight-carrying record for a mare of 55.5 kgs and became the first mare to win two Melbourne Cups.

With Makybe Diva now maturing into a Group 1 weight-for-age galloper, Freedman mapped out an ambitious 2005 autumn campaign for the mare that included runs in both Melbourne and Sydney.

In Melbourne she won the Australian Cup in track record time before heading to Sydney to win the BMW Stakes, in the process becoming the first mare to win a Melbourne Cup, Australian Cup and BMW Stakes in the same racing season.

Two unplaced runs in Japan followed before Makybe Diva was returned to Australia in pursuit of a third Melbourne Cup. Once again Freedman selected the Memsie Stakes as her comeback run, and on this occasion she scored impressively, powering home from last on the home turn to defeat Barely A Moment. She was then narrowly beaten in the Group 2 Dato Tan Chin Nam Stakes before taking the Group 2 Turnbull Stakes at Flemington. Makybe Diva's penultimate run was in the Cox Plate over a mile and a quarter at Moonee Valley, the race clearly recognised as the weight-for-age championship of Australia.

By this time, many believed the mare was unbeatable and so it proved. Punters rallied to her as an even-money favourite and, after making her now trademark long searching run from back in the field, she recorded a comfortable win. Much discussion followed regarding a possible start in the Melbourne Cup, where she was handicapped to carry 58 kgs, but with the Flemington track on the soft side, it was decided to run and attempt what seemed impossible for any horse, let alone a mare—three Melbourne Cups.

From The Correspondents

Makybe Diva didn't disappoint the large crowd in attendance at Flemington, storming to victory under a masterly ride from Glen Boss to defeat On A Jeune and Xcellent, breaking the weight carrying record for a mare that she had set the previous year, and becoming the only mare in history to complete the Cox Plate—Melbourne Cup double.

Makybe Diva retired with a Timeform rating of 129, making her one of Australia's highest-rated horses in recent times, and certainly the best staying filly or mare there in the last fifty years. Owner Tony Santic announced the retirement of Makybe Diva during the 2005 Melbourne Cup presentation. She finished her career with 15 wins from 26 race starts, A$14,526,685 in stakes earnings and seven Group 1 wins. Makybe Diva was a two-time winner of the Australian Horse of the Year title, just the third horse to win the title more than once, and was inducted into the Australian Racing Hall Of Fame on the 4th July 2006. Bronze statues of Makybe Diva have been erected at Flemington race course and at Port Lincoln, the home town of Tony Santic.

At the end of 2002 when Makybe Diva's career was about to blossom, another great mare, Sunline, was near the end of hers. The courageous front-running New Zealand-bred, -owned and -trained mare had amassed an imposing record of 32 victories from 48 race starts including 13 at Group 1 level and A$11,351,607 in stakes earnings.

Sunline commenced her career in New Zealand, and after winning her first four starts, she crossed the Tasman to contest the three-year-old fillies' series in Sydney, winning all three legs, culminating with her first Group 1 success in the Flight Stakes over a mile at Randwick. Sunline suffered her first defeat on her ninth start at Caulfield but she soon got back to winning ways, landing a second Group 1 against older horses in the Doncaster Handicap at Randwick during the autumn of 1999. Returning as a four-year-old in the spring of that year, Sunline scored the first of her Cox Plate wins, defeating a high-class field and relegating Tie The Knot and Sky Heights to the minor placings.

Sunline's outstanding four-year-old season continued in the autumn of 2000, winning the Coolmore Classic for mares with the maximum top weight of 60 kgs before just failing to hold off the lighter-weighted Over in the Doncaster Handicap, where Sunline carried 57.5 kgs.

Sunline finished that season with an effortless victory in the Group 1 All Aged Stakes at weight for age over the Randwick mile. Sunline's five-year-old campaign was her longest (11 runs) and perhaps her most successful. Sunline raced in four countries, New Zealand, Australia, Hong Kong and Dubai, posting four victories at Group 1 level at distances ranging from six furlongs to a mile and a quarter, among them the Hong Kong International Mile and a second Cox Plate by a record-equalling seven lengths. Sunline was also third in the Group 1 Dubai Duty Free Stakes at Nad Al Sheba, going under narrowly to Jim And Tonic and Fairy King Prawn.

Sunline was still competitive at the highest level in the season during which she turned seven, winning a second Coolmore Stakes and Doncaster Handicap, both with big weights under handicap conditions, and the All Aged Stakes at weight for age.

Significantly, Sunline just missed out on taking a record-equalling third Cox Plate, finishing second by half a length to Northerly in the 2001 renewal, a defeat that prevented her joining the great Kingston Town as the only horse to win Australia's premier weight-for-age contest three times. As it stands, Sunline is one of ten horses to have won back-to-back Cox Plates in the ninety-year history of the race, and is only the second mare to have achieved the feat, joining Flight who won consecutive renewals in 1945/46.

Sunline was retired following a brave fourth attempt in the 2002 Cox Plate, where she finished a close fourth behind Northerly, Defier and Godolphin's Grandera.

Much like Makybe Diva, Sunline posted a remarkable number of back-to-back victories in several feature races during her career, but unlike 'The Diva', Sunline also travelled and successfully competed at the highest level abroad. Sunline was New Zealand Horse of the Year on four occasions (1999-2002) and the Australian Horse of the Year three times (2000-2002). She is also an inductee into both the Australian and New Zealand Racing Hall Of Fame.

Bob Barry (TimeformUS) **Volponi (131)**

You really couldn't blame P. G. Johnson—Volponi's breeder, owner and trainer—for feeling sore about his horse's nickname. Volponi not only won the 2002 Breeders' Cup Classic, he ran away with it. The six and a half lengths the big bay put between himself and Medaglia d'Oro that cold and windy day at Arlington Park remains the biggest winning margin in the history of that contest. He was fast and tough and won Graded stakes on grass and dirt, but because his win at huge odds helped expose the biggest known betting scandal in the history of American racing, 'Special Agent' Volponi soon became a footnote to the story of the big race, instead of its star.

Along with his fellow Hall of Famer Allen Jerkens, Philip Johnson was one of the leading curmudgeons of the New York circuit, and he had been waiting fifty-eight years for a horse this good, only to end up having to listen, ad nauseum, to talk of those computer-geek bet-fixers any time someone said the word 'Volponi.' The crime would have likely escaped notice had the 5/2-favourite Medaglia d'Oro won, as that result would have splintered the Pick Six (a pool bet that involves picking the winners of six consecutive races) payouts. Instead, the big upset resulted in the entire $2.5 million winner's share going to a Maryland guy with an upstate New York bet-by-phone account, who had structured a winning ticket that when viewed with a horseplayer's eye, bore a stronger resemblance to larceny than to gambling. Hence: 'Special Agent' Volponi.

Johnson's Amherst Stable was named for the suburban street where he lived, and—owing to his distaste for the dubious charms of the wealthier clients—it specialized in well-bred mares purchased at rock-bottom prices. Johnson purchased the filly Prom Knight because he liked that she was by Irish Derby winner Sir Harry Lewis and loved that she cost only $8,000. Prom Knight raced once, got injured, and was retired. In 1997 she and stallion Cryptoclearance got together, $20,000 changed hands, and in 1998 along came Volponi. Breeders' Cup Classic winners don't come cheaper than that!

The horse was ostensibly named after a racing writer who had recently awarded the trainer his year-end 'Volponi Award', citing Johnson's skill in bringing horses back from long layoffs. If you suspect this makes Johnson a rank sentimentalist, or somehow needy for the affection of journalists, think again. Clearly, there was nothing to be done with 'Cryptoclearance' and 'Prom Knight' (I gave it ten minutes, and gave up). So this lover of thoroughbred bloodlines went back to the paternal grandsire, Fappiano, for inspiration. That great stallion had been named after one Giuseppe Carmine Fappiano, who was better known as Joseph C. Nichols, a long-time racing reporter with The New York Times. The horse may have been the namesake of Paul Volponi, but the inspiration for the naming was all Fappiano, rather than the racing writer (who has since graduated to writing teen fiction).

There is a long-held theory in racing, bordering on pure fact, that thoroughbreds cannot read tote boards. Ample evidence is provided almost daily, of course, but Volponi spent his entire two-year-old season as if he were trying to prove it all by himself. In his first four races, Volponi started as the post-time favorite four times, and settled for one of the minor awards all four times. In his fifth and final start that season, Johnson's odds-blind pupil was entered in the Grade 3 Pilgrim Stakes on the Belmont lawn, where he promptly broke his maiden by two lengths, at odds of 9-1.

The win in the Pilgrim suggested Volponi had a bright future on grass, but he spent the spring of his three-year-old season finishing mid-pack in Grade 3 turf events at Hawthorne and Belmont. Come the summer, Johnson ran him in a nine-furlong allowance race on Saratoga's dirt track, where Volponi blew away the field by more than thirteen lengths, prompting Johnson to enter him in America's oldest stakes race, the Travers. In this first particular entry, reeking with optimism, Johnson's reach exceeded his grasp. Volponi was buried, finishing more than sixteen lengths behind Point Given, who would go on to win Eclipse Awards as both three-year-old champion and Horse of the Year.

With nothing to show for Volponi's three-year-old season except that blowout win at Saratoga, Johnson kept him on the dirt through the fall. He beat a small allowance field over a mile, and followed that up with a win in the Grade 2 Pegasus Stakes, his first Graded win on dirt. Volponi finished 2001 with a fourth in the Grade 1 Cigar Mile at Aqueduct. While this fall campaign did not make anyone sit up and take notice, in his last three starts Volponi ran speed figures on a par with his big effort at Saratoga. It took all year, but he now seemed to be a fast and consistent dirt horse, and as a son of Cryptoclearance, whose runners tend to be late developers, this seemed to bode well for a four-year-old campaign on the dirt.

Volponi made his 2002 debut in May, winning an allowance sprint at odds on. But three weeks later, in another allowance race on dirt, he ran a dull fourth at odds of 2/5, prompting Johnson to put him back on the turf. Once again, showing an utter disregard for the tote board, Volponi won the Grade 2 Poker Handicap at Belmont by two lengths at 9-1. Up at Saratoga he ran two more good ones on the grass, beaten just a neck in another Grade 2, and then putting in a strong effort in the Grade 1, twelve furlong

Sword Dancer, finishing a close third. So while Volponi had finished his three-year-old season with some very strong dirt form, at four he was looking more and more like a committed turf runner.

Like graft to politics, and those Monarch butterflies to Mexico, racing returned to Belmont Park in the fall. The three co-conspirators in the 'Fix-Six' scandal (as New York's tabloids would come to describe it) were planning what they hoped would be an invisible heist. Essentially, it was a late-betting scheme utilising their 'Mister Inside' (a programmer with Autotote, the company that handles the wagers for sixty-five percent of horse races in North America), who would use his insider access to alter their oddly constructed bet (single selections in the first four races followed by 'all' in each of the last two) after the first four races had been run. Mister Inside knew two things: that betting hubs only sent detailed Pick Six data to the host tracks after most bets were already eliminated (it made for much smaller files), and that hitting a Pick Six with four singles was much easier to do if you got to change your selections after the races had been run.

But none of these criminal geniuses ever figured out how to construct a ticket that would stand up to close scrutiny should the unthinkable happen: that some combination of longshots would leave them holding the only winning ticket.

The 2002 Breeders' Cup was held at Arlington Park, just outside Johnson's hometown of Chicago. The trainer, 77 and weakened by a two-year battle against prostate cancer and the accompanying radiation treatments, was unsure whether to run Volponi in the Turf Mile or the Classic. Volponi's two prep races didn't help much: he ran second in both a Grade 2 turf race and a Grade 2 dirt race—both times as the favourite. In the end, Johnson opted for the Classic, which had a purse four times greater than the Mile.

Given Volponi's curious habit of running in inverse proportion to his odds, the 2002 Classic result was likely sealed upon completion of the post position draw, when he was assigned morning line odds of 50-1. Sure enough, as the gate popped open, Volponi broke well, tracked the leaders around the oval, blew past the favourites at the top of the stretch, and drew away as if he were a 1/5 shot. Asked in the winner's circle how he and Volponi had achieved this unlikely result, Johnson smiled and said, as if he believed it with all his heart: 'It was easy. He's a nice horse.'

The racing gods deserve their reputation, but every so often they get one right. Within the New York circuit, where Johnson spent the last 43 years of a 60-plus-year career, he was liked and respected by his peers (of which there were few), and was considered a father figure by his employees (his top assistant stayed 33 years). Johnson was happily married for 59 years, and all to the same woman. Not that this is ever germane in sporting matters, but Philip Johnson deserved this horse and this win. If there was ever such thing as a popular 44/1 winner, this was it.

The Fix-Six guys were all in prison by the time Volponi came back as a five-year-old, but the special agent never won another race. He continued to run fast figures in New York's top dirt races, but had bad racing luck. For his last race, Johnson gave his 'nice horse' the chance to defend his Classic win, but—in a rarity—the tank was empty that day, and Volponi was eased down the stretch, finishing last as smoke and ash from wildfires swirled around Santa Anita.

Johnson's wife, Mary Kay, died the following spring, and Johnson himself died during the Saratoga meet that summer, where they lowered the flag and observed a moment of silence. Volponi covered about 100 mares over two seasons in Kentucky, but he was sold to the Korean Racing Association late in 2005, and now leads the good life of an expat. He was the fifth-leading sire in Korea for 2012. There is no word yet as to any promising colts named after Korean racing writers, but there is always hope.

P.G. Johnson was a great trainer but a lousy bettor. So maybe he wasn't the best judge as to how his horse will be remembered in the States. Barring a Korean-bred Kentucky Derby winner, it won't be for Volponi's progeny.

Arcangues (who won the 1993 Classic at odds of 133/1) will always be the bigger upset, and some day some other horse will break his record for the winning margin in the Classic. But in a little more than two minutes that nasty day in Chicago, Volponi did more for tote security than any hundred racing executives ever did, and, for that alone, American punters should be eternally grateful.